Praise for Ira Glass and *This American Life*

"The best radio show host in America."   —*Time*

"A public radio sensation. As the medium's coolest commodity, *This American Life* captures the listener's imagination by mirroring our culture and society through the individual stories of people and the poignant, strange, or luminescent moments in which they find themselves."
                                                —Salon

"Radio's hippest show."   —*Mother Jones*

"It has this beat all to itself.... These stories float right into your brain and lodge there."   —*The Nation*

"Ira Glass finds—uncovers—drama and humor in the most pedestrian of places."   —David Mamet

"Mr. Glass is a journalist but also a storyteller who filters his interviews and impressions through a distinctive literary imagination, an eccentric intelligence, and a sympathetic heart."   —*The New York Times*

THE
NEW KINGS
OF NONFICTION

EDITED AND INTRODUCED BY

IRA GLASS

RIVERHEAD BOOKS

New York

RIVERHEAD BOOKS
Published by the Penguin Group
Penguin Group (USA) Inc.
375 Hudson Street, New York, New York 10014, USA
Penguin Group (Canada), 90 Eglinton Avenue East, Suite 700, Toronto, Ontario M4P 2Y3, Canada
(a division of Pearson Penguin Canada Inc.)
Penguin Books Ltd., 80 Strand, London WC2R 0RL, England
Penguin Group Ireland, 25 St. Stephen's Green, Dublin 2, Ireland (a division of Penguin Books Ltd.)
Penguin Group (Australia), 250 Camberwell Road, Camberwell, Victoria 3124, Australia
(a division of Pearson Australia Group Pty. Ltd.)
Penguin Books India Pvt. Ltd., 11 Community Centre, Panchsheel Park, New Delhi—110 017, India
Penguin Group (NZ), 67 Apollo Drive, Rosedale, North Shore 0745, Auckland, New Zealand
(a division of Pearson New Zealand Ltd.)
Penguin Books (South Africa) (Pty.) Ltd., 24 Sturdee Avenue, Rosebank, Johannesburg 2196,
South Africa

Penguin Books Ltd., Registered Offices: 80 Strand, London WC2R 0RL, England

THE NEW KINGS OF NONFICTION

The publisher does not have any control over and does not assume any responsibility for author or third-party websites or their contents.

First Riverhead trade paperback edition: October 2007

ISBN: 978-1-59448-267-0

PRINTED IN THE UNITED STATES OF AMERICA

10 9 8 7 6 5 4

CONTENTS

CONTENTS

Proceeds from the sale of this collection go to benefit the literacy program 826CHI. Hidden behind a shop that sells grappling hooks, sonic eavesdroppers, fake moustaches, and other useful gear for the international spy (deceptively called the Boring Store and located at 1331 Milwaukee Avenue in Chicago), 826CHI helps kids aged six to eighteen with their writing skills. To volunteer as a tutor or make a donation, visit their Web site: www.826chi.org.

THE
NEW KINGS
OF NONFICTION

INTRODUCTION

Ira Glass

★ ★ ★

Years ago, when I worked for public radio's daily news shows, I put together this story about a guy named Jack Davis. He was a Rush Limbaugh fan and a proud Republican, and he'd set out on an unusual mission. He wanted to go into the Chicago public housing projects to instruct the children there in the value of hard work and entrepreneurship. He'd do this with vegetables. His plan was to teach the kids at the Cabrini Green projects to grow high-end produce, they'd sell their crop to the fancy restaurants that are just blocks from Cabrini, and this would be a valuable life lesson in the joys of market capitalism.

So Jack set up a garden in the middle of the high-rises, and for the first few years, it didn't go so well. Jack was an accountant from the white suburbs and he didn't relate to the kids or understand the culture of the projects. He made a lot of parents mad. A kid would miss a day's work in the vegetable garden and Jack would dock his pay, to teach the consequences of sloth. Then all the windows in Jack's truck would get smashed. Jack's message was not getting through.

Hoping to turn this around, he enlisted this guy named Dan Underwood, who lived in Cabrini and whose children had been working in the garden. Everyone in the projects seemed to know Dan. He ran a double-Dutch jump-rope team for Cabrini kids that was ranked number one in the city, and a drum and color-guard squad, and martial arts classes. Kids loved Dan. He was fatherly. He was fun.

And while Jack was committed to the idea that they should run the vegetable garden like a real business, Dan saw it as just another after-school program. "These are children," he told me. "It's not like an adult coming to work at, you know, 8:00 and getting off at 4:30, and 'If you don't come, you don't get no money.' That won't work, not with a child." When a kid didn't show up to pick tomatoes, Dan would go to the family and find out why. He'd buy the kids pizza and take them on trips and get them singing in the van. What they needed was no mystery, as far as he was concerned. They were normal kids growing up in an unusually tough neighborhood, and they needed what any kid needs: some attention and some fun.

And sometimes, when he and Jack argued over how to run the program, they were both aware—uncomfortably aware, I think—how they were reenacting, in a vegetable garden surrounded by dingy high-rises, a bigger national debate. The white suburbanite was stomping around insisting that the project kids get a job and show up on time and not be coddled anymore, all for their own good, all to make them self-sufficient. The black guy was telling the interloper that he didn't know what he was talking about. A little coddling might be better for these kids than an enhanced appreciation of the work ethic and the free market.

When I was working on this story I thought that Jack and Dan would've made a great '70s TV show, one of those Norman Lear sitcoms where every week something happens to make all the characters argue about the big issues of the day. Sadly, we were twenty years too late for that, and Norman Lear had already set a show—*Good Times*—in Cabrini Green.

One interesting thing about this story was how my officemate at the time hated it. Or maybe *hate*'s too strong a word. He was suspicious of the story. And he was incredulous at how it seemed to lay out like a perfect little fable about modern America. "Are you making these stories up?" I remember him asking.

But I don't see anything wrong with a piece of reporting turning into a fable. In fact, when I'm researching a story and the real-life situation starts to turn into allegory—as it did with Dan and Jack—I feel incredibly lucky, and do everything in my power to expand that part of the story. Everything suddenly stands for something so much bigger, everything has more resonance, everything's more engaging. Turning your back on that is rejecting tools that could make your work more powerful. But for a surprising number of reporters, the stagecraft of telling a story—managing its fable-like qualities—is not just of secondary concern, but a kind of mumbo jumbo that serious-minded people don't get too caught up in. Taking delight in this part of the job, from their perspective, has little place in our important work as journalists. Another public radio officemate at that time—a Columbia University School of Journalism grad—would come back from the field with funny, vivid anecdotes she'd tell us in the hallway. Few of them ever appeared in her reports, which were dry as bones and hard to listen to.

She always had the same explanation for why she'd omit the entertaining details: "I thought that would be putting myself in the story." As if being interesting and expressing any trace of a human personality would somehow detract from the nonstop flow of facts she assumed her listeners were craving. There's a whole class of reporters—especially ones who went to journalism school, by the way—who have a strange kind of religious conviction about this. They actually get indignant; it's an affront to them when a reporter tries to amuse himself and his audience.

I say phooey to that. This book says phooey to that.

Most of the stories in this book come from a stack of favorite writing that I've kept behind my desk for years. It started as a place to toss articles I simply didn't want to throw away, and it's a mess. Old photocopies of photocopies. Pages I've torn from magazines and stapled together. Random issues of a Canadian magazine a friend edited for a while. Now and then, in working on a radio story with someone, I'll want to explain a certain kind of move they could try, or someone just needs inspiration. They need to see just how insanely good a piece of writing can be, and shoot for that. That's when I go to the stack.

As far as I'm concerned, we're living in an age of great nonfiction writing, in the same way that the 1920s and '30s were a golden age for American popular song. Giants walk among us. Cole Porters and George Gershwins and Duke Ellingtons of nonfiction storytelling. They're trying new things and doing pirouettes with the form. But nobody talks about it that way.

I don't pretend that the writers in my stack of stories are representative of a movement or a school of writing or anything like that. But they generally share a few traits. First and foremost, they're incredibly good reporters. And like the best reporters, they either find a new angle on something we all know about already, or—more often—they take on subjects that nobody else has figured out are worthy of reporting. They're botanists in search of plants nobody's given a name to yet. Take Malcolm Gladwell's *New Yorker* story "Six Degrees of Lois Weisberg," which at first reads like any other magazine story, until you take a moment to realize what it's about, which is nothing less than the question "how does everyone know everyone they know?" Or Lee Sandlin's story, which is attempting to redefine everything we think about World War II and, while he's at it, all other wars as well. Or Michael Pollan's story, where he buys a steer to illustrate in the most vivid way possible a thousand details most of us don't know about where our meat comes from. Or Mark Bowden's story, which addresses a very simple question, a question that's so simple that once you've heard it, you wonder why you've never heard anybody else ask it: what was Saddam Hussein really like?

And these writers are all entertainers, in the best sense of the word. I know that's not how we usually talk about great reporting, but it's a huge part of all these stories. Great scenes, great characters, great moments. Often they're funny. There's a cheerful embracing of life in this kind of journalism, and a curiosity about the world. What hits me most when I reread Gladwell's story is not his skill at laying out a series of very enjoyable anecdotes and his even greater skill at deploying scientific research that sheds light on those anecdotes. What hits me most is how the article could be half the length and still hit all its big ideas, and it's only longer because Gladwell has found so many things that interest and amuse him, and that's the engine that drives the whole enterprise. There's a whole section of the article about actors and Kevin Bacon and Burgess Meredith that actually repeats an idea he illustrates elsewhere. And pretty much everything in the story after section five is, to my way of thinking, just there for fun. That includes Gladwell thinking through the consequences of his findings for affirmative-action programs, a scene of Gladwell trying to pin down the inner life of one of his super-connected interviewees, and—best of all—the completely improbable and utterly amazing story of how his protagonist, Lois Weisberg, hooked up with her second husband.

Finally, near the very end of the article, Gladwell is trying to explain once and for all why some of us know such an extraordinary number of people and, like a man writing a fable, he arrives at the moral of his story, which he points out is "the same lesson they teach in Sunday school." Which is what I love about Gladwell. He stumbles onto some new phenomenon, and he's trying his damnedest, for page after page, to think through what it *means*. And part of his mission is sharing the sheer pleasure in thinking it through.

This is a special kind of pleasure, and another thing we don't usually talk about when we talk about what makes a piece of journalism great. It's the pleasure of discovery, the pleasure of trying to make sense of the world. Take this joyful passage from Jack Hitt's story about a personal-injury lawsuit so big that the four thousand plaintiffs—just to keep their claims straight—actually had to write their own constitution. As Hitt notes, it's nearly as long as the U.S. Constitution.

What first drew my attention was that absurd name. Stringfellow. Acid. Pits. Modern life rarely shunts nouns together with such Dickensian economy. After I first encountered that singular name in a newspaper article some four or five years ago, it began to appear in my life eerily, serendipitously. If I was in Washington, the *Post* had a short update; if in San Francisco, then the *Chronicle*. If, while dressing in a hotel, I caught an environmental lawyer on C-SPAN, then Stringfellow would be cited offhandedly and without explanation. One evening, seated at an intimate dinner party in New Haven, Connecticut, I casually mentioned my growing interest in Stringfellow. Across the table a head turned and said, "I've worked on that case." Then another guest spoke up. He, too, was indirectly involved. I was not following the case; it was pursuing me.

The newspaper reports I read created a sense of Cyclopean dimension: a specially constructed courtroom, private judges, secret negotiations, a quarter-million pages of pretrial documents, and legal processes of absurd intricacy. The case presented a problem unique in the history of American law. How does a court try four thousand cases that are generally similar but legally different? Judge Erik Kaiser came up with an innovative solution: he would bundle the four thousand plaintiffs into groups of roughly seventeen, and try the bundled cases consecutively. Consider the math: 4,000 divided by 17 = 235 trials. If each one lasted a little under a year—a conservative estimate—the entire process would be wrapped up in two centuries.

Two-thirds of the way into his story, it takes a remarkable turn, one I've rarely seen in any piece of reporting. There's no way for me to explain this turn without actually revealing the spoiler so jump down to the next paragraph right now if you don't want to know. Ready? Jack Hitt discovers that the premise of his story is completely wrong. Fantastic, right?

Or here's an excerpt from Bill Buford's hilarious and disturbing book *Among the Thugs*, where he spends months with soccer hooligans in England.

The thing about reporting is that it is meant to be objective. It is meant to record and relay the truth of things, as if truth were out there, hanging around, waiting for the reporter to show up. Such is the premise of objective journalism. What this premise excludes, as any student of modern literature will tell you, is that slippery relative fact of the person doing the reporting, the modern notion that there is no such thing as the perceived without someone to do the perceiving, and that to exclude the circumstances surrounding the story is to tell an untruth. . . .

I do not want to tell an untruth and feel compelled, therefore, to note that at this moment, the reporter was aware that the circumstances surrounding his story had become intrusive and significant and that, if unacknowledged, his account of the events that follow would be grossly incomplete. And his circumstances were these: the reporter was very, very drunk.

That's the will to entertain.

Part of what's exciting about *Among the Thugs* is that Buford is so honest about what happens between him and his interviewees, especially the awkwardness he feels as an outsider in the midst of this tribe of drunk, violent men. They hate him, and they don't trust him, and he doesn't pretend otherwise. There's a transparency to the reporting. Most of the book is Buford putting himself into one situation after another, and simply describing all the chance encounters he has along the way. It's an inspiring book to read if you want to try your hand at reporting, because it makes the job seem so damned straightforward, and I can't count the number of copies I've given away over the years to beginning journalists. Buford makes it clear how much of reporting is simply wandering from one place to another, talking to people and writing down what they say and trying to think of something, anything, that'll shed some light on what's happening in front of your face.

This explicitness about the process of reporting is true for many of the writers in this collection. It's a shame this technique is forbidden to most daily newspaper reporters and broadcast journalists, because a lot of the power of these stories comes from the writers telling you step by step what they're feeling and thinking, as they do their reporting. For example, here's how Michael Lewis explains his interest in the story of a fifteen-year-old named Jonathan Lebed—a minor who got into trouble with the Securities and Exchange Commission for trading stocks online: "When I first read the newspaper reports last fall, I didn't understand them. It wasn't just that I didn't understand what the kid had done wrong; I didn't understand what he had done."

Much later in the story Lewis interviews the Chairman of the SEC about Lebed's supposed crime, and he does something I'm not sure I've ever seen a reporter do in an interview with a government official. Lewis tells us what he's thinking, moment by moment, as the SEC Chair trots out one unconvincing argument after another. It's breathtaking, and skewers the guy in a way I've never seen before or since in an American newspaper. What's even more breathtaking is that somehow, Lewis doesn't come across as unfair. He doesn't seem like a hothead, or someone with an agenda. He comes off as a curious, reasonable guy, the most reasonable guy in the room in fact, a guy who's both annoyed and amused at the hokum being peddled. It's done so deftly you don't even realize how delicate it is, what he's pulling off. Especially when you consider the big policy questions he's juggling at the same time. In the middle of telling this great yarn, he's actually explaining an entirely original way to look at the regulation of the stock market and online trading, an analysis he invented himself over the course of his reporting. And he's made his explanation simple enough that people like you and me who may know absolutely nothing about the markets will understand what he's talking about and why it matters at all.

Which brings me to my next point. What I'm about to say doesn't apply to breaking news stories, which have their own rules and logic, but does apply to stories like the ones in this book, or on the radio show I host. When you're writing stories like these, I think you've really only got two basic building blocks. You've got the plot of the story, and you've got the ideas the story is driving at. Usually the plot is the easy part. You do whatever research you can, you talk to lots of people, and you figure out what happened. It's the ideas that kill you. What's the story mean? What bigger truth about all of us does it point to? You can knock your head against a wall for days thinking that through.

The writers in this book are geniuses when it comes to the ideas. In fact usually their stories would have trouble existing at all, without the scaffolding of ideas they've erected to hold the thing up. And some of the moves they pull to deploy their ideas! There's a section in Lawrence Weschler's story "Shapinsky's Karma" where every character in the story walks up to Weschler to tell him the meaning of the story he's writing about Shapinksy. Some of them even offer titles for his story. Susan Orlean's "The American Man, Age Ten" is a tour de force on this score, as she tries to think through what it means to be ten. She's profiling a random suburban kid named Colin Duffy. I could almost pick any three sentences from the story at random and they'll make my point, but this passage just kills me:

> The girls in Colin's class are named Cortnerd, Terror, Spacey, Lizard, Maggot, and Diarrhea. "They do have other names, but that's what we call them," Colin told me. "The girls aren't very popular."
>
> "They are about as popular as a piece of dirt," Japeth [Colin's friend] said. "Or you know that couch in the classroom? That couch is more popular than any girl. A thousand times more."

That is a very efficient way to explain a ten-year-old boy's attitude toward girls. I love the overall tone she invents to write this story. It's a voice that's halfway between hers and his.

> If Colin Duffy and I were to get married, we would have matching superhero notebooks. . . . We would eat pizza and candy for all of our meals. We wouldn't have sex, but we would have crushes on each other and, magically, babies would appear in our home. We would win the lottery and then buy land in Wyoming, where we would have one of every kind of cute animal. All the while, Colin would be working in law enforcement—probably the FBI. Our favorite movie star, Morgan Freeman, would visit us occasionally. We would listen to the same Eurythmics song

("Here Comes the Rain Again") over and over again and watch two hours of television every Friday night. We would both be good at football, have best friends, and know how to drive; we would cure AIDS and the garbage problem and everything that hurts animals. We would hang out a lot with Colin's dad. For fun, we would load a slingshot with dog food and shoot it at my butt. We would have a very good life.

Much later in the story, Orlean states more explicitly some of her conclusions about Colin's view of the world.

The collision in his mind of what he understands, what he hears, what he figures out, what popular culture pours into him, what he knows, what he pretends to know, and what he imagines makes an interesting mess. The mess often has the form of what he will probably think like when he is a grown man, but the content of what he is like as a little boy.

One thing I love about Weschler and Orlean (and, come to think of it, most of these writers) is their attitude toward the people they're writing about. Weschler is clearly skeptical of his protagonist, Akumal. Orlean is not in agreement with her ten-year-old. But they try to get inside their protagonists' heads with a degree of empathy that's unusual. Theirs is a ministry of love, in a way we don't usually discuss reporters' feelings toward their subjects. Or at least, they're willing to see what is lovable in the people they're interviewing. (Weschler's an interesting case when it comes to this, because he's mildly annoyed by his main character for the early part of his story, and then comes to have an obvious and real affection for him.)

David Foster Wallace's story kind of sneaks up on you in this regard. He's writing about right-wing talk radio, which is, depending on how you look at it, either very easy or very hard to write about well, since it's something everyone already has an opinion about. And after laying out a series of eye-opening details about how the whole talk industry actually works, at some point Wallace just starts to get very, very interested in the question of what sort of guy would be holding forth with these sorts of opinions on the radio. He then produces a set of unusually frank anecdotes and quotes to answer that question. The unusual honesty, by the way, is explained with this helpful footnote:

> The best guess re Mr. Z.'s brutal on-record frankness is that either (a) the host's on- and off-air personas really are identical, or (b) he regards speaking to a magazine correspondent as just one more part of his job, which is to express himself in a maximally stimulating way.

Part of what's most interesting about this story, I think, is Wallace's attitude toward Mr. Z. When he analyzes what Mr. Z. says on the air, he questions some of the most basic premises of Mr. Z.'s occupation. But it's all done in a way that's somehow still sympathetic to the guy.

This empathetic mission gives the writing a warmth, and—not incidentally—it helps Wallace and all these writers get away with saying certain unflattering things about their subjects, because it's clear the overall project of their writing is not a malicious or demeaning one. I like that. And as a reporter, I understand it. I have this experience when I interview someone, if it's going well and we're really talking in a serious way, and they're telling me these very personal things, I fall in love a little. Man, woman, child, any age, any background, I fall in love a little. They're sharing so much of themselves. If you have half a heart, how can you not?

Chuck Klosterman even makes Val Kilmer sympathetic. Klosterman is both an essayist and a reporter, and as an essayist, he has this fantastically agile brain. He tears through one idea after another with a speed and fierce confidence that I always find kind of inspiring. Some of the essays in his book *Sex, Drugs and Cocoa Puffs* I've read over and over, like the one explaining how *Star Wars* and *Reality Bites* are actually the same movie, and how that movie perfectly captures everything about Generation X, which is Klosterman's generation. ("There are no myths about Generation X," he writes. "It's all true.") When Klosterman does reporting, the superstructure of ideas and the aggressiveness with which he states those ideas are a big part of what makes the stories stand out. And the ideas are especially important when he writes about celebrities. I think celebrity journalism is one of the toughest assignments you can do, because the super-famous are usually guarded about what they reveal, and because they've been interviewed so many times before, what's left for you to explore? Klosterman's Val Kilmer story is a good example of someone taking a celebrity interview and creating a context and structure that gives the quotes and moments so much meaning. In general, Klosterman writes with a lot of sympathy for his subjects, while still simultaneously pointing out all sorts of things about them that they might find unflattering.

I wish there were a catchy name for stories like this. For one thing, it would've made titling this collection a lot easier. Sometimes people use the phrase "literary nonfiction" for work like this, but I'm a snob when it comes to that phrase. I think it's for losers. It's pretentious, for one thing, and it's a bore. Which is to say, it's exactly the opposite of the writing it's trying to describe. Calling a piece of writing "literary nonfiction" is like daring you to read it.

In choosing stories for this book, I haven't tried to include every great nonfiction writer who's working right now, or even all my favorites. I ended up rereading dozens of essays and stories I've loved, some of them by regular contributors to the radio program, some by people I've admired from afar. In the end I returned to my original premise—to select journalism I've found myself talking about and recommending over the years. And I decided to stick with stories that are built around original reporting of one sort or another, not essays.

Some of these stories are very well-known; some barely known. There's a whole class of stories I've included because the writers are trying to document such remarkable experiences they've had. Dan Savage tells how he got so sick of the homophobic policies of the Republican

Party that he decided to join the party himself and became a delegate to their state convention, where he caused various sorts of trouble. Coco Henson Scales describes what happens inside a trendy New York restaurant and—even more interesting—inside her head as the hostess there. In her story, celebrities show up and perform exactly as you'd want them to, but never get to see in print. It is possibly the greatest *New York Times* "Styles Section" feature that will ever be written.

Jim McManus's poker story is amazing because the facts shouldn't lay out the way they do. He enters his first poker tournament—the World Series of Poker—to write about it for *Harper's* magazine, and he ends up at the final table, pocketing a quarter-million dollars. This is the poker equivalent of showing up at the Olympics, never having competed on track or field, and taking home the bronze for the 100-meter dash. At one point, McManus squares off against one of his heroes, a guy whose poker manual he'd read and reread to prepare for the tournament, and—if that's not enough—they end up playing one of the hands the guy wrote about in his book. "I've studied the passage so obsessively," McManus writes, "I believe I can quote it verbatim." His *Harper's* article, by the way, was published two years before the full-blown poker craze hit America, which explains why he's so patiently explaining rules and customs of the game that are now familiar to most high school students.

☆ ☆ ☆

While this is the golden age of this kind of reporting and writing, it's also a golden age for crap journalism. And for some of the most amazing technological advances for stuffing it down your throat. A lot of daily reporting and news "commentary" just reinforces everything we already think about the world. It lacks the sense of discovery, the curiosity, the uncorny, human-size drama that's part of all these stories. A lot of daily reporting makes the world seem smaller and stupider.

In that environment, these stories are a kind of beacon. By making stories full of empathy and amusement and the sheer pleasure of discovering the world, these writers reassert the fact that we live in a world where joy and empathy and pleasure are all around us, there for the noticing. They make the world seem like an exciting place to live. I come out of them feeling like a better person—more awake and more aware and more appreciative of everything around me. That's a hard thing for any kind of writing to accomplish. In times when the media can seem so clueless and beside the point, that's a great comfort in itself.

JONATHAN LEBED'S EXTRACURRICULAR ACTIVITIES

Michael Lewis

On September 20, 2000, the Securities and Exchange Commission settled its case against a fifteen-year-old high-school student named Jonathan Lebed. The SEC's news release explained that Jonathan—the first minor ever to face proceedings for stock-market fraud—had used the Internet to promote stocks from his bedroom in the northern New Jersey suburb of Cedar Grove. Armed only with accounts at AOL and E*Trade, the kid had bought stock and then, "using multiple fictitious names," posted hundreds of messages on Yahoo! Finance message boards recommending that stock to others. He had done this eleven times between September 1999 and February 2000, the SEC said, each time triggering chaos in the stock market. The average daily trading volume of the small companies he dealt in was about sixty thousand shares; on the days he posted his messages, volume soared to more than a million shares. More to the point, he had made money. Between September 1999 and February 2000, his smallest one-day gain was twelve thousand dollars. His biggest was seventy-four thousand dollars. Now the kid had agreed to hand over his illicit gains, plus interest, which came to $285,000.

When I first read the newspaper reports last fall, I didn't understand them. It wasn't just that I didn't understand what the kid had done wrong; I didn't understand what he had done. And if the initial articles about Jonathan Lebed raised questions—what did it mean to use a fictitious name on the Internet, where every name is fictitious, and who were these people who traded stocks naively based on what they read on the Internet?—they were trivial next to the questions raised a few days later when a reporter asked Jonathan Lebed's lawyer if the SEC had taken all of the profits. They hadn't. There had been many more than the eleven trades described in the SEC's press release, the lawyer said. The kid's take from six months of trading had been nearly eight hundred thousand dollars. Initially the SEC had demanded he give it all up, but then backed off when the kid put up a fight. As a result, Jonathan Lebed was still sitting on half a million dollars.

At length, I phoned the Philadelphia office of the SEC, where I reached one of the investigators who had brought Jonathan Lebed to book. I was maybe the fiftieth journalist he'd spoken with that day, and apparently a lot of the others had had trouble grasping the finer points of securities law. At any rate, by the time I asked him to explain to me what, exactly, was wrong with broadcasting one's private opinion of a stock on the Internet, he was in no mood.

"Tell me about the kid."

"He's a little jerk."

"How so?"

"He is exactly what you or I hope our kids never turn out to be."

"Have you met him?"

"No. I don't need to."

Cedar Grove is one of those Essex County suburbs defined by the fact that it is not Newark. Its real-estate prices rise with the hills. The houses at the bottom of each hill are barely middle class; the houses at the top might fairly be described as opulent. The Lebeds' house sits about a third of the way up one of the hills.

When I arrived one afternoon not long ago, the first person to the door was Greg Lebed, Jonathan's fifty-four-year-old father. Black hair sprouted in many directions from the top of his head and joined together somewhere in the middle of his back. The curl of his lip seemed designed to shout abuse from a bleacher seat. He had become famous, briefly, when he ordered the world's media off his front lawn and said, "I'm proud of my son." Later, elaborating on *60 Minutes*, he said, "It's not like he was out stealing the hubcaps off cars or peddling drugs to the neighbors."

He led me to the family dining room, and without the slightest help from me, worked himself into a lather. He got out a photocopy of front-page stories from the *Daily News*. One side had a snapshot of Bill and Hillary Clinton beside the headline "Insufficient Evidence in Whitewater Case: CLINTONS CLEARED"; the other side had a picture of Jonathan Lebed beside the headline "Teen Stock Whiz Nailed." Over it all was scrawled in Greg's furious hand, "U.S. Justice at Work."

"Look at that!" he shouted. "This is what goes on in this country!".

Then, just as suddenly as he had erupted, he went dormant. "Don't bother with me," he said. "I get upset." He offered me a seat at the dining-room table. Connie Lebed, Jonathan's forty-five-year-old mother, now entered. She had a look on her face that as much as said: "I assume Greg has already started yelling about something. Don't mind him; I certainly don't."

Greg said testily, "It was that goddamn computer what was the problem."

"My problem with the SEC," said Connie, ignoring her husband, "was that they never called. One day we get this package from Federal Express with the whatdyacallit, the subpoenas inside. If only they had called me first." She will say this six times before the end of the day, with one of those marvelous harmonica-like wails that conveys a sense of grievance maybe better than any noise on the planet. If only they'da caaaawwwwlled me.

"The wife brought that goddamn computer into this house in the first place," Greg said, hurling a thumb at Connie. "Ever since that computer came into the house, this family was ruined."

Connie absorbed the full-frontal attack with an uncomprehending blink, and then said to me, as if her husband had never spoken: "My husband has a lot of anger. He gets worked up easily. He's already had one heart attack."

She neither expects nor receives the faintest reply from him. They obey the conventions of the stage. When one of them steps forward into the spotlight to narrate, the other recedes and freezes like a statue. Ten minutes into the conversation, Jonathan slouched in. Even that verb does not capture the mixture of sullenness and truculence with which he entered the room. He was long and thin and dressed in the prison costume of the American suburban teenager: pants too big, sneakers gaping, a pirate hoop dangling from one ear. He looked away when he shook my hand and said "Nice to meet you" in a way that made it clear that he couldn't be less pleased. Then he sat down and said nothing while his parents returned to their split-screen narration.

At first glance, it was impossible to link Jonathan in the flesh to Jonathan on the Web. I have a file of his Internet postings, and they're all pretty bombastic. Two days before the FedEx package arrived bearing the SEC's subpoenas, for instance, he logged on to the Internet and posted two hundred separate times the following plug for a company called Firetector (ticker symbol FTEC):

Subj: THE MOST UNDERVALUED STOCK EVER
Date: 2/03/00 3:43 p.m. Pacific Standard Time
From: LebedTGl

FTEC is starting to break out! Next week, this thing will EXPLODE....
Currently FTEC is trading for just $2 1/2! I am expecting to see FTEC at $20 VERY SOON.
Let me explain why....
Revenues for the year should very conservatively be around $20 million. The average company in the industry trades with a price/sales ratio of 3.45. With 1.57 million shares outstanding, this will value FTEC at ... $44.

It is very possible that FTEC will see $44, but since I would like to remain very conservative ... my short-term target price on FTEC is still $20!

The FTEC offices are extremely busy.... I am hearing that a number of HUGE deals are being worked on. Once we get some news from FTEC and the word gets out about the company ... it will take off to MUCH HIGHER LEVELS!

I see little risk when purchasing FTEC at these DIRT-CHEAP PRICES. FTEC is making TREMENDOUS PROFITS and is trading UNDER BOOK VALUE!!!

And so on. The author of that and dozens more like it now sat dully at the end of the family's dining-room table and watched his parents take potshots at each other and their government. There wasn't an exclamation point in him.

Not long after his eleventh birthday, Jonathan opened an account with America Online. He went onto the Internet, at least at first, to meet other pro-wrestling fans. He built a Web site dedicated to the greater glory of Stone Cold Steve Austin. But about the same time, by watching his father, he became interested in the stock market. In his thirty-plus years working for Amtrak, Greg Lebed had worked his way up to middle manager. Along the way, he accumulated maybe twelve thousand dollars of blue-chip stocks. Like half of America, he came to watch the market's daily upward leaps and jerks with keen interest.

Jonathan saved him the trouble. When he came home from school, he turned on CNBC and watched the stock-market ticker stream across the bottom of the screen, searching it for the symbols inside his father's portfolio. "Jonathan would sit there for hours staring at them," Connie said, as if Jonathan is miles away.

"I just liked to watch the numbers go across the screen," Jonathan said.

"Why?"

"I don't know," he said. "I just wondered, like, what they meant."

At first, the numbers meant a chance to talk to his father. He would call his father at work whenever he saw one of his stocks cross the bottom of the television screen. This went on for about six months before Jonathan declared his own interest in owning stocks. On September 29, 1996, Jonathan's twelfth birthday, a savings bond his parents gave him at birth came due. He took the eight thousand dollars and got his father to invest it for him in the stock market. The first stock he bought was America Online, at twenty-five dollars a share—in spite of a lot of adverse commentary about the company on CNBC.

"He said that it was a stupid company and that it would go to two cents," Jonathan chimed in, pointing at his father, who obeyed what now appeared to be the family rule and sat frozen at the back of some mental stage. AOL rose five points in a couple of weeks, and Jonathan had his father sell it. From this he learned that (a) you could make money quickly in the stock market, (b) his dad didn't know what he was talking about and (c) it paid him to exercise his own judgment on these matters. All three lessons were reinforced dramatically by what happened next.

What happened next was that CNBC—which Jonathan now rose at five every morning to watch—announced a stock-picking contest for students. Jonathan had wanted to join the contest on his own but was told that he needed to be on a team, and so he went and asked two friends to join him. Thousands of students from across the country set out to speculate their way to victory. Each afternoon CNBC announced the top five teams of the day.

To get your name read out loud on television, you obviously opted for highly volatile stocks that stood a chance of doing well in the short term. Jonathan's team, dubbing itself the Triple Threat, had a portfolio that rose 51 percent the first day, which put them in first place. They remained in the top three for the next three months, until in the last two weeks of the contest they collapsed. Even a fourth-place finish was good enough to fetch a camera crew from CNBC, which came and filmed the team in Cedar Grove. The Triple Threat was featured in the *Verona-Cedar Grove Times* and celebrated on television by the Cedar Grove Township Council.

"From then, everyone at work started asking me if Jonathan had any stock tips for them," said Greg.

"They still ask me," said Connie.

By the spring of 1998, Jonathan was thirteen, and his ambitions were growing. He had glimpsed the essential truth of the market: that even people who called themselves professionals are often incapable of independent thought and that most people, though obsessed with money, have little ability to make decisions about it. He knew what he was doing, or thought he did. He had learned to find everything he wanted to know about a company on the Internet; what he couldn't find, he ran down in the flesh. It became part of Connie Lebed's life to drive her son to various corporate headquarters to make sure they existed. He also persuaded her to open an account with Ameritrade. "He'd done so well with the stock contest, I figured, let's see what he can do," Connie said.

What he did was turn his eight-thousand-dollar savings bond into twenty-eight thousand dollars inside of eighteen months. During the same period, he created his own Web site devoted to companies with small market capitalization—penny stocks. The Web site came to be known as Stock-dogs.com. ("You know, like racing dogs.") Stock-dogs .com plugged the stocks of companies Jonathan found interesting or that people Jonathan met on the Internet found interesting. At its peak, Stock-dogs.com had maybe one thousand five hundred visitors a day. Even so, the officers of what seemed to Jonathan to be serious companies wrote to him to sell him on their companies. Within a couple of months of becoming an amateur stock-market analyst, he was in the middle of a network of people who spent every waking hour chatting about and trading stocks on the Internet. The mere memory of this clearly upset Greg.

"He was just a little kid," he said. "These people who got in touch with him could have been anybody."

"How do you know?" said Jonathan. "You've never even been on the Internet."

"Suppose some hacker comes in and steals his money!" Greg said. "Next day, you type in, and you got nothing left."

Jonathan snorted. "That can't happen." He turned to me. "Whenever he sees something on TV about the Internet, he gets mad and disconnects my computer phone line."

"Oh, yeah," Connie said, brightening as if realizing for the first time that she lived in the same house as the other two. "I used to hear the garage door opening at three in the morning. Then Jonathan's little feet running back up the stairs."

"I haven't ever even turned a computer on!" Greg said. "And I never will!"

"He just doesn't understand how a lot of this works," explained Jonathan patiently. "And so he overreacts sometimes."

Greg and Connie were born in New Jersey, but from the moment the Internet struck, they might as well have just arrived from Taiwan. When the Internet landed on them, it redistributed the prestige and authority that goes with a general understanding of the ways of the world away from the grown-ups and to the child. The grown-ups now depended on the child to translate for them. Technology had turned them into a family of immigrants.

"I know, I know," Greg said, turning to me. "I'm supposed to know how it works. It's the future. But that's his future, not mine!"

"Anyway," Connie said, drifting back in again. "That's when the SEC called us the first time."

The first time?

Jonathan was fourteen when Connie agreed to take him to meet with the SEC in its Manhattan offices. When he heard the news, Greg, of course, hit the roof and hopped on the high-speed train to triple bypass. "He'd already had one heart attack," Connie explained and started to go into the heart problems all over again, inspiring Greg to mutter something about how he wasn't the person who brought the computer into the house and so it wasn't his responsibility to deal with this little nuisance.

At any rate, Connie asked Harold Burk, her boss at Hoffmann-La Roche, the drug company where she worked as a secretary, to go with her and Jonathan. Together, they made their way to a long conference table in a big room at 7 World Trade Center. On one side of the table, five lawyers and an examiner from the SEC; on the other, a fourteen-year-old boy, his mother and a bewildered friend.

This is how it began:

SEC: Does Jonathan's father know he's here today?

MRS. LEBED: Yes.

SEC: And he approves of having you here?

MRS. LEBED: Right, he doesn't want to go.

SEC: He's aware you're here.

MRS. LEBED: With Harold.

SEC: And that Mr. Burk is here.

MRS. LEBED: He did not want to—this whole thing has upset my husband a lot. He had a heart attack about a year ago, and he gets very, very upset about things. So he really did not want anything to do with it, and I just felt like—Harold said he would help me.

The SEC seemed to have figured out quickly that they were racing into some strange mental cul-de-sac. They turned their attention to Jonathan or, more specifically, his brokerage statements.

SEC: Where did you learn your technique for day trading?

JONATHAN: Just on TV, Internet.

SEC: What TV shows?

JONATHAN: CNBC mostly—basically CNBC is what I watch all the time.

SEC: Do you generally make money on your day trading?

JONATHAN: I usually don't day trade; I just try to—since I was home these days and I was very bored. I wanted something to do, so I was just trading constantly. I don't think I was making money. . . .

SEC: Just looking at your April statement, it looks like the majority of your trading is day trading.

JONATHAN: I was home a lot at that time.

MRS. LEBED: They were on spring vacation that week.

Having established and then ignored the boy's chief motive for trading stocks—a desire to escape the tedium of existence—the authorities then sought to discover his approach to attracting attention on the Internet.

SEC: On the first page referring to a hard copy of Jonathan's Web site, Stock-dogs.com, where it says, "Our six- to twelve-month outlook, eight dollars," what does that mean? The stock is selling less than three but you think it's going to go to eight.

JONATHAN: That's our outlook for the price to go based on their earnings potential and a good value ratio. . . .

SEC: Are you aware that there are laws that regulate company projections?

JONATHAN: No.

Eventually, the SEC people crept up on the reason they had noticed Jonathan in the first place. They had been hot on the trail of a grown-up named Ira Monas, one of Jonathan Lebed's many Internet correspondents. Monas, eventually jailed on unrelated charges, had been employed in "investor relations" by a number of small companies. In that role, he had fed Jonathan Lebed information about the companies, some of which turned out to be false and some of which Jonathan had unwittingly posted on Stock-dogs.com.

The SEC asked if Monas had paid Jonathan to do this and thus help to inflate the price of his company's stocks. Jonathan said no, he had done it for free because he thought the information was sound. The SEC then expressed its doubt that Jonathan was being forthright about his relationship with Monas. One of the small companies Monas had been hired to plug was a cigar retail outlet called Havana Republic. As a publicity stunt, Monas announced that the company—in which Jonathan came to own one hundred thousand shares—would hold a "smoke-out" in Midtown Manhattan.

The SEC now knew that Jonathan Lebed had attended the smoke-out. To the people across the table from Jonathan, this suggested that his relationship with a known criminal was deeper than he admitted.

SEC: So you decided to go to the smoke-out?

JONATHAN: Yes.

SEC: How did you go about that?

JONATHAN: We walked down the street and took a bus.

SEC: Who is "we"?

JONATHAN: Me and my friend Chuck.

SEC: OK.

JONATHAN: We took a bus to New York.

SEC: You cut school to do this?

JONATHAN: It was after school. Then we got picked up at Port Authority, so then my mother and Harold came and picked us up and we went to the smoke-out.

SEC: Why were you picked up at the Port Authority?

JONATHAN: Because people, like, under eighteen across the country, from California . . .

MRS. LEBED: They pick up minors there at Port Authority.

SEC: So the cops were curious about why you were there?

JONATHAN: Yes.

SEC: And they called your mother?

JONATHAN: Yes.

SEC: And she came.

JONATHAN: Yes.

SEC: You went to the smoke-out.

JONATHAN: Yes.

SEC: Did you see Ira there?

JONATHAN: Yes.

SEC: Did you introduce yourself to Ira?

JONATHAN: No.

Here, you can almost hear the little sucking sound on the SEC's side of the table as the conviction goes out of this line of questioning.

> SEC: Why not?
> JONATHAN: Because I'm not sure if he knew my age, or anything like that, so I didn't talk to anyone there at all.

This mad interrogation began at ten in the morning and ended at six in the evening. When it was done, the SEC declined to offer legal advice. Instead, it said, "The Internet is a grown-up medium for grown-up-type activities." Connie Lebed and Harold Burk, both clearly unnerved, apologized profusely on Jonathan's behalf and explained that he was just a naive child who had sought attention in the wrong place. Whatever Jonathan thought, he kept to himself.

"When I came home that day, I closed the Ameritrade account," Connie told me.

"Then how did Jonathan continue to trade?" I asked.

Greg then blurted out, "The kid never did something wrong,"

"Don't ask me!" Connie said. "I got nothing to do with it."

"All right," Greg said, "here's what happened. When Little Miss Nervous over here closes the Ameritrade account, I open an account for him in my name with that other place, E*Trade."

I turned to Jonathan, who wore his expression of airy indifference.

"But weren't you scared to trade again?"

"No."

"This thing with the SEC didn't even make you a little nervous?"

"No."

"No?"

"Why should it?"

Soon after he agreed to defend Jonathan Lebed, Kevin Marino, his lawyer, discovered he had a problem. No matter how he tried, he was unable to get Jonathan Lebed to say what he really thought. "In a conversation with Jonathan, I was supplying way too many of the ideas," Marino says. "You can't get them out of him." Finally, he asked Jonathan and his parents each to write a few paragraphs describing their feelings about how the SEC was treating Jonathan. Connie Lebed's statement took the form of a wailing lament of the pain inflicted by the callous government regulators on the family. ("I am also upset, as you know, that I was not called.") Greg Lebed's statement was an angry screed directed at both the government and the media.

Jonathan's statement—a four-page e-mail message dashed off the night that Marino asked for it—was so different in both tone and substance from his parents' that it inspired wonder that it could have been written by even the most casual acquaintance of the other two.

It began:

I was going over some old press releases about different companies. The best performing stock in 1999 on the Nasdaq was Qualcomm (QCOM). QCOM was up around 2,000% for the year. On December 29th of last year, even after QCOM's run from 25 to 500, Paine Webber analyst Walter Piecky came out and issued a buy rating on QCOM with a target price of 1,000. QCOM finished the day up 156 to 662. There was nothing fundamentally that would make QCOM worth 1,000. There is no way that a company with sales under $4 billion, should be worth hundreds of billions. . . . QCOM has now fallen from 800 to under 300. It is no longer the hot play with all of the attention. Many people were able to successfully time QCOM and make a lot of money. The ones who had bad timing on QCOM, lost a lot of money.

People who trade stocks, trade based on what they feel will move and they can trade for profit. Nobody makes investment decisions based on reading financial filings. Whether a company is making millions or losing millions, it has no impact on the price of the stock. Whether it is analysts, brokers, advisors, Internet traders, or the companies, everybody is manipulating the market. If it wasn't for everybody manipulating the market, there wouldn't be a stock market at all. . . .

As it happens, those last two sentences stand for something like the opposite of the founding principle of the United States Securities and Exchange Commission. To a very great extent, the world's financial markets are premised on a black-and-white mental snapshot of the American investor that was taken back in 1929. The SEC was created in 1934, and the big question in 1934 was, How do you reassure the public that the stock market is not rigged? From mid-1929 to mid-1932, the value of the stocks listed on the New York Stock Exchange had fallen 83 percent, from ninety billion dollars to about sixteen billion. Capitalism, with reason, was not feeling terribly secure.

To the greater public in 1934, the numbers on the stock-market ticker no longer seemed to represent anything "real," but rather the result of manipulation by financial pros. So, how to make the market seem "real"? The answer was to make new stringent laws against stock-market manipulation—aimed not at ordinary Americans, who were assumed to be the potential victims of any manipulation and the ones who needed to be persuaded that it was not some elaborate web of perceptions, but at the Wall Street elite. The American financial elite acquired its own police force, whose job it was to make sure their machinations did not ever again unnerve the great sweaty rabble. That's not how the SEC put it, of course. The catch phrase used by the policy-making elites when describing the SEC's mission was "to restore public confidence in the securities markets." But it amounted to the same thing. Keep up appearances, so that the public did not become too cautious. It occurred to no one that the public might one day be as sophisticated in these matters as financial professionals.

Anyone who paid attention to the money culture could see its foundation had long lay exposed, and it was just a matter of time before the termites got to it. From the moment the Internet went boom back in 1996, Web sites popped up in the middle of nowhere—Jackson, Missouri; Carmel, California—and began to give away precisely what Wall Street sold for a living: earning forecasts, stock recommendations, market color. By the summer of 1998, Xerox or AT&T or some such opaque American corporation would announce earnings of twenty-two cents a share, and even though all of Wall Street had predicted a mere twenty cents and the company had exceeded all expectations, the stock would collapse. The amateur Web sites had been saying twenty-three cents.

Eventually, the Bloomberg News Service commissioned a study to explore the phenomenon of what were now being called "whisper numbers." The study showed the whisper numbers, the numbers put out by the amateur Web sites, were mistaken, on average, by 21 percent. The professional Wall Street forecasts were mistaken, on average, by 44 percent. The reason the amateurs now held the balance of power in the market was that they were, on average, more than twice as accurate as the pros—this in spite of the fact that the entire financial system was rigged in favor of the pros. The big companies spoon-fed their scoops directly to the pros; the amateurs were flying by radar.

Even a fourteen-year-old boy could see how it all worked, why some guy working for free out of his basement in Jackson, Missouri, was more reliable than the most highly paid analyst on Wall Street. The companies that financial pros were paid to analyze were also the financial pros' biggest customers. Xerox and AT&T and the rest needed to put the right spin on their quarterly earnings. The goal at the end of every quarter was for the newspapers and the cable television shows and the rest to announce that they had "exceeded analysts' expectations." The easiest way to exceed analysts' expectations was to have the analysts lower them. And that's just what they did, and had been doing for years. The guy in Carmel, California, confessed to Bloomberg that all he had to do to be more accurate on the earnings estimates than Wall Street analysts was to raise all of them 10 percent.

A year later, when the Internet bubble burst, the hollowness of the pros only became clearer. The most famous analysts on Wall Street, who just a few weeks before had done whatever they could to cadge an appearance on CNBC or a quote in the *Wall Street Journal* to promote their favorite dot-com, went into hiding. Morgan Stanley's Mary Meeker, who made fifteen million dollars in 1999 while telling people to buy Priceline when it was at $165 a share and Healtheon/WebMD when it reached $105 a share, went silent as they collapsed toward zero.

Financial professionals had entered some weird, new head space. They simply took it for granted that a "financial market" was a collection of people doing their best to get onto CNBC and CNNfn and into the Heard on the Street column of the *Wall Street Journal* and the Lex column of the *Financial Times*, where they could advance their narrow self-interests.

To anyone who wandered into the money culture after, say, January 1996, it would have seemed absurd to take anything said by putative financial experts at face value. There was no reason to get worked up about it. The stock market was not an abstraction whose integrity needed to be preserved for the sake of democracy. It was a game people played to make money. Who cared if anything anyone said or believed was "real"? Capitalism could now afford for money to be viewed as no different from anything else you might buy or sell.

Or, as Jonathan Lebed wrote to his lawyer:

> Every morning I watch *Shop at Home*, a show on cable television that sells such products as baseball cards, coins and electronics. Don West, the host of the show, always says things like, "This is one of the best deals in the history of *Shop at Home*! This is a no-brainer folks! This is absolutely unbelievable, congratulations to everybody who got in on this! Folks, you got to get in on the line, this is a gift, I just can't believe this!" There is absolutely nothing wrong with him making quotes such as those. As long as he isn't lying about the condition of a baseball card or lying about how large a television is, he isn't committing any kind of a crime. The same thing applies to people who discuss stocks.

Right from the start, the SEC treated the publicity surrounding the case of Jonathan Lebed at least as seriously as the case itself. Maybe even more seriously. The Philadelphia office had brought the case, and so when the producer from *60 Minutes* called to say he wanted to do a big segment about the world's first teenage stock-market manipulator, he called the Philadelphia office. "Normally we call the top and get bumped down to some flack," says Trevor Nelson, the *60 Minutes* producer in question. "This time I left a message at the SEC's Philadelphia office, and Arthur Levitt's office called me right back." Levitt, being the SEC chairman, flew right up from Washington to be on the show.

To the SEC, it wasn't enough that Jonathan Lebed hand over his winnings: he had to be vilified; people had to be made to understand that what he had done was a crime, with real victims. "The SEC kept saying that they were going to give us the name of one of the kid's victims so we could interview him," Nelson says. "But they never did."

I waited a couple of months for things to cool off before heading down to Washington to see Arthur Levitt. He was just then finishing up being the longest-serving chairman of the SEC and was taking a victory lap in the media for a job well done. He was now sixty-nine, but as a youth, back in the 1950s and 1960s, he had made a lot of money on Wall Street. At the age of sixty-two, he landed his job at the SEC—in part, because he had raised a lot of money on the street for Bill Clinton—where he set himself up to defend the interests of the ordinary investor. He had declared war on the financial elite and pushed through rules that stripped it of its natural market advantages. His single bravest act was Regulation FD, which required corporations to release significant information about themselves to everyone at once rather than through the Wall Street analysts.

Having first determined I was the sort of journalist likely to see the world exactly as he did, he set out to explain to me the new forces corrupting the financial markets. "The Internet has speeded up everything," he said, "and we're seeing more people in the markets who shouldn't be there. A lot of these new investors don't have the experience or the resources of a professional trader. These are the ones who bought that [expletive] that Lebed was pushing."

"Do you think he is a sign of a bigger problem?"

"Yes, I do. And I find his case very disturbing . . . more serious than the guy who holds up the candy store. . . . I think there's a considerable risk of an antibusiness backlash in this country. The era of the twenty-five-year-old billionaire represents a kind of symbol which is different from the Horatio Alger symbol. The twenty-five-year-old billionaire looks lucky, feels lucky. And investors who lose money buying stock in the company of the twenty-five-year-old billionaire . . ."

He trailed off, leaving me to finish the thought.

"You think it's a moral issue."

"I do."

"You think Jonathan Lebed is a bad kid?"

"Yes, I do."

"Can you explain to me what he did?"

He looked at me long and hard. I could see that this must be his meaningful stare. His eyes were light blue bottomless pits. "He'd go into these chat rooms and use twenty fictitious names and post messages. . . ."

"By fictitious names, do you mean e-mail addresses?"

"I don't know the details."

Don't know the details? He'd been all over the airwaves decrying the behavior of Jonathan Lebed.

"Put it this way," he said. "He'd buy, lie and sell high." The chairman's voice had deepened unnaturally. He hadn't spoken the line; he had acted it. It was exactly the same line he had spoken on *60 Minutes* when his interviewer, Steve Kroft, asked him to explain Jonathan Lebed's crime. He must have caught me gaping in wonder because, once again, he looked at me long and hard. I glanced away.

"What do you think?" he asked.

Well, I had my opinions. In the first place, I had been surprised to learn that it was legal for, say, an author to write phony glowing reviews of his book on Amazon but illegal for him to plug a stock on Yahoo! just because he happened to own it. I thought it was—to put it kindly—misleading to tell reporters that Jonathan Lebed had used "twenty fictitious names" when he had used four AOL e-mail addresses and posted exactly the same message under each of them so that no one who read them could possibly mistake him for more than one person. I further thought that without quite realizing what had happened to them, the people at the SEC were now lighting out after the very people—the average American with a bit of money to play with—whom they were meant to protect.

Finally, I thought that by talking to me or any other journalist about Jonathan Lebed when he didn't really understand himself what Jonathan Lebed had done, the chairman of the SEC displayed a disturbing faith in the media to buy whatever he was selling.

But when he asked me what I thought, all I said was, "I think it's more complicated than you think."

"Richard—call Richard!" Levitt was shouting out the door of his vast office. "Tell Richard to come in here!"

Richard was Richard Walker, the SEC's director of enforcement. He entered with a smile, but mislaid it before he even sat down. His mind went from a standing start to deeply distressed inside of ten seconds. "This kid was making predictions about the prices of stocks," he said testily. "He had no basis for making these predictions." Before I could tell him that sounds a lot like what happens every day on Wall Street, he said, "And don't tell me that's standard practice on Wall Street," so I didn't. But it is. It is still OK for the analysts to lowball their estimates of corporate earnings and plug the stocks of the companies they take public so that they remain in the good graces of those companies. The SEC would protest that the analysts don't actually own the stocks they plug, but that is a distinction without a difference: they profit mightily and directly from its rise.

"Jonathan Lebed was seeking to manipulate the market," said Walker.

But that only begs the question, If Wall Street analysts and fund managers and corporate CEOs who appear on CNBC and CNNfn to plug stocks are not guilty of seeking to manipulate the market, what on earth does it mean to manipulate the market?

"It's when you promote a stock for the purpose of artificially raising its price."

But when a Wall Street analyst can send the price of a stock of a company that is losing billions of dollars up fifty points in a day, what does it mean to "artificially raise" the price of a stock? The law sounded perfectly circular. Actually, this point had been well made in a recent article in *Business Crimes Bulletin* by a pair of securities law experts, Lawrence S. Bader and Daniel B. Kosove. "The casebooks are filled with opinions that describe manipulation as causing an 'artificial' price," the experts wrote. "Unfortunately, the casebooks are short on opinions defining the word 'artificial' in this context. . . . By using the word 'artificial,' the courts have avoided coming to grips with the problem of defining 'manipulation'; they have simply substituted one undefined term for another."

Walker recited, "The price of a stock is artificially raised when subjected to something other than ordinary market forces."

But what are "ordinary market forces"?

An ordinary market force, it turned out, is one that does not cause the stock to rise artificially. In short, an ordinary market force is whatever the SEC says it is, or what it can persuade the courts it is. And the SEC does not view teenagers' broadcasting their opinions as "an ordinary market force." It can't. If it did, it would be compelled to face the deep complexity of the modern market—and all of the strange new creatures who have become, with the help of the Internet, ordinary market forces. When the Internet collided with the stock market, Jonathan Lebed became a market force. Adolescence became a market force.

I finally came clean with a thought: the SEC let Jonathan Lebed walk away with five hundred grand in his pocket because it feared that if it didn't, it would wind up in court and it would lose. And if the law ever declared formally that Jonathan Lebed didn't break it, the SEC would be faced with an impossible situation: millions of small investors plugging their portfolios with abandon, becoming in essence professional financial analysts, generating embarrassing little explosions of unreality in every corner of the capital markets. No central authority could sustain the illusion that stock prices were somehow "real" or that the market wasn't, for most people, a site of not terribly productive leisure activity. The red dog would be off his leash.

I might as well have strolled into the office of the drug czar and lit up a joint.

"The kid himself said he set out to manipulate the market," Walker virtually shrieked. But, of course, that is not all the kid said. The kid said everybody in the market was out to manipulate the market.

"Then why did you let him keep five hundred grand of his profits?" I asked.

"We determined that those profits were different from the profits he made on the eleven trades we defined as illegal," he said.

This, I already knew, was a pleasant fiction. The amount Jonathan Lebed handed over to the government was determined by haggling between Kevin Marino and the SEC's Philadelphia office. The SEC initially demanded the eight hundred thousand dollars Jonathan had made, plus interest. Marino had countered with 125 grand. They haggled a bit and then settled at 285.

"Can you explain how you distinguished the illegal trades from the legal ones?"

"I'm not going to go through the case point by point."

"Why not?"

"It wouldn't be appropriate."

At which point, Arthur Levitt, who had been trying to stare into my eyes as intently as a man can stare, said in his deep voice, "This kid has no basis for making these predictions."

"But how do you know that?"

And the chairman of the SEC, the embodiment of investor confidence, the keeper of the notion that the numbers gyrating at the bottom of the CNBC screen are "real," drew himself up and said, "I worked on Wall Street."

Well. What do you say to that? He had indeed worked on Wall Street—in 1968.

"So did I," I said.

"I worked there longer than you."

Walker leapt back in. "This kid's father said he was going to rip the [expletive] computer out of the wall."

I realized that it was my turn to stare. I stared at Richard Walker. "Have you met Jonathan Lebed's father?" I said.

"No, I haven't," he said curtly. "But look, we talked to this kid two years ago, when he was fourteen years old. If I'm a kid and I'm pulled in by some scary government agency, I'd back off."

That's the trouble with fourteen-year-old boys—from the point of view of the social order.

They haven't yet learned the more sophisticated forms of dishonesty. It can take years of slogging to learn how to feign respect for hollow authority.

Still! That a fourteen-year-old boy, operating essentially in a vacuum, would walk away from a severe grilling by six hostile bureaucrats and jump right back into the market—how did that happen? It occurred to me, as it had occurred to Jonathan's lawyer, that I had taken entirely the wrong approach to getting the answer. The whole point of Jonathan Lebed was that he had invented himself on the Internet. The Internet had taught him how hazy the line was between perception and reality. When people could see him, they treated him as they would treat a fourteen-year-old boy. When all they saw were his thoughts on financial matters, they treated him as if he were a serious trader. On the Internet, where no one could see who he was, he became who he was. I left the SEC and went back to my hotel and sent him an e-mail message, asking him the same question I asked the first time we met: why hadn't he been scared off?

Straight away he wrote back:

It was about 2–3 months from when the SEC called me in for the first time until I started trading again. The reason I didn't trade for those 2–3 months is because I had all of my money tied up in a stock. I sold it at the end of the year to take a tax loss, which allowed me to start trading again. I wasn't frightened by them because it was clear that they were focused on whether or not I was being paid to profile stocks when the fact is I was not. I was never told by them that I was doing something wrong and I was never told by them not to do something.

By September 1999, Jonathan Lebed was playing at the top of his game. He had figured out the advantage, after he had bought shares in a small company, in publicizing his many interests. "I came up with it myself," he said of the idea. "It was obvious from the newspapers and CNBC. Of course stocks respond to publicity!"

After he had picked and bought his stock, he would write a single message about it and stick it up in as many places on Yahoo! Finance as he could between five and eight in the morning, when he left home for school. There were no explicit rules on Yahoo! Finance, but there were constraints. The first was that Yahoo! limited the number of messages he could post using one e-mail address. He would click onto Yahoo! and open an account with one of his four AOL screen names; a few minutes later, Yahoo!, mysteriously, would tell him that his messages could no longer be delivered. Eventually, he figured out that they must have some limit that they weren't telling people about. He got around it by grabbing another of his four AOL screen names and creating another Yahoo! account. By rotating his four AOL screen names, he found he could get his message onto maybe two hundred Yahoo! message boards before school.

He also found that when he went to do it the next time, with a different stock, Yahoo! would no longer accept messages from his AOL screen names. So he was forced to create four more screen names and start over again. Yahoo! never told him he shouldn't do this. "The account would be just, like, deleted," he said. "Yahoo! never had a policy; it's just what I figured out." The SEC accused Jonathan of trying to seem like more than one person when he promoted his stocks, but when you see how and why he did what he did, that is clearly false. (For instance, he ignored the feature on Yahoo! that enables users to employ up to seven different "fictitious names" for each e-mail address.) It's more true to say that he was trying to simulate an appearance on CNBC.

Over time, he learned that some messages had more effect on the stock market than others. "I definitely refined it," he said of his Internet persona. "In the beginning, I would write, like, very professionally.

But then I started putting stuff in caps and using exclamation points and making it sound more exciting. That worked better. When it's more exciting, it draws people's attention to it compared to when you write, like, dull or something." The trick was to find a stock that he could get excited about. He sifted the Internet chat rooms and the shopping mall with three things in mind: (1) "It had to be in the area of the stock market that is likely to become a popular play"; (2) "It had to be undervalued compared to similar companies"; and (3) "It had to be undiscovered—not that many people talking about it on the message boards."

Over a couple of months, I drifted in and out of Jonathan Lebed's life and became used to its staccato rhythms. His defining trait was that the strangest things happened to him, and he just thought of them as perfectly normal—and there was no one around to clarify matters. The threat of being prosecuted by the U.S. Attorney in Newark and sent away to a juvenile detention center still hung over him, but he didn't give any of it a second thought. He had his parents, his twelve-year-old sister, Dana, and a crowd of friends at Cedar Grove High School, most of whom owned pieces of Internet businesses and all of whom speculated in the stock market. "There are three groups of kids in our school," one of them explained to me. "There's the jocks, there's the druggies and there's us—the more business-oriented. The jocks and the druggies respect what we do. At first, a lot of the kids are, like, What are you doing? But once kids see money, they get excited."

The first time I heard this version of the social structure of Cedar Grove High, I hadn't taken it seriously. But then one day I went out with Jonathan and one of his friends, Keith Graham, into a neighboring suburb to do what they liked to do most when they weren't doing business— shoot pool. We parked the car and set out down an unprosperous street in search of the pool hall.

"Remember West Coast Video?" Keith said drolly.

I looked up. We were walking past a derelict building with West Coast Video stenciled on its plate glass.

Jonathan chuckled knowingly. "We owned, like, half the company."

I looked at him. He seemed perfectly serious. He began to tick off the reasons for his investment. "First, they were about to open an Internet subsidiary; second, they were going to sell DVDs when no other video chain . . ."

I stopped him before he really got going. "Who owned half the company?"

"Me and a few others. Keith, Michael, Tom, Dan."

"Some teachers, too," Keith said.

"Yeah, the teachers heard about it," Jonathan said. He must have seen me looking strangely at him because he added: "It wasn't that big a deal. We probably didn't have a controlling interest in the company, but we had a fairly good percentage of the stock."

"Teachers?" I said. "The teachers followed you into this sort of thing."

"Sometimes," Jonathan said.

"All the time," Keith said. Keith is a year older than Jonathan and tends to be a more straightforward narrator of events. Jonathan will habitually dramatize or understate some case and emit a strange frequency, like a boy not quite sure how hard to blow into his new tuba, and Keith will invariably correct him. "As soon as people at school found out what Jonathan was in, everybody got in. Like, right way. It was, like, if Jonathan's in on it, it must be good." And then the two boys moved on to some other subject, bored with the memory of having led some teachers in the acquisition of shares of West Coast Video. We entered the pool hall and took a table, where we were joined by another friend, John. Keith had paged him.

My role in Jonathan Lebed's life suddenly became clear: to express sufficient wonder at whatever he has been up to that he is compelled to elaborate.

"I don't understand," I said. "How would other kids find out what Jonathan was in?"

"It's high school," said Keith, in a tone reserved for people over thirty-five. "Four hundred kids. People talk."

"How would the teachers find out?"

Now Keith gave me a look that told me that I'm the most prominent citizen of a new nation called Stupid. "They would ask us!" he said.

"But why?"

"They saw we were making money," Keith said.

"Yeah," said Jonathan, who, odd as it sounds, exhibits none of his friend's knowingness. He just knows. "I feel, like, that most of my classes, my grades would depend not on my performance but on how the stocks were doing."

"Not really," Keith said.

"OK," Jonathan said. "Maybe not that. But, like, I didn't think it mattered if I was late for class."

Keith considered that. "That's true," he said.

"I mean," Jonathan said, "they were making, like, thousands of dollars off the trades, more than their salaries even. . . ."

"Look," I said, "I know this is a stupid question. But was there any teacher who, say, disapproved of what you were doing?"

The three boys considered this, plainly for the first time in their lives.

"The librarian," Jonathan finally said.

"Yeah," John said. "But that's only because the computers were in the library, and she didn't like us using them."

"You traded stocks from the library?"

"Fifth-period study hall was in the library," Keith said. "Fifth-period study hall was like a little Wall Street. But sometimes the librarian would say the computers were for study purposes only. None of the other teachers cared."

"They were trading," Jonathan said.

The mood had shifted. We shot pool and pretended that there was no more boring place to be than this world we live in. "Even though we owned like a million shares," Jonathan said, picking up the new mood, "it wasn't that big a deal. West Coast Video was trading at like thirty cents a share when we got in."

Keith looked up from the cue ball. "When you got in," he said.

"Everyone else got in at sixty-five cents; then it collapsed. Most of the people lost money on that one."

"Hmmm," Jonathan said, with real satisfaction. "That's when I got out."

Suddenly I realized that the SEC was right: there were victims to be found from Jonathan Lebed's life on the Internet. They were right here in New Jersey. I turned to Keith. "You're Jonathan's victim."

"Yeah, Keith," Jonathan said, laughing. "You're my victim."

"Nah," Keith said. "In the stock market, you go in knowing you can lose. We were just doing what Jon was doing, but not doing as good a job at it."

TOXIC DREAMS:
A CALIFORNIA TOWN FINDS
MEANING IN AN ACID PIT

Jack Hitt

✲ ✲ ✲

The Stringfellow Acid Pits were called into being on August 9, 1955, at a dull meeting of small-bore officials in Riverside County, California. The county's Board of Trade had convened to kick around a new idea, one you still hear among municipal officials in desperate places. The goal was to better facilitate "the program of enticing industries into our county"; the solution, board president Carl Davis said, was for the county to offer a dumping site for the toxic waste that the desired industries would inevitably produce. The board agreed. They approached J. B. Stringfellow, a high-school dropout who operated a granite quarry a mile or so outside the little town of Glen Avon. The county's proposal was to dump chemicals into the large stone cavities left by Stringfellow's excavations. The scientific thinking they adopted was: she'll hold.

The county imposed a few restrictions on Stringfellow; they discouraged, for example, any "fuming" liquids. But such burdensome government regulations were quickly forgotten, and the quarry began to fill up with an exquisite ragout, including "scrap thinner," "degreaser," "bonderlube," "paint booth waste," "lube line waste," "sump waste," "paint stripper," "chromated emulsion cleaner," and "paint line waste." One trucker would later testify (for there was, inevitably, a lawsuit) to the careful segregation of deadly chemicals at Stringfellow: if "one pond was full," he said, "we would go up to the next one."

A unique attraction offered by Stringfellow was "unsupervised night dumping." In 1971, local manufacturers received a brochure that read, "If your company finds it necessary to dump on a weekend or during the night, arrangements can be made by telephone with our office." Eventually even the phone call was eliminated, and the gate was simply left unlocked so that truckers could let themselves in at any hour of any day. The oversight system employed to prevent dumping violations was the honor code.

A list of the chemicals poured into Stringfellow fills thirteen pages in a court brief (for there were, inevitably, court briefs), including everything from acetylene chloride, butylated hydroxyanisole, and chlorobenzenesulfonic acid to uranium, xylene, and zinc phosphate. One pits veteran recalled in a deposition how the organics would sometimes get mixed into the acids and that Stringfellow, "as a result, caught fire."

Between September 1956 and November 1972, the quarry took in thirty-four million gallons of chemicals—hundreds of different chemicals—from about a hundred companies. In 1972, Mr. Stringfellow, fearing that the pits were leaking, agreed to shut the dump down. The huge uncovered lagoons languished, unprotected by even a fence.

In March 1978, the rainy season in southern California was worse than usual. With each downpour, the acid pits rose. The state announced that rather than allow the chemical mix to overrun the earthen levees that surrounded it, they were going to flush out some of the pits' contents. Eight hundred thousand gallons of Stringfellow brew were sluiced into the town's open culverts. It curled around the school, burbled past people's homes, and finally sloshed into ditches leading out of town. The sewers backed up with an odd viscous foam. Local kids thought the stuff was great; its stickiness made for hilariously goopy bubble beards when they smeared it on their faces.

That August, Love Canal, New York, was evacuated. Poisonous chemicals had been seeping onto playgrounds and into basements. President Carter declared the town a disaster area. "Toxic waste" became a household word. People in Glen Avon, newly conscious of environmental danger, began wondering about the weird foam they had seen, about the strange odors they sometimes smelled, about disabilities and ailments they had previously chalked up to bad luck. Everything, it seemed, could be traced to the same source: the dump.

A group of residents banded together, gave itself a name—Concerned Neighbors in Action—and started asking questions of state environmental officials. As the years passed, and answers were slow in coming, Concerned Neighbors became more activist—in 1980, they printed up a T-shirt with a wilted sunflower, a dying bird, and the slogan IT'S THE PITS. In 1984, state authorities announced the existence of an underground plume of Stringfellow slime, inching toward town. After the news, notices went up around town asking people if they had experienced any peculiar ailments or problems. They had. In April 1985, roughly one-third of the town's population joined in filing a massive lawsuit.

The suit's official title was *Penny Newman et al.* v. *J. B. Stringfellow et al.*, but the emphasis, on both sides, was on the "et al." The suit named as defendants J. B. Stringfellow, the state of California, and more than a hundred different dumpers that had used the pits.[1] The plaintiff pool consisted of nearly four thousand injured parties alleging damages that included property devaluation, physical ailment, and emotional distress.

On its surface, then, Stringfellow appears to be merely another wretched tale in the familiar genre of dump narratives: negligent corporate giants in cahoots with craven state lackeys secretly store a witches' brew of poisons near working-class town and don't fess up un-

---

1. Stringfellow boasts many of the standard villains of the classic toxic-waste story—Texaco, General Electric, Rockwell, Lockheed. But the list of offending companies goes on to include some ambitious newcomers: Rich Steel Pickling Company, Evr-Gard Coating Corp., George Industries, J&M Anodizing, Mask-Off Company, Basic Industries, Inc., Buck's of Upland, and, finally, a Mrs. Lucille Hubbs.

til children are stumping about on withered legs and the elderly are marooned inside oxygen tents. And one would expect the standard ending to this tale: locals sue the hell out of everybody and scoop up millions in well-deserved compensation. But, as I was to learn, there was very little that was standard about the Stringfellow story.

What first drew my attention to Glen Avon's woes was that absurd name. Stringfellow. Acid. Pits. Modern life rarely shunts nouns together with such Dickensian economy. After I first encountered that singular name in a newspaper article some four or five years ago, it began to appear in my life eerily, serendipitously. If I was in Washington, the *Post* had a short update; if in San Francisco, then the *Chronicle*. If, while dressing in a hotel, I caught an environmental lawyer on C-SPAN, then Stringfellow would be cited offhandedly and without explanation. One evening, seated at an intimate dinner party in New Haven, Connecticut, I casually mentioned my growing interest in Stringfellow. Across the table a head turned and said, "I've worked on that case." Then another guest spoke up. He, too, was indirectly involved. I was not following the case; it was pursuing me.

The newspaper reports I read created a sense of Cyclopean dimension: a specially constructed courtroom, private judges, secret negotiations, a quarter-million pages of pretrial documents, and legal processes of absurd intricacy. The more I studied Stringfellow, though, the less it seemed to me to be simply a complex of lawsuits. It became, in my mind, a diorama of the twentieth century and all its plagues: complexity, chaos, existential fear, tedium, colossal wads of money, and a neo-medieval conviction that the objective truth is attainable if only one can spend enough money and take enough depositions.

I wanted to look at Stringfellow up close—not only to wade into the particulars of the case but to enter the world that it had created. Four thousand people bound together for nearly two decades constitutes a kind of community, one that is very modern and American—built not upon tribal identification or religious tenets or a credo of common virtue but upon shared victimization. And beyond the plaintiffs, there were hundreds of others—lawyers, clerks, government functionaries—who had spent years wandering the Stringfellow landscape. And so, last fall, I decided to fly to California and explore their world.

The creative force that transfigured a neglected dump into a legal nightmare was the case's inherent complexity. For example, Stringfellow has all the superficial features of a straightforward class-action suit—corporate negligence, thousands injured—but it is not one. In a true class-action suit, such as Love Canal or the Dalkon Shield case, a large group of plaintiffs can sue as an individual, because each plaintiff has more or less the same complaint. Stringfellow was not so straightforward. The dump didn't contain just one chemical; it had hundreds of them. The chemicals didn't intrude into the plaintiffs' lives by an established path: some town residents said that the toxins leached into their water; some claimed that their soil had been contaminated; others claimed that the poisons wafted into their homes on the Santa Ana winds. What's more, each of the four thousand plaintiffs was suffering from a different set of ailments, ranging from young Phillip Leyva's "extreme retardation of bone maturation," "learning problem at school," and "uncontrollable crying" to Barbara Provonsha's "nightmares," "memory loss," and "tingling sensation in lips."

Stringfellow was so complex that it had to be seen as four thousand separate personal-injury cases—think of four thousand car accidents—packaged together. The case presented a problem unique in the history of American law. How does a court try four thousand cases that are generally similar but legally different? Judge Erik Kaiser came up with an innovative solution: he would bundle the four thousand plaintiffs into groups of roughly seventeen, and try the bundled cases consecutively. Consider the math: 4,000 divided by 17 = 235 trials. If each one lasted a little under a year—a conservative estimate—the entire process would be wrapped up in two centuries.

Kaiser's solution created enormous pressure to settle the case for money rather than adjudicate it for truth. If those first seventeen plaintiffs raked in an enormous settlement, then GE, Evr-Gard Coating, the state of California, and all the other dumpers could look forward to two hundred years of writing checks. And so from 1984 to 1993, as depositions were taken, motions were filed, and potential jurors were called (over two thousand of them), the assembled legal minds were behind closed doors, performing an elaborate minuet of settlement negotiation. A group of small dumpers caved in first, settling in 1989 for a million dollars. In 1990, Weyerhaeuser settled for the same amount. In November 1991, J. B. Stringfellow himself kicked in $8 million, and GE coughed up $5 million. By the time the first trial began, in January 1993, ninety-seven defendants had settled, for a total of $48 million. A month into the trial, another ten bought their way out, for a combined $44 million. Only two defendants remained—the state of California and a small die-casting company called Rainbow Canyon Manufacturing.

After a nine-month trial, the jury reached its verdict. Despite claims by the plaintiffs' lawyers that they won a moral victory, the decision could not have been encouraging to the people of Glen Avon: eight of the seventeen plaintiffs were awarded nothing at all, Rainbow Canyon Manufacturing was found blameless, and the state of California was ordered to pay the nine remaining plaintiffs a meager $159,147 in damages.

Nevertheless, under Kaiser's arrangement there would soon be another trial, with seventeen new plaintiffs, and then another, and another, until all four thousand had received justice. Meanwhile, in a federal courthouse in Los Angeles, an entirely separate case, to decide the pits' future, was under way. In this case, there were no plaintiffs: the hundred dumpers, along with old man Stringfellow and the state of California, were consuming hundreds of millions in legal fees battling among their many selves as to who would foot the estimated billion-dollar tab for the Stringfellow cleanup. In this dispute there is no resolution in sight.[2]

Stringfellow has but one precedent: *Jarndyce v. Jarndyce*, the famously unknowable and unending lawsuit in *Bleak House*. "The little

---

2. There are still other, ancillary suits born of Stringfellow, the most accessible of which turn on exotic distinctions in the hermeneutics of industrial insurance law.

plaintiff or defendant," wrote Dickens, "who was promised a new rocking-horse when Jarndyce and Jarndyce should be settled, has grown up, possessed himself of a real horse, and trotted away into the other world." Jarndyce was the author's metaphor for an ebbing empire consumed in furious, aimless argumentation. "This scarecrow of a suit has, in course of time," he wrote, "become so complicated that no man alive knows what it means."

The gorgeous convolutions of Stringfellow, of course, were what landed me in Riverside County, excited and ready, as Judge Kaiser began the preliminary hearings for trial two. But no one in the case could quite believe I had come. "There's nothing for you here," they said. By that, they meant that the case has no pizzazz, no O.J. True, the lawyers do not strut for the media; the witnesses do not have great hair; the crime is bloodless; Court TV will never broadcast the proceedings. Yet despite its turgid legalities, Stringfellow as a whole possesses a rare postmodern clarity. It is the platonic essence of a modern lawsuit: a mountain of money piled atop a tiny nugget of fear. Stringfellow needs no dream team. Stringfellow is the dream.

Judge Kaiser presided over *Newman v. Stringfellow* in a courtroom in the county seat of Riverside. Because of the complexities of the case, no municipal courthouse could contain the trial—during the early hearings, there were hundreds of defendants, which meant hundreds and hundreds of lawyers. To accommodate all the attorneys, the county appropriated a defunct, roomy beauty salon two blocks from the municipal building and rebuilt it into what is known, still, as the Stringfellow Courtroom.

My guide to the courtroom was Kira Morgan, the county's exhibits clerk. As she led me inside, she pointed out items of historical interest. The old plumbing for the salon's hair-washing sinks, she said, remained embedded in the low partitions that divided the room into four quadrants—jury, public, lawyers, judge. The lawyers, she said, sat at one of eight banquet tables arrayed on a raked stage facing the judge. On any given day during the trial, as many as forty lawyers, often pulling small carts crammed with their paperwork, packed themselves into the courtroom, outnumbering the jury and the public galleries combined.

As evidence clerk, though, Kira was anxious to tell me about the paper and props associated with the trial. "Usually all that's needed for the evidence in a case is just a box on a shelf," she said. "The closest thing I got to Stringfellow is probably a death penalty—I got one with a big trunk, a mannequin about five foot five, and a laundry bag with dirty clothes in it." Stringfellow, she explained, doesn't have an evidence box, or even an evidence shelf. She led me to a door in the corner of the courtroom. "Stringfellow," Kira said, "has its own room."

She pushed open the door. Boxes lined both walls, leaving a narrow alley. A thicket of picture boards—some monstrously large, seven by seven feet—leaned against a wall. Scattered throughout the room were soil-sample tubes and other pieces of evidence. Kira nodded at the floor, where a collection of large boulders lay quietly—evidence, apparently, of something.

"Boulders," she said.

Yet the overwhelming majority of what the jury saw was not in this room, Kira explained, but was stored in digital form. Multicolored computer graphics were presented via the most complex video system ever used in a courtroom: eighteen television monitors, two laser-disc players, three Telestrators (the machine John Madden uses to "draw" on the television screen during football games), an Elmo (a high-tech overhead projector), a videotape player, a video printer, and assorted laser-disc changers.

Because the matrix of causality in the case involved such a bewildering variety of dumpers, chemicals, and plaintiffs, much of the case was argued in the hypothetical realm of computer modeling. The plaintiffs hired a company with the Dickensian name of Failure Analysis Associates to reconfigure the evidence for the television screen. One computerized re-creation of this intricate chemical intrusion made assumptions involving more than fifteen thousand variables.

The complexity of Stringfellow had other unique manifestations. Take the plaintiffs: despite their lack of common ailments or history, they still had to devise a way to speak with one voice. So they wrote a full constitution, complete with checks and balances. The charter is divided into six articles—only one fewer than the U.S. Constitution. Article II delimits the powers of the Steering Committee and enumerates the duties of the Business, Property, Health, and Guardian ad Litem subcommittees. There are definitions of a quorum, methods for the conduct of business, and bylaws regarding the election of officers. Article VI details the proceedings for impeachment.

Some of the legal processes involved in the case are practically unknowable. When the stampede of settlements began, the lawyers had to devise a procedure allowing for possible protest from each of the four thousand plaintiffs. A few days after my tour of the courthouse, the two main plaintiffs' lawyers—Doug Welebir and John Grasberger—invited me to sit down with them at the enormous conference table in Welebir's San Bernardino office and discuss these intricate procedures.

Welebir described how the Glen Avon plaintiffs, via their own constitutional mechanism, had to approve each settlement offer; then, he explained, a separate judge—not Kaiser—had to decide whether the offer was fair to both sides.

"I'm not so sure about that," interrupted Grasberger.

"No, because then we had the challenge—" said Welebir.

"—Vis-à-vis the plaintiffs," said Grasberger.

"And vis-à-vis each other," Welebir said.

"No, no, no, no, no," said Grasberger.

"The state objected to our settlement," Welebir reminded his colleague.

"Well, yes, but that was a different track from the track I'm talking about," said Grasberger.

"Oh. Okay," Welebir said. He turned to me and smiled. "There's a lot of different tracks."

And each track, of course, had its own judge. Not only were sitting judges called upon but also retired judges, hired part-time, and even "special masters"—freelance judges, each of whom was assigned to take charge of one issue or aspect of the case. Asked to enumerate the case's pantheon of judges, Welebir and Grasberger grew nostalgic, joshing and tossing out catty memories. They ticked off the names—Trotter, Garst, Fields, Marceli, Irving—until they reached the most remote cul-de-sac of the process. They couldn't remember all the names. They said they'd get back to me.

The next day, I drove to Glen Avon itself. After my tour along the brightly bannered boulevards of Riverside, the off-ramp at Glen Avon opened onto wide, curbless thoroughfares. They seemed to match the distant russet hills—a scrub fire in search of a spark. The reason Riverside County located the dump here was still obvious. It is a poor town with hard, beaten dirt paths for sidewalks and dilapidated shops with misspelled signs. Judging from the billboards I saw—¡Gatorade: Quita la Sed!—the town is home to a sizable population of Mexican immigrants. The telephone poles were ancient T-bars, shredded by repairmen's cleats. Nailed to them were handwritten signs advertising the sale of Railroad Ties and Dirt. Down a side street I passed Dumpsters crammed with ruined sofas and flaccid mattresses. A murder of crows, fat and shiny, tried to stare me down. At the approach of my car, they lumbered off onto the dirt paths rather than take flight.

I stopped at a well-kept house with a trim lawn, the home of Penny Newman, the executive director of Concerned Neighbors in Action, and the namesake of *Newman v. Stringfellow*. She appeared at her door barefoot, in a cheerful yellow suit. We sat in her breakfast nook looking into her spic-and-span living room. As we chatted, she scrunched her toes into the warm cozy thickness of her brown carpet.

When I asked her to recall her first involvement with the case, she said it all began amid the lying and confusion that surrounded the events of 1978. The flood "galvanized the community to look at what was going on," she said. "Everybody was going off in their own direction and seeing things their own way. What Concerned Neighbors did was bring people together and focus on this one problem. It was a coalition of different groups that coordinated actions toward Stringfellow— the PTA, the Junior Women's Club, the Babysitting Cooperative. Women who were running the Scouts or Little League or organizing carnivals were all of a sudden dealing with this stuff.

"When you look back at it," she said, "you see how naive you were. You didn't associate everything that happened in the community with the site. It took a while before it all came together." During that time, Newman said, she didn't bother much with the science. Instead, she relied on common sense.

"We knew that lead is something that you shouldn't be exposed to. DDT had been banned. So it was on a very common-sense level, not on a very technical level" that Newman began to realize something was wrong at Stringfellow. "Then I got ahold of reports and started reading things. Once you decipher what they mean by different terms, they become real easy to read. It's just a bunch of bullshit. It's not really that hard. That's part of the trick used by government agencies and individuals to make it seem that it's more difficult than it is. It discourages people. If you know the secrets, then you become the expert and you can dictate what happens."

Newman wasn't interested in discussing her own ailments or those of her children, and just as her lawyers had done, she refused to let me speak to any of the other plaintiffs. The reason for their coyness, I surmised, was again the complexity of Stringfellow. Concerned Neighbors was not contending, as was argued in the classic dump narrative of Love Canal, that a single chemical caused a distinct disease. Instead they offered a new, untested argument. In Newman's own words: "We know that a high exposure to toxic chemicals can create a lot of problems. But what happens when you have a lower level of exposure over a longer period of time? What can we expect? Again, it was common sense. You just looked at the information."

But what, I wondered, was that information? Penny Newman's dependence on common sense, it was becoming apparent, amounted to a simple faith in unseen dangers, born out of a conviction that science is the government's handmaiden and that the government always lies. "They found this one chemical, PCBSA—they don't even have a standard protocol for testing it," she said. "They don't even know the health impacts. Basically they have no information on this thing." For Penny, no news was bad news—if it was in the dump, then it had injured them.

"It doesn't seem to be a carcinogen," she told me, "but there are significant health impacts. There's a lot of information in Russia. They've dealt with it quite a lot there."

Russia? That sounded frightening. "What," I asked, "were the symptoms?"

"Things like rashes. But we can't know because there isn't that much information about it. After a while," she explained patiently, "you reach a point where you don't need to know. You reach a point where you can just say, 'It's bad. Stop worrying about how many more particulates per whatever—it's bad.'"

Of the hundred corporations that rushed into settlement with Newman's group, only one firm stood its ground—Rainbow Canyon Manufacturing. The company, it turned out, was a mom-and-pop, the caster that had long ago gotten out of the business. The owners were in a retirement home, and any settlement money would come out of their daily bread. So they hired an attorney, a man named Robert Kelly.

I called him at his office. "You don't want to do this story," he growled into the phone. "This is fucking *Jarndyce v. Jarndyce*." But he agreed to talk with me anyway, and instructed me to meet him the next day at E2, a hot new bar in Santa Monica, a couple of blocks from the Pacific Ocean.

Kelly is a fireplug of a guy, a densely muscled man who arrived on a Yamaha motorcycle. He unzipped his bug-covered jumpsuit to reveal a crisp Savile Row suit. His opening prattle was pure *Goodfellas*, liberally sprinkled with "sumbitch" and "muthafucka." He shared with me the observation that one of the special masters on the case didn't have "the guts to slam a guy's dick in the door." We ordered beers, which arrived in tony eighteen-inch steins.

"Stringfellow was definitely a lawyer's full-employment policy," he said, pounding his hand on the table. He listed the excesses: fifteen lawyers showing up for a single deposition; xeroxing charges of twenty-eight cents a page over millions of pages; ridiculous negotiation fees. From an insider, Kelly had learned that one law firm charged its corporate client twelve million dollars to negotiate a six million-dollar settlement. According to Kelly's calculations, the lawyers' fees and expenses in the state case alone total roughly half a billion dollars, a figure that dwarfs even the most optimistic estimates of how much Glen Avon residents will receive.[3]

"The reason the corporations settled is because they hired corporate lawyers, and that's what corporate lawyers do—settle," he said with scorn. "Those law firms cut pretty good deals for themselves and fucked everybody else. A hundred corporations got screwed because they hired attorneys who were afraid to try a lawsuit. I was the only trial attorney! The plaintiffs are getting screwed, too, but then they should get screwed, because they aren't injured!"

At first, I assumed that Kelly was just engaging in good-old-boy hyperbole. But as I wrote down that last quotation, he went on railing at the plaintiffs. Slowly the words sunk in: the plaintiffs were not injured. Kelly's assertion, if true, explained why Penny Newman was so eager to cite the hunches of her common sense rather than the facts of science. It also explained why I was kept away from the plaintiffs. It also explained why everyone was so circumspect about their ailments. Could it be that a lawsuit always described in superlatives—largest, most complex, costliest, densest, hardest—was constructed on nothing more than fear? Could the folks of Glen Avon have built a castle in the air and then moved in?

Kelly admitted that the dump is a mess, but he pointed out that it is a mile and a half away from the plaintiffs' homes. He cited a three-year UCLA study of Glen Avon presented by the state of California during the trial. Its finding was unambiguous: Glen Avon residents had no medical problems out of proportion with any other town. The cause of Glen Avon's distress, according to Kelly, lay elsewhere. "This case," he said, "was propelled by chemical hysteria."

Kelly explained his own client's case. Rainbow was charged with illegally dumping chromium, which, according to the computer modeling

---

3. Such proportions are fairly routine in the world of toxic-waste legal wrangling. According to a 1992 Rand Corporation study, 88 percent of the money spent by insurers on Superfund claims goes to legal costs. The balance gets spent on cleanup.

by Failure Analysis, evaporated into the air and floated into people's homes. Kelly happily recalled for me the moment that, he said, clinched his case. "The plaintiffs put an expert on the stand to testify to the amount of chromium that could have got out of the dump. To put it into perspective for the jury, I made him add up all the exposure to the most heavily exposed person in town, a guy named Asher. Then I had him compare it to the amount of chromium in one vitamin supplement pill. Mr. Asher, over seven years, was exposed to twenty-four and a half micrograms. Each pill has twenty-five micrograms. The jury couldn't believe it."

He ordered another beer.

"Stringfellow is like Jarndyce because everyone who touched it got corrupted, except me. It just became an all-encompassing thing. Stringfellow was a dump that didn't threaten anybody. That's what's so amazing. People got involved in this lawsuit and then the lawsuit became what they did. Stringfellow was their life, and they did more and more useless work to further their belief."

After the disappointingly small award for the first seventeen plaintiffs (eight of them, you will recall, received not a dime; the best-compensated, John Longden, who actually played in the overflowing lagoons as a boy, was awarded only fifty thousand dollars), the plaintiffs lost some of their enthusiasm for pursuing the remaining 234 trials. While I was in Glen Avon, preparations were under way for the second trial (which would feature, Penny Newman assured me, a much more convincing hatch of seventeen plaintiffs). By this time, though, the state of California was the only defendant left—Rainbow had been cleared, and the rest of the polluters had bought their way out. Not long after I left, the state's lawyers offered $13.5 million to settle the case. And the plaintiffs, who had reportedly requested a settlement of $500 million, agreed. One head of the hydra had been cauterized.

Now that the town's lawsuit is over, one has to ask: Did Stringfellow destroy a community or create one? How did a little town focused on the future—Little League, Junior Women, the Babysitting Cooperative—sour into an alliance of fear, obsessed with the past and all its failures? With the exception of John Longden, the jury refused to find any link between Stringfellow and the physical health of the plaintiffs. But what about Glen Avon's spiritual health? During the trial, one plaintiff, Cynthia Baca, described what Stringfellow had come to mean. "It's like having this great big shadow, this great big monster," she testified. "You don't know when it's going to rear its ugly head." She started to cry. "It's scary."

What physical ailments the bulk of the four thousand people would have claimed, we'll never know. But the suffering that the first seventeen blamed on the dump reads like a page from Jean-Paul Sartre: fear of future illness, nightmares, sleeplessness, dizziness, emotional distress, insomnia, trouble concentrating, irritability, nagging fatigue, depression, anxiety.

Most communities learn to live with the low-grade fear and vague anxiety that characterize our century. In Glen Avon, Sartre's existential nausea is understood to have a distinct source. One teenage plaintiff said that Stringfellow had shrunk his skeleton. Because the dump made him small, he had no self-esteem, and so he quit Little League. Tieg Lancaster blamed Stringfellow for his learning disabilities, even though his father and brother shared the same problems. Others, like Helen Fontaine and David Asher, said that Stringfellow caused their depression. Cynthia Baca traced the death of her backyard chickens and goats to the pits. Her vegetables were gnarly and stunted. Her carrots looked arthritic, she said, and her corn sprouted "peculiar-looking kernels."

At one point during the trial, a twenty-one-year-old transient named Timothy Durette—not a plaintiff—got into the spirit of things by leaping to his feet in the visitors' gallery. He lowered his pants, pointed at a scar on his hip, and recited the familiar incantation: Stringfellow, Stringfellow, Stringfellow.[4]

---

4. Speaking of Stringfellow, the eponymous hero himself passed away during the state trial, on July 18, 1993. The obituaries noted ironically that the old high-school dropout and former quarryman had opposed the dump until the state assured him it was safe. "When we went to restaurants," his widow was quoted as saying, "he would use the

"There was no bodily injury to virtually all of them," the jury fore-man, Rudolph Klutschkowski, told reporters just after the trial ended in the summer of 1993. "And the Glen Avon people who have emotional distress are people who have had ten years of litigation put on them. We just didn't see physical injuries. Once the lawsuits are over, many of their emotional problems go away."

Last winter's settlement with the state of California may have ended Glen Avon's lawsuit, but it hasn't ended the legal work. There is a total of about $125 million—including interest—in the plaintiffs' pot, almost all of it from the pretrial settlements. The plaintiffs' attorneys will take nearly a third as their fee, plus as much as $30 million in expenses. This will leave about half of the fund for the victims. The division of the spoils is itself a tangled affair, again because each resident has a different complaint. To adjudicate the process, the plaintiffs hired a very special master known as a "distribution master." Ever since Love Canal divid-ing spoils among complicated client populations has become a new and lucrative subspecialty of the law. The most exalted practitioner of this peculiar science—which goes by the comely name "mass tort claims resolution facilities"—is Francis McGovern of the University of Ala-bama at Tuscaloosa. The Glen Avon plaintiffs have retained McGovern to distribute their money.

I spent a few weeks trying to track down Professor McGovern. I spoke to him briefly by telephone in Barcelona, then managed to talk to him at more length when he stopped off for a couple of days in Alabama before jetting off to another continent. He is in great demand in these complex times.

"There are two models for claims-resolution facilities," he explained to me. "There's the model of Social Security, where you give everyone flat amounts. At the other extreme is the model of the tort system,

name String instead of Stringfellow because people would glare at him." The settlement bankrupted him. At the time of his death, Mr. Stringfellow, sixty-six, had taken work in a Costa Mesa shipyard, scraping boats.

where you individualize the amount of money quite extensively." But the system has a catch. The more precise the accounting of each individual case, the higher the administrative fee for McGovern, and the less the plaintiffs get.

Transaction costs, he admitted, can run as high as 50 percent of the total pot of money. "So, generally speaking," he said, "most people trade off a little exquisiteness of individualism for a lower transaction cost."

Not always, though. "You do run into cases where people want the exquisiteness," McGovern said. It is in these cases that McGovern gets to really show his stuff. With the use of increasingly powerful computers, McGovern believes that he can approach, with infinitely more refined precision, the always unreachable certainty of absolute truth.

In fact, McGovern said, if the variables are few enough, he can really save people a lot of hassle. "Less than twenty variables derives a 95 percent degree of certainty," he said. "That is, you can predict what award the case will bring in the normal marketplace of litigation with a 95 percent degree of certainty."[5] In other words, with McGovern's model, the entire trial, the burden of determining right and wrong, can be skipped and the two sides can get right down to cutting and cashing checks.

Even after McGovern finishes his recondite mathematics, Stringfellow will continue. The case in the federal courts—where the hundreds

---

5. According to one economic analysis, the formula to determine whether or not defendants will prefer a mass tort resolution facility involves the following calculation:

$$\left[C_d + \left(\frac{D_H + C_p}{2}\right)\right]\left[\frac{D_H - C_p}{D_H}\right]N > \left[C_d + \left(\frac{D_H + D^*}{2}\right)\right]\left[\frac{D_H - D^*}{D_H}\right]N_c$$

$$+ \left[C_f + D_{cf}\right]\left[\frac{D^*}{D_H}\right]N$$

$$\left[C_d + \left(\frac{D^* + C_p}{2}\right)\right]\left[D^* - C_p\right] > \left[C_f + D_{cf}\right]\left[D^*\right]$$

of dumpers and the state of California have been squabbling for ten years about who is responsible for the cleanup and care of the site—is nowhere near resolution. The state's argument alone is supported by 4,185 exhibits, one of which is forty-one thousand pages long.

The district judge assigned to the case is Reagan-appointee James Ideman, known among court regulars as judge "Idleman." In January 1985, Ideman appointed Judge Harry Peetris to take over the entire case as the special master for Stringfellow. Stringfellow, in short, has its own federal judge-for-hire. These days, Peetris charges $400 an hour, and, as you read this, the meter on his wisdom is running. So far Peetris has collected well over a million dollars and is on his way to two million. His assistant, Karen Koe, charges $150 an hour for her contribution, which includes carrying judge Peetris's notes and fielding his calls. She's closing in on $500,000. The case also maintains its own private deputy attorney general, Don Robinson. By his own estimate, Robinson has logged nine man-years. ("Mr. Tangle knows more of Jarndyce and Jarndyce than anybody," wrote Dickens. "He is famous for it—supposed never to have read anything else since he left school.")

The federal decision, when it comes, is not likely to be final. There have been successful constitutional challenges to the very concept of the special master. If such an argument is successful here, the entire case, after decades of lawsuits and millions to Peetris and his amanuensis, could be handed back to yet another federal judge with instructions to start over.

Chances are good that as long as there are chemicals in the Stringfellow quarry there will be lawsuits about the cleanup. So, on my last day in California, I called the state's engineer in charge of Stringfellow. His name is Rich Bailey, and he agreed to show me the site itself.

As friendly as his first name and quick to offer it to a stranger, Rich is six feet of mainly arms and legs. For that matter, so am I, and thus, inside his rented Ford subcompact, we looked like two bugs stuck in a specimen jar. We passed through a sliding gate bright with warnings and rolled out onto a gravel road circumscribing the seventeen acres of Stringfellow at a comfy, oh, three miles per hour.

At a glance, Stringfellow didn't look very menacing: nothing more than a glade rioting in yellow blossoms, fat dandelions that looked more like midsize sunflowers—yellow, erect, heliotropic, healthy.

"Blasted things," said Rich, cracking his knuckles on the windshield with a flick. "The wild sunflowers look nice, but we don't want 'em 'cause they'll root down through my cap." Rich's cap, he explained, is the layer of clay and lime authorized by Governor Jerry Brown in 1978 to cover the open lagoons and keep rainwater from washing through the pits and on toward town. The roots of the flowers weaken the cap and let in seepage.

Rich is a straightforward guy, unpracticed at bureaucratic euphemism. Without my asking, he admitted that the cap is lousy. "It wouldn't pass standard now, but it was a had-to-do-something-back-then kind of issue." When I asked Rich what kind of cap he'd put on there today if money were no object, his eyes ambled out across his fallen meadow, and he began to speak a fresh and lovely language. It was the first time I had heard such a voice since I had entered the wonderland of Stringfellow—the flat, uninflected honesty of an engineer.

"I'd be thinking extremely fine grain, you know, low permeable clay, maybe three foot, or synthetic material, perhaps, and then top it probably with a foot of good soil over, say, six inches of kiln dust." We silently nodded our heads like two old buddies who'd just lathed a particularly knotty piece of oak. Rich relaxed a bit. He pointed out a cluster of gray boxes at the lower end of the site. They pump out the rain seepage—about thirteen gallons per minute—and then relay it to a nearby treatment center until the next downpour leaks through.

Back at the fence, Rich and I clambered out to stretch our legs and look at the site in the open air. Since the remaining Stringfellow legal battles are all about the cleanup, I wanted to know how long it might take. I asked Rich: For how many years will the pumps have to chug? How long will Stringfellow be a place? Rich puffed out his cheeks, kicked some rocks, and stared into a powder-blue California sky. "If the status quo is maintained," he said, "and assuming extrapolation of all the trend data, then for it to reach nondetectable background levels would take over four hundred and fifty years." We both stared in silence at the waving flowers.

But Rich didn't want to end our conversation on such a catastrophic note. He volunteered the information that the local Chamber of Commerce had always been a little ticked about the lawsuit. It just focused everybody's attention on the negative, he said, and what kind of life is that? Rich told me that there had been some recent exploratory efforts to consider building a rock 'n' roll amphitheater over Stringfellow—sort of a lemons-into-lemonade kind of deal. He cautioned, though, that any plan would have to be compatible with the site, and to his mind only one alternative use for Stringfellow is even remotely practical.

"If you mixed in a solidifying agent in situ," he said, "and then you eliminated the exposure path of waste and put some soil on top of it—I mean, put on a new cap and added control for in-flowing water and vapor emissions—well, then, I could see a golf course."

But the Stringfellow Acid Pits will not easily give themselves up to such a tidy and lasting solution. The methods being tossed around for stabilizing the leaking dump suggest that the Chamber of Commerce's bright future is a long way off. A 1991 EPA study looked at a number of different alternatives. One called for sinking heatable rods into the dump and toasting Stringfellow to three thousand six hundred degrees, thus turning it into a giant glass ball. Another suggested mixing in concrete with what one newspaper account described as "fifty-foot egg-beaters" so that the brew would harden and remain entombed. Yet another method called for plying the dump with nutrients to attract microorganisms that would consume the chemicals. But it was concluded that nature has not yet evolved a life-form robust enough to adapt to the poisonous diversity of Stringfellow. In fact, this report was the first official hint that nothing really would work—that the best solution, the only solution, was to hire people like Rich Bailey, and a dynasty of curators after him, to check the pumps and mow the dandelions for the next half millennium.

SIX DEGREES OF LOIS WEISBERG

Malcolm Gladwell

1

Everyone who knows Lois Weisberg has a story about meeting Lois Weisberg, and although she has done thousands of things in her life and met thousands of people, all the stories are pretty much the same. Lois (everyone calls her Lois) is invariably smoking a cigarette and drinking one of her dozen or so daily cups of coffee. She will have been up until two or three the previous morning, and up again at seven or seven thirty, because she hardly seems to sleep. In some accounts—particularly if the meeting took place in the winter—she'll be wearing her white, fur-topped Dr. Zhivago boots with gold tights; but she may have on her platform tennis shoes, or the leather jacket with the little studs on it, or maybe an outrageous piece of costume jewelry, and, always, those huge, rhinestone-studded glasses that make her big eyes look positively enormous. "I have no idea why I asked you to come here, I have no job for you," Lois told Wendy Willrich when Willrich went to Lois's office in downtown Chicago a few years ago for an interview. But by the end of the interview Lois did have a job for her, because for Lois meeting someone is never just about meeting someone. If she likes you, she wants to recruit you into one of her grand schemes—to sweep you

62

up into her world. A while back, Lois called up Helen Doria, who was then working for someone on Chicago's city council, and said, "I don't have a job for you. Well, I might have a little job. I need someone to come over and help me clean up my office." By this, she meant that she had a big job for Helen but just didn't know what it was yet. Helen came, and, sure enough, Lois got her a big job.

Cindy Mitchell first met Lois twenty-three years ago, when she bundled up her baby and ran outside into one of those frigid Chicago winter mornings because some people from the Chicago Park District were about to cart away a beautiful sculpture of Carl von Linné from the park across the street. Lois happened to be driving by at the time, and, seeing all the commotion, she slammed on her brakes, charged out of her car—all five feet of her—and began asking Cindy questions, rat-a-tat-tat: "Who are you? What's going on here? Why do you care?" By the next morning, Lois had persuaded two *Chicago Tribune* reporters to interview Cindy and turn the whole incident into a cause célèbre, and she had recruited Cindy to join an organization she'd just started called Friends of the Parks, and then, when she found out that Cindy was a young mother at home who was too new in town to have many friends, she told her, "I've found a friend for you. Her name is Helen, and she has a little boy your kid's age, and you will meet her next week and the two of you will be best friends." That's exactly what happened, and, what's more, Cindy went on to spend ten years as president of Friends of the Parks. "Almost everything that I do today and 80 to 90 percent of my friends came about because of her, because of that one little chance meeting," Cindy says. "That's a scary thing. Try to imagine what would have happened if she had come by five minutes earlier."

It could be argued, of course, that even if Cindy hadn't met Lois on the street twenty-three years ago she would have met her somewhere else, maybe a year later or two years later or ten years later, or, at least, she would have met someone who knew Lois or would have met someone who knew someone who knew Lois, since Lois Weisberg is connected, by a very short chain, to nearly everyone. Weisberg is now the

Commissioner of Cultural Affairs for the City of Chicago. But in the course of her seventy-three years she has hung out with actors and musicians and doctors and lawyers and politicians and activists and environmentalists, and once, on a whim, she opened a secondhand jewelry store named for her granddaughter Becky Fyffe, and every step of the way Lois has made friends and recruited people, and a great many of those people have stayed with her to this day. "When we were doing the jazz festival, it turned out—surprise, surprise—that she was buddies with Dizzy Gillespie," one of her friends recalls. "This is a woman who cannot carry a tune. She has no sense of rhythm. One night Tony Bennett was in town, and so we hang out with Tony Bennett, hearing about the old days with him and Lois."

Once, in the midfifties, on a whim, Lois took the train to New York to attend the World Science Fiction Convention and there she met a young writer by the name of Arthur C. Clarke. Clarke took a shine to Lois, and next time he was in Chicago he called her up. "He was at a pay phone," Lois recalls. "He said, 'Is there anyone in Chicago I should meet?' I told him to come over to my house." Lois has a throaty voice, baked hard by half a century of nicotine, and she pauses between sentences to give herself the opportunity for a quick puff. Even when she's not smoking, she pauses anyway, as if to keep in practice. "I called Bob Hughes, one of the people who wrote for my paper." Pause. "I said, 'Do you know anyone in Chicago interested in talking to Arthur Clarke?' He said, 'Yeah, Isaac Asimov is in town. And this guy Robert, Robert . . . Robert Heinlein.' So they all came over and sat in my study." Pause. "Then they called over to me and they said, 'Lois'—I can't remember the word they used. They had some word for me. It was something about how I was the kind of person who brings people together."

This is in some ways the archetypal Lois Weisberg story. First, she reaches out to somebody—somebody outside her world. (At the time, she was running a drama troupe, whereas Arthur C. Clarke wrote science fiction.) Equally important, that person responds to her. Then there's the fact that when Arthur Clarke came to Chicago and wanted to meet someone Lois came up with Isaac Asimov. She says it was a fluke that Asimov was in town. But if it hadn't been Asimov it would have been someone else. Lois ran a salon out of her house on the North Side in the late 1950s, and one of the things that people remember about it is that it was always, effortlessly, integrated. Without that salon, blacks would still have socialized with whites on the North Side—though it was rare back then, it happened. But it didn't happen by accident: it happened because a certain kind of person made it happen. That's what Asimov and Clarke meant when they said that Lois has this thing—whatever it is—that brings people together.

2

Lois is a type—a particularly rare and extraordinary type, but a type nonetheless. She's the type of person who seems to know everybody, and this type can be found in every walk of life. Someone I met at a wedding (actually, the wedding of the daughter of Lois's neighbors, the Newbergers) told me that if I ever went to Massapequa I should look up a woman named Marsha, because Marsha was the type of person who knew everybody. In Cambridge, Massachusetts, the word is that a tailor named Charlie Davidson knows everybody. In Houston, I'm told, there is an attorney named Harry Reasoner who knows everybody. There are probably Lois Weisbergs in Akron and Tucson and Paris and in some little town in the Yukon Territory, up by the Arctic Circle. We've all met someone like Lois Weisberg. Yet, although we all know a Lois Weisberg type, we don't know much about the Lois Weisberg type. Why is it, for example, that these few, select people seem to know everyone and the rest of us don't? And how important are the people who know everyone? This second question is critical, because once you begin even a cursory examination of the life of someone like Lois Weisberg you start to suspect that he or she may be far more important than we would ever have imagined—that the people who know everyone, in some oblique way, may actually run the world. I don't mean that they are the sort who head up the Fed or General Motors or Microsoft, but that, in a very down-to-earth, day-to-day way, they make the world work. They spread ideas and information. They connect varied and isolated parts of society. Helen Doria says someone high up in the Chicago government told her that Lois is "the epicenter of the city administration," which is the right way to put it. Lois is far from being the most important or the most powerful person in Chicago. But if you connect all the dots that constitute the vast apparatus of government and influence and interest groups in the city of Chicago you'll end up coming back to Lois again and again. Lois is a connector.

Lois, it must be said, did not set out to know everyone. "She doesn't network for the sake of networking," says Gary Johnson, who was Lois's boss years ago, when she was executive director of the Chicago Council of Lawyers. "I just think she has the confidence that all the people in the world, whether she's met them or not, are in her Rolodex already, and that all she has to do is figure out how to reach them and she'll be able to connect with them."

Nor is Lois charismatic—at least, not in the way that we think of extroverts and public figures as being charismatic. She doesn't fill a room; eyes don't swivel toward her as she makes her entrance. Lois has frizzy blond hair, and when she's thinking—between her coffee and her cigarette—she kneads the hair on the top of her head, so that by the end of a particularly difficult meeting it will be standing almost straight up. "She's not like the image of the Washington society doyenne," Gary Johnson says. "You know, one of those people who identify you, take you to lunch, give you the treatment. Her social life is very different. When I bump into her and she says, 'Oh, we should catch up,' what she means is that someday I should go with her to her office, and we'd go down to the snack bar and buy a muffin and then sit in her office while she answered the phone. For a real treat, when I worked with her at the Council of Lawyers she would take me to the dining room in the Wieboldt's department store." Johnson is an old-school Chicago intellectual who works at a fancy law firm and has a corner office with one of those Midwestern views in which, if you look hard enough, you can almost see Nebraska, and the memory of those lunches at Wieboldt's seems to fill him with delight. "Now, you've got to understand that the Wieboldt's department store—which doesn't exist anymore—was a notch below Field's, where the suburban society ladies have their lunch, and it's also a notch below Carson's," he says. "There was a kind of room there where people who bring their own string bags to go shopping would have a quick lunch. This was her idea of a lunch out. We're not talking Pamela Harriman here."

In the mideighties, Lois quit a job she'd had for four years, as director of special events in the administration of Harold Washington, and somehow hooked up with a group of itinerant peddlers who ran the city's flea markets. "There was this lady who sold jewelry," Lois said. "She was a person out of Dickens. She was bedraggled. She had a houseful of cats. But she knew how to buy jewelry, and I wanted her to teach me. I met her whole circle of friends, all these old gay men who had antique stores. Once a week, we would go to the Salvation Army." Lois was arguably the most important civic activist in the city. Her husband was a judge. She lived in a huge house in one of Chicago's nicest neighborhoods. Yet somehow she managed to be plausible as a flea-market peddler to a bunch of flea-market peddlers, the same way she managed to be plausible as a music lover to a musician like Tony Bennett. It doesn't matter who she's with or what she's doing; she always manages to be in the thick of things. "There was a woman I knew—Sandra—who had a kid in school with my son Joseph," Lois told me. Lois has a habit of telling stories that appear to be tangential and digressive but, on reflection, turn out to be parables of a sort. "She helped all these Asians living uptown. One day, she came over here and said there was this young Chinese man who wanted to meet an American family and learn to speak English better and was willing to cook for his room and board. Well, I'm always eager to have a cook, and especially a Chinese cook, because my family loves Chinese food. They could eat it seven days a week. So Sandra brought this man over here. His name was Shi Young. He was a graduate student at the Art Institute of Chicago." Shi Young lived with Lois and her family for two years, and during that time Chicago was in the midst of political turmoil. Harold Washington, who would later become the first black mayor of the city, was attempting to unseat the remains of the Daley political machine, and Lois's house, naturally, was the site of late-night, top-secret strategy sessions for the pro-Washington reformers of Chicago's North Side. "We'd have all these important people here, and Shi Young would come down and listen," Lois recalls. "I didn't think anything of it." But Shi Young, as it turns out, was going back up to his room and writing up what he heard for the *China Youth Daily*, a newspaper with a circulation in the tens of millions. Somehow, in the improbable way that the world works, a portal was opened up, connecting Chicago's North Side reform politics and the readers of the *China Youth Daily*, and that link was Lois's living room. You could argue that this was just a fluke—just as it was a fluke that Isaac Asimov was in town and that Lois happened to be driving by when Cindy Mitchell came running out of her apartment. But sooner or later all those flukes begin to form a pattern.

3

In the late 1960s, a Harvard social psychologist named Stanley Milgram conducted an experiment in an effort to find an answer to what is known as the small-world problem, though it could also be called the Lois Weisberg problem. It is this: How are human beings connected? Do we belong to separate worlds, operating simultaneously but autonomously, so that the links between any two people, anywhere in the world, are few and distant? Or are we all bound up together in a grand, interlocking web? Milgram's idea was to test this question with a chain letter. For one experiment, he got the names of a hundred and sixty people, at random, who lived in Omaha, Nebraska, and he mailed each of them a packet. In the packet was the name and address of a stockbroker who worked in Boston and lived in Sharon, Massachusetts. Each person was instructed to write his name on a roster in the packet and send it on to a friend or acquaintance who he thought would get it closer to the stockbroker. The idea was that when the letters finally arrived at the stockbroker's house Milgram could look at the roster of names and establish how closely connected someone chosen at random from one part of the country was to another person chosen at random in another part. Milgram found that most of the letters reached the stockbroker in five or six steps. It is from this experiment that we got the concept of six degrees of separation.

That phrase is now so familiar that it is easy to lose sight of how surprising Milgram's finding was. Most of us don't have particularly diverse groups of friends. In one well-known study, two psychologists asked people living in the Dyckman public-housing project, in uptown Manhattan, about their closest friend in the project; almost 90 percent of the friends lived in the same building, and half lived on the same floor. In general, people chose friends of similar age and race. But if the friend lived down the hall, both age and race became a lot less important. Proximity overpowered similarity. Another study, involving students at the University of Utah, found that if you ask someone why he is friendly with someone else he'll say that it is because they share similar attitudes. But if you actually quiz the pairs of students on their attitudes you'll find out that this is an illusion, and that what friends really tend to have in common are activities. We're friends with the people we do things with, not necessarily with the people we resemble. We don't seek out friends; we simply associate with the people who occupy the same physical places that we do: people in Omaha are not, as a rule, friends with people who live in Sharon, Massachusetts. So how did the packets get halfway across the country in just five steps? "When I asked an intelligent friend of mine how many steps he thought it would take, he estimated that it would require a hundred intermediate persons or more to move from Nebraska to Sharon," Milgram wrote. "Many people make somewhat similar estimates, and are surprised to learn that only five intermediaries will—on the average—suffice. Somehow it does not accord with intuition."

The explanation is that in the six degrees of separation not all degrees are equal. When Milgram analyzed his experiments, for example, he found that many of the chains reaching to Sharon followed the same asymmetrical pattern. Twenty-four packets reached the stockbroker at his home, in Sharon, and sixteen of those were given to him by the same person, a clothing merchant whom Milgram calls Mr. Jacobs. The rest of the packets were sent to the stockbroker at his office, and of those the majority came through just two men, whom Milgram calls Mr. Brown and Mr. Jones. In all, half of the responses that got to the stockbroker were delivered to him by these three people. Think of it. Dozens of people, chosen at random from a large Midwestern city, sent out packets independently. Some went through college acquaintances. Some sent their packets to relatives. Some sent them to old workmates. Yet in the end, when all those idiosyncratic chains were completed, half of the packets passed through the hands of Jacobs, Jones, and Brown. Six degrees of separation doesn't simply mean that everyone is linked to everyone else in just six steps. It means that a very small number of people are linked to everyone else in a few steps, and the rest of us are linked to the world through those few.

There's an easy way to explore this idea. Suppose that you made a list of forty people whom you would call your circle of friends (not including family members or coworkers), and you worked backward from each person until you could identify who was ultimately responsible for setting in motion the series of connections which led to that friendship. I met my oldest friend, Bruce, for example, in first grade, so I'm the responsible party. That's easy. I met my college friend Nigel because he lived down the hall in the dormitory from Tom, whom I had met because in my freshman year he invited me to play touch football. Tom, then, is responsible for Nigel. Once you've made all the connections, you will find the same names coming up again and again. I met my friend Amy when she and her friend Katie came to a restaurant where I was having dinner. I know Katie because she is best friends with my friend Larissa, whom I know because I was told to look her up by a mutual friend, Mike A., whom I know because he went to school with another friend of mine, Mike H., who used to work at a political weekly with my friend Jacob. No Jacob, no Amy. Similarly, I met my friend Sarah S. at a birthday party a year ago because she was there with a writer named David, who was there at the invitation of his agent, Tina, whom I met through my friend Leslie, whom I know because her sister Nina is best friends with my friend Ann, whom I met through my old roommate Maura, who was my roommate because she had worked with a writer named Sarah L., who was a college friend of my friend Jacob. No Jacob, no Sarah S. In fact, when I go down my list of forty friends, thirty of them, in one way or another, lead back to Jacob. My social circle is really not a circle but an inverted pyramid. And the capstone of the pyramid is a single person, Jacob, who is responsible for an overwhelming majority of my relationships. Jacob's full name, incidentally, is Jacob Weisberg. He is Lois Weisberg's son.

This isn't to say, though, that Jacob is just like Lois. Jacob may be the capstone of my pyramid, but Lois is the capstone of lots and lots of people's pyramids, and that makes her social role different. In Milgram's experiment, Mr. Jacobs the clothing merchant was the person to go through to get to the stockbroker. Lois is the kind of person you would use to get to the stockbrokers of Sharon and also the cabaret singers of Sharon and the barkeeps of Sharon and the guy who gave up a thriving career in orthodontics to open a small vegetarian falafel hut.

4

There is another way to look at this question, and that's through the popular parlor game Six Degrees of Kevin Bacon. The idea behind the game is to try to link in fewer than six steps any actor or actress, through the movies they've been in, to the actor Kevin Bacon. For example, O. J. Simpson was in *Naked Gun* with Priscilla Presley, who was in *The Adventures of Ford Fairlane* with Gilbert Gottfried, who was in *Beverly Hills Cop II* with Paul Reiser, who was in *Diner* with Kevin Bacon. That's four steps. Mary Pickford was in *Screen Snapshots* with Clark Gable, who was in *Combat America* with Tony Romano, who, thirty-five years later, was in *Starting Over* with Bacon. That's three steps. What's funny about the game is that Bacon, although he is a fairly young actor, has already been in so many movies with so many people that there is almost no one to whom he can't be easily connected. Recently, a computer scientist at the University of Virginia by the name of Brett Tjaden actually sat down and figured out what the average degree of connectedness is for the quarter-million or so actors and actresses listed in the Internet Movie Database: he came up with 2.8312 steps. That sounds impressive, except that Tjaden then went back and performed an even more heroic calculation, figuring out what the average degree of connectedness was for everyone in the database. Bacon, it turns out, ranks only 668th. Martin Sheen, by contrast, can be connected, on average, to every other actor, in 2.63681 steps, which puts him almost 650 places higher than Bacon. Elliott Gould can be connected even more quickly, in 2.63601. Among the top fifteen are people like Robert Mitchum, Gene Hackman, Donald Sutherland, Rod Steiger, Shelley Winters, and Burgess Meredith.

Why is Kevin Bacon so far behind these actors? Recently, in the journal *Nature*, the mathematicians Duncan Watts and Steven Strogatz published a dazzling theoretical explanation of connectedness, but a simpler way to understand this question is to look at who Bacon is. Obviously, he is a lot younger than the people at the top of the list are and has made fewer movies. But that accounts for only some of the difference. A top-twenty person, like Burgess Meredith, made 114 movies in the course of his career. Gary Cooper, though, starred in about the same number of films and ranks only 878th, with a 2.85075 score. John Wayne made 183 movies in his fifty-year career and still ranks only 116th, at 2.7173. What sets someone like Meredith apart is his range. More than half of John Wayne's movies were Westerns, and that means he made the same kind of movie with the same kind of actors over and over again. Burgess Meredith, by contrast, was in great movies, like the Oscar-winning *Of Mice and Men* (1939), and in dreadful movies, like *Beware! The Blob* (1972). He was nominated for an Oscar for his role in *The Day of the Locust* and also made TV commercials for Skippy peanut butter. He was in four *Rocky* movies, and also played Don Learo in Godard's *King Lear*. He was in schlocky made-for-TV movies, in B movies that pretty much went straight to video, and in pictures considered modern classics. He was in forty-two dramas, twenty-two comedies, eight adventure films, seven action films, five sci-fi films, five horror flicks, five Westerns, five documentaries, four crime movies, four thrillers, three war movies, three films noir, two children's films, two romances, two mysteries, one musical, and one animated film. Burgess Meredith was the kind of actor who was connected to everyone because he managed to move up and down and back and forth among all the different worlds and subcultures that the acting profession has to offer. When we say, then, that Lois Weisberg is the kind of person who "knows everyone," we mean it in precisely this way. It is not merely that she knows lots of people. It is that she belongs to lots of different worlds.

In the 1950s, Lois started her drama troupe in Chicago. The daughter of a prominent attorney, she was then in her twenties, living in one of the suburbs north of the city with two small children. In 1956, she decided to stage a festival to mark the centenary of George Bernard Shaw's birth. She hit up the reclusive billionaire John D. MacArthur for money. ("I go to the Pump Room for lunch. Booth one. There is a man, lurking around a pillar, with a cowboy hat and dirty, dusty boots. It's him.") She invited William Saroyan and Norman Thomas to speak on Shaw's legacy; she put on Shaw plays in theaters around the city; and she got written up in *Life*. She then began putting out a newspaper devoted to Shaw, which mutated into an underground alternative weekly called the *Paper*. By then, Lois was living in a big house on Chicago's near North Side, and on Friday nights people from the *Paper* gathered there for editorial meetings. William Friedkin, who went on to direct *The French Connection* and *The Exorcist*, was a regular, and so were the attorney Elmer Gertz (who won parole for Nathan Leopold) and some of the editors from *Playboy*, which was just up the street. People like Art Farmer and Thelonious Monk and Dizzy Gillespie and Lenny Bruce would stop by when they were in town. Bruce actually lived in Lois's house for a while. "My mother was hysterical about it, especially one day when she rang the doorbell and he answered in a bath towel," Lois told me. "We had a window on the porch, and he didn't have a key, so the window was always left open for him. There were a lot of rooms in that house, and a lot of people stayed there and I didn't know they were there." Pause. Puff. "I never could stand his jokes. I didn't really like his act. I couldn't stand all the words he was using."

Lois's first marriage—to a drugstore owner named Leonard Solomon—was breaking up around this time, so she took a job doing public relations for an injury-rehabilitation institute. From there, she went to work for a public-interest law firm called BPI, and while she was at BPI she became concerned about the fact that Chicago's parks were neglected and crumbling, so she gathered together a motley collection of nature lovers, historians, civic activists, and housewives, and founded the lobbying group Friends of the Parks. Then she became alarmed on discovering that a commuter railroad that ran along the south shore of Lake Michigan—from South Bend to Chicago—was about to shut down, so she gathered together a motley collection of railroad enthusiasts and environmentalists and commuters, and founded South Shore Recreation, thereby saving the railroad. Lois loved the railroad buffs. "They were all good friends of mine," she says. "They all wrote to me. They came from California. They came from everywhere. We had meetings. They were really interesting. I came this close"—and here she held her index finger half an inch above her thumb—"to becoming one of them." Instead, though, she became the executive director of the Chicago Council of Lawyers, a progressive bar association. Then she ran Congressman Sidney Yates's reelection campaign. Then her sister June introduced her to someone who got her the job with Mayor Washington. Then she had her flea-market period. Finally, she went to work for Mayor Daley as Chicago's Commissioner of Cultural Affairs.

If you go through that history and keep count, the number of worlds that Lois has belonged to comes to eight: the actors, the writers, the doctors, the lawyers, the park lovers, the politicians, the railroad buffs, and the flea-market aficionados. When I asked Lois to make her own list, she added musicians and the visual artists and architects and hospitality-industry people whom she works with in her current job. But if you looked harder at Lois's life you could probably subdivide her experiences into fifteen or twenty worlds. She has the same ability to move among different subcultures and niches that the busiest actors do. Lois is to Chicago what Burgess Meredith is to the movies.

Lois was, in fact, a friend of Burgess Meredith. I learned this by accident, which is the way I learned about most of the strange celebrity details of Lois's life, since she doesn't tend to drop names. It was when I was with her at her house one night, a big, rambling affair just off the lakeshore, with room after room filled with odds and ends and old photographs and dusty furniture and weird bric-a-brac, such as a collection of four hundred antique egg cups. She was wearing blue jeans and a flowery-print top and she was smoking Carlton Menthol 100s and cooking pasta and holding forth to her son Joe on the subject of George Bernard Shaw, when she started talking about Burgess Meredith. "He was in Chicago in a play called *Teahouse of the August Moon*, in 1956," she said, "and he came to see my production of *Back to Methuselah*, and after the play he came up to me and said he was teaching acting classes, and asked would I come and talk to his class about Shaw. Well, I couldn't say no." Meredith liked Lois, and when she was running her alternative newspaper he would write letters and send in little doodles, and later she helped him raise money for a play he was doing called *Kicks and Company*. It starred a woman named Nichelle Nichols, who lived at Lois's house for a while. "Nichelle was a marvellous singer and dancer," Lois said. "She was the lead. She was also the lady on the first . . ." Lois was doing so many things at once—chopping and stirring and smoking and eating and talking—that she couldn't remember the name of the show that made Nichols a star. "What's that space thing?" She looked toward Joe for help. He started laughing. "Star something," she said. "Star . . . *Star Trek*! Nichelle was Lieutenant Uhura!"

5

On a sunny morning not long ago, Lois went to a little café just off the Magnificent Mile, in downtown Chicago, to have breakfast with Mayor Daley. Lois drove there in a big black Mercury, a city car. Lois always drives big cars, and, because she is so short and the cars are so big, all that you can see when she drives by is the top of her frizzy blond head and the lighted ember of her cigarette. She was wearing a short skirt and a white vest and was carrying a white cloth shopping bag. Just what was in the bag was unclear, since Lois doesn't have a traditional relationship to the trappings of bureaucracy. Her office, for example, does not have a desk in it, only a sofa and chairs and a coffee table. At meetings, she sits at the head of a conference table in the adjoining room, and, as often as not, has nothing in front of her except a lighter, a pack of Carltons, a cup of coffee, and an octagonal orange ceramic ashtray, which she moves a few inches forward or a few inches back when she's making an important point, or moves a few inches to the side when she is laughing at something really funny and feels the need to put her head down on the table.

Breakfast was at one of the city's tourist centers. The Mayor was there in a blue suit, and he had two city officials by his side and a very serious and thoughtful expression on his face. Next to him was a Chicago developer named Al Friedman, a tall and slender and very handsome man who is the chairman of the Commission on Chicago Landmarks. Lois sat across from them, and they all drank coffee and ate muffins and batted ideas back and forth in the way that people do when they know each other very well. It was a "power breakfast," although if you went around the table you'd find that the word "power" meant something very different to everyone there. Al Friedman is a rich developer. The Mayor, of course, is the administrative leader of one of the largest cities in the country. When we talk about power, this is usually what we're talking about: money and authority. But there is a third kind of power as well—the kind Lois has—which is a little less straightforward. It's social power.

At the end of the 1980s, for example, the City of Chicago razed an entire block in the heart of downtown and then sold it to a developer. But before he could build on it the real-estate market crashed. The lot was an eyesore. The Mayor asked for ideas about what to do with it. Lois suggested that they cover the block with tents. Then she heard that Keith Haring had come to Chicago in 1989 and worked with Chicago high-school students to create a giant five-hundred-foot-long mural. Lois loved the mural. She began to think. She'd long had a problem with the federal money that Chicago got every year to pay for summer jobs for disadvantaged kids. She didn't think it helped any kid to be put to work picking up garbage. So why not pay the kids to do arts projects like the Haring mural, and put the whole program in the tents? She called the program Gallery 37, after the number of the block. She enlisted the help of the Mayor's wife, Maggie Daley, whose energy and clout were essential in order to make the program a success. Lois hired artists to teach the kids. She realized, though, that the federal money was available only for poor kids, and, Lois says, "I don't believe poor kids can advance in any way by being lumped together with other poor kids." So Lois raised money privately to bring in middle-income kids, to mix with the poor kids and be put in the tents with the artists. She started small, with 260 "apprentices" the first year, 1990. This year, there were more than three thousand. The kids study sculpture, painting, drawing, poetry, theater, graphic design, dance, textile design, jewelry-making, and music. Lois opened a store downtown, where students' works of art are sold. She has since bought two buildings to house the project full-time. She got the Parks Department to run Gallery 37 in neighborhoods around the city, and the Board of Education to let them run it as an after-school program in public high schools. It has been copied all around the world. Last year, it was given the Innovations in American Government Award by the Ford Foundation and the Harvard school of government.

Gallery 37 is at once a jobs program, an arts program, a real-estate fix, a schools program, and a parks program. It involves federal money and city money and private money, stores and buildings and tents,

Maggie Daley and Keith Haring, poor kids and middle-class kids. It is everything, all at once—a jumble of ideas and people and places which Lois somehow managed to make sense of. The ability to assemble all these disparate parts is, as should be obvious, a completely different kind of power from the sort held by the Mayor and Al Friedman. The Mayor has key allies on the city council or in the statehouse. Al Friedman can do what he does because, no doubt, he has a banker who believes in him, or maybe a lawyer whom he trusts to negotiate the twists and turns of the zoning process. Their influence is based on close relationships. But when Lois calls someone to help her put together one of her projects, chances are she's not calling someone she knows particularly well. Her influence suggests something a little surprising—that there is also power in relationships that are not close at all.

6

The sociologist Mark Granovetter examined this question in his classic 1974 book *Getting a Job*. Granovetter interviewed several hundred professional and technical workers from the Boston suburb of Newton, asking them in detail about their employment history. He found that almost 56 percent of those he talked to had found their jobs through a personal connection, about 20 percent had used formal means (advertisements, headhunters), and another 20 percent had applied directly. This much is not surprising: the best way to get in the door is through a personal contact. But the majority of those personal connections, Granovetter found, did not involve close friends. They were what he called "weak ties." Of those who used a contact to find a job, for example, only 16.7 percent saw that contact "often," as they would have if the contact had been a good friend; 55.6 percent saw their contact only "occasionally"; and 27.8 percent saw the contact "rarely." People were getting their jobs not through their friends but through acquaintances.

Granovetter argues that when it comes to finding out about new jobs—or, for that matter, gaining new information or looking for new ideas—weak ties tend to be more important than strong ties. Your friends, after all, occupy the same world that you do. They work with you, or live near you, and go to the same churches, schools, or parties. How much, then, do they know that you don't know? Mere acquaintances, on the other hand, are much more likely to know something that you don't. To capture this apparent paradox, Granovetter coined a marvellous phrase: "the strength of weak ties." The most important people in your life are, in certain critical realms, the people who aren't closest to you, and the more people you know who aren't close to you the stronger your position becomes.

Granovetter then looked at what he called "chain lengths"—that is, the number of people who had to pass along the news about your job before it got to you. A chain length of zero means that you learned about your job from the person offering it. A chain length of one means that you heard about the job from someone who had heard about the job from the employer. The people who got their jobs from a zero chain were the most satisfied, made the most money, and were unemployed for the shortest amount of time between jobs. People with a chain of one stood second in the amount of money they made, in their satisfaction with their jobs, and in the speed with which they got their jobs. People with a chain of two stood third in all three categories, and so on. If you know someone who knows someone who knows someone who has lots of acquaintances, in other words, you have a leg up. If you know someone who knows someone who has lots of acquaintances, your chances are that much better. But if you know someone who has lots of acquaintances—if you know someone like Lois—you are still more fortunate, because suddenly you are just one step away from musicians and actors and doctors and lawyers and park lovers and politicians and railroad buffs and flea-market aficionados and all the other weak ties that make Lois so strong.

This sounds like a reformulation of the old saw that it's not what you know, it's who you know. It's much more radical than that, though. The old idea was that people got ahead by being friends with rich and powerful people—which is true, in a limited way, but as a practical lesson in how the world works is all but useless. You can expect that Bill Gates's godson is going to get into Harvard and have a fabulous job waiting for him when he gets out. And, of course, if you play poker with the Mayor and Al Friedman it is going to be a little easier to get ahead in Chicago. But how many godsons can Bill Gates have? And how many people can fit around a poker table? This is why affirmative action seems pointless to so many people: it appears to promise something—entry to the old-boy network—that it can't possibly deliver. The old-boy network is always going to be just for the old boys.

Granovetter, by contrast, argues that what matters in getting ahead is not the quality of your relationships but the quantity—not how close you are to those you know but, paradoxically, how many people you know whom you aren't particularly close to. What he's saying is that the key person at that breakfast in downtown Chicago is not the Mayor or Al Friedman but Lois Weisberg, because Lois is the kind of person who it really is possible for most of us to know. If you think about the world in this way, the whole project of affirmative action suddenly starts to make a lot more sense. Minority-admissions programs work not because they give black students access to the same superior educational resources as white students, or access to the same rich cultural environment as white students, or any other formal or grandiose vision of engineered equality. They work by giving black students access to the same white students as white students—by allowing them to make acquaintances outside their own social world and so shortening the chain lengths between them and the best jobs.

This idea should also change the way we think about helping the poor. When we're faced with an eighteen-year-old high-school dropout whose only career option is making five dollars and fifty cents an hour in front of the deep fryer at Burger King, we usually talk about the importance of rebuilding inner-city communities, attracting new jobs to depressed areas, and reinvesting in neglected neighborhoods. We want to give that kid the option of another, better-paying job, right down the street. But does that really solve his problem? Surely what

that eighteen-year-old really needs is not another marginal induce-
ment to stay in his neighborhood but a way to get out of his neighborhood altogether. He needs a school system that provides him with the
skills to compete for jobs with middle-class kids. He needs a mass-
transit system to take him to the suburbs, where the real employment
opportunities are. And, most of all, he needs to know someone who
knows someone who knows where all those good jobs are. If the world
really is held together by people like Lois Weisberg, in other words,
how poor you are can be defined quite simply as how far you have to
go to get to someone like her. Wendy Willrich and Helen Doria and
all the countless other people in Lois's circle needed to make only one
phone call. They are well-off. The dropout wouldn't even know where
to start. That's why he's poor. Poverty is not deprivation. It is isolation.

7

I once met a man named Roger Horchow. If you ever go to Dallas and
ask around about who is the kind of person who might know everyone,
chances are you will be given his name. Roger is slender and composed.
He talks slowly, with a slight Texas drawl. He has a kind of wry, ironic
charm that is utterly winning. If you sat next to him on a plane ride
across the Atlantic, he would start talking as the plane taxied to the
runway, you would be laughing by the time the seat-belt sign was turned
off, and when you landed at the other end you'd wonder where the time
had gone.

I met Roger through his daughter Sally, whose sister Lizzie went to
high school in Dallas with my friend Sara M., whom I know because
she used to work with Jacob Weisberg. (No Jacob, no Roger.) Roger
spent at least part of his childhood in Ohio, which is where Lois's second husband, Bernie Weisberg, grew up, so I asked Roger if he knew
Bernie. It would have been a little too apt if he did—that would have
made it all something out of *The X-Files*—but instead of just answering,
"Sorry, I don't," which is what most of us would have done, he paused

for a long time, as if to flip through the Ws in his head, and then said, "No, but I'm sure if I made two phone calls . . ."

Roger has a very good memory for names. One time, he says, someone was trying to talk him into investing his money in a business venture in Spain, and when he asked the names of the other investors he recognized one of them as the same man with whom one of his exgirlfriends had had a fling during her junior year abroad, fifty years before. Roger sends people cards on their birthdays: he has a computerized Rolodex with sixteen hundred names on it. When I met him, I became convinced that these techniques were central to the fact that he knew everyone—that knowing everyone was a kind of skill. Horchow is the founder of the Horchow Collection, the first high-end mail-order catalogue, and I kept asking him how all the connections in his life had helped him in the business world, because I thought that this particular skill had to have been cultivated for a reason. But the question seemed to puzzle him. He didn't think of his people collection as a business strategy, or even as something deliberate. He just thought of it as something he did—as who he was. One time, Horchow said, a close friend from childhood suddenly resurfaced. "He saw my catalogue and knew it had to be me, and when he was out here he showed up on my doorstep. I hadn't seen him since I was seven. We had zero in common. It was wonderful." The juxtaposition of those last two sentences was not ironic; he meant it.

In the book *The Language Instinct*, the psychologist Steven Pinker argues against the idea that language is a cultural artifact—something that we learn "the way we learn to tell time." Rather, he says, it is innate. Language develops "spontaneously," he writes, "without conscious effort or formal instruction," and "is deployed without awareness of its underlying logic. . . . People know how to talk in more or less the sense that spiders know how to spin webs." The secret to Roger Horchow and Lois Weisberg is, I think, that they have a kind of social equivalent of that instinct—an innate and spontaneous and entirely involuntary affinity for people. They know everyone because—in some deep and less than conscious way—they can't help it.

8

Once, in the very early 1960s, after Lois had broken up with her first husband, she went to a party for Ralph Ellison, who was then teaching at the University of Chicago. There she spotted a young lawyer from the South Side named Bernie Weisberg. Lois liked him. He didn't notice her, though, so she decided to write a profile of him for the *Hyde Park Herald*. It ran with a huge headline. Bernie still didn't call. "I had to figure out how I was going to get to meet him again, so I remembered that he was standing in line at the reception with Ralph Ellison," Lois says. "So I called up Ralph Ellison"—whom she had never met—"and said, 'It's so wonderful that you are in Chicago. You really should meet some people on the North Side. Would it be OK if I have a party for you?'" He said yes, and Lois sent out a hundred invitations, including one to Bernie. He came. He saw Dizzy Gillespie in the kitchen and Ralph Ellison in the living room. He was impressed. He asked Lois to go with him to see Lenny Bruce. Lois was mortified; she didn't want this nice Jewish lawyer from the South Side to know that she knew Lenny Bruce, who was, after all, a drug addict. "I couldn't get out of it," she said. "They sat us down at a table right at the front, and Lenny keeps coming over to the edge of the stage and saying"—here Lois dropped her voice down very low—"'Hello, Lois.' I was sitting there like this." Lois put her hands on either side of her face. "Finally I said to Bernie, 'There are some things I should tell you about. Lenny Bruce is a friend of mine. He's staying at my house. The second thing is I'm defending a murderer.'" (But that's another story.) Lois and Bernie were married a year later.

The lesson of this story isn't obvious until you diagram it culturally: Lois got to Bernie through her connections with Ralph Ellison and Lenny Bruce, one of whom she didn't know (although later, naturally, they became great friends) and one of whom she was afraid to say that she knew, and neither of whom, it is safe to speculate, had ever really been connected with each other before. It seems like an absurdly roundabout way to meet someone. Here was a thirtyish liberal Jewish intellectual from the North Side of Chicago trying to meet a thirtyish liberal Jewish intellectual from the South Side of Chicago, and to get there she charted a cross-cultural social course through a black literary lion and an avant-garde standup comic. Yet that's a roundabout journey only if you perceive the worlds of Lenny Bruce and Ralph Ellison and Bernie Weisberg to be impossibly isolated. If you don't—if, like Lois, you see them all as three points of an equilateral triangle—then it makes perfect sense. The social instinct makes everyone seem like part of a whole, and there is something very appealing about this, because it means that people like Lois aren't bound by the same categories and partitions that defeat the rest of us. This is what the power of the people who know everyone comes down to in the end. It is not—as much as we would like to believe otherwise—something rich and complex, some potent mixture of ambition and energy and smarts and vision and insecurity. It's much simpler than that. It's the same lesson they teach in Sunday school. Lois knows lots of people because she likes lots of people. And all those people Lois knows and likes invariably like her, too, because there is nothing more irresistible to a human being than to be unqualifiedly liked by another.

Not long ago, Lois took me to a reception at the Museum of Contemporary Art in Chicago—a brand-new, Bauhaus-inspired building just north of the Loop. The gallery space was impossibly beautiful—cool, airy, high-ceilinged. The artist on display was Chuck Close. The crowd was sleek and well groomed. Black-clad young waiters carried pesto canapés and glasses of white wine. Lois seemed a bit lost. She can be a little shy sometimes, and at first she stayed on the fringes of the room, standing back, observing. Someone important came over to talk to her. She glanced up uncomfortably. I walked away for a moment to look at the show, and when I came back her little corner had become a crowd. There was her friend from the state legislature. A friend in the Chicago Park District. A friend from her neighborhood. A friend in the consulting business. A friend from Gallery 37. A friend from the local business-development group. And on and on.

They were of all ages and all colors, talking and laughing, swirling and turning in a loose circle, and in the middle, nearly hidden by the commotion, was Lois, clutching her white bag, tiny and large-eyed, at that moment the happiest person in the room.

SHAPINSKY'S KARMA

Lawrence Weschler

I was up late one night last fall, absorbed in Serge Guilbaut's provoca-
tive revisionist tract *How New York Stole the Idea of Modern Art*,
when, at eleven thirty, the phone rang. A stranger on the line introduced himself as Akumal Ramachander, from Bangalore, India. He
was calling from Washington, D.C., he informed me in a spirited voice.
He'd just been in Warsaw a few weeks earlier, where he'd had many
fascinating experiences. He'd read a book I'd written on Poland, and
could see that I'd given the situation there much thought. He was going
to be in New York City later in the week, and would it be all right if we
got together? It all sounded mildly diverting, so we set a rendezvous.

A few days later, on schedule, Ramachander appeared in my
office—a youngish, fairly slight gentleman with short-cropped black
hair and a round face. His conversation caromed all over the place
(Gdansk, Reagan, Sri Lanka, Lech Walesa, Indira Gandhi, the Sikhs,
Margaret Thatcher, Satyajit Ray, London); he told me that he was some
sort of part-time correspondent for the local paper of one of those Indian towns almost no one in America has ever heard of. He'd taught
English at an agricultural college but had generally been something of
a drifter, he explained—that is, until recently, for he'd just discovered

his true calling. "My destiny!" he insisted. "We Indians believe in karma, in destiny, in discovering the true calling for our lives. It has nothing to do with making money, this 'making a living' you have here in America. No, it is the spirit calling, and we answer. Not in some silly mystical way but as if the purpose of life were revealed—sometimes, as in my case, all-of-a-suddenly, like that! And this is what has now happened."

And what calling, I asked him, had he suddenly uncovered?

"Shapinsky!"

And who, or what, I hazarded, was Shapinsky?

"Harold Shapinsky," he replied. "Abstract Expressionist painter, generation of de Kooning and Rothko, an undiscovered marvel, an absolute genius, completely unknown, utterly unappreciated. He lives here in New York City, with his wife, in a tiny one-bedroom apartment, where he continues to paint, as he has been doing for over forty years, *like an angel*." Ramachander scribbled an address and a phone number on a scrap of paper, shoved it at me, and continued, "You *must* visit this Shapinsky fellow. He's a true find, a major discovery. It is my destiny to bring him to the attention of the world."

I was somewhat speechless.

Ramachander was not: "You will see—this is an extraordinary discovery. As I say, I don't care about money. What's money? I do it because of my destiny."

Well, at length Ramachander departed. (He was, he told me, headed for Europe a few days hence.) I tacked Shapinsky's address and phone number to my bulletin board but didn't get around to calling him right away, and then one thing led to another, and I pretty much forgot about the whole incident.

A few weeks later, at seven in the morning, the phone in my apartment rang me awake. "Hello, Mr. Weschler. Akumal here. In Utrecht, Holland. You won't believe the good news! I took slides of Shapinsky's work to the Stedelijk Museum in Amsterdam, and the curator there was amazed. He told me that I'd brought him the work of a great artist, that Shapinsky is a major find. I must tell you, I'm beginning to believe this is one of the great discoveries of the last five years. The curator was extremely supportive, and eager to see how things develop."

Myself, I wasn't really eager to believe any of it. I hung up and went back to sleep.

A few days later, the phone rang again—at ten in the morning this time. "Akumal again here, Mr. Weschler! Only, in London today. More good news! I visited the Tate this morning. Just walked in with no appointment, demanded to see the curator of modern art, refused to leave the waiting room until he finally came out—to humor me, I suppose, this silly little Indian fellow, you know—but presently he was *blown away*. He bows to me and says, 'Mr. Ramachander, you are right. Shapinsky is a terrific discovery.' I'm becoming more and more convinced myself that he's the discovery of the decade. Anyway, he gave me the name of a gallery—the Mayor Gallery. James Mayor, one of the top dealers in London, Cork Street—Warhol, Lichtenstein, Rauschenberg, first-rate. I went over there, and he, too, was flabbergasted. He's thinking about scheduling a show for the spring."

I still didn't know quite what to make of any of this; I assumed that it was all a bit daft, some elaborate fantastication, and, anyway, I remained too busy with other projects to take time to call and visit Shapinsky, if Shapinsky actually existed.

A few days later, the phone rang, again at seven in the morning, and, used to the pattern by now, I managed to preempt my new friend with a "Hello, Akumal."

"British television!" Ramachander exclaimed, utterly unimpressed by my prescience. "I showed the slides to some people over at British Channel 4 and they loved them, and right on the spot they committed themselves to doing a special, an hour-long documentary, to be ready in time for the show at the Mayor Gallery. Did I tell you? A one-man show to open on May twenty-first, Shapinsky's sixtieth birthday. They love the story, the idea of this unknown genius Abstract Expressionist and of the little Indian fellow and his destiny. They'll be flying me back to New York in several weeks with a camera crew to re-create our meeting—Shapinsky and myself—and then the following month they're going to fly Shapinsky and his wife and me to Bangalore, in India, so I can show them around my digs. This meeting of East and West, you see—that's the ticket. So maybe I'll see you in New York, yes?"

I set the phone back in its cradle, resolving to give the whole matter a bit more thorough consideration once I'd reawakened at some more decent hour. But just as I was nodding back off the phone rang again.

"The Ludwig Museum! I forgot to tell you. Just before Channel 4, I went to Cologne and showed the slides to the excellent lady in charge of the Ludwig Museum there. She couldn't get over them. She can't wait to see the show at the Mayor Gallery. Everyone agrees.

"I'm beginning to see it clearly now: Shapinsky is one of the top finds of the century!"

✳ ✳ ✳

Several weeks later (I'd anticipated the visitation with a notation in my desk diary), the phone rang at my office, and of course it was Akumal, this time in New York, in Shapinsky's apartment—I simply had to drop whatever I was doing immediately, he told me, and come see for myself.

So I did. The address on Seventieth Street, east of Second Avenue, turned out to be a Japanese restaurant. Off to one side was a dark entry passage behind a glass door. I pushed a doorbell and was buzzed in—a five-story walk-up; steep stairs and dim, narrow corridors. I could hear something of a commotion upstairs as I approached. Rounding the corner onto the fifth-floor landing, I was momentarily blinded by a panning klieg light: the tiny apartment was indeed overflowing with a bustling film crew. I craned my neck into the bustle. The foyer was almost entirely taken up by a single bed (the only bed in the apartment, I later discovered), which was covered with coats and equipment; the next room was an almost equally crammed kitchen; and just beyond that I could see into a tiny bedroom, which was serving as the studio. A very dignified and dapper-looking English gentleman had spread several paintings about the floor of the studio and was crouched down making a careful selection as the television crew peered over his shoulder. I managed to step in. In the far corner I spotted Akumal, who was beaming. Next to him stood a soft, slightly stooped, fairly rumpled, gray-bearded old man, wrapped in a moth-eaten wool sweater and puffing cherry-sweet tobacco smoke into the air from the bowl of a well-chewed pipe.

"Ah!" Akumal exclaimed, suddenly catching sight of me. "Mr. Weschler! I want you to meet Harold Shapinsky."

Shapinsky looked up, mildly (understandably) dazed.

★ ★ ★

The dapper Englishman got up off his haunches, wiped his hands, gave one last approving glance at the paintings arrayed before him, and then looked over at Shapinsky, smiling. "Yes," he said. "I think that will do. That will do superbly."

"Cut!" shouted the film director. "Good. Very good." The kliegs went dark.

"James Mayor," Akumal said, introducing the distinguished-looking Englishman, whose identity I'd already surmised.

Shapinsky puffed on his pipe and nodded.

The cameraman asked if he could have Shapinsky and his wife stand by the window for a moment, and Mayor walked over beside me. "Most amazing story," he said. "I mean, an artist of this caliber living like this, dirt poor, completely unknown—*living in a virtual garret* five stories above a Japanese restaurant I've been to literally dozens of times. Quite good Japanese restaurant, by the way, that." Mayor is in his late thirties, trim, conventionally handsome, with a shock of black hair cresting to a peak over his forehead. "I must say, when Akumal brought me in those slides I was astonished," he continued. "I mean, this art business can get one pretty jaded after a while. One gets to feeling one's seen it all. You begin to despair of ever again encountering anything original, powerful, real. I haven't felt a buzz like this in a long time."

Akumal and the director of the film, Greg Lanning, joined us. Lanning explained that he'd now like to shoot a sequence of Mayor and

Shapinsky talking together. Everything really was intolerably cramped. I asked Akumal if he'd like to join me for a little walk, and he agreed.

"Well," I told Akumal outside, "you've certainly gone and caught my attention. But do you think we might slow down and wind this tape back a bit? First of all, seriously, *who are you*?"

"Ah, yes." He laughed. "It's been just as I predicted, hasn't it? Wonderful destiny! Manifest destiny—isn't that one of your expressions here in America? Manifest *karma*, if you'll allow me. As I told you, I am a lowly professor of elementary English at the College of Agricultural Sciences in Bangalore. I am there every day from eight to three, teaching my classes of forty students grammar, spelling, sentence structure, conversational skills—only, I'm on leave just now, as you can see."

He was born in Bombay on the tenth of July, 1949, and his family presently moved to Calcutta. His father was a clerk in the army. His family was lower middle class, struggling to advance slightly higher, into the middle class proper. When his father and mother were married, they were so poor they couldn't afford a single night in the fanciest hotel in Bombay—they couldn't even afford tea there—so they went over and just rode up and down in the lifts. "That was their sort of honeymoon celebration. When I was growing up, there were six of us in two rooms."

Walking and talking at a brisk clip, Akumal continued, "My parents are both polyglots—they speak five Indian languages each, I speak seven—and they would encourage my reading. Especially my mother: I remember coming upon her in my room one day; she was reading my copy of *Death of a Salesman* and she was weeping. I was very bookish. I almost went blind with all my reading. There was no electricity, and to save my eyes my father made a huge clamor and got electricity for the entire block. He was not able to complete his schooling himself, so he sacrificed enormously so that his children would be able to: he sent me to a fine school where I perfected my English. Eventually, I even managed to teach English for many years before ever going to England my first time, which was in 1980.

"I was especially in love with beauty. In India, even the poorest will adorn themselves with colorful saris or simple jewelry—you may be economically deprived, we say, but God has given you eyes in your head to see—and from a very early age I was entranced, mesmerized by the flowing movements of all those intense colors. One of my earliest memories in Calcutta was going to the fields not far from Fort William, along the banks of the Hooghly River. This was my art school. Because there, each summer, thousands—no, hundreds of thousands—of butterflies would gather, and I would run among them, chasing them, all those brilliant hues floating about. I never actually tried to catch any. It was just the swarming of all that color. And that was my initial association when I saw the slides of Shapinsky's paintings for the first time. They reminded me of the butterflies back in Calcutta, and the rhythms of classical Indian dance, too—another great passion of mine. I knew I must be in the presence of a profound art if it could inspire associations like that."

Akumal went on to relate that his family had moved to Bangalore when he was sixteen. He received his bachelor's degree in physics and chemistry *and* mathematics from the National College in Bangalore in 1968, shifted fields and campuses and attained a master's degree from Bangalore's Central College in 1971. In addition to teaching, he wrote poetry in Hindi and fiction in English. In 1973, an early draft of an antiwar play of his somehow got him an invitation to Weimar, East Germany—his first trip abroad—and there he was "bowled over by Brecht." I say "somehow": Akumal was actually very specific—exhaustively so—about the circumstances, but my concentration had begun to buckle under the weight of his relentlessly detailed recapitulations. All of Akumal's accounts are exhaustive: it's not so much that he is incapable of compression as that he seems authentically dazzled by the particulate density of every aspect of his fate. Anyway, he returned to India and became something of a gadfly in Bangalore, one of the fastest-growing provincial cities in India, endlessly exhorting the editors of the local papers to expand their cultural coverage, especially of international film and literature. He haunted the British Council Library. He arranged for the first translation of Darwin's *Origin of Species* into

Kannada, the local language. He acted as a literary agent on behalf of various local poets and essayists. He managed to finagle a special four-page supplement on the films of the Polish director Krzysztof Zanussi during a Bangalore film festival in 1979. Zanussi eventually saw the supplement, and had Akumal invited to the 1980 Gdansk film festival, at the height of the Solidarity period—the first of several trips Akumal took to Poland. Somewhere along the line, he met Lelah Dushkin, a sociology professor at Kansas State University, who managed to arrange an invitation for Akumal to come to Kansas to lecture on Indian politics and cinema, so that early in the fall of 1984 Akumal found himself in Chicago, fresh from Poland (where he had just attended another film festival), en route to Manhattan, Kansas.

This is where the story proper begins—a story that Akumal has now told hundreds of times, each time the same way, with the same formulaic cadences and ritualized digressions, except for the addition, at the end of each new telling, of the name and reaction of the person he told it to the immediately prior time. It's like one of those Borges fictions, in which to hear the story is to become part of it. And the story always begins with Akumal's fresh astonishment, his sheer amazement at the wondrous coincidence of it all. Because, as he points out, if he hadn't been on his way to Kansas he would never have been in Chicago, and if he hadn't been in Chicago he would never have accompanied his host, the distinguished Indian poet (and MacArthur Fellowship recipient) A. K. Ramanujan, to a retirement party for Maureen Patterson, the South Asia bibliographer at the University of Chicago, and in that case he would never have had an impulse "to befriend one young man who was standing somewhat shyly in the corner"—an impulse that arose "because the man had an interesting, kind face"—and then he would never have met one of Maureen Patterson's graduate assistants, who proved to be David, the twenty-four-year-old son of Harold and Kate Shapinsky. "It could all easily never have happened," Akumal invariably points out here. "It was all built on the most precarious of coincidences. But, then again, it had to happen, because it was my karma to discover Harold Shapinsky, and it was Shapinsky's karma to be discovered by me."

David Shapinsky was in Chicago doing graduate work in American diplomatic history, so their conversation initially revolved around international relations, alighting on the subject of Poland, and thence on to the subject of a young Polish artist whose work Akumal had taken to promoting since his most recent trip to Gdansk, and some of whose etchings he had back in his suitcase at Ramanujan's. (He had bought them in Poland to assist the poor artist, and was now reselling them as he went along to finance his trip; beyond that, he was virtually without funds.)

"David didn't mention anything about his father that night," Akumal explained to me as we completed perhaps our twelfth lap of the block the afternoon he recounted the whole story to me for the first time. "That took another coincidence—the next day, we just happened to run into each other at the University of Chicago library, and he asked me if I'd mind going with him for coffee. Presently, he told me about his father and invited me up to his room to look at some slides of his father's paintings and see if I might be willing to promote his father's work as well. He is a loving son, and he was pained by the oblivion into which his father had fallen. I was interested, but I really didn't know much about Abstract Expressionism—I mean, I of course had Alvarez's anthology of twentieth-century English poetry, which has a Pollock on the cover, and I'd read a piece in *The Economist* for June 1978, a review of a book about ancient Indian popular painting in which the writer suggested that these artists must have unconsciously anticipated Pollock. So I knew about Pollock, though I'd never heard of de Kooning. And I had no idea how I would react to this work of David's father. In David's room, though, looking at the slides, I got butterflies—the butterflies of my Calcutta youth!

"Over the next few days, I got very excited. I told David to call his parents and tell them to sit tight just a big longer—that a crazy Indian from Bangalore was on his way to promote Harold's paintings. And I made David a two-part bet. I bet him that within a year I would secure a show for his father's paintings at a major world-class gallery—possibly not in America, possibly in Europe. I wasn't sure about New

York—they're funny in New York, you can never tell. And, secondly, we would force the *Encyclopedia Britannica* to revise its entry on Abstract Expressionism to establish the name Shapinsky in its rightful place among de Kooning, Pollock, Rothko, and the others. We bet a dinner at the fanciest restaurant we could think of, and then I was off to Kansas.

"From Kansas, I called a friend of mine in New Jersey, an Indian fellow named Sudhir Vaikkattil. An exceptional photographer, he was an earlier discovery of mine. I told him not to ask any questions but to call the Shapinskys right away, go over there, and take new slides of the work and of them. I'd be joining up with him in a few weeks. I told him not to worry, that somehow I'd find money to pay for the materials—although at that moment I was, frankly, penniless. I called Harold—this was our first conversation—and told him about Sudhir and the need for the new slides. And—this was fantastic—you know what he said? He said, 'Well, I hope he gets in touch with me.' This was a wonderful omen. In India, we have a proverb—'The thirsty man goes to the well, the well doesn't go to the thirsty man.' As I suspected, this confirmed that Shapinsky was a well, not a thirsty man. He is incredibly serene. He is *siddhipurush*—this is a Sanskrit expression meaning a wise man, self-actualized, unflappable, unfazed."

Akumal soon completed his lectures in Kansas and flew on, for some reason (he told me why; I just got lost somewhere in here), to Los Angeles and then to Washington, D.C. There, as elsewhere, he managed to find some Indian patrons. "I sing for them," Akumal explained to me matter-of-factly. "Oh, I didn't tell you? Yes, I am a great fan of Indian semiclassical music, and I can sing unaccompanied. Homesick Indians all over the world love to have me stay with them in their homes as long as I sing for my keep." He now launched his siege of the Smithsonian, armed with David's slides. There was a whole series of coincidences here as well, including a fellow named Asman ("This was a wonderful omen, because, you see, *asman* in Hindustani means the sky, and, of course, I was reaching for the sky, and also, in Bangalore, I am known as Chander, the Moon, so the Asman-Chander—you get the idea"), whom Akumal encountered somewhere along the way toward Dean Anderson, "the number two man at the Smithsonian." Anderson was impressed by the slides and dumbfounded that Shapinsky wasn't listed in any of the reference books on his extensive shelf. He promised to pass the slides on to the curators over at the Hirshhorn and get back to Akumal with their response as quickly as possible. On one of the days in here, Akumal happened upon a copy of my book on Poland in a bookstore and noted, from the jacket copy, that I'd also occasionally written on art ("another wonderful omen"), which is why he called me later (very much later) that night. As he pointed out, admiring his own tactical acumen, he'd limited his conversation in that first phone call to the subject of Poland. This was partly, he now told me, because he'd spent much of the interim that afternoon calling New York galleries. "I must tell you I've made a major discovery," he'd told one receptionist after another, "an extraordinary Abstract Expressionist of the generation of Pollock, Rothko, and de Kooning, and I would like to make an appointment to come in and show you some slides." In a few cases, he managed to get past the flak-catchers, but it didn't much help. "Harold *who*?" was a common response. One prominent dealer, Ivan Karp, went as far as to assert, "He couldn't be very major if I've never heard of him." Akumal called thirty-two galleries and got not one appointment. A few days later, on October thirtieth, undaunted, he boarded a bus for Manhattan. He immediately called on the Shapinskys. They became fast friends, and later that very afternoon he showed up in my office, making his subtle (as it developed, almost too subtle) pitch.

The next day, Akumal called Anderson at the Smithsonian. "The people here are amazed," Akumal recalls Anderson's telling him. "They say either Shapinsky is an outstanding genius of twentieth-century art or he is a first-class derivative artist. They want more time." Akumal pointed out that all Western art was derivative of the East, if you wanted to get picky about things, and anyway art history was not a relay race. He asked whether Anderson would mind if he began showing the slides to art people in Europe. Anderson said of course not, and shortly thereafter Akumal boarded a flight to Amsterdam on the first leg of his pre-booked, prepaid return to Bangalore.

We'd now accomplished a half-dozen more laps of the block, and we decided to peer in and see how the TV shoot was going. It was going like most such things—at a snail's pace—and Akumal would not be needed for a bit longer, so we decided to head out for a few more rounds.

"The next coincidence occurred on the plane," Akumal continued. "The KLM in-flight magazine happened to include an article about the Stedelijk Museum, mentioning a curator named Alexander van Gravenstein, so once I arrived in Holland I immediately took to calling him, and eventually obtained an appointment. When I arrived at his office, he invited me down to the museum cafeteria, and I was momentarily alarmed, because I literally didn't have a cent in my pocket and, you know, there is this phrase 'going Dutch,' and, this being Amsterdam and everything, I figured I might be expected to pay for my own coffee. But he was very generous—another good omen—and he just picked up the tab. And after he looked at the slides, he said, 'You have brought me the work of a great artist. The work of the late forties and fifties is especially original.' He gave me the name of Xavier Fourcade, a dealer in New York City, but I decided not to tell him how I'd already called the thirty-two New York galleries, all to no avail."

Buoyed by that exchange, Akumal borrowed money from some Dutch friends and took the boat to England, arriving in London early in the morning and being met by an Indian friend who was studying at Cambridge. Over dinner, their conversation turned to the Booker Prize for fiction and the fact that it had recently been won by Anita Brookner, who happened to be a professor of art. "I took this as an omen," Akumal recounted. "And I excused myself momentarily from the table. I went over to the pay phone and looked up her number in the phone book. It was listed—*another* good omen. And since it wasn't too late—before ten, anyway—I placed the call. She answered herself, and I quickly explained my situation and she was very gracious, at the end suggesting that the man to get in touch with was her friend Alan Bowness, the director of the Tate." When Akumal returned to the dining table, his Cambridge friend was aghast that he'd actually called Miss Brookner, but "once in a while you just have to be bold."

The next morning, Akumal presented himself at the reception desk at the Tate, insisting on seeing the director. No, he did not have an appointment, but he did have urgent business. Bowness, it turned out, was not in, but Akumal would not be budged. Finally, the receptionist managed to get Ronald Alley, the keeper of the modern art collection, to come down and attend to this immovable Indian. "I pulled out the slides, and as he looked through them he almost immediately said, 'You have made a major discovery.' I said yes. He suggested that what Shapinsky needed now was a first-class gallery, and asked if I'd like a referral. Of course, I said yes again. He went over to his phone and called James Mayor and told him he'd be sending over someone with some very interesting work. I thanked him, left the building, flagged a cab, and immediately proceeded to the Mayor Gallery."

Salman Rushdie, the bestselling author of *Midnight's Children* and *Shame*, who was to become another student and chronicler of this affair, has pointed out, correctly, that this was the turning point in Akumal's Shapinsky quest. As Rushdie says, "Now, for the first time, Akumal had become that most *pukka* of persons, a man who has been properly introduced." (*Pukka* is Hindustani for "complete," "whole," "together.")

Mayor had hardly had time to put his phone back in its cradle when Akumal arrived at his door, pulling out his slides. And Mayor, too, was impressed. He asked for a couple of weeks to think it over, but a few days later, on December fourth, he told Akumal that he would like to schedule a Shapinsky retrospective for the spring. Akumal asked him to frame his request as a letter. Mayor did, and the next evening Akumal told the whole story to Salman Rushdie, whom he'd met a few years earlier when a lecture tour brought the writer to Bangalore.

Akumal now took a boat back to Holland, made his quick and highly successful side trip to the Ludwig Museum in Cologne, and then prepared to resume his flight back to Bangalore, again virtually out of funds. Dutch television had become interested in his story and wanted to scoop the world with news of the Shapinsky discovery. Unfortunately, the sole slot it had available was for a few days after Akumal's prepaid and nonchangeable flight back. Akumal called Rushdie to ask what he should do.

Rushdie offered some tentative advice, but the real import of this call in terms of the saga was that it served to remind Rushdie of the whole affair. This was important, because that evening it just happened—"another incredible coincidence"—that Rushdie was going to be dining with his friend Tariq Ali. Ali, who comes from an area of pre-Partition India that is now in Pakistan, had been one of the foremost student activists in Europe during the Vietnam War period; he'd been instrumental in establishing the Bertrand Russell–Jean-Paul Sartre war-crimes tribunal in Stockholm; and he'd gone on to become a prolific and highly regarded political writer. Ali had also recently been named one of the executive producers of a documentary-film company named Bandung Productions, which was loosely affiliated with Britain's new television network, Channel 4. One of Ali's colleagues from Channel 4 was at the dinner, and Rushdie naturally regaled the group with his improbable tale of Akumal and Shapinsky. As he did so, he warmed to his subject, finally insisting that Bandung and Channel 4 commit themselves on the spot to doing a documentary on Akumal's discovery—or else, he assured them, he'd go to the BBC with the tale the very next morning. He made one proviso—that whoever took the project should take on Akumal's expenses for the interim as well. He was tired of seeing his friend ricocheting around the world so precariously close to bankruptcy. The dinner reconvened as an instant committee of the whole, they all agreed to Rushdie's proposal and his terms, and Akumal was called the next morning.

And now, a scant three months later, here we were, Akumal and I, negotiating loops around the real-life set of the resultant movie. We decided to go back upstairs, and this time Akumal's services were required. I spoke briefly with the Shapinskys, arranged for a meeting a few days later, when things would have quieted a bit, and took my leave.

✮ ✮ ✮

Akumal telephoned me the next morning at my office to tell me that he and the film crew would be off to Chicago later that day to shoot a re-creation of the meeting with David ("We're going to reassemble the entire party," he said enthusiastically. "Miss Patterson is going to get to retire all over again"), but first he was going to the Museum of Modern Art to talk to William Rubin, the formidable director of the museum's Department of Painting and Sculpture.

"Do you have an appointment?" I asked.

"Of course not," Akumal shot back. "But, then, I haven't had appointments most other places, either. I'll drop by afterward to tell you how things went."

Twenty minutes later, someone stepped into my office to tell me that there was a Mr. Ramachander asking for me in the lobby. "Well," I said sympathetically as I guided Akumal back to my office a few moments later, "it must have been a short meeting."

"Ah," Akumal replied sheepishly. "It's Wednesday. I forgot. The museum is closed on Wednesdays. But"—he brightened—"I've made a wonderful new discovery." He reached into his satchel and pulled out a bag. "Croissants! Sort of like French flaky breakfast rolls. You can just go in and buy them at a place right around the corner. Very tasty. Here." He offered me one and then reached again into his satchel, this time pulling out a folder.

"I wanted to show you all the letters," he explained. He had apparently been collecting testimonials as he went along.

"Dear Mr. Akumal," the one from Ronald Alley began, under the Tate Gallery letterhead. "Thank you for showing me the slides of Harold Shapinsky's paintings. I am sorry to say he was completely unknown to me, but he is clearly an Abstract Expressionist artist of real interest whose work deserves to be widely known. His pictures have great freshness and beautiful colour, and I think people are going to be very surprised that an artist of this quality could have slipped into total obscurity."

There was one from Dr. Partha Mitter, the eminent Asian Studies scholar from the University of Sussex: "I was deeply moved by [Shapinsky's] immensely joyous paintings which appeared to celebrate life and its manifold creations. They exude power and dynamism, and their range of primary colours and sinuous lines evokes striking impressions of organic forms."

It must have been by way of Mitter that Akumal was able to get to Norbert Lynton, the celebrated historian of twentieth-century art who is also a professor at Sussex. (Lynton's *The Story of Modern Art* was conceived of, and is currently used in classrooms throughout the world, as an adjunct volume to E. H. Gombrich's classic *The Story of Art*.) "I write to thank you for coming in and showing me your slides of the work of Shapinsky," Lynton's letter began. "Some days have passed since then: and though I had intended to write to you sooner the delay has not been without value, in that I find my recollection of many of Shapinsky's works crystal clear, a sure sign (I know from past experience) of artistic significance. He is certainly a painter of outstanding quality. . . . The slides suggest a rare quality of fresh and vivid (as opposed to mournfully soulful) Abstract Expressionism, a marvelous sense of colour, and also a rare feel for positioning marks and areas of colour on the canvas or paper. When you see Shapinsky, please . . . bring him respectful, admiring greetings from me."

There were several other letters in the file as well, and Akumal beamed as I read them. "It's all quite fantastic, isn't it?" he said. "So, don't you think you should come to the opening?"

I told him that I might try to make it to London for the opening, which was two months away. We left it at that.

Then he asked me if I would mind writing a letter, just to say that I, too, had now seen the slides, and that I might be coming to the opening.

I told him I'd try to remember to.

He said it was okay; he could wait—he had a few minutes before he had to go catch the airport bus.

So far, I really hadn't had a chance to talk with Shapinsky, or, for that matter, to get a good look at his work, but now that the traveling documentary show had hit the road and quiet had returned to East Seventieth Street I went over for a chat the next day. Actually, several such visits were necessary: Shapinsky turned out to be as reserved and measured and withdrawn as Akumal was voluble and extravagant and outgoing. He was always gentle and polite, but he was subdued; indeed, at times his restraint verged on the spooky. He answered questions in a flat, becalmed voice with simple sentences often consisting of just one or two words ("Yes, marvelous," "Truly gratifying"). Though his answers eventually got longer, they often seemed preset—not that he was being evasive or had adopted some sort of party line but, rather, that his life seemed to hold little curiosity for him, few fresh surprises, no new vantages. His accounts had none of the free-associative, scattershot unpredictability that characterized Akumal's. I could see what Akumal had meant when he spoke of Shapinsky's serenity, but it seemed clearly a serenity that had a cost—there seemed to be a certain exhaustion behind the equanimity.

I was struck on each new visit to the Shapinskys by the extraordinary spareness of their circumstances. One day, there happened to be three dirty cups in the kitchen sink, and there were not enough clean ones to go around until Kate had washed one of them. Another time, I took along a couple of friends, and there were not enough chairs in the apartment for all of us to sit on until Shapinsky lifted an ancient stereo off a rickety stool, set the stereo on the floor, and brought the stool over to the table. At night, I learned, they pulled a rolled-up thin mattress out of the closet and spread it across the floor to sleep on. During my visits, Kate would occasionally sit with us in the kitchen, knitting (she was always more spry and animated than he); other times, she would repair to the little foyer, on the other side of the thin wall, and operate her sewing machine, using the single bed as a layout table, while tossing anecdotes and amplifications back into the kitchen.

Harold Shapinsky was born in Brooklyn in 1925, which is to say that, contrary to Akumal's telescoped version, he was a good fifteen years younger than most of the first-generation Abstract Expressionists. (For that matter, he was younger than many of the second-generation New York School painters as well.) His parents were first-generation Russian-Jewish immigrants, and his father worked as a designer in the garment industry. Harold was the third of four boys. Music was highly prized in the family—one of his older brothers became a classical cellist, and the other played double bass—but the visual arts were encouraged hardly at all. Indeed, as Harold's precocious drawing talent started garnering notice it began to be actively discouraged. A musician, after all, could always gain employment somewhere, but what possible livelihood could there be for a painter?

Nevertheless, from an early age Shapinsky inhabited a highly visual universe. As a small boy, he was always attracted to the museums—especially the Brooklyn Museum, where he was particularly taken with ancient figurines, Egyptian friezes, and Coptic reliefs. But he also found visual stimulation in contexts other than the formally artistic. For example, he was fascinated by the patterns chalked out across the swatches of fabric his father brought home from his work in the garment industry—"the complex jumble of shapes," he recalls, "and especially the spaces in between." He also spent hours poring over weather maps in the newspaper, his imagination stirred by what he calls "the compression of distances and scale, the layering, the sense of pressures building and spilling into winds, the gracefully sweeping front lines, the three-dimensional density expressed through the simplest of abstract graphic means." He says that the fabric swatches and the maps influenced his later work.

When Shapinsky was in his early teens, his parents divorced, and his home life, which he seldom discusses directly, appears to have become quite strained and unhappy. His mother would find his paintings and throw them out; even more distressing, his stepfather—after she remarried—would find his paintings and paint right over them, in an act of not even thinly veiled jealousy. Shapinsky persevered. He became fascinated by modern European painting—especially Cézanne and Picasso—and he says that by the age of fifteen, in 1940, he had resolved to become a painter. By that time, he had been out of school a year—he had been forced to drop out of junior high to help support his family. He worked at a succession of jobs, and continued to draw and paint in the evenings. His early portraits were highly influenced by the neo-classical Picasso. In 1945, he received some sort of scholarship to the Art Students League, where he studied with Harry Sternberg and Cameron Booth. (I derive this fact from a photostat of a handwritten two-page "résumé," the only documentation the Shapinskys were able to muster when James Mayor requested a curriculum vitae to be used in preparing the show.) That year, at twenty, Shapinsky moved to Manhattan—to an unheated three-room, five-flight walk-up on the lower East Side, for which he paid twelve dollars and fifty cents a month. (Forty years later, he and his wife share a space almost as small in a similar walk-up, although it's in a somewhat nicer neighborhood and costs a lot more.)

These were to be the high good times of Shapinsky's life—in many ways, its only good times, at least up until October of 1984. He got a job in a ceramics factory and gradually rose to become head of its decorating department. But that was just part-time. All the rest of his time, his energy, and whatever little money he was able to save were poured into his painting. "It was a wonderful period," he recalls. "There was a tremendous camaraderie among the artists. We were putting our all into painting, into the activity of painting itself. We'd get together at the old Waldorf Cafeteria at Sixth Avenue and Eighth Street, and we'd talk about the mission of painting. Nobody gave a thought to money, or to exhibiting, or even to selling the work. It was a pure scene."

The first-generation Abstract Expressionists were just making their breakthroughs—one-two-three, one after the other, like that! And Shapinsky watched as it was happening all about him. "I saw my first Gorky show at the Julien Levy Gallery in 1946, right around the time I was myself turning decidedly toward abstraction," he says. "Although I never met him, Gorky was a great encouragement: he had a beautiful touch—such a warm feeling to him. I met and became friends with Franz Kline around 1947. I saw my first Jackson Pollock show in 1948, at Betty Parsons. Although I saw de Kooning himself a good deal on the street and about town, I didn't see my first de Kooning painting till 1950 or so. But the point is, everybody was painting. We weren't Abstract Expressionists—that designation would only come later. We were just *painters*."

Shapinsky met Kate Peters at an all-night New Year's Eve party as 1947 became 1948. She was, she says, "a dancer and a shiksa." She was the renegade bohemian offshoot of an established New England family. Her father was an architect and had a bit of the artist in him. But her parents, too, had divorced. Her mother had remarried, and her stepfather was Hugh Lofting, the author of the Doctor Dolittle stories, though he didn't seem to like children very much, or at any rate had little use for her. Her insistence on becoming a dancer received little support from her family, but she kept at it, studying with Doris Humphrey and José Limón, among others. Like many dancers, she hung around the artists. She *had* met Gorky, baby-sitting for his children not long before his suicide. "He'd walk me home afterward to the Sixteenth Street Y," she says. "He was angry at the world. He had a great big dog. His little girls called his paintings 'broken toys.'" At that party, Kate says, she was immediately attracted to Harold—"He was so thin and gaunt, he had a face like El Greco's Jesus Christ"—but she didn't think she had a chance, because of her New England background. She was wrong. ("She had marvelous form," Shapinsky recalls of his first impression.)

A few weeks later, he tracked her down: she was nude, modeling on a dais at the Art Students League. He borrowed a large drawing pad, scrawled in big letters Meet Me in the Cafeteria, and held the pad up before her. The class broke into applause. And after class she did meet him in the cafeteria. They went off to a pizza joint ("No," she corrects him, "it was a health-food place"), and the dinner cost two dollars, cleaning him out completely. "It was worth it, worth every penny," he says now, smiling over at her fondly. Their courtship was gradual, proceeding by fits and starts, and, like many affairs among artists of the period, it took a long time to formalize. They weren't officially married until 1955, and David, their only child, didn't arrive until 1960.

Shapinsky continued to scramble, hoarding whatever time he could for his painting, though he never seemed to have enough. A great break came when he happened to hear, in the fall of 1948, that a school named Subjects of the Artist was being established on Eighth Street by the painters William Baziotes, David Hare, Mark Rothko, and Robert Motherwell. (They were subsequently joined by Barnett Newman.) After work one evening, he went over to see about the possibility of a scholarship—he certainly couldn't afford the tuition. Baziotes happened to be there, and they had a long talk before class. "Finally," Shapinsky recalls, "Bill said to me, 'Well, let's see what you can do.' So I ran downstairs, found a paint shop, bought some black and white enamel and a board, hauled the things back up, squatted on the floor, and set to work. A while later, Bill came over, and he liked it and said he thought I had a good chance. A few minutes later, Motherwell came over and started watching. Something went wrong, though, and I became dissatisfied and began scraping the paint away, gouging it and starting over. Motherwell liked how I treated the painting as a process. So they offered me a tuition scholarship on the spot. It was worth thousands—or anyway, it was worth thousands *to me* at that time. I began hanging out there morning, noon, and night. There weren't very many students, actually—maybe about a dozen—and my work received a lot of attention, caused a lot of talk. David Smith liked it. Bradley Tomlin liked it. Sometimes I would draw with chalk directly on the wall—I liked its hardness, the challenge of opening up a space. One time, Mark Rothko, who was terribly nearsighted, was talking to the class, and he began to speak appreciatively about one of my wall drawings as an example. He reached up to get a better look and tried to pull it off the wall—only, it *was* the wall. It was very embarrassing. Baziotes meant the most to me as a teacher, although they all had an impact. He was warm and enthusiastic—the others were more intellectual—and he helped encourage me to continue dealing with issues in my painting that were just beginning to be formulated. That sense of painting as a process. There were Friday-night lectures—Jean Arp came and spoke, Adolph Gottlieb, others."

The school closed toward the end of the winter of 1949. Shapinsky dragged his stuff back to his cramped cold-water flat and continued working. He was pouring all his money into paint and brushes and boards. He was literally living on peanuts, consuming a packet a day. Finally, it all became too much. "I collapsed," Shapinsky recalls. "One day, I couldn't get out of bed in the morning. I couldn't move. It was terrible. If my brother hadn't come a few days later to see what had become of me, I don't know, I might have . . . Anyway, he came, he saw my condition and bundled me up and brought me back out to Long Island for the summer, where they pampered me, fattened me up, let me lie out on the beach, and I slowly recovered."

His brother, however, forgot to pay the rent on the cold-water flat— the twelve dollars and fifty cents a month. It may be that it didn't even occur to him. In the first of a series of terrible setbacks for Shapinsky, the landlord simply came up and cleared out the apartment, tossing several years' worth of work into the garbage. Although almost everything was lost, including all the large paintings, a few smaller pieces were salvaged at the last minute. (Some of them would eventually be slated for inclusion in the Mayor show.) Shapinsky was devastated by the news.

Had Akumal been with us the afternoon that Shapinsky related this sad incident, he might (good student of karma that he is) have noted the date—the summer of 1949. Karma metes out mysterious compensations, uncanny reincarnations: somewhere on the other side of the globe, Akumal Ramachander was being born.

Shapinsky returned to the city around Christmastime of 1949 to take a job as extra help at the post office. Around New Year's, he learned that Motherwell had founded a school in his own studio, on Fourth Avenue, as a sort of follow-up to Subjects of the Artist, and Shapinsky began attending the sessions. He returned to full strength, poured himself into the work once again. At the end of the year, Motherwell selected one of Shapinsky's paintings for an invitational show at the Kootz Gallery.

Samuel Kootz had five artists in his stable and eight slots on his annual calendar, so he was always having to come up with creative ways to fill the extra spaces while not unduly favoring any one or three particular artists. That December of 1950, he invited the five artists themselves—Baziotes, Hare, Hans Hofmann, Gottlieb, and Motherwell—to select three artists each for a "Fifteen Unknowns" show. During one of my visits, Shapinsky foraged from deep within a kitchen drawer a flyer for the show. Most of the unknowns have returned to oblivion, but there are some surprises. Hofmann selected John Grillo. Gottlieb included Clement Greenberg, in his sometime role as a painter, and Helen Frankenthaler—a year before her first one-woman show, at Tibor de Nagy. The Kootz invitational received some good notices, and Shapinsky was among those singled out. In the *Times*, for example, Stuart Preston cited his "deft profiling of creamy shapes, waving like flames in a crossbreeze."

As second-generation Abstract Expressionists go, Shapinsky had staked his claim early. Indeed, in a sense he could have been conceived of as a transitional figure, too young for the first generation but so thoroughly identified with it in terms of ambitions and conceptions of the activity of painting as to be more of a precursor than a simple member of the second generation. But all this speculation soon proved moot. A few months before the opening of the Kootz show came the outbreak of hostilities in Korea, and Shapinsky was drafted. He got a night's leave to attend the opening but had to be back in barracks the next morning. He wasn't sent abroad—in fact, he logged most of his hitch in Fort Dix, New Jersey—but he was effectively sequestered from the scene just as it was beginning to catch fire, or, rather, at the very moment that the torch was being passed from the first generation to the second. Thus, he missed the celebrated Ninth Street Exhibition, in 1951, in which several charter members of the Artists Club invited sixty-one artists to install one work each in an empty storefront in the Village. According to Irving Sandler, one of the period's premier chroniclers, in his book *The New York School*, the show included at least thirteen of the younger artists—Frankenthaler, Robert Goodnough, Grace Hartigan, Alfred

Leslie, Joan Mitchell, and Milton Resnick among them. It is not inconceivable that Shapinsky would have been included had he been around. He might, at any rate, have been able to capitalize on his Kootz exposure, to insure that he would be part of the transition.

Instead, he was discharged, in the summer of 1952, into what he experienced as a radically altered environment. "The whole spirit had changed," he says, with something between a shudder and a sigh. "Money was beginning to flow in, and it was ruining everything. Politics was setting in. Everything was breaking apart. It was all becoming who you know, cliques, kowtowing, bootlicking. There was a mad scramble for galleries. It just got worse and worse." And Shapinsky began to fall inexorably away. "I couldn't stand all those cocktail parties," he recalls. He and Kate became more and more reclusive. "I tried to do my own work as quietly as possible, enjoy my family, my friends, visit the museums, study the masters, return to my studio, paint." He'd show once in a long while—a single painting or two in an obscure exhibition at some out-of-the-way gallery. But these shows were marginal, peripheral, in a scene, on an island, where centrality was everything. He looked on, aghast, as the art scene was transmogrified. "Painting became a business," he says. "The painters became like factories. Their product was the new—something new for each season. Most of it nowadays is like newspaper headlines. That's what the galleries seem to want—it creates a big splash, but then it doesn't mean anything. The work can be quite competent technically, but it's dead. You don't feel the artist's hand. It's all superficial. It's launching bandwagons and chasing after them. Nobody is concerned about *feeling* anymore, about the journey."

One day, he finally took me into his little bedroom studio to show me some paintings. "Look," he said. "*Feeling is everything.*" One after another, he pulled out works from 1946, 1958, 1963, 1982, 1970, 1948. . . . It was amazing: isolated, utterly alone, working for no one but himself, unconcerned about wider acceptance, not kowtowing to any gallery or potential moneyed patrons, Shapinsky had almost managed to make time stand still. The paintings *were* quite lovely. The ones he showed me (like all those slated for the Mayor Gallery show) were small, and many of them were on paper. Shapinsky explained that he would have loved to work on large canvases, but he could never afford the canvas or the paint; he never had the room to stretch any large canvases, or the space to store the resultant paintings. So he condensed his art, working in what the Abstract Expressionists would have considered a miniature format—eighteen by twenty-four inches. Remarkably, however, he seemed able to compress a great deal of energy into those limited spaces, so that there is occasionally an almost epic quality to the small images—or, rather, they start out lyric and seem to hover, to modulate toward the epic.

But the main thing about them was this sense of their being frozen in time. Perhaps, ironically, one of the functions of occasional gallery shows for an artist is to force him or her to focus and summarize and then to push forward to the next thing. Shapinsky never seemed to feel that pressure. In 1953, Robert Rauschenberg was erasing his de Kooning. Color-field painting, Pop Art, Op Art, Minimalism—they would all now come and go, and none of them would be in any way reflected in Shapinsky's stubborn, obliviously resolute passion. For almost forty years, Shapinsky would continue to do 1946–50 New York Abstract Expressionist painting. And Shapinsky's words, as he now spoke about his paintings, also seemed to come barreling out of some sort of time warp. "It's all a struggle with fluidity and spontaneity," he told me that day. "It's a journey—when you start, you don't know where it will take you, how it will all come out, how *you* will come out." *Now* he was becoming animated. "Sometimes I just start by throwing the brush at the blank surface. Then I try to respond to that mark. I enter into a dialogue with the surface. Then I try to deal with the surface tension. With enough tension, the piece comes alive, it begins to breathe, it swells, there's a fullness. I try to *puncture* the surface, to go deep inside, to build up the layers. I love to listen to music as I work—Mahler, for example, Bach, jazz—and, as they say, painting becomes a sort of visual music. It's abstract, but there's a sense of the world in it. I love to take walks in the park, see the way the branches intersect and sway, the swooping of the birds. I love looking down on the city from rooftops—the clean verticals and horizontals, the movement of traffic. All that gets filtered in. But, above all, it's *feeling*—feeling that is then carefully composed and constructed and integrated. Feeling that breaks apart and then comes together again. It's feeling, and a human touch, an existential trace."

Time passed. Shapinsky became a father. He held various jobs. For a while, he was an antiquarian bookseller. He taught art to children, ran an arts workshop with his dancer wife. He became a neighborhood activist, organizing the Sixth Street Block Association in the East Village. He continued to paint. And his health broke again. A back injury from his army days gave him chronic problems. He contracted a severe, lingering case of pneumonia, was bedridden literally for years during the late sixties and early seventies. He suffered from hypoglycemia. For a period, he almost went blind: much of his work from the seventies is even more miniature than usual—intricate murals on sheafs of eight-and-a-half-by-eleven-inch paper. He trembled. It was thought that he might have multiple sclerosis. Perhaps it was partly a physical manifestation of his frustration and despair at having been left behind as the train pulled out of the station—that, and the perversity of somehow being condemned to continue living right there inside the station amid all the noise and bustle of the new trains as they came and left: to wait there, eternally cordoned off.

The family was poor. One evening, David Shapinsky recounted for me over the phone how for long stretches he and his parents had lived below the poverty line. "It wasn't the lack of material comforts," he said, "but rather, the recurrent anxiety that come the end of the month there wouldn't be enough money to pay the rent and we might end up being thrown out on the street."

"I learned very early that sometimes you buy things just to make yourself feel better—and they don't," Kate told me one day. "Things you can buy usually don't matter." Kate began knitting sweaters and sewing patchwork quilt vests and jackets, and selling her wares to Henri Bendel. What with one thing and another, they got by. And Shapinsky continued to paint. Time passed—everywhere but in his painting world,

where it seemed to stay 1948. He'd become like one of those tribes se-
creted deep in the jungle by the headwaters of some lush, narrow New
Guinean stream, a little cusp of the world where the Stone Age still
holds sway—and then, one day, over the godforsaken, fog-enshrouded
pass, in stumbled Akumal.

In the ensuing weeks, I showed a set of transparencies of the twenty-
two paintings selected for the Mayor Gallery show to various dealers
around New York. A consensus quickly formed among those dealers.
There was no question but that Shapinsky could paint. "This is the work
of a real painter," André Emmerich, of the André Emmerich Gallery,
told me. "Technically, these are very proficient, smart paintings. This
one here"—he picked out the transparency of *Poe*, a black-and-white
piece from 1949–50—"is excellent." Other dealers singled out other
paintings as "charming," "beautiful," or "strong." "Really a very fine
painter," I heard over and over. But almost everyone followed up such
observations with a string of misgivings. For one thing, the paintings
were too small. "You simply couldn't work this small and be a true Abstract Expressionist," Emmerich declared. "The whole point about Abstract Expressionism was that sense of Action painting, and that
required scale." I started to point out Shapinsky's explanation for the
small size of his works—the problem of storage, for example—but Emmerich wasn't buying that. "Canvases roll up," he said. "I could probably store all of Morris Louis's lifework in this little room." (The room
was little, but, in fairness, it was still larger than Shapinsky's entire
apartment.)

The most frequent recurring misgiving, however, was some varia-
tion on the theme that Shapinsky's lifework was very close, uncannily
close—indeed, uncomfortably close—to that of Willem de Kooning. "It's
funny," Emmerich commented. "Future art historians might well have
been excused if they'd accidentally attributed these works to de Kooning. That wouldn't have surprised me at all." Sidney Janis, of the Sidney
Janis Gallery, agreed—the works seemed enormously derivative. Over

and over, dealers would reach for their de Kooning catalogues and track the parallel years. "Look," one said. "See, here de Kooning is doing that sort of thing six months before Shapinsky—and he's doing it better." Shapinsky faced something of a double bind with these comparisons, because on those occasions—and there were several—when it appeared that Shapinsky had anticipated de Kooning (some of his paintings from 1947, for example, displayed the loose, lazy, languid curves of the very late de Kooning; and one Shapinsky, dated 1955–56, seemed to radically simplify the complexities of prior work, indulging in wide swaths of luminous, uninterrupted color, a full year before de Kooning was doing the same thing), the dealers uniformly challenged the accuracy of Shapinsky's dating, suggesting that he had probably got it wrong, if only accidentally. Since Shapinsky was judged derivative as his work went into the analysis, all the work *had* to be derivative by definition, and certain dates therefore *had* to be mistaken, since de Kooning, the man whom Shapinsky was ipso facto deriving everything from, hadn't yet reached that point. Q.E.D.

Irving Blum and his partner, Joseph Helman, of the Blum Helman Gallery, were the most blunt in their evaluation of Shapinsky's significance. "It's just too dicey!" Blum exclaimed. "The early paintings are versions of de Kooning and the late paintings are versions of the early paintings. There were dozens of guys like this. He's just another one of those close-but-no-cigar cases."

"Look," Helman said, pulling the current copy of the magazine *Flash Art* from a nearby shelf and flipping through the pages quickly. "Look at all these neo-Expressionist surrealists operating today. Dozens of painters with virtually identical imagery. Look, look, here, this one, this other one—a whole page of them here. Now, if one of these guys goes on and develops, if he keeps pushing, if he breaks through, if he can demonstrate his power and strength over and over again, if he can keep it up—well, then you're talking about someone worth considering. But by itself—nothing. You can go back and look through some issues of *Art News* from the late forties and early fifties, and I'm sure you'd find the same sort of things—dozens of Shapinskys. De Kooning had a lot of clones—he was an enormously influential figure, an over-powering presence; he exerted a tremendous force field, warping all sorts of careers around him—but *he* moved on. He changed over the years across a sustained career of dazzling inventiveness. Just because somebody was painting like him at one particular point in time doesn't make him his equal, not by a long shot."

I pointed out that they had both agreed that some of the Shapinskys were good paintings. Didn't that count for anything?

"You can't separate the issue of being derivative from the issue of being good," Helman replied. "They're deft, they're flashy, but . . ."

What about the European museum people and art writers who had vouched for the work?

"They never understood Abstract Expressionism in the first place," Blum said.

Helman agreed. "Most of the Europeans missed it when it was happening, and now they're misreading it in retrospect."

Blum asked me how much Mayor was going to be charging, and I told him I'd heard between fifteen and thirty thousand a painting, average around twenty-five.

"Look," Blum said. "That's big stakes. And this could all just be a bubble, hype feeding on itself. It can be smashed flatter than a pancake in an instant—and it may well be. These paintings will not bear the weight." Blum paused for a moment, and then continued, "The scene today is enormously protected, enormously serious: too much money is at stake."

Outside the office, as I left, the gallery walls were graced by a gorgeous selection of recent paintings by the thirty-three-year-old Donald Sultan—so recent, in fact, that you could smell some of the panels as they dried. Blum Helman had sold the show out before it had even opened, at sixty thousand dollars a pop. The whole question of art and money has become terribly vexed this past decade—we are living through a period of cultural inflation—but it seemed to me that some of these dealers were being a bit harsh. Given that a painting's true value bears almost no relation to its financial worth, its financial worth may just be whatever the market will bear. It had yet to be seen what the market would bear in Shapinsky's case. Hype, at any rate, is always the other gallery's publicity. As far as Shapinsky goes, as he nears the end of his career—in many ways a noble career, which has produced certain paintings of merit, of beauty—I couldn't see what was so terribly offensive about his finally being rewarded.

The questions of Shapinsky's relationship to de Kooning and of his true historical place in the transition between the early generations of Abstract Expressionism in New York were interesting ones in their own right, however, completely independent of any implications they might have for the market in Shapinsky's paintings. They were difficult questions to research, however, partly because there was virtually no history of exhibitions or critical commentary on Shapinsky's case to refer to. And now many of the principal witnesses were dead or unavailable for comment. De Kooning, in particular, has for many years maintained a policy of refusing to be interviewed.

I did reach William Baziotes's widow, Ethel. It turned out that she had barely met Shapinsky while Baziotes was alive, but she well recalls her husband's talking about his young colleague during the years before his death, in 1963. "The teachers and fellow artists liked him enormously," she recalls. "They felt his gifts were evident, so much so that Franz Kline gave him several works—and there is no higher praise a painter can give a fellow artist than that. They thought of him as a younger brother. They trusted him. They knew he would not confuse the issues or choose the easy way. Bill felt that Shapinsky had a grave mind. It had known many hells, he used to say—he seemed to need to fight alone, to be terribly singular. His dark, painful youth, Bill felt, had conditioned him to move obliquely. Bill felt that Shapinsky would take a sober course at great cost but that he would stay the course. He used to say that once in a while he had come upon a student like that, and that had made it all worthwhile."

I then called Robert Motherwell, at his home in Connecticut. I summed up the recent developments and asked him if he remembered Shapinsky.

"Oh, yes," he said, but hesitantly, seeming to reach far back. "Extraordinary, the way things like that return on you. Yes, yes. Harold Shapinsky: big horn glasses, very pale, thin." He paused. "There was no question with him that the talent and the dedication were real. There were a lot of students moving through those schools, and many of them were just passing through, but Shapinsky was clearly the real McCoy. However, the main thing I remember about him was how terribly intense he was—a combination of extreme intensity and shyness. He'd tremble; he'd quiver with all that intensity. It was too bad, because whereas that sort of temperament might have worked ten years earlier— many of those first-generation people were loners, they were into profound psychological and existential self-exploration—that just wasn't the way things were developing after 1950. By then, people were becoming looser, more optimistic, more sunny, more social."

Our conversation turned to how Shapinsky had fallen away. I mentioned his having been drafted.

"That's odd," Motherwell said. "He must have been registered with some other draft board than the one in Greenwich Village. The draft board in the Village, if they heard you were an artist they assumed you must be some sort of Communist—or, at any rate, you were manifestly unreliable—and they had no use for the likes of you in their army, so it meant an almost automatic deferment." (I subsequently asked Shapinsky about this, and it was true: he had been registered in Brooklyn, at his mother's address.) Motherwell agreed that Shapinsky's forced absence from the scene couldn't have helped his career. "But he would probably have been temperamentally unsuited in any case," he said. "He was so wound up. He couldn't have been one of the boys; it would have been like asking Kafka to be one of the boys. That second generation, they loved to party. I can't imagine Shapinsky enjoying a party or talking for hours at a time on the phone. I was married to one of them, Helen Frankenthaler, for twelve years, and I used to marvel at how much time she and her fellow artists spent on the phone. That first generation—there wasn't a single phone person. No, I take that back. Barnett Newman used to love talking on the phone. But Shapinsky just never could have been made to fit into the way things developed through the fifties."

I also visited with Irving Sandler, the chronicler of the history of the New York art scene since the war, at his apartment, in New York University faculty housing. "In my own work, I have a zillion loose threads," he said, smiling, as I laid out the basic contours of my Shapinsky subject. "Graduate students are going to be picking them up for years." Sandler had never heard of Shapinsky but seemed delighted at the prospect of widening his horizon. "What I love about the Shapinsky story as you've told it to me is that it manages to fulfill two of the most prevalent art-world fantasies of the time," he said. "One of them we all used to talk about was the fantasy of the late discovery at the very end of a career, after years and years of unsung labor. And the other one was the fantasy of the lonely secret master, slaving away somewhere completely apart: that here all of us were, expecting Master to emerge from our midst—we were, after all, the center—but in fact he was patiently working off in some barn or up in some garret, far away from it all." Sandler, however, was less than overwhelmed by the transparencies I now began to show him. "They're good paintings," he said. "Some of them are very good. But they're de Kooning. There were a lot of artists like this, but this one is almost the most de Kooning–like of any of them." Sandler then spoke for a little while about de Kooning's impact on the second generation. He read me a passage from a recent monograph he had written on Al Held, about the way de Kooning had labored heroically to create a new language, one that the second generation could now take for granted, could simply pick up and *start making sentences with*. Shapinsky fitted in there somewhere. Sandler continued to riffle through the transparencies, marveling at the dates. "His uniqueness is that he's still doing it. The conviction carries all the way through: the later ones are as fresh as the early ones. *He still believes it.*"

Weeks were passing quickly now, and the London opening was less than a month away. I went over to the Shapinskys' apartment once again. (They had ended up not joining the film crew on its transit to Bangalore to film Akumal in situ.) I wanted to get a clearer focus on Shapinsky's own sense of his relationship to de Kooning.

Shapinsky was in his subdued mode again, puffing on his cherry-scented tobacco. It was difficult to narrow in on the issue—or, rather, Shapinsky's statements remained calmly consistent with his earlier claim that he had seen virtually no de Kooning work before 1950 or so. "I knew we were working in the same general terrain," he explained. "People kept telling me so. So I guess I bent over backward not to see his work. One time, he and Noguchi came by the Subjects of the Artist, and they were walking around looking at some of the students' work when they came upon one of my canvases—I happened to be on the other side of the room at the moment—and they spent a long time talking about it very intently with each other. That kind of thing didn't happen very often; it was sort of embarrassing. Later, de Kooning would call down to me from the window of his studio, inviting me up, but I intentionally made excuses, because I didn't want to be worried about the overlap."

He paused, and then said, "No, I really don't see de Kooning's having been that big an influence. Gorky, perhaps, a bit more. And several of the Europeans, definitely—Cézanne, Kandinsky, Miró. And above all Picasso. We were all of us drawing on the same sources, but Picasso was paramount. Everything you tried to do, Picasso had already done. It drove some people crazy, and they tried to reject Picasso. But I thought he was fantastic, and he was most important."

I decided to leave things at that and asked him and Kate if they were getting excited about the coming weeks.

"Oh, yes," Shapinsky said, with about as little excitement as I suspect it's possible for a human being to muster. "It is all very gratifying." He was silent for a moment. "The work will be seen."

"I can't get over it myself," Kate said, with more than enough animation for both of them. "I find myself on the phone talking to

London—me, London!—and I can't believe this is really happening. At first, it was really scary—the prospect of life's becoming a little easier came as quite a shock. I have a rich fantasy life. I wrote whole novels in my head about what was going on, entire scenarios of calamities playing themselves out. But it looks as if everything is going to be all right."

I asked them how they'd imagined that things might go in the days before Akumal.

"I always had the feeling that something like this would occur sooner or later," Shapinsky said. "That the work would someday be seen."

Kate said, "I used to cry at night. I'd pray and pray to my grandfather, who was a minister. It was so unfair, so terrible to live with this man who was creating so much beauty, and not have anyone know about it. The worst came about a year ago. I heard about an old artist who died; all his lifework was just tossed out onto the street, stray people passing by were picking at it. . . . That really got to me. I prayed all the harder. Akumal was like the answer to my prayers. Seriously, I think he's an angel." She said that Akumal had at first refused to accept any reward for all his labors but that she and Harold had insisted, during his most recent trip, and he'd finally agreed to accept a percentage of whatever they would be realizing from Harold's art from now on.

We made arrangements to meet in London. (This was going to be their first trip to Europe.) "Yes," Shapinsky said in his monotone. "It should be a big event."

"He's not like this all the time," Kate confided, smiling lovingly over at him. "Sometimes, lately, he just starts dancing. Sometimes he turns the radio to a disco station and suddenly he's *dancing*."

I had just arrived at my London hotel and was emptying the contents of my bags into the drawers and closets, and absentmindedly listening to a television program called *The Antiques Road Show*. It was apparently part of a series of such programs, and it essentially played out endless permutations on the same basic formula. Doughty plebian matrons of one sort or another would bring in examples of antique bric-a-brac, describe how they'd happened to come by them ("Oh, it were up in me attic, sir, just lying about for years"), and the supercilious experts, dressed to the nines in the most distinguished Bond Street finery, would then lavish their silken expertise upon the proffered objects—a tea set, a china bowl, a pewter jug, a dresser, a pocket watch—in ostentatious displays of virtuoso discernment. At first, I thought it was a Monty Python skit, but it was all in dead earnest—these were real people. The show generally proceeded as a sort of morality play: those who came on too confidently were obviously destined for a fall. One woman stood before a large early-nineteenth-century English landscape painting and smugly predicted that it was a Constable, offering as proof positive a letter of evaluation she'd procured from a putative expert named Thomas Keating. The television expert, however, was not impressed: he evaluated not only the painting but the prior expert's letter as well. "Really, very typical late Keating letter, this. Because he goes on to conclude it to be 'possibly a sketch by Constable' and in fact he gives you every reason to believe that it is an extremely important painting. Now, you know, Tom Keating during his lifetime was a likeable rogue— really, frightfully sad about the heart attack and all—but I can tell you without the shadow of a doubt that this painting has nothing to do with John Constable. Were it a Constable—three million pounds plus. But no, madam, it's not a Constable. It's not an F. W. Watts. *It's not even a John Paul.* Maybe it's a *Paul.*" The most humble of all the petitioners—a squat farm woman who could barely mumble her own name, so awestruck did she seem in the presence of her tuxedoed expert—had somehow managed to cart in an antique chest of drawers the size of a prize bull. The expert was beside himself: "This is the most important piece of furniture we've had on the *Road Show*, and doubtless the most valuable. It's a commode—that's the official term, French term. French shape, English built. To begin with, note the exquisite construction, and how it's been covered over with the most extraordinary collection of veneers. How ever did you come by it?" The woman's tongue remained hopelessly tied. "This is—please, madam, pray, sit down here, yes—this is a piece of national, no of *international* stature. It was made between 1770 and 1785 by one of three or four people, maybe even by Pierre Langlois himself before he went back to France in 1773. Should you choose to put this commode up for sale—naturally very carefully, with a great deal of expert advice—you ought easily to realize forty thousand pounds, and soon it should be worth twice that." The farm woman started to cry.

The phone rang. "Welcome! I've got wonderful news. The *Observer* Sunday magazine is going to be featuring a full-color spread on the discovery with an article by Salman Rushdie. In addition, *Time Out* will be running a major story by Tariq Ali. And that's not all. Chatto and Windus, the top-class publishers, will be bringing out a big illustrated autobiography of Shapinsky."

"Hi, Akumal," I said. "I didn't know Shapinsky could write."

"No, no. *I'm* going to write it."

"Well, sounds as if you've been keeping yourself busy and productive."

"Yes, everybody's talking about the discovery. I'd come over to visit with you right now, except that I'm afraid I must head over to the airport. I've got three friends coming in from India for the opening. It will be quite an international affair. There will also be six friends from Holland, three from West Germany, and one from America."

A couple of days later, on May twenty-first, Shapinsky's sixtieth birthday (and not even seven months since Akumal phoned me that first morning), I set out for Mayor's. Cork Street is a short nub of a thoroughfare, teeming with fashionable art establishments. Leslie Waddington seems to own most of them—four or five bear his name—and this May they were showing, among other artists, Alexander Calder, Sam Francis, David Hockney, Henry Moore, and Claes Oldenburg. John Kasmin runs another—the British outpost of Knoedler—right next door to Mayor's, and his current fare consisted of recent ceramic-and-steel wall constructions by Frank Stella. When I got to Mayor's, its large street window announced, in big white painted letters, Harold Shapinsky. Inside, Mayor and his partner, Andrew Murray, were making subtle adjustments to the lighting, and waiting for Akumal and the Shapinskys, who were going to drop by and give their final approval. The front two rooms contained the twenty-two Shapinsky paintings, framed and displayed to full advantage. Beyond the second room, a large, vaultlike space opened out and down (with a corkscrew stairway curling to the floor below), and that space was filled with Rauschenbergs, Lichtensteins, Twomblys, Rosenquists, and Warhols—remaining evidence of the preceding show, "A Tribute to Leo Castelli." Before long, Akumal and the Shapinskys arrived. This was the first time the Shapinskys had seen the show, and Kate was thrilled. Harold took it all in calmly, puffing contemplatively on his pipe, admiring the work. "Very good painting, that one," he ventured, in his flat monotone, before moving on to the next. "This one, too—fine painting. Nice sense of swell."

Akumal came over to me, flushed with freshly building excitement. "I brought you advance copies of the texts of Salman's and Tariq's articles," he said. "And here." He reached over and pulled a catalogue of the show out of a bulging box. "You'll want to have a look at this, too. And, oh!" He riffled quickly through his folder. "Look at this." He produced another letter from Ronald Alley, this one handwritten on Tate Gallery stationery. "Now that I have actually seen some originals of Harold Shapinsky's work I feel I must congratulate you again on your discovery," Alley had written Akumal some weeks earlier. "Colour slides can be very misleading, and I had expected to find lyrical work with glowing colours. Instead his pictures turn out to be much more thickly painted—definitely paintings rather than drawings—and, above all, much tougher and more dramatic. One senses a real drama and tension, even anguish, behind the works, which though small are very highly charged." As if in harmony with my reading, Shapinsky, on the other side of the room, was commenting, "Nice tension in this one here. Very gratifying."

David Shapinsky now entered the gallery, a surprisingly young man with delicate features, blondish hair, wire-rim glasses, and, yes, a very kind face. Kate greeted him warmly, and Harold came over as well. I could see that in this slightly offbeat, mildly daft family, David plays the role of the steady anchor, the responsible center, and had probably been doing so for some time.

Akumal, Kate, Harold, and David presently set out to find a suit for Harold for the opening; he didn't seem to own one. After they'd left, James Mayor and I found ourselves talking about Akumal and his mania for letters. "Did he have you write them, too?" Mayor asked me. "Most extraordinary; every time we have a conversation, he seems to want me to write it up as a letter—on the spot. I've got a title for your piece. You should call it 'The Man of Few Words and the Man of Many Letters.'"

I left the gallery, intending to return to my hotel where I could look through the various texts Akumal had gathered for me in preparation for the evening's opening. But first I dropped in on the Stella exhibition next door. Kasmin was sitting the desk himself. "So," he asked, "what exactly is going on over there? Who is this Shapinsky fellow?" I gave him the quick capsule version: Shapinsky, forty years, Akumal, no interest in New York, the Tate, and now a big show. "How remarkable," Kasmin interjected. "That's the sort of thing that usually just happens to the widow. I've got a title for you. You should call your piece 'The Man Who Became His Own Widow.'"

Back at the hotel, I flipped through the various texts Akumal had gathered, beginning with the catalogue—a handsome, thirty-two-page booklet in square format with an elegant plain gray cover, twenty-two illustrations, four of them in color, a preface by Ronald Alley, and an extended essay by Marta Jakimowicz-Shah, a Polish artist friend of Akumal's who now lives in India. Alley's preface was laudatory in a careful, measured sort of way, concluding, "I am delighted that Shapinsky is at last beginning to get the recognition that he greatly deserves. Such a shame he has had to wait so long. As for Akumal, he amazes me more and more. Speaking for myself, it has usually been my experience when I try to help someone that the outcome is total disaster; but at least this time everything seems to have come out right." Well, not quite everything, I soon realized. Ms. Jakimowicz-Shah's catalogue essay, anyway, was, well, problematic: absolutely without any critical distance as it celebrated Shapinsky's virtually unparalleled importance.

Rushdie's and Ali's articles likewise tended to go a bit overboard in proclaiming Shapinsky's significance, but neither of them claimed any expertise in art. Both were mainly enthralled by the saga of the discovery itself. The circumstance of the discovery, the character of Shapinsky's art, his reticent nature—all seemed to act as a sort of Rorschach inkblot, with each of the various writers projecting his own rich themes of signification upon the material. For example, Tariq Ali, a formidable political pamphleteer, discerned a moral in the Marxist tradition: "It is almost a truism these days to suggest that Art is big business. Late capitalism has completed the transformation of works of art into commodities. Most art galleries in the West function as ruthless business enterprises." Shapinsky in this version came off as a sort of martyr to the vagaries of art capitalism who through Akumal's fluky intervention may yet receive some measure of justice at the last moment. "One can safely assert," Ali concludes, "that there are many Shapinskys in different parts of the world (including Britain), most of whom will never be 'discovered'! It is only when the priorities of the existing social order are irreversibly altered that they will ever stand a chance."

Salman Rushdie, for his part, found a different moral in the story. He had recently been involved in a fairly heated exchange with, among others, Conor Cruise O'Brien, growing out of an article Rushdie published in the British literary quarterly *Granta*. In that article, entitled "Outside the Whale," he'd attacked the current spate of Raj fictions—the television serializations of *The Far Pavilions* and *The Jewel in the Crown*, and the films of *Gandhi* and *A Passage to India*—describing them as "only the latest in a very long line of fake portraits inflicted by the West on the East." It was not surprising, therefore, that the aspect of the Akumal-Shapinsky story that seemed to appeal most to Salman Rushdie was the theme of The Tables Turned. "For centuries now," he wrote in the last paragraph of his *Observer* piece, "it has been the fate of the peoples of the East to be 'discovered' by the West, with dramatic and usually unpleasant consequences. The story of Akumal and Shapinsky is one small instance in which the East has been able to repay the compliment, and with a happy ending, too."

Ronald Alley, in his catalogue preface, glancingly hinted at another Rorschach reading. He recounted how, early in the saga, Akumal had been taking his slides around to show to people. "He even telephoned about thirty galleries in New York and asked if he could bring the slides round, but not one said yes," Alley wrote. "I suppose they thought that the chances of a visiting Indian finding an unknown Abstract Expressionist painter in New York who was any good at all were so remote as to be not worth thinking about." His next paragraph began, "When I saw the slides I was amazed," and from the silent interstice between those two sentences welled up the theme of The Smug, Closed, and Self-Satisfied New York Art Scene, with its subtheme of Europe Still Open and Curious. Ironically, this theme received its fullest exposition in Rushdie's piece, his rage at the smugness of the Empire notwithstanding. "There has been a certain amount of gleeful hand-rubbing going on, because the Shapinsky case reflects so badly on the New York art scene," he reported. "New York has been ruling the roost for so long that this piece of European revenge must taste sweet indeed."

The shopping expedition had been a success: Shapinsky was decked out in a smart new suit when I finally caught sight of him in the midst of the throng at the Mayor opening—a debonair gray flannel outfit with sleek, fresh creases tapering down to a pair of blue canvas deck shoes. The cherry aroma from his pipe wafted about the assembly throughout the evening, which Shapinsky spent quietly enduring the sometimes effusive adulation of his new admirers. In the face of this onslaught, his composure attained almost epic proportions. As for Kate, she was wearing one of her patchwork vests, a lovely medley of black-and-white rectangles with an occasional highlight of bright, bright red. Toward the end of the evening, when the crowd had thinned, she pulled out a ball of wool and resumed her knitting. All the careful work that Mayor and Murray had put into modulating the lighting on the paintings went more or less unnoticed; in fact, this was one of those openings so crowded that the paintings themselves are virtually unseeable. In any case, this particular evening the lighting was drowned out by the roving television kliegs of the crew from Bandung Productions, capturing a few last shots for their documentary, which would be broadcast in a week.

"This is really more of a literary crowd than an art one," one of the guests told me. "But, then again, there really isn't much of an art scene here in London. The English like to look at words, not pictures."

"The whole thing is quite romantic in a shaggy-dog sort of way," I overheard one woman saying. "Aladdin's lamp and that sort of thing."

"But where has this fellow Shapinsky *been*?" her companion replied. "It all reminds me of those blind white fish swimming about deep in those underground caverns in Kentucky or wherever it is they do all that."

"Yes, look at him! He even *looks* like Rip Van Winkle, newly emerged from his sleep, his eyes still blinking in the glaring daylight."

"The Japanese soldier on that island outpost who's only just found out the war is over—say, what?"

At one point, I met Ronald Alley, who turned out to be a tall man in his late fifties, with a gentle, dignified bearing. "Originally," he recalled for me, "I went downstairs that morning simply to try and rescue my colleague from the siege of what she was describing to me as a very persistent Indian caller. I mean, you get people turning up like that from time to time, and I do try to go down and see them whenever I can, partly out of courtesy but partly in the hope that something like this might happen. It almost never does, but this"—he included the whole thronged room in his gesture—"sort of justifies the whole enterprise, doesn't it?"

For me, the opening provided an occasion to speak with several Indians who were able to offer me a much deeper understanding of

Akumal's passion. (That passion appeared all the more remarkable to me when I learned, as I did in passing, that Akumal was suddenly deep in debt again, pending the eventual success of the show, because he had paid for part of the travel fares and lodging for several members of his Indian, Dutch, German, and American contingents.) Up to that evening, I'd seen Akumal's quest as by turns comic, resourceful, vaguely frenzied, but always inspired. Through these new conversations, I began to get a sense of some of the darker imperatives underlying his intensity. One of his group from Bangalore, a beautiful woman draped in a luminous blue-and-green sari, noted that Akumal had always been like this, that it was sometimes exhausting to be with him for more than fifteen minutes at a stretch, but that to understand him "one has to realize how stultifying, for example, is his daily regimen at the school where he teaches, as is the case in most Indian academic settings." She continued, "You also must try to imagine how incredibly hard it is in India for someone from the lower middle class just to survive, let alone rise. I think Akumal derives a lot of his energy from this being betwixt and between."

A few moments later, Salman Rushdie amplified on this theme. "I think with Akumal there is a sort of desperation in part of his makeup," he said. "To describe him as a teacher of English at an agricultural college is gravely to diminish him—but that is his status in Bangalore. It is a terrible thing when someone's picture of himself does not coincide with the world's. You have to realize that the gulf between the classes is much greater in India, and for Akumal to have pulled himself up by his own bootstraps, as he has done, has all along required the continuous projection of the kind of frenetic energy he's now been demonstrating in this affair."

I asked Rushdie how Akumal had gotten access to him in the first place.

"Well, I was in Bangalore briefly during a lecture tour a few years ago," Rushdie said. "My hosts had escorted me to my hotel and had just left the room when there was an immediate knocking on the door. I figured that it was my hosts returning with one last bit of instruction, or something; when I opened the door, I was instead confronted by the hugest garland of flowers I'd ever seen, deep inside which, barely visible, stood Akumal. He barged into the room in this overwhelming, unstoppable frenzy of vast smiles and flashing eyes, proclaiming that he was my 'number one fan in Bangalore,' and describing how he'd been pestering the editors of all the local papers for weeks, demanding that they include features and supplements on my coming visit, so that now, here, this was the result—whereupon he thrust a bunch of newspapers at me, all with big photographs and long stories. It was a unique and fairly winning sort of approach. I would then see him occasionally on his visits to Europe, although I must say I was a bit incredulous when he launched into this story about his discovery of an American painter. I mean, Akumal sometimes strikes one as a bit of an operator. But it's impossible not to warm to his evident enthusiasm for life, his disarming openness, and his obviously genuine devotion to the arts. And he's pulled it off. Well, I hope that maybe this success will bring him a measure of peace."

A few minutes later, I was talking with Tariq Ali, an expansive and friendly man, with none of the archness of his occasionally polemical prose. "When Akumal first told Salman the story about Shapinsky, Salman says, he thought Akumal was making this artist up," Ali reported. "Well, when Salman subsequently told me about Akumal, I thought *he* was making *Akumal* up—I mean, I figured he'd gone a bit over the top. Akumal sounded so much like a character in one of his own fictions. But I eventually saw the slides and met the man. It was all true, and the story seemed a natural for Bandung."

We watched for a few minutes as Akumal buzzed about the room, bringing his contingents over to meet James Mayor or Ronald Alley or Salman Rushdie. "The thing about India," Ali continued, "is that this synthesis of almost two hundred years of British rule and native tradition means that there are a lot of people like Akumal—people with this very wide range of worldly, cosmopolitan interests who are condemned to live fairly narrow, constricted, provincial lives. I think part of his nervous energy comes from this being between classes, between cultures.

It was a very moving experience going to Bangalore with the film crew to shoot that part of the documentary. People would come up to us and ask what we were doing. We'd tell the story, and they'd be quite dumbfounded. 'Are you serious?' they would ask. 'All this is happening because of our Akumal?' Or his students in the English class: 'Our Professor Ramachander has accomplished this?' I mean, Bangalore is a large and growing city, but in many ways it's like a Chekhovian small town, with Akumal as the village eccentric, the character from the local coffeehouse scene who suddenly makes good in the world. I mean, he's been doing this sort of thing all along in Bangalore, but everybody there is just amazed by the *scale* this time around."

Akumal had gone over to talk with Shapinsky. "A character from Naipaul meets a character from Bellow," Ali said.

On the evening the Shapinsky show was opening at the Mayor Gallery, a couple of miles away, at the Aldwych Theatre, Paul Eddington was starring in a revival of Tom Stoppard's metaphysical farce *Jumpers*, About halfway through the first act, Eddington, playing the role of a second-rate philosophy professor, delivers himself of the following contention: "Of the five proofs of God's existence put forward by St. Thomas Aquinas, three depended on the simple idea that if an apparently endless line of dominoes is knocking itself over one by one then somewhere there is a domino which was *nudged*." It occurred to me on several occasions during the next few days, as I kept returning for visits to a teeming Mayor Gallery, that in the case of Akumal's discovery of Shapinsky *two* lines of dominoes had needed to be nudged. For this was a story of how the lifelines of two individuals—marginal, utterly peripheral figures in their own societies—had, most improbably, managed to intersect, and then of the entirely improbable chain reaction that their intersection had subsequently set off. Actually, *three* coincidental factors were playing themselves out in this story: Akumal, Shapinsky, and the specific, highly peculiar (one might use the word "marginal" here as well) situation of the art world itself in 1985. To shift metaphors,

Akumal and Shapinsky were like two stray crystals dropped into a flask: it was only because of the special conditions obtaining inside the flask—the specific momentary chemical dynamics of the supersaturated medium—that these two crystals were able to conjoin and blossom in such a surprising way. I am convinced that had Akumal met Shapinsky in 1975, say, or even 1980, his quest would have gone nowhere.

There are two major reasons for this. The first involves a sea change that has been occurring in the dominant aesthetic sensibility over the last decade. Fifteen years ago, Minimalism was at its height. The past decade has seen a resurgence of interest in both figurative and expressive imagery. This has proved true both retrospectively (witness the sudden rediscovery of the late Picasso at the Guggenheim in 1984, a phase of the Master's career that had been almost entirely dismissed until just a couple of years before; and the considerable popularity of the de Kooning retrospective that was up at the Whitney at about the same time) and with regard to the most up-to-date in gallery fashions as well (witness the proliferation of neo-Expressionist imagery throughout the world over the past five years). It is hardly surprising that the time was ripe for a comprehensive reconsideration of the second generation of Abstract Expressionists, and, indeed, precisely that was beginning to happen: completely unbeknownst to Akumal during that afternoon in September 1984, when he was first being exposed to Shapinsky's work via those primitive slides in David Shapinsky's apartment, a major traveling exhibition entitled "Action/Precision" and featuring work from the fifties by six of the second-generation luminaries— Norman Bluhm, Michael Goldberg, Grace Hartigan, Al Held, Alfred Leslie, and Joan Mitchell—was touring the country. (The exhibition was organized by the Newport Harbor Art Museum.) The show's unusually lovely catalogue features several excellent essays touching on this sea change in aesthetic sensibility—a change that, of course, has had a bearing on Shapinsky's reception as well. Robert Rosenblum, for example, recalls what it was like in the midfifties, as the tide began pulling out for interest in that sort of work: "For me and many of my contemporaries, Rauschenberg, Johns, Stella swiftly became the Holy Trinity that led us from the Old Testament to the New, liberating us from the burden of living under the oppressive yoke of the coarse and sweaty rhetoric of Action painting, whose supreme deity, de Kooning, suddenly loomed large for many younger spectators and artists as a conservative force, a tyrant of past authority who demanded the instant embalming of any youthful, liberated spirit . . . a suffocating father image." Paul Schimmel notes how "the rich and diverse paintings of [the six artists in this show] were relegated to obscurity because they embraced and expanded upon the revolutions of their predecessors rather than reacting against them." Rosenblum talks about how at the time he thought he could "write off most of the work by the six artists in this show as irritating anachronisms, the product of loyal but growingly irrelevant satellites." This "temporary blackout of visibility" for the second-generation Abstract Expressionists lasted almost thirty years. But suddenly they were back. "And now how do they look?" Rosenblum asks. "For one thing, they look surprisingly up-to-date, riding in unexpectedly as ancestral figures behind the latest neo-Expressionist wave from Germany, Italy, or our own shores, a wave that once more permits us to wallow and frolic in the primordial ooze of oil paint. Seen as a whole, these pictures have the tonic quality of sheer sensuous enjoyment. . . . For anyone who was getting chilled by the laboratory calibrations of so much Minimal and Conceptual art and by the puritanical ban on color and palpable textures, this is the perfect antidote, a drunkenly deep breath of visual oxygen."

Akumal was thus going to find himself hawking just the right sort of elixir for 1985: the atmosphere in which he would be moving stood a good chance of welcoming Shapinsky's sort of oxygen. But the previous decade had also seen a second transformation in the art world—one that would have an even more dramatic impact on Akumal's and Shapinsky's fortunes. This had to do with the changing character of the art market. Prices across the board, as I suggested earlier, had shot completely out of sight.

The explanation for this is extremely simple: the market for art had exploded in size—the number of players (collectors) in the game had multiplied many times over. The explanation for *that* is more complex. For one thing, the baby-boom generation had come of age, gone to college in record numbers, and been exposed to the humanities and, in particular, the contemporary arts; and now many of its members were becoming professionals and earning substantial incomes, with the result that collecting seemed worthwhile to them both as an avocation and, increasingly, as an investment. Sidney Janis recently observed, "More money is being spent these days because more money is being made." Around the same time, corporations began to enter the art market, building up vast company collections as exercises both in good public relations and in shrewd investment. There was a tremendous increase in the number of museums and a tremendous upsurge in museum attendance. According to a recent article in the Los Angeles *Times*, West Germany will witness the launching of thirty new museums by 1990; another article in *Progressive Architecture* cites similar figures for the United States. Japan is involved in a parallel frenzy. Each of these new museum projects features dozens of empty walls, a board of trustees, and a carefully tended hive of supporting collectors. The infrastructure of art commerce—the network of galleries, art journals, and auction houses—has developed great sophistication, including extremely supple engines of publicity. Literally tens, and perhaps hundreds, of thousands of potential consumers are being funneled into the system. At recent contemporary-art auctions of the sort that just five years ago were being attended by only a few hundred collectors, well over a thousand people are jammed into auditoriums filled to standing-room-only capacity—and that's not even counting many of the highest bidders who choose to avoid the crush by phoning in their entries.

A friend of mine, the director of one of Europe's finest small museums, recently told me, "There's simply not enough work of superior quality anymore to go around—work, that is, by the *grands maîtres*—so the prices, of course, go way up, and prices for the next layer of artists, the *petits maîtres*, rise up in turn, to answer the demand. Paintings by artists I had barely even heard of until a few months before are going for fifty thousand dollars at auction."

This situation was recently encapsulated in a succinct formula by the Paris-based art critic Souren Melikian. In an article entitled "The Ten-Percent Law," which appeared in *Art & Auction*, he wrote, "Over the last twelve months a new law has been verified with increasing frequency in the Impressionist and Modern masters field. Artists regarded rightly or (not infrequently) wrongly as second fiddles to famous artists are worth one-tenth of those from whom they supposedly took their cue." This assertion might at first appear to knock the wind out of any enthusiasms the *petits maîtres* could have been expected to arouse; but, on second glance, when one recognizes that individual works by *grands maîtres* are now selling for many millions of dollars, 10 percent looms back up as a figure worth reckoning with, or for. Melikian cited several examples in his article. A work by Charles Angrand (1854–1910), a neo-Impressionist artist who "greatly admired van Gogh, who returned the compliment," recently sold for two hundred thousand dollars—one-tenth of what a van Gogh with a similar composition would fetch. This ratio also obtains between the works of Roger de La Fresnaye (1855–1925) and those of Braque, as it does between the works of Paul Sérusier (1863–1927) and those of Gauguin.

Lucy Havelock-Allan, the director of contemporary art at Sotheby's auction house in New York, recently confirmed for me that a similar trend was beginning to be noticeable in the contemporary market—though not yet at quite the same percentage rate. She noted that artists like Esteban Vícente, Conrad Marca-Relli, and Joan Mitchell are all getting personal record prices for their works these days. "One reason people are looking at works by artists like these is that they can't afford de Kooning, especially the de Kooning of the late forties and the fifties, and they know they never will be able to," she explained. "Theodoros Stamos, for example, languished at around twenty thousand dollars for years, then last year a painting of his sold for forty thousand, and this year we saw a fine one go for over ninety thousand—this for a work that ten years ago would have been lucky to bring five thousand."

Almost in passing, Melikian includes the interesting observation that the 10-percent law "has nothing to do with beauty, as nonspecialists would call it, or 'quality,' as the sophisticated professionals like to put it." He cites the example of a "stunning" 1892 landscape by Maurice Denis (1870–1943) that recently sold for $25,400, or roughly "one-tenth of any Neo-Impressionist painting of similar size, even of third-rate quality, by Monet, of which the great man committed more than a few." Melikian concluded, "In art-market thinking, there is no such thing as a masterpiece by a painter who is not currently dubbed a great master."

This last proviso would not have bothered James Mayor, if he read the article. With the prices of de Koonings what they had come to be, he still had a lot of room to maneuver. I spoke earlier of the Rorschach responses that Shapinsky's story seemed to summon. To these must be added Mayor's own calculations. Mayor may well have been—indeed, no doubt he *was*—authentically taken with Shapinsky's work. But he must also have realized that if he could just get Shapinsky included in the lists of the *petits maîtres* working in de Kooning's wake, his prices would have a vast horizon. This was especially the case in Europe, for when Europeans began collecting American art in a serious fashion, in the sixties, they initially went after Warhol, Oldenburg, Stella, Rauschenberg, and Johns, and later, Pollock, but not so much after de Kooning, because, ironically, they saw him more as a transitional European figure, and *Americans* were what they wanted. By the time they realized their mistake, de Kooning's prices were out of reach for all but the wealthiest among them. Collectors with a speculative turn of mind would realize this, too: as long as the current bubble in *all* art prices lasted (and there was no particular reason to believe that it would burst anytime soon), and assuming Mayor was going to be successful in establishing Shapinsky's status as a second-generation Abstract Expressionist, Shapinsky's paintings at twenty thousand dollars each might prove a good investment. As Ronald Alley explained to me while we huddled together at the opening, "There's a tremendous interest in Abstract Expressionism now, and the prices of the famous names have gone straight through the ceiling. Here's a chap who's been producing work of enormous quality, and his prices are starting from scratch. I mean, it seems to me it's a dealer's dream, and a collector's dream."

I wasn't the least bit surprised, therefore, a few days later (I'd returned to New York in the meantime) to be awakened—at 8:00 a.m.—by a phone call from Akumal telling me, "Wonderful news! The show has already sold completely out." The review in the London *Times* by the redoubtable John Russell Taylor had been a rave. ("An extremely good and original abstract expressionist . . . his forms have an extraordinary interior energy . . . exquisitely subtle harmonies.") A few days afterward, however, the Shapinsky juggernaut had received a bit of a jolt when the *Guardian* published a scathing review by its critic, Waldemar Januszczak, not so much on Shapinsky (whose paintings apparently left the critic fairly unmoved either way) as on Akumal and Tariq Ali and Salman Rushdie, and all their hype. All three of them immediately dispatched letters to the editor, and all three letters were published two days later, *along with a cartoon.* "It didn't really bother us," Akumal told me. "I was a little surprised, the fellow being of Polish stock and all, but even the Poles once in a while . . . And, anyway, it just doubled the ratings for the documentary on Channel 4 the next evening. The folks *there* were very pleased. And the BBC have invited the *Guardian* critic and Tariq to square off in a live televised debate next Sunday, and that should be interesting." The screening of the documentary had gone extremely well, and now Akumal was being stopped on the street, at bus stops, and so forth—especially by fellow Indians who were eager to congratulate him on his discovery.

I called up the gallery to see how things were going there. Andrew Murray answered the phone in the gallery's basement storeroom. "James and I are holed up down here, I'm afraid," he said. "It's the only place where there's any room. It's like a railway station up there—all chockablock. The limousines are queued up around the corner!"

Mayor picked up another extension. "There's a waiting list for Shapinsky! The last several purchases went to big world-class collectors, your household names. I've never seen anything like it. The press is all over Shapinsky. We had Greek television in here yesterday morning, Canadian national radio in the afternoon, the Jerusalem *Post*, two of the biggest German art periodicals. This morning, Shapinsky was being interviewed by a pair of Chinese reporters. Not Hong Kong—Beijing!"

I asked them how Shapinsky was holding up under all this. "He's starting to talk," Murray reported. "It's bizarre—he's turned positively loquacious."

Mayor confirmed this improbable finding: "He seems to think he's back in the Waldorf Cafeteria or something."

The following week, I got another call from Akumal. "You'll never guess what happened to me." I didn't even try. "I met a man from California who'd read about the controversy in the *Guardian* and went to see the show. He'd just been over to the gallery and the paintings had bowled him over, and now he wants me to fly to Hollywood to meet a producer friend of his, so we can talk about the possibility of making a movie." Akumal seemed even more excited, however, by the fact that two of India's leading weekly magazines were going to be doing major stories on the discovery. "And I have another important bit of news," he added. "Norbert Lynton was in the gallery again yesterday, and he inscribed a copy of his book, *The Story of Modern Art*. Listen to the inscription. I have it right here: 'All good wishes to Akumal, who is doing his best to force us all to rewrite our art histories.' So, you see, I think it's a good omen. I may yet win the second half of my bet with David." It occurred to me that whether or not Akumal succeeded in forcing Shapinsky into the *Encyclopedia Britannica*, he himself stood a good chance of transmigrating one of these days straight into the *Oxford English Dictionary*. "Akumal: *n.* A genie, a fairy godfather, a doer of good deeds, esp. with regard to artists who regard him as a sort of patron saint, *e.g.*, 'Marcel had been slaving away at his easel for years, all to no avail; he was beginning to wonder if he'd ever meet his *Akumal*.'"

"You know what the moral of the story is?" Akumal asked me. All the others had given me theirs. I wondered what Akumal's would be. "That sometimes the good can win," he said.

"Yeats—the poet I admire much more than Eliot—he wrote a poem called 'The Second Coming,' and two lines of that poem go, 'The best lack all conviction, while the worst are full of passionate intensity.' There is pure motive and there is impure motive. I see it as my mission to give the best some passionate intensity. And, you see, this is a story that celebrates the unity of the human race. Think about it: there are Dutchmen, Americans, Englishmen, Poles, Germans, Indians, Pakistanis—all united by a karma to bring a little good into this world. Don't you think it's wonderful? No matter what happens now, Harold will have a few years to paint in peace. He'll be having a big show at a gallery in Cologne—did I tell you? Fifteen paintings at increased prices, later this year—it's all arranged. But it doesn't matter anymore if not a single other one of his paintings sells, because now Harold and Kate will have a little comfort. They're even talking about moving here to England."

Akumal was silent for a moment, seeming to bask in the light of his good works. "With me, you see," he concluded, finally, "it was always *pure motive*."

POSTSCRIPT (1988)

Shortly after the events described in these pages, Akumal returned to India, to Bangalore, to his parents' home, where he subsided into a sixteen-hour-a-day sleeping depression. I can picture him there, the talk of his neighborhood, children huddled in the shade outside the house gossiping about the guy inside who sleeps all day long and about the rumors of his earlier worldly adventures.

He slept for weeks on end, and then he roused himself, and a few months later my phone was ringing at 7:00 a.m. and it was of course Akumal, who had just arrived back in town—in fact, he was still at the airport.

"Gee, Akumal," I said groggily. "You must be suffering from jet lag."

"No," Akumal replied, laughing. "Are you kidding? Me? The *jet* has lag. I never get lag."

We arranged to meet a few days later at my office, and there he regaled me with a new saga, one that was barely more probable than the first. It turned out he'd made another discovery. He'd received dozens of calls and letters following the Shapinsky opening, he explained, young artists likewise eager to have themselves revealed to a thirsting world, but most of them he'd let slide. "This thing of discovering people is quite taxing," he explained. One inquiry, however, had for some reason held his attention (for several reasons, actually, all of which he rehearsed at length for me and none of which I can any longer remember). This was the plea of another son on behalf of his painter-father—in this case, a father who'd been dead for some years. Patrick Carr invited Akumal out to his mother's place to have a look at the paintings of his late father, David Carr.

Now, David Carr *had* been known in the British art world, but principally as a collector and an enthusiast—his own production (faux-naïf renditions of Irish peasants and fishmongers and more complex, neo-Cubist studies of factory workers and their machines) had been virtually private. Akumal was thunderstruck ("completely floored") by these paintings, and he immediately set to work. By the time he returned to New York, he'd already managed to arrange for a major retrospective at the Mayor Gallery; the publication by the well-regarded firm of Quartet Books of a full-color, hardbound, coffee-table volume, with an introduction by Ronald Alley; and, of course, a full-length television documentary (this time with BBC-2 rather than Channel 4). All of these events have since come off flawlessly, and Carr's revival seems well assured.

The Shapinskys, for their part, did indeed prosper following the success of Harold's London show. They transposed themselves to England for about half a year but eventually returned to New York City, abandoning their East Side garret for somewhat more commodious circumstances in the Chelsea district. Somewhat nonplussed by his sudden success, Shapinsky himself seemed to retreat for a time into the fabrication of dozens and presently hundreds of miniature paper-and-tinfoil sculptures—this mad progeny came to occupy virtually all the shelves and then all the floor space as well in his new apartment. After a while, though, Shapinsky returned to his painting, which he now seemed to tackle with renewed vigor and zest.

Akumal and James Mayor, however, were still having trouble cracking the New York City gallery scene. Most dealers remained dubious (the eerie stasis of Shapinsky's style, its proximity to de Kooning's, etc.), and not a few of them continued to resent the London provenance of this whole Shapinsky renaissance (or, rather, naissance).

Following his triumph with Carr, Akumal therefore decided that it was time to give his Shapinsky discovery another push. Here I get a little foggy as to the exact chronology (and chutzpahlogy), but somehow Akumal managed to befriend Kathy Ford, the wife of automobile tycoon Henry Ford II, and to enlist her support in the cause. At one point he was even talking about the possibility of having a Shapinsky show in the living room of her own Palm Beach, Florida, mansion—so that they could display Shapinsky's marvelous canvases directly to the potential buyers in that elite community, bypassing the hopelessly hidebound New York art scene altogether. As things actually developed, Shapinsky had a one-man show at Bruce Helander's Palm Beach gallery, which is how it came to pass that on a January 1987 evening, Akumal and Harold Shapinsky found themselves being celebrated at the gala opening of their new show by over eight hundred of the upper crustiest of *le tout Palm Beach*, including the Fords, Peter and Sandy Brant (owners of the White Birch Polo Farms and publisher of *Art in America*, respectively), and Hector and Susan Barrantes (the well-known Argentine polo player and his wife, the mother of Sarah Ferguson, the recently endowed Duchess of York). Another vision well worth conjuring.

By the time of the Helander show, Shapinsky canvases were fetching as much as thirty-four thousand dollars each—and once again the show proved a financial success (it had been half sold out before it even opened, partly on the strength of Mrs. Ford's contacts). The reviews were mixed to good, but the most remarkable of all was a rave by Kenworth Moffett, the former curator of contemporary art at the Boston Museum of Fine Arts, who now publishes a newsletter of his own, entitled *Moffett's Artletter* ($150 for ten issues, artists half price). In discussing Shapinsky with his subscribers, Moffett went *way* out on a limb. He characterized the objection of most New York dealers, the similarity between Shapinsky's and de Kooning's work, as "beside the main point, which is that Shapinsky is better than de Kooning. I think if a show were hung with alternating pairs of the best pictures of Shapinsky and de Kooning, Shapinsky would win every time. He is simply a much more talented artist. His pictures have more movement and intensity. They have better color and drawing: They have more life." And then, further on: "Maybe Shapinsky's presence will help people finally see de Kooning's work for what it is. In any event, Shapinsky, despite his modesty, has been unusually good from the start and has been consistently good for forty years. He has known how to sustain his intensity. If de Kooning first invented the style, Shapinsky is the one who filled it up with feeling."

Mr. and Mrs. Murry Robinson, who purchased a Shapinsky from Helander, proceeded to donate it to the National Gallery of Art in Washington, D.C. On one of his subsequent visits to New York, Akumal handed me a copy of the letter with which the National Gallery's director, the redoubtable J. Carter Brown, accepted the gift:

I am happy to report that at today's meeting, the Board of Trustees of the National Gallery of Art accepted with pleasure your gift of *Untitled*, 1948, by Harold Shapinsky.

The story of the discovery of Shapinsky is fascinating and having now seen *Untitled*, I must say that the discovery is long overdue. In fact, this work will make an important addition to our twentieth-century holdings. The art of the Abstract Expressionists is a crucial strength of our collection, and Shapinsky's splendid painting will fit in exceedingly well.

Thank you very much for your generous gift to the National Gallery. It is always a particular pleasure for us when collectors become involved with the Gallery, and I hope that in the coming months members of our curatorial staff can visit you either in

Providence or in Palm Beach to view your collection and to discuss present and future projects.

To a skeptic this letter might reveal J. Carter Brown to be not only an erudite connoisseur but also a suave diplomat.

Helander now contacted his New York colleague Nathan Shippee, who runs a gallery in the prestigious Fuller Building at the corner of Madison and Fifty-seventh. Shippee, like many who read my piece when it first ran in the *New Yorker* in December 1985, had imagined the whole story to be an elaborate fiction. He was now pleased to discover otherwise, and after seeing some slides and canvases, he scheduled a New York opening for Shapinsky at his gallery in the fall of 1988. Ironically (although Akumal would surely begrudge the concept, he'd insist it had simply been fate, karma, all along), the opening will occur three stories directly below the room into which André Emmerich had earlier insisted to me that he'd have been able to fit Morris Louis's entire life production.

Having righted and relaunched the Shapinsky juggernaut, Akumal set himself to other tasks. One day, a few months later, he barged in on me at my office, bearing a medium-smallish white cube carton that came flying out of his arms as he entered the room, smashing against my filing cabinet and then rolling onto the floor. "Oh dear," he said, picking up the box, which he then proceeded to drop—indeed, almost to spike—all over again. After a few more elaborate stumbles and fumbles, Akumal triumphantly opened his little package: a package that turned out to contain in its hollow—otherwise utterly unprotected—a single, entirely undamaged, not even pockmarked, egg. I surmised that the egg must be hard-boiled. But Akumal proceeded to take a nearby coffee mug, crack the egg, and pour out its liquid (though completely scrambled) contents. "My newest discovery!" Akumal announced enthusiastically.

It turned out that Patrick Carr, the painter's son, was some sort of inventor in his own right, and this particular product of his laboratory, a virtually weightless ingeniously molded polystyrene-like packing box that could be mass-produced and sold in flats "so easy to assemble that any grandmother could do it," or so Akumal insisted, was going to "revolutionize the packaging industry." This was going to be Akumal's new project—this, and the career of that Polish graphic designer, Stasys Eidrigevicius, whose work Akumal had already been flogging when first we'd met. In fact, he was heading back to Warsaw to bring himself up-to-date on Eidrigevicius.

The next time he was back in New York, Akumal brought me up-to-date. He'd managed to secure a one-man show for Eidrigevicius in the very heart of New York's Soho, something I had never for a minute doubted he would. I asked him how things were going with the box. "Superbly!" Akumal exulted. As karma would have it, his friend Shippee, before turning to art dealing, had been in the packaging business himself and retained all sorts of contacts. "So we've now been able to show the box to the president of one of the top companies in the country, and he was completely high on it, totally sold out!"

If the box takes off, I commented to Akumal, he'd be able to retire. "Are you kidding?" he said. "I'll be even more busy."

I've decided that "Akumal" would never work as a noun. It is going to have to be a verb.

POST-POSTSCRIPT (1998)

If I'm not sure what became of that box scheme, it's only because, as the years passed, there were so many others. While the Shapinskys settled into a relatively comfortable life of middling late-career success (Kate herself even achieved a certain renown displaying her own abstract geometric miniature quilt tapestries), Akumal was hardly one to rest on his laurels. He discovered a young black American opera singer in Warsaw and promoted the living daylights out of the poor lucky man. He composed and had himself recorded singing a sort of jazz sutra. And he even created a book of his own—an improbable children's story pitched somewhere between *Charlotte's Web* and *The Gulag Archipelago*, the tale (lavishly illustrated by Stasys) of a little girl on a pig farm who rescues the runt of the litter, raises it to full thriving health, and then, under enormous pressure from her father, gives it up for transport to the slaughterhouse. That night, wracked by guilt, the girl dreams that she herself is turning into a pig, and by morning she has indeed become one, at which point, at story's end, she's being hauled off to the slaughterhouse. Good night and sweet dreams! Owing to the strength of Stasys's startlingly vivid imagery and Akumal's indefatigable promotions, the vegetarian tract eventually made it into numerous foreign editions. Akumal even turned it into a musical which achieved a full-fledged Warsaw production.

I haven't heard from Akumal in a while, but the other day I received a flyer announcing a major Stasys retrospective in Bangalore, India. So I have to assume all's right with the world.

THE AMERICAN MAN, AGE TEN

Susan Orlean

In her introduction to her collection *The Bullfighter Checks Her Makeup,* Susan Orlean explains the origin of this story. Her editor at *Esquire* magazine asked her to write a profile of Macauley Culkin, who was then just ten years old.

"Then my editor told me that he was planning to use the headline 'The American Man, Age Ten.' On a whim, I told my editor that I would do the piece if I could find a typical American ten-year-old man to profile instead—someone who I thought was more deserving of that headline."

Her editor said sure.

"I was completely dismayed. First of all, I had to figure out what I'd had in mind when I made the suggestion. Obviously there is no such thing as a 'typical' boy or girl, and even if I could establish some very generous guidelines for what constitutes typicalness—say, a suburban kid from a middle-class family who went to public school and didn't have an agent, a manager, or a chauffeur—there was the problem of choosing one such kid. I considered going to a shopping mall and just snatching the first ten-year-old I found, but instead I asked my friends to ask their friends if they knew anyone with a ten-year-old, and eventually I got the name of a boy who lived in the New Jersey suburbs. I liked Colin Duffy right away because he seemed unfazed by the prospect of my observing him for a couple of weeks. He was a wonderful kid, and I still marvel at how lucky I was to have stumbled on someone so endearing, but the truth is that if you set out to write about a ten-year-old boy, any boy would do."

If Colin Duffy and I were to get married, we would have matching superhero notebooks. We would wear shorts, big sneakers, and long, baggy T-shirts depicting famous athletes every single day, even in the winter. We would sleep in our clothes. We would both be good at Nintendo Street Fighter II, but Colin would be better than me. We would have some homework, but it would never be too hard and we would always have just finished it. We would eat pizza and candy for all of our meals. We wouldn't have sex, but we would have crushes on each other and, magically, babies would appear in our home. We would win the lottery and then buy land in Wyoming, where we would have one of every kind of cute animal. All the while, Colin would be working in law enforcement—probably the FBI. Our favorite movie star, Morgan Freeman, would visit us occasionally. We would listen to the same Eurythmics song ("Here Comes the Rain Again") over and over again and watch two hours of television every Friday night. We would both be good at football, have best friends, and know how to drive; we would cure AIDS and the garbage problem and everything that hurts animals. We would hang out a lot with Colin's dad. For fun, we would load a slingshot with dog food and shoot it at my butt. We would have a very good life.

Here are the particulars about Colin Duffy: He is ten years old, on the nose. He is four feet eight inches high, weighs seventy-five pounds, and appears to be mostly leg and shoulder blade. He is a handsome kid. He has a broad forehead, dark eyes with dense lashes, and a sharp, dimply smile. I have rarely seen him without a baseball cap. He owns several, but favors a University of Michigan Wolverines model, on account of its pleasing colors. The hat styles his hair into wild disarray. If you ever managed to get the hat off his head, you would see a boy with a nimbus of golden-brown hair, dented in the back, where the hat hits him.

Colin lives with his mother, Elaine; his father, Jim; his older sister, Megan; and his little brother, Chris, in a pretty pale blue Victorian house on a bosky street in Glen Ridge, New Jersey. Glen Ridge is a serene and civilized old town twenty miles west of New York City. It does not have much of a commercial district, but it is a town of amazing lawns. Most of the houses were built around the turn of the century and are set back a gracious, green distance from the street. The rest of the town seems to consist of parks and playing fields and sidewalks and backyards—in other words, it is a far cry from South-Central Los Angeles and from Bedford-Stuyvesant and other, grimmer parts of the country where a very different ten-year-old American man is growing up today.

There is a fine school system in Glen Ridge, but Elaine and Jim, who are both schoolteachers, choose to send their children to a parents' cooperative elementary school in Montclair, a neighboring suburb. Currently, Colin is in fifth grade. He is a good student. He plans to go to college, to a place he says is called Oklahoma City State College University. OCSCU satisfies his desire to live out west, to attend a small college, and to study law enforcement, which OCSCU apparently offers as a major. After four years at Oklahoma City State College University, he plans to work for the FBI. He says that getting to be a police officer involves tons of hard work, but working for the FBI will be a cinch, because all you have to do is fill out one form, which he has already gotten from the head FBI office. Colin is quiet in class but loud on the playground. He has a great throwing arm, significant foot speed, and a lot of physical confidence. He is also brave. Huge wild cats with rabies and gross stuff dripping from their teeth, which he says run rampant throughout his neighborhood, do not scare him. Otherwise, he is slightly bashful. This combination of athletic grace and valor and personal reserve accounts for considerable popularity. He has a fluid relationship to many social groups, including the superbright nerds, the ultra-jocks, the flashy kids who will someday become extremely popular and socially successful juvenile delinquents, and the kids who will be elected president of the student body. In his opinion, the most popular boy in his class is Christian, who happens to be black, and Colin's favorite television character is Steve Urkel on *Family Matters*, who is black, too, but otherwise he seems uninterested in or oblivious to race. Until this year, he was a Boy Scout. Now he is planning to begin karate lessons. His favorite schoolyard game is football, followed closely by prison dodgeball, blob tag, and bombardo. He's crazy about athletes, although sometimes it isn't clear if he is absolutely sure of the difference between human athletes and Marvel Comics action figures. His current athletic hero is Dave Meggett. His current best friend is named Japeth. He used to have another best friend named Ozzie. According to Colin, Ozzie was found on a doorstep, then changed his name to Michael and moved to Massachusetts, and then Colin never saw him or heard from him again.

He has had other losses in his life. He is old enough to know people who have died and to know things about the world that are worrisome. When he dreams, he dreams about moving to Wyoming, which he has visited with his family. His plan is to buy land there and have some sort of ranch that would definitely include horses. Sometimes when he talks about this, it sounds as ordinary and hard-boiled as a real estate appraisal; other times it can sound fantastical and wifty and achingly naive, informed by the last inklings of childhood—the musings of a balmy real estate appraiser assaying a wonderful and magical landscape that erodes from memory a little bit every day. The collision in his mind of what he understands, what he hears, what he figures out, what popular culture pours into him, what he knows, what he pretends to know, and what he imagines makes an interesting mess. The mess often has the form of what he will probably think like when he is a grown man, but the content of what he is like as a little boy.

He is old enough to begin imagining that he will someday get married, but at ten he is still convinced that the best thing about being married will be that he will be allowed to sleep in his clothes. His father once observed that living with Colin was like living with a Martian who had done some reading on American culture. As it happens, Colin is not especially sad or worried about the prospect of growing up, although he sometimes frets over whether he should be called a kid or a grown-up; he has settled on the word *kid-up*. Once, I asked him what the biggest advantage to adulthood will be, and he said, "The best thing is that grown-ups can go wherever they want." I asked him what he meant, exactly, and he said, "Well, if you're grown up, you'd have a car, and whenever you felt like it, you could get into your car and drive somewhere and get candy."

Colin loves recycling. He loves it even more than, say, playing with little birds. That ten-year-olds feel the weight of the world and consider it their mission to shoulder it came as a surprise to me. I had gone with Colin one Monday to his classroom at Montclair Cooperative School. The Co-op is in a steep, old, sharp-angled brick building that had served for many years as a public school until a group of parents in the area took it over and made it into a private, progressive elementary school. The fifth-grade classroom is on the top floor, under the dormers, which gives the room the eccentric shape and closeness of an attic. It is a rather informal environment. There are computers lined up in an adjoining room and instructions spelled out on the chalkboard—BRING IN: (1) A CUBBY WITH YOUR NAME ON IT, (2) A TRAPPER WITH A 5-POCKET ENVELOPE LABELED SCIENCE, SOCIAL STUDIES, READING/LANGUAGE ARTS, MATH, MATH LAB/COMPUTER; WHITE LINED PAPER; A PLASTIC PENCIL BAG; A SMALL HOMEWORK PAD, (3) LARGE BROWN

GROCERY BAGS—but there is also a couch in the center of the classroom, which the kids take turns occupying, a rocking chair, and three canaries in cages near the door.

It happened to be Colin's first day in fifth grade. Before class began, there was a lot of horsing around, but there were also a lot of conversations about whether Magic Johnson had AIDS or just HIV and whether someone falling in a pool of blood from a cut of his would get the disease. These jolts of sobriety in the midst of rank goofiness are a ten-year-old's specialty. Each one comes as a fresh, hard surprise, like finding a razor blade in a candy apple. One day, Colin and I had been discussing horses or dogs or something, and out of the blue he said, "What do you think is better, to dump garbage in the ocean, to dump it on land, or to burn it?" Another time, he asked me if I planned to have children. I had just spent an evening with him and his friend Japeth, during which they put every small, movable object in the house into Japeth's slingshot and fired it at me, so I told him that I wanted children but that I hoped they would all be girls, and he said, "Will you have an abortion if you find out you have a boy?"

At school, after discussing summer vacation, the kids began choosing the jobs they would do to help out around the classroom. Most of the jobs are humdrum—putting the chairs up on the tables, washing the chalkboard, turning the computers off or on. Five of the most humdrum tasks are recycling chores—for example, taking bottles or stacks of paper down to the basement, where they would be sorted and prepared for pickup. Two children would be assigned to feed the birds and cover their cages at the end of the day.

I expected the bird jobs to be the first to go. Everyone loved the birds; they'd spent an hour that morning voting on names for them (Tweetie, Montgomery, and Rose narrowly beating out Axl Rose, Bugs, Ol' Yeller, Fido, Slim, Lucy, and Chirpie). Instead, they all wanted to recycle. The recycling jobs were claimed by the first five kids called by Suzanne Nakamura, the fifth-grade teacher; each kid called after that responded by groaning, "Suzanne, aren't there any more recycling jobs?" Colin ended up with the job of taking down the chairs each morning. He accepted the task with a sort of resignation—this was going to be just a job rather than a mission.

On the way home that day, I was quizzing Colin about his worldviews.

"Who's the coolest person in the world?"

"Morgan Freeman."

"What's the best sport?"

"Football."

"Who's the coolest woman?"

"None. I don't know."

"What's the most important thing in the world?"

"Game Boy." Pause. "No, the world. The world is the most important thing in the world."

★ ★ ★

Danny's Pizzeria is a dark little shop next door to the Montclair Cooperative School. It is not much to look at. Outside, the brick facing is painted muddy brown. Inside, there are some saggy counters, a splintered bench, and enough room for either six teenagers or about a dozen ten-year-olds who happen to be getting along well. The light is low. The air is oily. At Danny's, you will find pizza, candy, Nintendo, and very few girls. To a ten-year-old boy, it is the most beautiful place in the world.

One afternoon, after class was dismissed, we went to Danny's with Colin's friend Japeth to play Nintendo. Danny's has only one game, Street Fighter II Champion Edition. Some teenage boys from a nearby middle school had gotten there first and were standing in a tall, impenetrable thicket around the machine.

"Next game," Colin said. The teenagers ignored him.

"Hey, we get next game," Japeth said. He is smaller than Colin, scrappy, and, as he explained to me once, famous for wearing his hat backward all the time and having a huge wristwatch and a huge bedroom. He stamped his foot and announced again, "Hey, we get next game."

One of the teenagers turned around and said, "Fuck you, *next game*," and then turned back to the machine.

"Whoa," Japeth said.

He and Colin went outside, where they felt bigger.

"Which street fighter are you going to be?" Colin asked Japeth.

"Blanka," Japeth said. "I know how to do his head-butt."

"I hate that! I hate the head-butt," Colin said. He dropped his voice a little and growled, "I'm going to be Ken, and I will kill you with my dragon punch."

"Yeah, right, and monkeys will fly out of my butt," Japeth said.

Street Fighter II is a video game in which two characters have an explosive brawl in a scenic international setting. It is currently the most popular video arcade game in America. This is not an insignificant amount of popularity. Most arcade versions of video games, which end up in pizza parlors, malls, and arcades, sell about two thousand units. So far, some fifty thousand Street Fighter II and Street Fighter II Championship Edition arcade games have been sold. Not since Pac-Man, which was released the year before Colin was born, has there been a video game as popular as Street Fighter. The home version of Street Fighter is the most popular home video game in the country, and that, too, is not an insignificant thing. Thirty-two million Nintendo home systems have been sold since 1986, when it was introduced in this country. There is a Nintendo system in seven of every ten homes in America in which a child between the ages of eight and twelve resides. By the time a boy in America turns ten, he will almost certainly have been exposed to Nintendo home games, Nintendo arcade games, and Game Boy, the handheld version. He will probably own a system and dozens of games. By ten, according to Nintendo studies, teachers, and psychologists, game prowess becomes a fundamental, essential male social marker and a schoolyard boast.

The Street Fighter characters are Dhalsim, Ken, Guile, Blanka,

E. Honda, Ryu, Zangief, and Chun Li. Each represents a different country, and they each have their own special weapon. Chun Li, for instance, is from China and possesses a devastating whirlwind kick that is triggered if you push the control pad down for two seconds and then up for two seconds, and then you hit the kick button. Chun Li's kick is money in the bank, because most of the other fighters do not have a good defense against it. By the way, Chun Li happens to be a girl—the only female Street Fighter character.

I asked Colin if he was interested in being Chun Li. There was a long pause. "I would rather be Ken," he said.

The girls in Colin's class at school are named Cortnerd, Terror, Spacey, Lizard, Maggot, and Diarrhea. "They do have other names, but that's what we call them," Colin told me. "The girls aren't very popular."

"They are about as popular as a piece of dirt," Japeth said. "Or, you know that couch in the classroom? That couch is more popular than any girl. A thousand times more." They talked for a minute about one of the girls in their class, a tall blonde with cheerleader genetic material, who they allowed was not quite as gross as some of the other girls. Japeth said that a chubby, awkward boy in their class was boasting that this girl liked him.

"No way," Colin said. "She would never like him. I mean, not that he's so . . . I don't know. I don't hate him because he's fat, anyway. I hate him because he's nasty."

"Well, she doesn't like him," Japeth said. "She's been really mean to me lately, so I'm pretty sure she likes me."

"Girls are different," Colin said. He hopped up and down on the balls of his feet, wrinkling his nose. "Girls are stupid and weird."

"I have a lot of girlfriends, about six or so," Japeth said, turning contemplative. "I don't exactly remember their names, though."

The teenagers came crashing out of Danny's and jostled past us, so we went inside. The man who runs Danny's, whose name is Tom, was leaning across the counter on his elbows, looking exhausted. Two little boys, holding Slush Puppies, shuffled toward the Nintendo, but Colin and Japeth elbowed them aside and slammed their quarters down on the machine. The little boys shuffled back toward the counter and stood gawking at them, sucking on their drinks.

"You want to know how to tell if a girl likes you?" Japeth said. "She'll act really mean to you. That's a sure sign. I don't know why they do it, but it's always a sure sign. It gets your attention. You know how I show a girl I like her? I steal something from her and then run away. I do it to get their attention, and it works."

They played four quarters' worth of games. During the last one, a teenager with a quilted leather jacket and a fade haircut came in, pushed his arm between them, and put a quarter down on the deck of the machine.

Japeth said, "Hey, what's that?"

The teenager said, "I get next game. I've marked it now. Everyone knows this secret sign for next game. It's a universal thing."

"So now we know," Japeth said. "Colin, let's get out of here and go bother Maggie. I mean Maggot. Okay?" They picked up their backpacks and headed out the door.

Psychologists identify ten as roughly the age at which many boys experience the gender-linked normative developmental trauma that leaves them, as adult men, at risk for specific psychological sequelae often manifest as deficits in the arenas of intimacy, empathy, and struggles with commitment in relationships. In other words, this is around the age when guys get screwed up about girls. Elaine and Jim Duffy, and probably most of the parents who send their kids to Montclair Cooperative School, have done a lot of stuff to try to avoid this. They gave Colin dolls as well as guns. (He preferred guns.) Japeth's father has three motorcycles and two dirt bikes but does most of the cooking and cleaning in their home. Suzanne, Colin's teacher, is careful to avoid sexist references in her presentations. After school, the yard at Montclair Cooperative is filled with as many fathers as mothers—fathers who hug their kids when they come prancing out of the building and are dismayed when their sons clamor for Supersoaker water guns and war toys or take pleasure in beating up girls.

In a study of adolescents conducted by the Gesell Institute of Human Development, nearly half the ten-year-old boys questioned said they thought they had adequate information about sex. Nevertheless, most ten-year-old boys across the country are subjected to a few months of sex education in school. Colin and his class will get their dose next spring. It is yet another installment in a plan to make them into new, improved men with reconstructed notions of sex and male-female relationships. One afternoon I asked Philip, a schoolmate of Colin's, whether he was looking forward to sex education, and he said, "No, because I think it'll probably make me really, really hyper. I have a feeling it's going to be just like what it was like when some television reporters came to school last year and filmed us in class and I got really hyper. They stood around with all these cameras and asked us questions. I think that's what sex education is probably like."

At a class meeting earlier in the day:

COLIN'S TEACHER, SUZANNE: Today was our first day of swimming class, and I have one observation to make. The girls went into their locker room, got dressed without a lot of fuss, and came into the pool area. The boys, on the other hand, the *boys* had some sort of problem doing that rather simple task. Can someone tell me what exactly went on in the locker room?

KEITH: There was a lot of shouting.

SUZANNE: Okay, I hear you saying that people were being noisy and shouting. Anything else?

CHRISTIAN: Some people were screaming so much that my ears were killing me. It gave me, like, a huge headache. Also, some of the boys were taking their towels, I mean, after they had taken their clothes off, they had their towels around their waists and then they would drop them really fast and then pull them back up, really fast.

SUZANNE: Okay, you're saying some people were being silly about their bodies.

CHRISTIAN: Well, yeah, but it was more like they were being silly about their pants.

Colin's bedroom is decorated simply. He has a cage with his pet parakeet, Dude, on his dresser, a lot of recently worn clothing piled haphazardly on the floor, and a husky brown teddy bear sitting upright in a chair near the foot of his bed. The walls are mostly bare, except for a Spiderman poster and a few ads torn out of magazines he has thumbtacked up. One of the ads is for a cologne, illustrated with several small photographs of cowboy hats; another, a feverish portrait of a woman on a horse, is an ad for blue jeans. These inspire him sometimes when he lies in bed and makes plans for the move to Wyoming. Also, he happens to like ads. He also likes television commercials. Generally speaking, he likes consumer products and popular culture. He partakes avidly but not indiscriminately. In fact, during the time we spent together, he provided a running commentary on merchandise, media, and entertainment:

"The only shoes anyone will wear are Reebok Pumps. Big T-shirts are cool, not the kind that are sticky and close to you, but big and baggy and long, not the kind that stop at your stomach."

"The best food is Chicken McNuggets and Life cereal and Frosted Flakes."

"Don't go to Blimpie's. They have the worst service."

"I'm not into Teenage Mutant Ninja Turtles anymore. I grew out of that. I like Donatello, but I'm not a fan. I don't buy the figures anymore."

"The best television shows are on Friday night on ABC. It's called TGIF, and it's *Family Matters*, *Step by Step*, *Dinosaurs*, and *Perfect Strangers*, where the guy has a funny accent."

"The best candy is Skittles and Symphony bars and Crybabies and Warheads. Crybabies are great because if you eat a lot of them at once you feel so sour."

"Hyundais are Korean cars. It's the only Korean car. They're not that good because Koreans don't have a lot of experience building cars."

"The best movie is *City Slickers*, and the best part was when he saved his little cow in the river."

"The Giants really need to get rid of Ray Handley. They have to get somebody who has real coaching experience. He's just no good."

"My dog, Sally, costs seventy-two dollars. That sounds like a lot of money but it's a really good price because you get a flea bath with your dog."

"The best magazines are *Nintendo Power*, because they tell you how to do the secret moves in the video games, and also *Mad* magazine and *Money Guide*—I really like that one."

"The best artist in the world is Jim Davis."

"The most beautiful woman in the world is not Madonna! Only Wayne and Garth think that! She looks like maybe a . . . a . . . slut or something. Cindy Crawford looks like she would look good, but if you see her on an awards program on TV she doesn't look that good. I think the most beautiful woman in the world probably is my mom."

★ ★ ★

Colin thinks a lot about money. This started when he was about nine and a half, which is when a lot of other things started—a new way of walking that has a little macho hitch and swagger, a decision about the Teenage Mutant Ninja Turtles (con) and Eurythmics (pro), and a persistent curiosity about a certain girl whose name he will not reveal. He knows the price of everything he encounters. He knows how much college costs and what someone might earn performing different jobs. Once, he asked me what my husband did; when I answered that he was a lawyer, he snapped, "You must be a rich family. Lawyers make four hundred thousand dollars a year." His preoccupation with money baffles his family. They are not struggling, so this is not the anxiety of deprivation; they are not rich, so he is not responding to an elegant, advantaged world. His allowance is five dollars a week. It seems sufficient for his needs, which consist chiefly of quarters for Nintendo and candy money. The remainder is put into his Wyoming fund. His fascination is not just specific to needing money or having plans for money: It is as if money itself, and the way it makes the world work, and the realization that almost everything in the world can be assigned a price, has possessed him. "I just pay attention to things like that," Colin says. "It's really very interesting."

He is looking for a windfall. He tells me his mother has been notified that she is in the fourth and final round of the Publisher's Clearinghouse Sweepstakes. This is not an ironic observation. He plays the New Jersey lottery every Thursday night. He knows the weekly jackpot; he knows the number to call to find out if he has won. I do not think this presages a future for Colin as a high-stakes gambler; I think it says more about the powerful grasp that money has on imagination and what a large percentage of a ten-year-old's mind is made up of imaginings. One Friday, we were at school together, and one of his friends was asking him about the lottery, and he said, "This week it was four million dollars. That would be I forget how much every year for the rest of your life. It's a lot, I think. You should play. All it takes is a dollar and a dream."

★ ★ ★

Until the lottery comes through and he starts putting together the Wyoming land deal, Colin can be found most of the time in the backyard. Often, he will have friends come over. Regularly, children from the neighborhood will gravitate to the backyard, too. As a technical matter of real-property law, title to the house and yard belongs to Jim and Elaine Duffy, but Colin adversely possesses the backyard, at least from 4:00 each afternoon until it gets dark. As yet, the fixtures of teenage life—malls, video arcades, friends' basements, automobiles—either hold little interest for him or are not his to have.

He is, at the moment, very content with his backyard. For most intents and purposes, it is as big as Wyoming. One day, certainly, he will grow and it will shrink, and it will become simply a suburban backyard and it won't be big enough for him anymore. This will happen so fast that one night he will be in the backyard, believing it a perfect place, and by the next night he will have changed and the yard as he imagined it will be gone, and this era of his life will be behind him forever.

Most days, he spends his hours in the backyard building an Evil Spider-Web Trap. This entails running a spool of Jim's fishing line from every surface in the yard until it forms a huge web. Once a garbageman picking up the Duffys' trash got caught in the trap. Otherwise, the Evil Spider-Web Trap mostly has a deterrent effect, because the kids in the neighborhood who might roam over know that Colin builds it back there. "I do it all the time," he says. "First I plan who I'd like to catch in it, and then we get started. Trespassers have to beware."

One afternoon when I came over, after a few rounds of Street Fighter at Danny's, Colin started building a trap. He selected a victim for inspiration—a boy in his class who had been pestering him—and began wrapping. He was entirely absorbed. He moved from tree to tree, wrapping; he laced fishing line through the railing of the deck and then back to the shed; he circled an old jungle gym, something he'd outgrown and abandoned a few years ago, and then crossed over to a bush at the back of the yard. Briefly, he contemplated making his dog, Sally, part of the web. Dusk fell. He kept wrapping, paying out fishing line an inch at a time. We could hear mothers up and down the block hooting for their kids; two tiny children from next door stood transfixed at the edge of the yard, uncertain whether they would end up inside or outside the web. After a while, the spool spun around in Colin's hands one more time and then stopped; he was out of line.

It was almost too dark to see much of anything, although now and again the light from the deck would glance off a length of line, and it would glint and sparkle. "That's the point," he said. "You could do it with thread, but the fishing line is invisible. Now I have this perfect thing and the only one who knows about it is me." With that, he dropped the spool, skipped up the stairs of the deck, threw open the screen door, and then bounded into the house, leaving me and Sally the dog trapped in his web.

AMONG THE THUGS

Bill Buford

★ ★ ★

This is excerpted from an early chapter of *Among the Thugs*. Bill Buford's story begins when he witnesses soccer hooligans on a violent spree in the British trains. As an American living in England, he's astonished to learn just how common this is. "I had read about the violence and, to the extent that I thought about it, had assumed that it was an isolated thing or mysterious in the way that crowd violence is meant to be mysterious: unpredictable, spontaneous, the mob." This, however, was a regular part of British life, a weekly occurrence. After matches, fans tore apart trains and smashed shop windows.

Buford starts attending matches and tries to get close to the "lads," and at first he only manages to establish a rapport with one of them, an overweight, heavy-drinking fellow named Mick. Mick is not what Buford expected from the soccer fans at all. He'd figured that the violence was a protest of some sort, and that the fans would be guys on the dole. But Mick is neither unemployed, alienated nor disenfranchised. He's a skilled electrician with his pockets full of twenty-pound notes. Which is handy because it's expensive, never missing a soccer match. Some fans have money.

Others get to every game, Mick explains, by going "on the jib"—sneaking on trains, stealing food, swiping game tickets, doing everything possible so the whole venture will cost them nothing.

Mick's team is Manchester United, whose fans were so unruly that they were banned from games outside of England—by the team itself. "I wanted to find out what these supporters were like," Buford writes. "It seemed an extraordinary thing for the team's management to ban its own fans." Buford decides to travel to Italy on a charter flight with Mick and other Manchester United fans, a flight not sanctioned by the team of course, to watch a match against a squad called Juventus, in the city of Turin. When the fans' plane touches down, there are soldiers waiting in formation and a police escort for their buses. The fans have been drinking for hours.

Clayton had a number of troubles but his greatest one was his trousers. In all likelihood Clayton will have trouble with his trousers for the rest of his life. His stomach was so soft and large—no adjective seems big enough to describe its girth—that his trousers, of impressive dimensions to begin with, were not quite large enough to be pulled up high enough to prevent them from slipping down again. Clayton emerged from the airplane and waddled down the ramp, clasping his belt buckle, wrestling with it, trying to wiggle it over his considerable bulk. He was singing, "We're so proud to be British." His eyes were closed, and his face was red, and he repeated his refrain over and over again, although nobody else was singing with him.

Mick was not far behind. He had finished his bottle of vodka and was drinking a can of Carlsberg Special Brew that he had snapped up from the drinks trolley as he bumped past it on his way out. Mick paused, started to utter something, in the puffy, considered way that characterizes the speech of a man who has consumed a liter of spirits in the span of ninety minutes. And then Mick belched. It was a spectacular belch, long and terrible, a brutal, slow bursting of innumerable noxious gastric bubbles.

The others followed. They were also singing—on their own or arm in arm with friends—and their songs, like Clayton's, were all about being English and what a fine thing that was. Something had happened to the group shortly after landing; there had been a definitive change. As the plane approached the terminal, someone had spotted the army: it was waiting for them, standing in formation.

The army!

They wore strange uniforms and brightly colored berets; the soldiers were not English—that was the point; the soldiers were *foreign*.

The effect was immediate: these were no longer supporters of Manchester United; they were now defenders of the English nation. People stood up and, as if on cue, began changing their clothes, switching their urban, weekday dress for costumes whose principal design was the Union Jack. All at once, heads and limbs began poking through Union Jack T-shirts and Union Jack swimming suits, and one pair (worn unusually around the forehead) of Union Jack boxer shorts. The moment seemed curiously prepared for, as if it had been rehearsed. Meanwhile, everyone had started singing "Rule Britannia"—sharp, loud, spontaneous—and they sang it again, louder and louder, until finally, as the terminal grew near, it was not being sung but shouted.

A police escort is an exhilarating thing. I couldn't deny that I was sharing the experience of those around me, who now felt themselves to be special people. After all, who is given a police escort? Prime ministers, presidents, the Pope—*and* English football supporters. By the time the buses reached the city—although there was little traffic, the sirens had been turned on the moment we left the parking lot—the status of their occupants had been enlarged immeasurably. Each intersection we passed was blocked with cars and onlookers. People had gathered on every street, wondering what all the fuss was about, wanting to get a look. The sound of twenty sirens is hard to miss. Who in the city of Turin could not have known that the English had arrived?

The English themselves, moved by the effect they were having, started to sing, which they managed to do more loudly than the brain-penetrating sirens that heralded their entrance into the city. To sing so powerfully was no small achievement, although to describe the noise that emerged from the bus as singing is to misrepresent it. One song was "England." This was repeated over and over again. There were no more words. Another, more sophisticated, was based on the tune of "The Battle Hymn of the Republic." Its words were:

> Glory, glory, Man United
> Glory, glory, Man United
> Glory, glory, Man United
> Yours troops are marching on! on! on!

Each "on" was grunted a bit more emphatically than the one before, accompanied by a gesture involving the familiar upturned two fingers. There was an especially simple tune, "Fuck the Pope"—simple because the words consisted exclusively of the following: *Fuck the Pope*. "Fuck the Pope" was particularly popular, and, despite the sirens and speed, at least two buses (the one I was in and the one behind us) succeeded in chanting "Fuck the Pope" in some kind of unison.

I noticed Clayton. He was several rows in front. Somehow Clayton, like an unwieldy truck, had reversed himself into a position in which the opened window by his seat was filled by his suddenly exposed and very large buttocks—his trousers, this time, deliberately gathered around his knees, the cheeks of his suddenly exposed and very large buttocks clasped firmly in each hand and spread apart. Just behind him was a fellow who was urinating through his window. People were standing on the seats, jerking their fists up and down, while screaming profanities at pedestrians, police, children—any and all Italians.

Then someone lobbed a bottle.

It was bound to happen. There were bottles rolling around on the floor or being passed from person to person, and it was inevitable that, having tried everything else—obscene chants, abuse, peeing—someone would go that much further and pick up one of the empty bottles and hurl it at an Italian. Even so, the use of missiles of any kind was a significant escalation, and there was the sense, initially at least, that bottle throwing was "out of order."

"What the fuck did you do that for?" someone shouted, angry, but not without a sense of humor. "What are you, some kind of hooligan?"

A meaningful threshold had been crossed. Moments later there was the sound of another bottle breaking. And a second, and a third, and then bottles started flying out of most windows—of each of the four buses.

I wondered: if I had been a citizen of Turin, what would I have made of all this?

After all, here I'd be, at the foot of the Alps, in one of the most northern regions of Italy, surrounded by an exquisite, historic brick architecture, a city of churches and squares and arcades and cafés, a civilized city, an intellectual city, the heart of the Communist Party, the home of Primo Levi and other writers and painters, and, during my lunch hour, when perhaps I, a Juventus supporter like everyone else, had gone out to pick up my ticket for the match that evening, I heard this powerful sound, the undulating whines of multiple sirens. Were they ambulances? Had there been a disaster? All around me people would have stopped and would be craning their necks, shielding their eyes from the sun, until finally, in the distance we would have spotted the oscillating blue and white lights of the approaching police. And when they passed—one, two, three, four buses—would my response be nothing more than one of fascination, as in the window of each bus, I would see faces of such terrible aggression—remarkable aggression, intense, inexplicably vicious? Perhaps my face would be splattered by the spray of someone's urine. Perhaps I would have to jump out of the way of a bottle being hurled at my head. And perhaps, finally, I would have responded in the manner chosen by one Italian lad, who, suddenly the target of an unforeseen missile, simply answered in kind: he hurled a stone back.

The effect on those inside the buses was immediate. To be, suddenly, the target came as a terrible shock. The incredulity was immense:

"Those bastards," one of the supporters exclaimed, "are throwing stones at the windows," and the look on his face conveyed such urgent dismay that you could only agree that a stone-throwing Italian was a very bad person indeed. The presumption—after all a window could get broken and someone might get hurt—was deeply offensive, and everyone became very, very angry. Looking around me, I realized that I was no longer surrounded by raving, hysterically nationalistic social deviants; I was now surrounded by raving, hysterically nationalist social deviants *in a frenzy*. They were wild, and anything that came to hand—bottles, jars of peanuts, fruit, cartons of juice, anything—was summarily hurled through the windows. "Those bastards," the lad next to me said, teeth clenched, lobbing an unopened beer can at a cluster of elderly men in dark jackets. "Those bastards."

Everyone was now very excited.

And then: a rainbow. The streets, which had been getting tighter and tighter, opened, at last, on to a square: Piazza San Carlo. Light, air, the sky, and the bus slowly, undeniably, coming to rest. We had arrived.

✷ ✷ ✷

And so four coaches of supporters arrived to attend the match that they had been banned from attending only to discover that many people had gotten there before them. Where had they come from? The square was packed. As we pulled in, someone waved to us, one hand wild above his head, the other clinging to his penis, urinating into a fountain. There could be no doubt about his nationality, or, for that matter, any of the others', familiar bloated examples of an island race who, sweltering under the warm Italian sun, had taken off their shirts, a great, fatty manifestation of the history of pub opening hours, of gallons and gallons of lager and incalculable quantities of bacon-flavored crisps. They were singing: "Manchester, la-la-la, Manchester, la-la-la." They had the appearance of people who had been at the square, singing and drinking and urinating into the fountain, for many days. The pavement was covered with large empty bottles.

I spotted Mick who, ever vigilant, had discovered the place to buy cheap beer very cheaply and who, ever generous, appeared with three two-liter bottles of lager, including one for me. Then Mick made for the middle of the throng, shouting "C'mon, you Reds"—red for the red of Manchester United's Red Devils—and he vanished, only his upturned two-liter bottle remaining visible above everyone's heads.

I wandered around the square. I was not uncomfortable, mainly because I had decided that I wasn't going to allow myself to be uncomfortable. If I had allowed myself to be uncomfortable then it would follow that I would start to feel ridiculous and ask myself questions like: Why am I here? Now that the journey to Turin was properly completed, I had, I realized, done little more than gawk and drink. Mick had disappeared, although I thought I could pick out his bellowing amid the noise around me. Apart from him, however, I knew nobody. Here I was, my little black notebook hidden away in my back trouser pocket, hoping to come up with a way of ingratiating myself into a group that, from what I could see, was not looking for new members. For a moment I had the unpleasant experience of seeing myself as I must have appeared: as an American who had made a long journey to Italy that he shouldn't have known about so that he could stand alone in the middle of what was by now several hundred Manchester United supporters who all knew each other, had probably known each other for years, were accustomed to traveling many miles to meet every week and who spoke with the same thick accent, drank the same thick beer, and wore many of the same preposterous, vaguely designed, High Street clothes.

What was worse, word had got around that I was in Turin to write about the supporters—a piece of news that few had found particularly attractive. Two people came up and told me that they never read the *Express* (the *Express*?) and that when they did they found only rubbish in it. When I tried to explain that I wasn't writing for the *Express*, I could see that they didn't believe me or—a more unpleasant prospect—thought that, therefore, I must be writing for the *Sun*. Another, speaking sotto voce, tried to sell me his story ("The *Star*'s already offered me a thousand quid"). In its way this was a positive development, except that someone else appeared and started jabbing me vigorously in the chest: You don't look like a reporter. Where was my notebook? Where was my camera? What's an American doing here anyway?

There had been other journalists. In Valencia, a Spanish television crew had offered ten pounds to any supporter who was prepared to throw stones, while jumping up and down and shouting dirty words. At Portsmouth, someone had appeared from the *Daily Mail*, working "undercover," wearing a bomber jacket and Doc Marten boots, but he was chased away by the supporters: it was pointed out that no one had worn a bomber jacket and a pair of Doc Marten boots for about ten years, except for an isolated number of confused Chelsea fans. And last year in Barcelona there was a journalist from the *Star*. His was the story that I found most compelling. He had been accepted by most members of the group, but had then kept asking them about the violence. This, I was told, just wasn't done. When is it going to go off? he would ask. Is it going to go off now? Will it go off tonight? No doubt he had a deadline and a features editor waiting for his copy. When the violence did occur, he ran, which was not unreasonable: he could get hurt. In the supporters' eyes, however, he had done something very bad: he had—in their inimitable phrasing—"shitted himself." When he returned to complete his story, he was set upon. But they didn't stab him. He wasn't disfigured in any lasting way.

The story about the *Star* journalist was not particularly reassuring—so great, they didn't stab him; lucky reporter—and I made a mental note not to shit myself under any circumstances. Even so, the story revealed an important piece of information.

Until then, everyone I had spoken to went out of his way to establish that, while he might *look* like a hooligan, he was not one in fact. He was a football supporter. True: if someone was going to pick a fight, he wasn't going to run—he was English, wasn't he?—but he wouldn't go looking for trouble. Everyone was there for the laugh and the trip abroad and the drink and the football.

I did not want to hear this. And when I heard it, I refused to believe it. I had to. The fact was that I had come to Italy to see trouble. It was expensive and time-consuming, and that was why I was there. I didn't encourage it—I wasn't in the position to do so—and I wasn't admitting my purpose to anyone I met. I may not have been admitting it to myself. But *that* was why I was there, prepared to stand on my own with five hundred people staring at me wondering what I was doing. I was waiting for them to be bad. I wanted to see violence. And the fact that the *Star* journalist had witnessed some, that it had finally "gone off," suggested I might be in the right spot after all.

Violence or no violence, mine was not an attractive moral position. It was, however, an easy one, and it consisted in this: not thinking. As I entered this experience, I made a point of removing moral judgment, like a coat. With all the drink and the luxurious Italian sun, I wouldn't need it. Once or twice, facing the spectacle of the square, the thought occurred to me that I should be appalled. If I had been British I might have been. I might have felt the burden of that peculiar nationalist liability that assumes you are responsible for everyone from your own country ("I was ashamed to be British"—or French or German or American). But I'm not British. Mick and his friends and I were not of the same kind. And although I might have felt that I should be appalled, the fact was: I wasn't. I was fascinated.

And I wasn't alone.

A group of Italians had gathered near the square. I walked over to them. There were about a hundred, who, afraid of getting too close, had huddled together, staring and pointing. Their faces all had the same look of incredulity. They had never seen people act in this way. It was inconceivable that an Italian, visiting a foreign city, would spend hours in one of its principal squares, drinking and barking and peeing and shouting and sweating and slapping his belly. Could you imagine a busload from Milan parading around Trafalgar Square showing off their tattoos? "Why do you English behave like this?" one Italian asked me, believing that I was of the same nationality. "Is it something to do with being an island race? Is it because you don't feel European?" He looked confused; he looked like he wanted to help. "Is it because you lost the Empire?"

I didn't know what to say. Why were these people behaving in this way? And who were they doing it for? It would make sense to think that they were performing for the benefit of the Italians looking on—the war dance of the invading barbarians from the north and all that—but it seemed to me that they were performing solely for themselves. Over the last hour or so, I could see that the afternoon was turning into a highly patterned thing.

It looked something like this: once a supporter arrived, he wandered around, usually with a friend, periodically bellowing or bumping into things or joining in on a song. Then a mate would be spotted and they would greet each other. The greeting was achieved through an exchange of loud, incomprehensible noises. A little later they would spot another mate (more noise) and another (more noise), until finally there were enough people—five, six, sometimes ten—to form a circle. Then, as though responding to a toast, they would all drink from a very large bottle of very cheap lager or a very large bottle of very cheap red wine. This was done at an exceptional speed, and the drink spilled down their faces and on to their necks and down their chests, which, already quite sticky and beading with perspiration, glistened in the sun. A song followed. From time to time, during a particularly important refrain, each member of the circle squatted slightly, clenching his fists at his sides, as if, poised so, he was able to sing the particular refrain with the extra oomph that it required. The posture was not unlike shitting in public. And then the very large bottle with its very cheap contents was drunk again.

The circle broke up and the cycle was repeated. It was repeated again. And again. All around the square, little clusters of fat, sticky men were bellowing at each other.

Mick reappeared and pointed to the far end of the square, where a silver Mercedes was moving slowly through a street crowded with supporters, Italian onlookers, and police. The driver, in a shiny purple track suit, was a black man with a round fleshy face and a succession of double chins. In the back seat were two others, both black. One, I would learn, was named Tony Roberts. The other was Roy Downes.

No one had mentioned Tony to me before, but he was impossible to forget once you saw him. He was thin and tall—he towered above everyone else—and had an elaborate, highly styled haircut. The fact was Tony looked exactly like Michael Jackson. Even the color of his skin was Michael Jackson's. For a brief electric instant—the silver Mercedes, the driver, the ceremony of the arrival—I thought Tony *was* Michael Jackson. What a discovery: to learn that Michael Jackson, that little red devil, was actually a fan of Manchester United. But, then, alas, yes, I could see that, no, Tony was not Michael Jackson. Tony was only someone who had spent a lot of time and money trying to look like Michael Jackson.

There was Tony's wardrobe. This is what I saw of it during his stay in Turin (approximately thirty hours):

One: a pale yellow jump suit, light and casual and worn for comfort during the long hours in the Mercedes.

Two: a pastel-blue T-shirt (was there silk in the mix?), a straw hat, and cotton trousers, his "early summer" costume, worn when he briefly appeared on the square around four o'clock.

Three: his leather look (lots of studs), chosen for the match.

Four: a light woolen jacket (chartreuse) with complementary olive-green trousers for later in the evening, when everyone gathered at a bar.

Five: and finally, another travel outfit for the return trip (a pink cotton track suit with pink trainers).

Later, during the leather phase, I asked Tony what he did for a living, and he said only that he sometimes "played the ticket game": large-scale touting, buying up blocks of seats for pop concerts or the sporting events at Wimbledon and Wembley and selling them on at inflated prices. I heard also that he was, from time to time, a driver for Hurricane Higgins, the snooker star; that he was a jazz dancer, that he had "acted" in some porn films. His profession, I suspect, was the same as that of so many of the others, a highly lucrative career of doing "this and that," and it wasn't worth looking too deeply into what constituted either the "this" or the "that."

Roy Downes was different. Ever since Mick had mentioned Roy, I had been trying to find out as much about him as I could. I had learned that he had just finished a two-year prison sentence in Bulgaria, where he had been arrested before the match between Manchester United and Leviski Spartak (having just cracked the hotel safe) and that, ever since, people said he wasn't the same: that Roy had become serious, that he never laughed, that he rarely spoke. I had heard that Roy always had money—rolls and rolls of twenty- and fifty-pound notes. That he had a flat in London, overlooking the river. That he saw his matches from the seats and never stood in the terraces with the other supporters, and that he got his tickets free from the players. That he was a lounge lizard: the best place to leave messages for Roy was Stringfellows, a basement bar and nightclub on Upper St. Martin's Lane in London, with Bob Hoskins bouncers in dinner jackets and lots of chrome and mirrors and a small dance floor filled, on the wintry Tuesday night when I later went there (perhaps an off night), with sagging men who had had too much to drink and young secretaries in tight black skirts. (I was let in, stepping past the bouncers and into a bad black-and-white movie, having said— with a straight face—that Roy sent me.)

I couldn't get anybody to tell me what Roy did. Maybe they didn't know or didn't need to know. Or maybe they all knew and didn't want to say. After all, how many of your friends can pick a safe?

Actually I did know one other thing about Roy, but at the time I didn't know that I knew it. I had told a friend about getting caught up in a football train in Wales, and he mentioned an incident he had witnessed that same month. He had been traveling from Manchester, in a train already filled with supporters. When it stopped at Stoke-on-Trent, more fans rushed into his carriage. They were from West Ham and, shouting, "Kill the nigger cunts," they set upon two blacks who were sitting nearby. My friend could see only the backs of the West Ham supporters, their arms rising in the air and then crashing down again, the two blacks somewhere in the middle, when he heard: "They've got a stick, kill the bastards"—the stick evidently referring to a table leg that one of the blacks had managed to break off to defend himself. By the time my friend ran off to find a member of the Transport Police, there was blood on the floor and the seats and some was splattered across the windows. One of the blacks had had his face cut up. But it was the other one they were after. He was stabbed repeatedly—once in the lower chest, a few inches below his heart. A finger was broken, his forehead badly slashed and several of his ribs were fractured. The list of injuries is taken from the "Statement of Witness" that my friend prepared, and on it are the victims' names, meaningful to me only when I returned from Italy. They were Anthony Roberts and Roy Downes. Roy had been the one they were after, the one who had been repeatedly stabbed.

Roy's car drove around the square, with him waving from the window like a politician, and disappeared. When I spotted him again, about an hour later, Roy was standing on one of the balconies, arms apart, leaning on the rail, surveying the supporters below. He was small but muscular—wiry, lean—and good-looking, with strong features and very black skin. He looked, as I had been led to expect, grim and serious. What he saw on the square below him seemed to make him especially grim and serious. In fact he was so grim and serious that I thought it might have been just a little overdone. He looked like he had chosen to be grim and serious in the way that you might pick out a particular article of clothing in the morning; it was what he had decided on instead of wearing red.

It was not an opportunity to miss, and I bounced up the stairs and introduced myself. I was writing a book; I would love to chat. I babbled away—friendly, Californian, with a cheerful, gosh-isn't-the-world-a-wonderful-place kind of attitude, until finally Roy, who did not look up from the square, asked me to shut up, please. There was, please, no need to talk so much: he already knew all about me.

No one had told me to shut up before. How did he know whatever it was he knew? I suppose I was impressed. This was a person for whom style was no small thing.

Roy, at any rate, wasn't having a lot to do with me, despite my good efforts. These efforts, painful to recall, went something like this.

After expressing my surprise that I was a person worth knowing anything about, I, bubbling and gurgling away, suggested that Roy and I get a drink.

Roy, still surveying the square, pointed out that he didn't drink.

That was fine, I said, carrying on, cheerful to the end: then perhaps, after his long journey, he might be interested in joining me for a bite to eat.

No.

Right, I said, a little tic I had developed for responding to a situation that was not right but manifestly wrong. I pulled out a pack of cigarettes—I wanted badly to smoke—while taking in the scene below us: there was Mick, standing by himself, a large bottle of something in one hand and a large bottle of something else in the other, singing "C'mon, you Reds," bellowing it, unaccompanied, his face deeply colored, walking around and around in a circle.

I offered Roy a cigarette.

Roy didn't smoke.

Right, I said, scrutinizing the scene below us with more attention, pointing out how everyone was having such a jolly good time, to which Roy, of course, did not reply. In fact the scene below us was starting to look like a satanic Mardi Gras. There must have been about eight hundred people, and the noise they were making—the English with their songs; the Italians with their cars, horns blaring—was very loud. In normal circumstances, the noise was so loud it would have made conversation difficult. In my current circumstances, nothing could have made conversation any worse.

I carried on. Whatever came into my head found itself leaving my mouth, with or without an exclamatory *Right!* I talked about football, Bryan Robson, the Continental style—in fact about many things I knew little about—until finally, after a brief aside about something completely inconsequential, I tried to talk to Roy about Roy. I don't recall what I said next; actually I fear I do, which is worse, because I think it was something about Roy's being both black and short and what a fine thing that was to be. And then I paused. The pause I remember precisely because at the end of it Roy looked at me for the first time. I thought he was going to spit. But he didn't. What he did was this: he walked away.

With a slight swagger, hands in his pockets, Clint Eastwood had just strolled off and disappeared down the stairs and walked out of my story.

I wasn't cut out to be a journalist.

It was time I met more people. I hadn't gotten through to Roy. Maybe I would later. Maybe it didn't matter. I had had so many I-am-not-going-to-think-about-why-I-am-here lagers that I didn't care if people were going to talk to me. The choices were not complicated: either I would find myself in conversation, or I would find myself not in conversation.

I found myself neither in conversation nor not in conversation but looking into a particularly ugly mouth. I can't recall how I arrived before this mouth—zigzagging across the square—but once in its presence I couldn't take my eyes off it.

In it, there were many gaps, the raw rim of the gums showing where once there must have been teeth. Of the teeth still intact, many were chipped or split; none was straight: they appeared to have grown up at odd, unconventional angles or (more likely) been redirected by a powerful physical influence at some point in their career. All of them were highly colored—deep brown or caked with yellow or, like a pea soup, mushy green and vegetable soft with decay. This was a mouth that had suffered many slings and arrows along with the occasional thrashing and several hundredweight of tobacco and Cadbury's milk chocolate. This was a mouth through which a great deal of life had passed at, it would appear, an uncompromising speed.

The mouth belonged to Gurney. Mick had told me about Gurney. What he hadn't told me about was the power of Gurney's unmitigated ugliness. It was ugliness on a scale that elicited concern: I kept wanting to offer him things—the telephone number of my dentist or a blanket to cover his head. It was hard not to stare at Gurney. Gurney was one of the older supporters and was well into his thirties. He was looked up to, I discovered, by the younger lads. I never understood why they looked up to him or what they hoped to find when they did. Like Roy, Gurney didn't trust me, at least initially, but I was getting used to not being trusted. His Cockney followers were less suspicious. When I came upon them, they were in the middle of singing one of those songs (squatting slightly). They were in good spirits and, straightaway, started questioning me.

No, I wasn't from the *Express*—I had never read the *Express*.

Yes, I was here to write about football supporters.

Yes, I know you are not hooligans.

What was I doing here, then? Well, that was obvious, wasn't it? I was here to get very, very pissed.

And, with that, I had become one of them, or enough of one of them for them to feel comfortable telling me stories. They wanted me to understand how they were organized; it was the "structure" that was important to understand.

There were, it was explained, different kinds of Manchester United supporters, and it was best to think of each kind as belonging to one of a series of concentric circles. The largest circle was very large: in it you would find *all* the supporters of Manchester United, which, as everyone kept telling me, was one of the best-supported teams in English football, with crowds regularly in excess of forty thousand.

Within that large circle, however, there were smaller ones. In the first were the members of the *official* Manchester United Supporters' Club—at its peak more than twenty thousand. The official Manchester United Supporters' Club, started in the seventies, hired trains from British Rail—"football specials"—for conveying fans to the matches, produced a regular magazine, required annual dues, and in general kept the "good" supporters informed of developments in the club and tried to keep the "bad" supporters from ever learning about them.

In the second circle was the *un*official supporters' club, the "bad" supporters: the firm.

The firm was divided between those who lived in Manchester and those who did not. Those who did not came from just about everywhere in the British Isles—Newcastle, Bolton, Glasgow, Southampton, Sunderland: these people were the Inter-City Jibbers. Mick had mentioned them: they got their name from taking only the Inter-City fast commuter trains and never the football specials hired by the official supporters' club.

The Inter-City Jibbers themselves were also divided, between those who were not from London and those who were: the Cockney Reds.

I remembered Mick's account of being on the jib. I had much to learn, and most of it I would learn the next day on my return to England. But initially I was skeptical. How was it possible that so many people could travel on the jib? From what I understood about traveling on the jib, it meant not only not paying but actually making money as well.

Roars of laughter followed. Being on the jib was very simple, I was told, and involved no more than defeating the Hector. The Hector was the British Rail ticket collector, and at the mention of the Hector, everyone started singing the Hector song:

> *Ha ha ha*
> *He he he*
> *The Hector's coming*
> *But he can't catch me.*
> *On the racks*
> *Under the seats*
> *Into the bogs*
> *The Hector's coming*
> *But he can't catch me.*
> *Ha ha ha*

He he he
The ICJ is on the jib again
Having a really g-o-o-o-o-o-o-o-o-o-o-o-d time.

There were tricks: passing one good ticket between members of a group, making the sound of endless vomiting while hiding in the loo, pretending not to understand English. It was Gurney's ploy to engage the ticket collector in a battle of wills, giving him everything but a ticket: a sandwich, a cigarette, the ashtray, his shoe, a sock, then his other sock, bits of dirt scraped from beneath his toenails, his shirt, the darkly colored lint from his navel, his belt until—the final destination getting closer the longer the exchange went on—the ticket collector, fed up, got on with the rest of his job. The ICJ had learned two principles about human nature—especially human nature as it had evolved in Britain.

The first was that no public functionary, and certainly not one employed by British Rail or London Transport, wants a difficult confrontation—there is little pride in a job that the functionary believes to be underpaid and knows to be unrewarding and that he wants to finish so that he can go home.

The second principle was the more important: everyone—including the police—is powerless against a large number of people who have decided not to obey *any* rules. Or put another way: with numbers there are no laws.

It is easy to imagine the situation. You're there, working by yourself at the ticket booth of an Underground station, and two hundred supporters walk past you without paying. What do you do? Or you're working the cash register in a small food shop—one room, two refrigerators, three aisles—and you look up and see that, out of nowhere, hundreds of lads are crowding through your door, pushing and shoving and shouting, until there is no room to move, and that each one is filling his pockets with crisps, meat pies, beer, biscuits, nuts, dried fruit, eggs (for throwing), milk, sausage rolls, liter-bottles of Coke, red wine, butter (for throwing), white wine, Scotch eggs, bottles of retsina, apples, yogurt (for throwing), oranges, chocolates, bottles of cider, sliced ham, mayonnaise (for throwing) until there is very little remaining on your shelves. What do you do? Tell them to stop? Stand in the doorway? You call the police but as the supporters pour out through the door—eggs, butter, yogurt, and mayonnaise already flying through the air, splattering against your front window, the pavement outside, the cars in the parking lot, amid chants of "Food fight! Food fight!"—they split up, some going to the left, others to the right, everybody disappearing.

Gurney and his crew had arrived in Turin by a large minibus that they had hired in London. The bus was called Eddie; the group was called Eddie and the Forty Thieves.

Forty Thieves?

They explained. Their adventures began in Calais. At the first bar they entered, the cashier was on a lunch break, and they popped open a cash register with an umbrella and came away with four thousand francs. They carried on, traveling south and then along the French coast, robbing a succession of small shops on the way, never paying for gas or food, entering and leaving restaurants en masse, always on the lookout "for a profit." I noticed that each member of the Eddie-and-the-Forty-Thieves team was wearing sunglasses—filched, I was told, from a French gas station that had a sideline in tourist goods that, it would appear, also included brightly colored Marilyn Monroe T-shirts. All of them were wearing Rolex watches.

Most of the supporters on the square had not been on the plane. How had they gotten here?

They went through a list.

Daft Donald hadn't made it. He had been arrested in Nice (stealing from a clothing shop), and, proving his nickname, was found to be in possession of one can of mace, eighteen Stanley knives (they fell out when he was searched), and a machete.

Robert the Sneak Thief had been delayed—his ferry had been turned back following a fight with Nottingham Forest fans—but he had gotten a flight to Nice and would be coming by taxi.

A taxi from Nice to Turin?

Robert, I was told, always had money (if you see what I mean), and, although I didn't entirely (see what he meant), I didn't have the chance to find out more because they were well down their list.

Sammy? ("Not here but he won't miss Juventus." "Sammy? Impossible.")

Mad Harry? ("Getting too old.")

Teapot? ("Been here since Friday.")

Berlin Red? ("Anybody seen Berlin Red?")

Scotty? ("Arrested last night.")

Barmy Bernie? ("Inside." "Barmy Bernie is inside again?") Whereupon there followed the long, moving story of Barmy Bernie, who, with twenty-seven convictions, had such a bad record that he got six months for loitering. Everyone shook his head in commiseration for the sad, sad fate of Barmy Bernie.

Someone from another group appeared, showing me a map with an inky blue line tracing the route to Turin. It began in Manchester, then continued through London, Stockholm, Hamburg, Frankfurt, Lyon, Marseilles, and finally stopped here. A great adventure, not unlike, I reflected, the Grand Tour that young men had made in the eighteenth and nineteenth centuries, and it had cost them—all eleven of them—a total of seven pounds.

Seven pounds, I exclaimed, understanding the principle. What went wrong?

They assured me they would be in profit on the return.

The circle of supporters who now surrounded me had grown to a considerable size, with one or two regularly disappearing and returning with cans of lager. I had ceased to be the CIA. I was no longer the hack from the *Express*. I appeared to have ended my tenure as an undercover officer of the British Special Branch. And I was starting to be accepted. I would learn later that I had earned a new status; I had become a "good geezer." Yes, that's what I was: a good geezer. What a thing.

I was also someone to whom people needed to tell their stories. There was an implicit responsibility emerging. I was being asked to set the record straight. I was the "repoyta." I was given instructions, imperatives, admonitions. I was told:

That they weren't hooligans.

That it was a disgrace that there were so many obstacles keeping them from supporting their team properly.

That they weren't hooligans.

That the management of Manchester United was a disgrace.

That they weren't hooligans.

Until finally I was telling them, yes, yes, I know, I know, I know: you're just here for the drink and the laugh and the football, and, for the first time, despite myself, I wanted to believe it. I was starting to like them, if only because they were starting to like me (the irrational mechanism of the group at work, and I was feeling grateful just to be accepted by it). And it *was* true that no one had been violent. People had been loud, grotesque, disgusting, rude, uncivilized, unpleasant to look at and, in some instances, explicitly repellent—but not violent. And it was possible that they wouldn't be. It didn't suit my purposes that everyone here should be nothing more than a fanatical fan of the game, but it was conceivable that there really would be no violence, that this was simply how normal English males behaved. It was a terrifying notion, but not an impossible one.

The thing about reporting is that it is meant to be objective. It is meant to record and relay the truth of things, as if truth were out there, hanging around, waiting for the reporter to show up. Such is the premise of objective journalism. What this premise excludes, as any student of modern literature will tell you, is that slippery relative fact of the person doing the reporting, the modern notion that there is no such thing as the perceived without someone to do the perceiving, and that to exclude the circumstances surrounding the story is to tell an untruth. These circumstances might include the fact that you've rushed to an airplane, had too much to drink on it, arrived, realized that you are dressed for the tropics when in fact it is about to snow, that you have forgotten your socks, that you have only one contact lens, that you're not going to get the interview anyway, and then, at four-thirty, that you've got to file your story, having had to make most of it up. It could be argued that the circumstances have more than a casual bearing on the truth reported.

I do not want to tell an untruth and feel compelled therefore to note that at this moment, the reporter was aware that the circumstances surrounding his story had become intrusive and significant and that, if unacknowledged, his account of the events that follow would be grossly incomplete. And his circumstances were these: the reporter was very, very drunk.

He could not, therefore, recall much about the bus ride apart from a dim, watery belief that there were fewer people in the bus this time. The other thing he remembers is that he arrived.

When the buses of United supporters pulled up into the cool evening shadow cast by the Stadio Comunale, a large crowd was already there. The fact of the crowd—that it would be waiting for the English—was hard to take in at first.

Thousands of Italian supporters converged on the bus. They surrounded it and were pounding on its sides—jeering, ugly, and angry.

The bus started to rock from side to side. The Italians were trying to push the bus, our bus—the bus that had me inside it—onto its side.

I had not appreciated the importance of the match that evening, the semifinals for the Cup-Winners Cup. It had sold out the day the tickets—seventy thousand of them—had gone on sale, and at that moment all seventy thousand ticket holders seemed to be in view. In my ignorance, I had also not expected to see the English supporters, who were meant to be the hooligans, confronted by Italians who, to my untutored eye, looked like hooligans: their conduct—rushing towards the buses, brandishing flags—was so exaggerated that it was like a caricature of a nineteenth-century mob. Was this how they normally greeted the supporters of visiting teams?

It took a long time for the buses to empty, and fill the area set aside for them outside the stadium, enclosed by a chain-link fence. At some point, during this long wait, the Italian supporters at the very top of the stadium—the top row that could overlook the grounds outside—realized that there was a gaggle of English below them. I remember the moment, looking up into the evening's pink sky, and watching the long, long slow arc of an object hurled from far above as it came closer and closer, gaining speed as it approached, until finally, in those milliseconds before it disclosed its target, I could actually make out what it was—a beer bottle—and then *crash*: it shattered within three feet of one of the supporters.

Distant muted laughter from on high.

I feared what would follow. An English supporter went down, his forehead cut open. Eventually we all became targets, helpless underneath a barrage that consisted principally of beer bottles and oranges. There were so many bottles and so many oranges that the pavement, covered with juice and pulp and skins, was sticky to look at and sparkled from the shattered glass.

When finally we were ushered through a tunnel that led to the ground, police in front and police behind, it became apparent that, while the English supporters may have been accommodated, their accommodation wasn't in the most salubrious part of the stadium. We were heading for the bottom steps of the terraces, directly beneath the very people who had been hurling missiles at us while we waited outside.

I did not like the look of this.

I kept thinking of the journalist from the *Daily Star*, the one who ran off when things got violent. He emerged in my mind now as an unequivocally sympathetic figure. He had, the supporters said, shit himself, and it was worth noting that this phrase had now entered my vocabulary.

I was not, I found myself muttering, going to shit myself.

One by one, we walked from out of the darkness of the tunnel into the blinding light of the ground—the sun, though setting, was at an angle and still shining bright—and it was hard to make out the figures around us. There were not many police—I could see that—and it appeared that Italians had spilled onto the pitch in front of the terraces where we were meant to stand, separated only by a chain-link perimeter fence. Once again things were coming at us from the air: not just bottles and pieces of fruit but also long sticks—the staffs of Juventus flags—firecrackers, and smoke bombs. The first one out of the tunnel, drunk and arrogant and singing about his English pride, was hit on the back of the head by an eight-foot flagpole and he dropped to the concrete terrace. Out of the corner of my eye I saw a Union Jack had been set alight, its flames fanned as it was swirled in the air. I saw this only out of the corner of my eye because I was determined not to look up at the Italians above me, who were hurling things down, or down to the Italians below, who were hurling things up. I had the suspicion that if I happened to make eye contact with anybody I would be rewarded with a knock on the head. Also I didn't want to lose my concentration. Looking straight ahead, I was concentrating very hard on chanting my new refrain.

I will not shit myself. I will not shit myself.

Somehow the match started, was played, ended. And, while it could be said that there was no single serious incident, it could also be said that there was no moment without one. Several people were hurt, and one supporter was taken away to the hospital.

It was a peculiar setting for watching a sporting event, although, oddly, it didn't seem so at the time. The day had consisted of such a strange succession of events that, by this point in the evening, it was the most natural thing in the world to be watching a football game surrounded by policemen: there was one on my left, another on my right, two directly behind me, and five in front. It didn't bother me; it certainly didn't bother the supporters, who, despite the distractions, were watching the match with complete attentiveness. And when Manchester United tied, the goal was witnessed, as it unfolded, by everyone there (except me; I was looking over my shoulder for missiles), and jubilation shot through them, their cheers and songs suddenly tinny and small in that great cavity of the Juventus football ground, its seventy thousand Italians now comprehensively silent. The United supporters jumped up and down, fell over each other, embraced.

But the euphoria was brief. In the final two minutes Juventus scored again. The exhilaration felt but minutes before by that small band of United supporters was now felt—magnified many times—by the seventy thousand Italian fans who, previously humiliated, directed their powerful glee into our corner. The roar was deafening, invading the senses like a bomb.

And with that explosive roar, the mood changed.

What happened next is confusing to recall. Everything started moving at great speed. Everything would continue to move at great speed for many hours. I remember that riot police started kicking one of the supporters who had fallen down. I remember hearing that Sammy had arrived and then coming upon him. He was big, well-dressed, with heavy horn-rimmed glasses that made him look like a physics student, standing underneath the bleachers, his back to the match, an expensive leather bag and camera hanging over his shoulder, having (like Robert) just come from France by taxi.

And I remember some screaming: there had been a stabbing (I didn't see it) and, with the screaming, everyone bolted—animal speed, instinct speed—and pushed past the police and rushed for the exit. But the gate into the tunnel was locked, and the United supporters slammed into it.

It was impossible to get out.

Throughout this last period of the match, I had been hearing a new phrase: "It's going to go off."

It's going to go off, someone said, and his eyes were glassy, as though he had taken a drug.

If this keeps up, I heard another say, then it's going to go off. And the phrase recurred—it's going to go off, it's going to go off—spoken softly, but each time it was repeated it gained authority.

Everyone was pressed against the locked gate, and the police arrived moments later. The police pulled and pushed in one direction, and the supporters pushed in another, wanting to get out. It was shove and counter shove. It was crushing, uncomfortable. The supporters were humorless and determined.

It's going to go off.

People were whispering.

I heard: "Watch out for knives. Zip up your coat."

I heard: "Fill up your pockets."

I heard: "It's going to go off. Stay together. It's going to go off."

I was growing nervous and slipped my notebook into my shirt, up against my chest, and buttoned up my jacket. A chant had started: "United. United. United." The chant was clipped and sure. "United. United. United." The word was repeated, *United*, and, through the repetition, its meaning started changing, pertaining less to a sporting event or a football club and sounding instead like a chant of unity—something political. It had become the chant of a mob.

"United. United. United. United. United. United . . ."

And then it stopped.

There was a terrible screaming, a loud screaming, loud enough to have risen above the chant. The sound was out of place; it was a woman's screaming.

Someone said that it was the mother of the stabbed boy.

The screaming went on. It appeared that a woman had been caught by the rush to get away and swept along by it. I spotted her: she was hemmed in and thrashing about, trying to find some space, some air. She couldn't move towards the exit and couldn't move away from it, and she wasn't going to be able to: the crush was too great, and it wouldn't stay still, surging back and forth by its own volition, beyond the control of anyone in it. She was very frightened. Her scream, piercing and high-pitched, wouldn't stop. She started hyperventilating, taking in giant gulps of air, and her screams undulated with the relentless rhythm of her over-breathing. It was as if she were drowning in her own high-pitched oxygen, swinging her head from side to side, her eyes wild. I thought: Why hasn't she passed out? I was waiting for her to lose consciousness, for her muscles to give up, but she didn't pass out. The scream went on. Nobody around me was saying a word. I could tell that they were thinking what I was thinking, that she was going to have a fit, that she was going to die, there, now, pressed up against them. It went on, desperate and unintelligible and urgent.

And then someone had the sense to lift her up and raise her above his shoulders—it was so obvious—and he passed her to the person in front of him. And he passed her to the person in front of him. And in this way, she was passed, hand to hand, above everyone's heads, still screaming, still flailing, slowly making her way to the exit, and then, once there, the gate was opened to let her out.

And it was all that was needed. Once the gate had been opened, the English supporters surged forwards, pushing her heavily to one side.

I was familiar with the practice of keeping visiting supporters locked inside at the end of a match until everyone had left and of using long lines of police, with horses and dogs, to direct the visitors to their buses. The plan in Turin had been the same, and the police were there, outside the gate, in full riot regalia, waiting for the United supporters. But they weren't ready for what came charging out of the tunnel.

For a start, owing to the trapped woman, the supporters came out earlier than expected and when they emerged, they came out very fast, with police trailing behind, trying to keep up. They came as a mob, with everyone pressed together, hands on the shoulders of the person in front, moving quickly, almost at a sprint, racing down the line of police, helmets and shields and truncheons a peripheral blur. The line of police led to the buses, but just before the bus door someone in the front veered sharply and the mob followed. The police had anticipated this and were waiting. The group turned again, veering in another direction, and rushed out into the space between two of the buses. It came to a sudden stop, and I slammed into the person in front of me, and people slammed into me from behind: the police had been there as well. Everyone turned around. I don't know who was in front—I was trying only to keep up—and nothing was being said. There were about two hundred people crushed together, but they seemed able to move in unison, like some giant, strangely coordinated insect. A third direction was tried. The police were not there. I looked behind: the police were not there. I looked to the left and the right: there were no police anywhere.

What was the duration of what followed? It might have been twenty minutes; it seemed longer. It was windy and dark, and the trees, blowing back and forth in front of the street lamps, cast long, moving shadows. I was never able to see clearly.

I knew to follow Sammy. The moment the group broke free, he had handed his bag and camera to someone, telling him to give them back later at the hotel. Sammy then turned and started running backwards. He appeared to be measuring the group, taking in its size.

The energy, he said, still running backwards, speaking to no one in particular, the energy is very high. He was alert, vital, moving constantly, looking in all directions. He was holding out his hands, with his fingers outstretched.

Feel the energy, he said.

There were six or seven younger supporters jogging beside him, and it would be some time before I realized that there were always six or seven younger supporters jogging beside him. When he turned in one direction, they turned with him. When he ran backwards, they ran backwards. No doubt if Sammy had suddenly become airborne there would have been the sight of six or seven younger supporters desperately flapping their arms trying to do the same. The younger supporters were in fact very young. At first I put their age at around sixteen, but they might have been younger. They might have been fourteen. They might have been nine: I take pleasure, even now, in thinking of them as nothing more than overgrown nine-year-olds. They were nasty little nine-year-olds who, in some kind of prepubescent confusion, regarded Sammy as their dad.

Sammy had stopped running backwards and had developed a kind of walk-run, which involved moving as quickly as possible without breaking into an outright sprint. Everybody else did the same. The idea, it seemed, was to be inconspicuous—not to be seen to be actually running, thus attracting the attention of the police—but nevertheless to jet along as fast as you could. The effect was ridiculous: two hundred English supporters, tattooed torsos tilted slightly forwards, arms straight, hurtling stiffly down the sidewalk, believing that nobody was noticing them.

Everyone crossed the street, decisively, without a word spoken. A chant broke out—"United, United, United"—and Sammy waved his hands up and down, as if trying to bat down the flames of a fire, urging people to be quiet. A little later there was another one-word chant. This time it was "England." They couldn't help themselves. They wanted so badly to act like normal football supporters—they wanted to sing and behave drunkenly and carry on doing the same rude things that they had been doing all day long—and they had to be reminded that they couldn't. Why this pretense of being invisible? There was Sammy again, whispering, insistent: no singing, no singing, waving his hands up and down. The nine-year-olds made a shushing sound to enforce the message.

Sammy said to cross the street again—he had seen something—and his greasy little companions went off in different directions, fanning out, as if to hold the group in place, and then returned to their positions beside him. It was only then that I appreciated fully what I was witnessing: Sammy had taken charge of the group—moment by moment giving it specific instructions—and was using his obsequious little lads to ensure that his commands were being carried out.

I remembered, on my first night with Mick, hearing that leaders had their little lieutenants and sergeants. I had heard this and I had noted it, but I hadn't thought much of it. It sounded too much like toyland, like a war game played by schoolboys. But here, now, I could see that everything Sammy said was being enforced by his entourage of little supporters. The nine-year-olds made sure that no one ran, that no one sang, that no one strayed far from the group, that everyone stayed together. At one moment, a cluster of police came rushing towards us, and Sammy, having spotted them, whispered a new command, hissing that we were to disperse, and the members of the group split up—some crossing the street, some carrying on down the center of it, some falling behind—until they had got past the policemen, whereupon Sammy turned around, running backwards again, and ordered everyone to regroup: and the little ones, like trained dogs, herded the members of the group back together.

I trotted along. Everyone was moving at such a speed that, to ensure I didn't miss anything, I concentrated on keeping up with Sammy. I could see that this was starting to irritate him. He kept having to notice me.

What are you doing here? he asked me, after he had turned around again, running backwards, doing a quick head count after everyone had regrouped.

He knew precisely what I was doing there, and he had made a point of asking his question loudly enough that the others had to hear it as well.

Just the thing, I thought.

Fuck off, one of his runts said suddenly, peering into my face. He had a knife.

"Didja hear what he said, mate? He said fuck off. What the fuck are you doing here anyway, eh? Fuck off."

It was not the time or the occasion to explain why I was there, and, having got this far, I wasn't about to turn around now.

I dropped back a bit, just outside of striking range. I looked about me. I didn't recognize anyone. I was surrounded by people I hadn't met; worse, I was surrounded by people I hadn't met who kept telling me to fuck off. I felt I had understood the drunkenness I had seen earlier in the day. But this was different. If anyone here was drunk, he was not acting as if he was. Everyone was purposeful and precise, and there was a strong quality of aggression about them, like some kind of animal scent. Nobody was saying a word. There was a muted grunting and the sound of their feet on the pavement; every now and then, Sammy would whisper one of his commands.

I had no idea where we were, but, thinking about it now, I see that Sammy must have been leading his group around the stadium, hoping to find Italian supporters along the way. When he turned to run backwards, he must have been watching the effect his group of two hundred walk-running Frankensteins was having on the Italian lads, who spotted the English rushing by and started following them, curious, attracted by the prospect of a fight or simply by the charisma of the group itself, unable to resist tagging along to see what might happen.

And then Sammy, having judged the moment to be right, suddenly stopped, and, abandoning all pretense of invisibility, shouted: "Stop."

Everyone stopped.

"Turn."

Everyone turned. They knew what to expect. I didn't. It was only then that I saw the Italians who had been following us. In the half-light, streetlight darkness I couldn't tell how many there were, but there were enough for me to realize—holy shit!—that I was now unexpectedly in the middle of a very big fight: having dropped back to get out of the reach of Sammy and his lieutenants I was in the rear, which, as the group turned, had suddenly become the front.

Adrenaline is one of the body's more powerful chemicals. Seeing the English on one side of me and the Italians on the other, I remember seeming quickly to take on the properties of a small helicopter, rising several feet in the air and moving out of everybody's way. There was a roar, everybody roaring, and the English supporters charged into the Italians.

In the next second I went down. A dark blur and then smack: I got hit on the side of the head by a beer can—a full one—thrown powerfully enough to knock me over. As I got up, two policemen, the only two I saw, came rushing past, and one of them clubbed me on the back of the head. Back down I went. I got up again, and most of the Italians had already run off, scattering in all directions. But many had been tripped up before they got away.

Directly in front of me—so close I could almost reach out to touch his face—a young Italian, a boy really, had been knocked down. As he was getting up, an English supporter pushed the boy down again, ramming his flat hand against the boy's face. He fell back and his head hit the pavement, the back of it bouncing slightly.

Two other Manchester United supporters appeared. One kicked the boy in the ribs. It was a soft sound, which surprised me. You could hear the impact of the shoe on the fabric of the boy's clothing. He was kicked again—this time very hard—and the sound was still soft, muted. The boy reached down to protect himself, to guard his ribs, and the other English supporter then kicked him in the face. This was a soft sound as well, but it was different: you could tell that it was his face that had been kicked and not his body and not something protected by clothing. It sounded gritty. The boy tried to get up and he was pushed back down— sloppily, without much force. Another Manchester United supporter appeared and another and then a third. There were now six, and they all started kicking the boy on the ground. The boy covered his face. I was surprised that I could tell, from the sound, when someone's shoe missed or when it struck the fingers and not the forehead or the nose.

I was transfixed. I suppose, thinking about this incident now, I was close enough to have stopped the kicking. Everyone there was off-balance—with one leg swinging back and forth—and it wouldn't have taken much to have saved the boy. But I didn't. I don't think the thought occurred to me. It was as if time had dramatically slowed down, and each second had a distinct beginning and end, like a sequence of images on a roll of film, and I was mesmerized by each image I saw. Two more Manchester United supporters appeared—there must have been eight by now. It was getting crowded and difficult to get at the boy: they were bumping into each other, tussling slightly. It was hard for me to get a clear view or to say where exactly the boy was now being kicked, but it looked like there were three people kicking him in the head, and the others were kicking him in the body—mainly the ribs but I couldn't be sure. I am astonished by the detail I can recall. For instance, there was no speech, only that soft, yielding sound—although sometimes it was a gravelly, scraping one—of the blows, one after another. The moments between the kicks seemed to increase in duration, to stretch elastically, as each person's leg was retracted and then released for another blow.

The thought of it: eight people kicking the boy at once. At what point is the job completed?

It went on.

The boy continued to try to cushion the blows, moving his hands around to cover the spot were he had just been struck, but he was being hit in too many places to be able to protect himself. His face was now covered with blood, which came from his nose and his mouth, and his hair was matted and wet. Blood was all over his clothing. The kicking went on. On and on and on, that terrible soft sound, with the boy saying nothing, only wriggling on the ground.

A policeman appeared, but only one. Where were the other police? There had been so many before. The policeman came running hard and knocked over two of the supporters, and the others fled, and then time accelerated, no longer slow motion time, but time moving very fast.

We ran off. I don't know what happened to the boy. I then noticed that all around me there were others like him, others who had been tripped up and had their faces kicked.

In the vernacular of the supporters, it had now "gone off." With that first violent exchange, some kind of threshold had been crossed, some notional boundary: on one side of that boundary had been a sense of limits, an ordinary understanding—even among this lot—of what you didn't do; we were now someplace where there would be few limits, where the sense that there were things you didn't do had ceased to exist. It became very violent.

I caught up with Sammy. Sammy was transported. He was snapping his fingers and jogging in place, his legs pumping up and down, and he was repeating the phrase, It's going off, it's going off. Everyone around him was excited. It was an excitement that verged on being something greater, an emotion more transcendent—joy at the very least, but more like ecstasy. There was an intense energy about it; it was impossible not to feel some of the thrill. Somebody near me said that he was happy. He said that he was very, very happy, that he could not remember ever being so happy, and I looked hard at him, wanting to memorize his face so that I might find him later and ask him what it was that made for this happiness, what it was like. It was a strange thought: here was someone who believed that, at this precise moment, following a street scuffle, he had succeeded in capturing one of life's most elusive qualities. But then he, dazed, babbling away about his happiness, disappeared into the crowd and the darkness.

There was more going on than I could assimilate: there were violent noises constantly—something breaking or crashing—and I could never tell where they were coming from. In every direction something was happening. I have no sense of sequence.

There was a row of tables where programs were sold, along with flags, T-shirts, souvenirs, and as the group went by each table was lifted up and overturned. There were scuffles. Two English supporters grabbed an Italian and smashed his face into one of the tables. They grabbed him by the hair on the back of his head and slammed his face into the table again. They lifted his head up a third time, pulling it higher, holding it there—his face was messy and crushed—and slammed it into the table again. Once again the terrible slow motion of it all, the time, not clock time, that elapsed between one moment of violence and the next one, as they lifted his head up—were they really going to do it again?—and smashed it into the table. The English supporters were methodical and serious; no one spoke.

An ambulance drove past. Its siren made me realize that there were still no police.

The group crossed a street, a major intersection. It had long abandoned the pretense of invisibility and had reverted to the arrogant identity of the violent crowd, walking, without hesitation, straight into the congested traffic, across the hoods of the cars, knowing that they would stop. At the head of the traffic was a bus, and one of the supporters stepped up to the front of it, and from about six feet, hurled something with great force—it wasn't a stone; it was big and made of a metal, like the manifold of a car engine—straight into the driver's windshield. I was just behind the one who threw this thing. I don't know where he got it from, because it was too heavy to have been carried for any distance, but no one had helped him with it; he had stepped out of the flow of the group, and in those moments between throwing his heavy object and turning back to his mates, he had a peculiar look on his face. He knew he had done something that no one else had done yet, that it had escalated the violence, that the act had crossed another boundary of what was permissible. He had thrown a missile that was certain to cause serious physical injury. He had done something bad—extremely bad—and his face, while acknowledging the badness of it, was actually saying something more complex. It was saying that what he had done wasn't all that bad, really; in the context of the day, it wasn't that extreme, was it? What his face expressed, I realized—his eyes seemed to twinkle—was no more than this: I have just been naughty.

He had been naughty and he knew it and was pleased about it. He was happy. Another happy one. He was a runt, I thought. He was a little shit, I thought. I wanted to hurt him.

The sound of the shattering windshield—I realize now—was a powerful stimulant, physical and intrusive, and it had been the range of sounds, of things breaking and crashing, coming from somewhere in the darkness, unidentifiable, that was increasing steadily the strength of feeling of everyone around me. It was also what was making me so uneasy. The evening had been a series of stimulants, assaults on the senses, that succeeded, each time, in raising the pitch of excitement. And now, crossing this intersection, traffic coming from four directions, supporters trotting on top of cars, the sound of this thing going through the windshield, the crash following its impact, had the effect of increasing the heat of the feeling: I can't describe it any other way; it was almost literally a matter of temperature. There was another moment of disorientation—the milliseconds between the sensation of the sound and knowing what accounted for it, an adrenaline moment, a chemical moment—and then there was the roar again, and someone came rushing at the bus with a pole (taken from one of the souvenir tables?) and smashed a passenger's window. A second crashing sound. Others came running over and started throwing stones and bottles with great ferocity. They were, again, in a frenzy. The stones bounced off the glass with a shuddering thud, but then a window shattered, and another shattered, and there was screaming from inside. The bus was full, and the passengers were not lads like the ones attacking them but ordinary family supporters, dads and sons and wives heading home after the match, on their way to the suburbs or a village outside the city. Everyone inside must have been covered with glass. They were shielding their faces, ducking in their seats. There were glass splinters everywhere: they would cut across your vision suddenly. All around me people were throwing stones and bottles, and I felt afraid for my own eyes.

We moved on.

I felt weightless. I felt nothing would happen to me. I felt that anything might happen to me. I was looking straight ahead, running, trying to keep up, and things were occurring along the dark peripheries of my vision: there would be a bright light and then darkness again and the sound, constantly, of something else breaking, and of movement, of objects being thrown and of people falling.

A group of Italians appeared, suddenly stepping forward into the glare of a street lamp. They were different from the others, clearly intending to fight, full of pride and affronted dignity. They wanted confrontation and stood there waiting for it. Someone came towards us swinging a pool cue or a flag-pole, and then, confounding all sense, it was actually grabbed from out of his hands—it was Roy; Roy had appeared out of nowhere and had taken the pole out of the Italian's hands—and broken it over his head. It was flamboyantly timed, and the next moment the other English supporters followed, that roar again, quickly overcoming the Italians, who ran off in different directions. Several, again, were tripped up. There was the sight, again, of Italians on the ground, wriggling helplessly while English supporters rushed up to them, clustering around their heads, kicking them over and over again.

Is it possible that there were simply no police?

Again we moved on. A trash bin was thrown through a car show-room window, and there was another loud crashing sound. A shop: its door was smashed. A clothing shop: its window was smashed, and one or two English supporters lingered to loot from the display.

I looked behind me and I saw that a large vehicle had been over-turned, and that further down the street flames were issuing from a building. I hadn't seen any of that happen: I realized that there had been more than I had been able to take in. There was now the sound of sirens, many sirens, different kinds, coming from several directions.

The city is ours, Sammy said, and he repeated the possessive, each time with greater intensity: It is *ours*, *ours*, *ours*.

A police car appeared, its siren on—the first police car I had seen—and it stopped in front of the group, trying to cut it off. There was only one car. The officer threw open his door, but by the time he had gotten out the group had crossed the street. The officer shouted after us, helpless and angry, and then dropped back inside his car and chased us down, again cutting us off. Once again, the group, in the most civilized manner possible, crossed the street: well-behaved foot-ball supporters on their way back to their hotel, flames receding be-hind us. The officer returned to his car and drove after us, this time accelerating dangerously, once again cutting off the group, trying, it seemed to me, to knock down one of the supporters, who had to jump out of the way and who was then grabbed by the police officer and hurled against the hood, held there by his throat. The officer was very frustrated. He knew that this group was responsible for the damage he had seen; he knew, beyond all reasonable doubt, that the very lad whose throat was now in his grip had been personally responsible for mayhem of some categorically illegal kind, but the officer had not personally seen him do anything. He hadn't personally seen the group do anything. He had not seen anyone commit a crime. He saw only the results. He kept the supporter pinned there, holding him by the throat, and then in disgust he let him go.

A fire engine passed, an ambulance, and finally the police—many police. They came from two directions. And once they started arriving, it seemed that they would never stop. There were vans and cars and motorcycles and paddy wagons. And still they came. The buildings were illuminated by their flashing blue lights. But the group of supporters from Manchester, governed by Sammy's whispered commands, simply kept moving, slipping past the cars, dispersing when needing to disperse and then regrouping, turning this way, that way, crossing the street again, regrouping, reversing, with Sammy's greasy little lieutenants bringing up the rear, keeping everyone together. They were well-behaved fans of the sport of football. They were once again the law-abiding supporters they had always insisted to me that they were.

CRAZY THINGS SEEM NORMAL, NORMAL THINGS SEEM CRAZY

Chuck Klosterman

When I was leaving Val Kilmer's ranch house, he gave me a present. He found a two-page poem he had written about a melancholy farmer, and he ripped it out of the book it was in (in 1988, Val apparently published a book of free-verse poetry called *My Edens After Burns*). He taped the two pages of poetry onto a piece of cardboard and autographed it, which I did not ask him to do. "This is my gift to you," he said. I still possess this gift. Whenever I stumble across those two pages, I reread Val Kilmer's poem. Its theme is somewhat murky. In fact, I can't even tell if the writing is decent or terrible; I've asked four other people to analyze its merits, and the jury remain polarized. But this is what I will always wonder: Why did Val Kilmer give me *this* poem? Why didn't he just give me the entire book? Was Kilmer trying to tell me something?

The man did not lack confidence.

CRAZY THINGS SEEM NORMAL,
NORMAL THINGS SEEM CRAZY
JULY 2005

"I just like looking at them," Val Kilmer tells me as we stare at his bison. "I liked looking at them when I was a kid, and I like looking at them now." The two buffalo are behind a fence, twenty-five feet away. A fifteen-hundred-pound bull stares back at us, bored and tired; he stomps his right hoof, turns 180 degrees, and defecates in our general direction. "Obviously, we are not seeing these particular buffalo at their most noble of moments," Kilmer adds, "but I still like looking at them. Maybe it has something to do with the fact that I'm part Cherokee. There was such a relationship between the buffalo and the American Indian—the Indians would eat them, live inside their pelts, use every part of the body. There was almost no separation between the people and the animal."

Val Kilmer tells me he used to own a dozen buffalo, but now he's down to two. Val says he named one of these remaining two ungulates James Brown, because it likes to spin around in circles and looks like the kind of beast who might beat up his wife. I have been talking to Kilmer for approximately three minutes; it's 5:20 p.m. on April Fool's Day. Twenty-four hours ago, I was preparing to fly to Los Angeles to interview Kilmer on the Sunset Strip; this was because Val was supposedly leaving for Switzerland (for four months) on April 3. Late last night, these plans changed entirely: suddenly, Val was not going to be in L.A. Instead, I was instructed to fly to New Mexico, where someone would pick me up at the Albuquerque airport and drive me to his six-thousand-acre ranch. However, when I arrived in Albuquerque this afternoon, I received a voicemail on my cell phone; I was now told to rent a car and drive to the ranch myself. Curiously, his ranch is not outside Albuquerque (which I assumed would be the case, particularly since Val himself suggested I fly into the Albuquerque airport). His ranch is actually outside of Santa Fe, which is seventy-three miles away. He's also no longer going to Switzerland; now he's going to London.

The drive to Santa Fe on I-25 is mildly Zen: there are public road signs that say Gusty Winds May Exist. This seems more like lazy philosophy than travel advice. When I arrive in New Mexico's capital city, I discover that Kilmer's ranch is still another thirty minutes away, and the directions on how to arrive there are a little confusing; it takes at least forty-five minutes before I find the gate to his estate. The gate is closed. There is no one around for miles, the sky is huge, and my cell phone no longer works; this, I suppose, is where the buffalo roam (and where roaming rates apply). I locate an intercom phone outside the green steel gate, but most of the numbers don't work. When an anonymous male voice finally responds to my desperate pleas for service, he is terse. "Who are you meeting?" the voice mechanically barks. "What is this regarding?" I tell him I am a reporter, and that I am there to find Val Kilmer, and that Mr. Kilmer knows I am coming. There is a pause, and then he says something I don't really understand: "Someone will meet you at the bridge!" The gate swings open automatically, and I drive through its opening. I expect the main residence to be near the entrance, but it is not; I drive at least two miles on a gravel road. Eventually, I cross a wooden bridge and park the vehicle. I see a man driving toward me on a camouflaged ATV four-wheeler. The man looks like a cross between Jeff Bridges and Thomas Haden Church, which means that this is the man I am looking for. He parks next to my rental car; I roll down the window. He is smiling, and his teeth are huge. I find myself staring at them.

"Welcome to the West," the teeth say. "I'm Val Kilmer. Would you like to see the buffalo?"

✳ ✳ ✳

"I've never been that comfortable talking about myself, or about acting," the forty-five-year-old Kilmer says. It's 7:00 p.m. We are now sitting in his lodge, which is more rustic than I anticipated. We are surrounded by unfinished wood and books about trout fishing, and an African kudu head hangs from the wall. There seem to be a lot of hoofed animals on this ranch, and many of them are dead. Kilmer's friendly ranch hand (a fortyish woman named Pam Sawyer) has just given me a plateful of Mexican food I never really wanted, so Val is eating it for me. He is explaining why he almost never gives interviews and why he doesn't like talking about himself, presumably because I am interviewing him and he is about to talk about himself for the next four hours. "For quite a while, I thought that it didn't really matter if I defended myself [to journalists], so a lot of things kind of snowballed when I didn't rebuke them. And I mainly didn't do a lot of interviews because they're hard, and I was sort of super-concerned. When you're young, you're always concerned about how you're being seen and how you're being criticized."

I have not come to New Mexico to criticize Val Kilmer. However, he seems almost disturbingly certain of that fact, which is partially why he invited me here. Several months ago, I wrote a column where I made a passing reference about Kilmer being "Advanced." What this means is that I find Kilmer's persona compelling, and that I think he makes choices other actors would never consider, and that he is probably my favorite working actor. This is all true. However, Kilmer took this column to mean that I am his biggest fan on the planet, and that he can trust me entirely, and that I am among his closest friends. From the moment we look at his buffalo, he is completely relaxed and cooperative; he immediately introduces me to his children, Mercedes (age thirteen) and Jack (age ten). They live with their British mother (Kilmer's ex-wife Joanne Whalley, his costar from *Willow*) in Los Angeles, but they apparently spend a great chunk of time on this ranch; they love it here, despite the fact that it doesn't have a decent television. Along with the bison, the farmstead includes horses, a dog, two cats, and (as of this afternoon) five baby chickens, one of which will be eaten by a cat before the night is over. The Kilmer clan is animal crazy; the house smells like a veterinarian's office. Jack is predominantly consumed with the chicks in the kitchen and the trampoline in the backyard. Mercedes is an artist and a John Lennon fan; she seems a little too smart to be thirteen. When I ask her what her favorite Val Kilmer movie is, she says, "Oh, probably *Batman Forever*, but only because it seems like it was secretly made by Andrew Lloyd Webber."

For the first forty-five minutes I am there, the five of us—Kilmer, his two kids, Pam the ranch hand, and myself—occupy the main room of the ranch house and try to make casual conversation, which is kind of like making conversation with friendly strangers in a wooden airport. Mercedes has a lot of questions about why Kilmer is "Advanced," and Val mentions how much he enjoys repeating the word *Advanced* over and over and over again. He tells me about an *Afterschool Special* he made in 1983 called "One Too Many," where he played a teenage alcoholic alongside Mare Winningham (his first teenage girlfriend) and Michelle Pfeiffer (a woman he would later write poetry for). I mention that he seems to play a lot of roles where he's a drug-addled drunk, and he agrees that this is true. In fact, before I got here, I unconsciously assumed Val would be a drug-addled drunk during this interview, since every story I've ever heard about Kilmer implies that he's completely crazy; he supposedly burned a cameraman with a cigarette on the set of *The Island of Dr. Moreau*. There are a few directors (most notably Joel Schumacher) who continue to paint him as the most egocentric, unreasonable human in Hollywood. As far as I can tell, this cannot possibly be accurate. If I had to describe Kilmer's personality in one word (and if I couldn't use the word *Advanced*), I would have to employ the least incendiary of all potential modifiers: Val Kilmer is *nice*. The worst thing I could say about him is that he's kind of a name-dropper; beyond that, he seems like an affable fellow with a good sense of humor, and he is totally not fucked up.

But he is *weird*.

He's weird in ways that are expected, and he's weird in ways that are not. I anticipated that he might seem a little odd when we talked about the art of acting, mostly because (a) Kilmer is a Method actor, and (b) all Method actors are insane. However, I did not realize how much insanity this process truly required. That started to become clear when I asked him about *The Doors* and *Wonderland*, two movies where Kilmer portrays self-destructive drug addicts with an acute degree of realism; there is a scene late in *Wonderland* where he wordlessly (and desperately) waits for someone to offer him cocaine in a manner that seems painfully authentic. I ask if he ever went through a drug phase for real. He says no.

He says he's never freebased cocaine in his life; he was simply interested in "exploring acting," but that he understands the mind-set of addiction. The conversation evolves into a meditation on the emotional toll that acting takes on the artist. To get a more specific example, I ask him about the "toll" that he felt while making the 1993 Western *Tombstone*. He begins telling me about things that tangibly happened to Doc Holliday. I say, "No, no, you must have misunderstood me—I want to know about the toll it took on *you*." He says, "I know, I'm talking about those feelings." And this is the conversation that follows:

CK: You mean you think you literally had the same experience as Doc Holliday?

KILMER: Oh, sure. It's not like I believed that I actually shot somebody, but I absolutely know what it feels like to pull the trigger and take someone's life.

CK: So you're saying you understand how it feels to shoot someone as much as a person who has actually committed a murder?

KILMER: I understand it more. It's an actor's job. A guy who's lived through the horror of Vietnam has not spent his life preparing his mind for it. Most of these guys were borderline criminal or poor, and that's why they got sent to Vietnam. It was all the poor, wretched kids who got beat up by their dads, guys that didn't get on the football team, guys who couldn't finagle a scholarship. They didn't have the emotional equipment to handle that experience. But this is what an actor trains to do. So—standing onstage—I can more effectively represent that kid in Vietnam than a guy who was there.

CK: I don't question that you can more effectively *represent* that experience, but that's not the same thing. If you were talking to someone who's in prison for murder, and the guy said, "Man, it really fucks you up to kill another person," do you think you could reasonably say, "I completely know what you're talking about"?

KILMER: Oh yeah. I'd know what he's talking about.

203

CK: You were in *Top Gun*. Does this mean you completely understand how it feels to be a fighter pilot?

KILMER: I understand it more. I don't have a fighter pilot's pride. Pilots actually go way past actors' pride, which is pretty high. Way past rock 'n' roll pride, which is even higher. They're in their own class.

CK: Let's say someone made a movie about you—Val Kilmer— and they cast Jude Law[1] in the lead role. By your logic, wouldn't this mean that Jude Law—if he did a successful job—would therefore understand what it means to be Val Kilmer more than you do?

KILMER: No, because I'm an actor. Those other people that are in those other circumstances don't have the self-knowledge.

CK: Well, what if it was a movie about your young life? What if it was a movie about your teen years?

KILMER: In that case, I guess I'd have to say yes. No matter what the circumstances are, it's all relative. I think Gandhi had a sense of mission about himself that was spiritual. He found himself in political circumstances, but he became a great man. Most of that story in the film *Gandhi* is about the politics; it's about the man leading his nation to freedom. But I know that Sir Ben Kingsley understood the story of Gandhi to be that personal journey of love. It would be impossible to portray Gandhi as he did—which was perfectly—without having the same experience he put into his body. You can't *act* that.

CK: Okay, so let's assume you had been given the lead role in *The Passion of the Christ*. Would you understand the feeling of being crucified as much as someone who had been literally crucified as the Messiah?

---

1. I have no idea why I would cast Jude Law in this role, particularly if Heath Ledger were available.

KILMER: Well, I just played Moses [in a theatrical version of *The Ten Commandments*]. Of course.

CK: So you understand the experience of being Moses? You understand how it feels to be Moses? Maybe I'm just taking your words too literally.

KILMER: No, I don't think so. That's what acting is.

I keep asking Kilmer if he is joking, and he swears he is not. However, claiming that he's not joking might be part of the joke. A few weeks after visiting the ranch, I paraphrased the preceding conversation to Academy Award–winning conspiracy theorist Oliver Stone, the man who directed Kilmer in 1991's *The Doors* and 2004's *Alexander*. He did not find our exchange surprising.

"This has always been the issue with Val," Stone said via cell phone as his son drove him around Los Angeles. "He speaks in a way that is propelled from deep inside, and he doesn't always realize how the things he says will sound to other people. But there *is* a carryover effect from acting. You can never really separate yourself from what you do, and Val is ultrasensitive to that process."

Stone says Kilmer has substantially matured over the years, noting that the death of Kilmer's father in 1993 had an immediate impact on his emotional flexibility. "We didn't have the greatest relationship when we made *The Doors*," he says. "I always thought he was a technically brilliant actor, but he was difficult. He can be moody. But when we did *Alexander,* Val was an absolute pleasure to work with. I think part of his problems with *The Doors* was that he just got sick of wearing leather pants every day."

Kilmer and his two kids are playing with the cats. Because there are two of these animals (Ernest and Refrigerator), the living room takes on a *Ghost and the Darkness* motif. While they play with the felines, Val casually mentions he awoke that morning at 4:00 a.m. to work on a screenplay, but that he went back to bed at 6:00 a.m. His schedule is unconventional. A few hours later, I ask him about the movie he's writing.

"Well, it's a woman's story," he says cautiously. "It's about this woman who was just fighting to survive, and everything happened to her."

I ask him if this is a real person; he says she is. "Her first husband died. Her own family took her son away from her. She marries a guy because he promises to help her get the son back, and then he doesn't. The new husband is a dentist, but he won't even fix her teeth. She ends up divorcing him because he gets captured in the Civil War. She meets a homeopathic guy who's probably more of a mesmerist hypnotist. For the first time in her life, at forty-two years old, she's feeling good. But then she slips on the ice and breaks every bone in her body, and the doctor and the priest say she should be dead. But she has this experience while she's praying and she gets up. People literally thought they were seeing a ghost. And then she spent the rest of her life trying to articulate what had happened to her. How was she healed? That's what the story is about: the rest of her life. Because she lived until she was ninety and became the most famous lady in the United States."

His vision for this film is amazingly clear, and he tells me the story with a controlled, measured intensity. I ask him the name of the woman. He says, "Mary Baker Eddy. She died in 1910." We talk a little more about this idea (he'd love to see Cate Blanchett in the lead role), but then the conversation shifts to the subject of *Common Sense* author Thomas Paine, whom Kilmer thinks should be the subject of Oliver Stone's next movie.

It is not until the next morning that I realize Mary Baker Eddy was the founder of the *Christian Science Monitor*, and that Val Kilmer is a Christian Scientist.

"Well, that is what I am trying to be," he says while we sit on his back porch and look at the bubbling blueness of the Pecos River. "It is quite a challenging faith, but I don't think I'm hedging. I just think I am being honest."

There are many facets to Christian Science, but most people only concern themselves with one: Christian Scientists do not take medicine. They believe that healing does not come from internal processes or from the power of the mortal mind; they believe healing comes from the Divine Mind of God. Growing up in Los Angeles, this is how Kilmer was raised by his parents. This belief becomes more complex when you consider the context of the Kilmer family: the son of an engineer and a housewife, Val had two brothers. They lived on the outskirts of L.A., neighbors to the likes of Roy Rogers. Over time, the family splintered. Val's parents divorced, and he remains estranged from his older brother over a business dispute that happened more than ten years ago ("We have a much better relationship not speaking," Val says). His younger brother, Wesley, died as a teenager; Wesley had an epileptic seizure in a swimming pool (Val was seventeen at the time, about to go to school at Juilliard). I ask him if his brother's epilepsy was untreated at the time of his death.

"Well, this is a complicated answer," he says. "He was treated periodically. There is a big misnomer with Christian Science; I think maybe that misnomer is fading. People used to say, 'Christian Science. Oh, you're the ones that don't believe in doctors,' which is not a true thing. It's just a different way of treating a malady. It could be mental, social, or physical. In my little brother's case, when he was diagnosed, my parents were divorced. My father had him diagnosed and Wesley was given some medical treatment for his epilepsy. When he was in school, they would stop the treatment. Then periodically, he would go back and forth between Christian Science and the medical treatment."

I ask him what seems like an obvious question: Isn't it possible that his brother's death happened when he was being untreated, and that this incident could have been avoided?

"Christian Science isn't responsible for my little brother's death," he says, and I am in no position to disagree.

We're still sitting on his porch, and his daughter walks past us. I ask Val if he would not allow her to take amoxicillin if she had a sore throat; he tells me that—because he's divorced—he doesn't have autonomous control over that type of decision. But he says his first move in such a scenario would be to pray, because most illness comes from fear. We start talking about the cult of Scientology, which he has heard is "basically Christian Science without God." We begin discussing what constitutes the definition of religion; Kilmer thinks an institution cannot be classified as a religion unless God is involved. When I argue that this is not necessarily the case, Val walks into the house and brings out the *Oxford English Dictionary*; I'm not sure how many working actors own their own copy of the OED, but this one does. The print in the OED is minuscule, so he begins scouring the pages like Sherlock Holmes. He pores over the tiny words with a magnifying glass that has an African boar's tusk as a handle. He finds the definition of *religion*, but the OED's answer is unsatisfactory. He decides to check what *Webster's Second Unabridged Dictionary* has to say, since he insists that *Webster's Second* was the last dictionary created without an agenda. We spend the next fifteen minutes looking up various words, including *monastic*.

So this, I suppose, is an illustration of how Val Kilmer is weird in unexpected ways: he's a Christian Scientist, and he owns an inordinate number of reference books.

I ask Val Kilmer if he agrees that his life is crazy. First he says no, but then he (kind of) says yes.

"I make more money than the whole state of New Mexico," he says. "If you do the math, I've probably made as much as six hundred thousand or eight hundred thousand people in this state. And I know that's crazy. You know, I live on a ranch that's larger than Manhattan. That's a weird circumstance." Now, this is something of a hyperbole; the island of Manhattan is 14,563 acres of real estate, which is more than twice as large as Val's semiarid homestead. But his point is still valid—he's got a big fucking backyard, and that's a weird circumstance. "The thing I'm enjoying more is that there are lots of things that fame has brought me that I can use to my advantage in a quiet way. For example, a friend of mine is an amazing advocate for trees. He's so incredible and selfless. He's planted [something like] twenty million trees in Los Alamos. I actually got to plant the twenty-millionth tree. And we got more attention for doing that simply because I've made some movies and I'm famous."

Kilmer's awareness of his fame seems to partially derive from his familiarity with other famous people. During the two days we spend together, he casually mentions dozens of celebrities he classifies as friends—Robert DeNiro, Nelson Mandela, Steve-O. Val tells me that he passed on the lead role in *The Insider* that eventually went to Russell Crowe; he tells me he dreams of making a comedy with Will Ferrell, whom he considers a genius. At one point, Kilmer does a flawless Marlon Brando impersonation, even adjusting the timbre of his voice to illustrate the subtle difference between the '70s Brando from *Last Tango in Paris* and the '90s Brando from *Don Juan DeMarco*. We talk about his longtime camaraderie with Kevin Spacey, and he says that Spacey is "proof that you can learn how to act. Because he was horrible when he first started, and now he's so good." We talk about the famous women he's dated; the last serious relationship he had was with Darryl Hannah, which ended a year ago. During the 1990s, he was involved with Cindy Crawford, so I ask him what it's like to sleep with the most famous woman in the world. His short answer is that it's awesome. His long answer is that it's complicated.

"Cindy is phenomenally comfortable in the public scene," Kilmer says. "I never accepted that responsibility. If you're the lead in a film, you have a responsibility to the company and the studio. With a great deal of humor, Cindy describes herself as being in advertising. She's an icon in it; we actually talked about her image in relation to the product. And I was uncomfortable with that. We got in a huge fight one night because of a hat she was wearing. The hat advertised a bar, and I used to be so unreasonable about that kind of thing. I had a certain point of view about the guy who owned the bar, and I was just being unreasonable. I mean, she knows what she's doing, and she's comfortable with it. But I knew we were going to go to dinner and that we'd get photographed with this hat, and I was just hard to deal with. It was a really big deal."

This is the kind of insight that makes talking to an established movie star so unorthodox: Kilmer remembers that his girlfriend wearing a certain hat was a big deal, but he doesn't think it was a big deal that the girlfriend was Cindy Crawford. Crazy things seem normal, normal things seem crazy. He mentions that he is almost embarrassed by how cliché his life has become, despite the fact that the manifestation of this cliché includes buffalo ownership. However, there are certain parts of his life that even he knows are strange. This is most evident when—apropos of nothing—he starts talking about Bob Dylan.

"I am a friend of Bob's, as much as Bob has friends," Kilmer says. "Bob is a funny guy. He is the funniest man I know." Apparently, Dylan loved *Tombstone* so much that he decided to spend an afternoon hanging out in Kilmer's hotel room, later inviting Val into the recording studio with Eric Clapton and casting him in the film *Masked and Anonymous.* Much like his ability to mimic Brando, Kilmer is able to impersonate Dylan's voice with detailed exactness and loves re-creating conversations the two of them have had. What he seems to admire most about Dylan is that—more than anything else—Bob Dylan never appears to care what anyone thinks of him. And that is something Val Kilmer still cares about (even though he'd like to argue otherwise).

"I never cultivated a personality," he says, which is something I am skeptical of, but something I cannot disprove. "Almost everyone that is really famous has cultivated a personality. I can safely say that no one who has ever won an Oscar didn't want to win an Oscar. I think that Bob Dylan would have loved to win a Grammy during all those years when he knew he was doing his best work. Advanced or not, he was certainly ahead of his time, and he was more worthy than whoever won. . . . Dylan was doing stuff that was so new that everyone hated it. Like when he started playing the electric guitar, for example: he toured for a year, and he was booed every night. Onstage, I could never take three performances in a row and be booed. I just don't think I'm that strong. I think that I would just go to the producers of the play and say, 'Well, we tried, but we failed to entertain here.' But Dylan spent a year being booed. They were throwing bottles at him. And he still can't play it! Forty years later, he is still trying to play the electric guitar. I mean, he has a dedication to an ideal that I can't comprehend."

On the shores of the Pecos River, nothing is as it seems: Kevin Spacey was once a terrible actor, Bob Dylan remains a terrible guitar player, and Val Kilmer is affable and insecure. Crazy things seem normal, normal things seem crazy. Gusty winds may exist.

HOST

David Foster Wallace

★ ★ ★

1

Mr. John Ziegler, thirty-seven, late of Louisville's WHAS, is now on the air, "Live and Local," from 10:00 P.M. to 1:00 A.M. every weeknight on southern California's KFI, a 50,000-watt megastation whose hourly ID and Sweeper, designed by the station's Imaging department and featur-

FCC regulations require a station ID to be broadcast every hour. This ID comprises a station's call letters, band and frequency, and the radio market it's licensed to serve. Just about every serious commercial station (which KFI very much is) appends to its ID a Sweeper, which is the little

There are also separate, subsidiary tag lines that KFI develops specially for its local programs. The main two it's using for the *John Ziegler Show* so far are "Live and Local" and "Hot, Fresh Talk Served Nightly."

tag line by which the station wishes to be known. KABC, the other giant AM talk station in Los Angeles, deploys the entendre-rich "Where America Comes First." KFI's own main Sweeper is "More *Stimulating* Talk Radio," but it's also got secondary Sweepers that it uses to intro the half-hour news, traffic updates at seventeen and forty-six past the hour, and station promos. "Southern California's Newsroom," "The Radio Home of Fox News," and "When You See News Break, Don't Try to Fix It Yourself—Leave That to Professionals" are the big three that KFI's running this spring. The content and sound of all IDs, Sweepers, and promos are the responsibility of the station's Imaging department, apparently so named because they involve KFI's image in the LA market. Imaging is sort of the radio version of branding—the Sweepers let KFI communicate its special personality and 'tude in a compressed way.

ing a gravelly basso whisper against licks from Ratt's 1984 metal classic "Round and Round," is "KFI AM-640, Los Angeles—More *Stimulating* Talk Radio." This is either the eighth or ninth host job that Mr. Ziegler's had in his talk-radio career, and far and away the biggest. He moved out here to LA over Christmas—alone,

> The whisperer turns out to be one Chris Corley, a voiceover actor best known for movie trailers. Corley's C^2 Productions is based in Fort Myers FL.

towing a U-Haul—and found an apartment not far from KFI's studios, which are in an old part of the Koreatown district, near Wilshire Center.

The John Ziegler Show is the first local, nonsyndicated late-night program that KFI has aired in a long time. It's something of a gamble for everyone involved. Ten o'clock to one qualifies as late at night in southern California, where hardly anything reputable's open after nine.

It is currently right near the end of the program's second segment on the evening of May 11, 2004, shortly after Nicholas Berg's taped beheading by an al-Qaeda splinter in Iraq. Dressed, as is his custom, for golf, and wearing a white-billed cap w/corporate logo, Mr. Ziegler is seated by himself in the on-air studio, surrounded by monitors and sheaves of Internet downloads. He is trim, clean-shaven, and handsome in the somewhat bland way that top golfers and local TV newsmen tend to be. His eyes, which off-air

> (By the standards of the U.S. radio industry this makes him almost movie-star gorgeous.)

are usually flat and unhappy, are alight now with passionate conviction. Only some of the studio's monitors concern Mr. Z.'s own program; the ones up near the ceiling take muted, closed-caption feeds from Fox News, MSNBC, and what might be C-SPAN. To his big desk's upper left is a wall-mounted digital clock that counts down seconds. His computer monitors' displays also show the exact time.

Across the soundproof glass of the opposite wall, another monitor in the Airmix room is running an episode of *The Simpsons*, also muted, which both the board op and the call screener are watching with half an eye.

Pendent in front of John Ziegler's face, attached to the same type of hinged, flexible stand as certain student desk lamps, is a Shure-brand broadcast microphone that is sheathed in a gray foam filtration sock to soften popped p's and hissed sibilants. It is into this microphone that the host speaks:

"And I'll tell you why—it's because we're *better* than they are."

A Georgetown B.A. in government and philosophy, scratch golfer, former TV sportscaster, possible world-class authority on the O.J. Simpson trial, and sometime contributor to MSNBC's *Scarborough Country*, Mr. Ziegler is referring here to America versus what he terms "the Arab world." It's near the end of his "churn," which is the industry term for a host's opening monologue, whose purpose is both to introduce a show's nightly topics and to get listeners emotionally stimulated enough that they're drawn into the program and don't switch away. More than any other mass medium, radio enjoys a captive audience—if only because so many of the listeners are driving—but in a major market there are dozens of AM stations to listen to, plus of course FM and satellite radio, and even a very seductive and successful station rarely gets more than a five or six percent audience share.

"We're not perfect, we suck a lot of the time, but we are *better* as a people, as a culture, and as a society than they are, and we need to recognize that, so that we can possibly even *begin* to deal with the evil that we are facing."

When Mr. Z.'s impassioned, his voice rises and his arms wave around (which obviously only those in the Airmix room can see). He also fidgets, bobs slightly up and down in his executive desk chair, and weaves. Although he must stay seated and can't pace around the room, the host does not have to keep his mouth any set distance from the microphone, since the board op, 'Mondo Hernandez, can adjust his levels on the mixing board's channel 7 so that Mr. Z.'s volume always stays in range and never peaks or fades. 'Mondo, whose price for letting outside parties hang around Airmix is one large bag of cool ranch Doritos per evening, is an immense twenty-one-year-old man with a ponytail, stony Mesoamerican features, and the placid, grand-motherly eyes common to giant mammals everywhere. Keeping the

'Mondo's lay explanation of what *peaking* is consists of pointing at the red area to the right of the two volumeters' bobbing needles on the mixing board: "It's when the needles go into the red." The overall mission, apparently, is to keep the volume and resonance of a host's voice high enough to be stimulating but not so high that they exceed the capacities of an AM analog signal or basic radio receiver. One reason why callers' voices sound so much less rich and authoritative than hosts' voices on talk radio is that it is harder to keep telephone voices from peaking.

Another reason is mike processing, which evens and fills out the host's voice, removing raspy or metallic tones, and occurs automatically in Airmix. There's no such processing for the callers' voices.

studio signal from *peaking* is one of 'Mondo's prime directives, along with making sure that each of the program's scheduled commercial spots is loaded into Prophet and run at just the right time, whereupon he must confirm that the ad has run as scheduled in the special

Prophet is the special OS for KFI's computer system—"like Windows for a radio station," according to Mr. Ziegler's producer.

Airmix log he signs each page of, so that the station can bill advertis-ers for their spots. 'Mondo, who started out two years ago as an un-paid intern and now earns ten dollars an hour, works 7:00–1:00 on weeknights and also board-ops KFI's special cooking show on Sun-days. As long as he's kept under forty hours a week, which he some-how always just barely is, the station is not obliged to provide 'Mondo with employee benefits.

The Nick Berg beheading and its Internet video compose what is known around KFI as a "Monster," meaning a story that has both high news value and tremendous emotional voltage. As is SOP in political talk radio, the emotions most readily accessed are anger, outrage, indignation, fear, despair, disgust, contempt, and a certain kind of a apocalyptic glee all of which the Nick Berg thing's got in

---

Here is a sample bit of "What the *John Ziegler Show* is All About," a long editorial intro to the program that Mr. Ziegler delivered snippets of over his first several nights in January:

> The underlying premise of the *John Ziegler Show* is that, thanks to its Socialistic leanings, incompetent media, eroding moral foundation, aging demographics, and undereducated masses, the United States, as we know it, is doomed. In my view, we don't know how much longer we still have to enjoy it, so we shouldn't waste precious moments constantly worrying or complaining about it. However, because not everyone in this country is yet convinced of this seemingly obvious reality, the show does see merit in pointing out or documenting the demise of our nation and will take great pains to do so. And because most everyone can agree that there is value in attempting to delay the sinking of the *Titanic* as long as possible, whenever feasible the *John Ziegler Show* will attempt to do its part to plug whatever holes in the ship it can. With that said, the show realizes that, no matter how successful it (or anyone else) may be in slowing the downfall of our society, the final outcome is still pretty much inevitable, so we might as well have a good time watching the place fall to pieces.

Be advised that the intro's stilted, term-paperish language, which looks kind of awful in print, is a great deal more effective when the spiel is delivered out loud—the stiffness gives it a slight air of self-mockery that keeps you from being totally sure just how seriously John Ziegler takes what he's saying. Meaning he gets to have it both ways. This half-pretend pretension, which is ingenious in all sorts of ways, was pioneered in talk radio by Rush Limbaugh, although with Limbaugh the semi-self-mockery is more tonal than syntactic.

---

spades. Mr. Ziegler, whose program is in only its fourth month at KFI, has been fortunate in that 2004 has already been chock-full of Monsters—Saddam's detention, the Abu Ghraib scandal, the Scott Peterson murder trial, the Greg Haidl gang-rape trial, and preliminary hearings in the rape trial of Kobe Bryant. But tonight is the most angry, indignant, disgusted, and impassioned that Mr. Z.'s gotten on-air so far, and the consensus in Airmix is that it's resulting in some absolutely first-rate talk radio.

John Ziegler, who is a talk-radio host of unflagging industry, broad general knowledge, mordant wit, and extreme conviction, makes a particular specialty of media criticism. One object of his disgust and contempt in the churn so far has been the U.S. networks' spineless, patronizing decision not to air the Berg videotape and thus to deny Americans "a true and accurate view of the barbarity, the utter *depravity*, of these people." Even more outrageous, to Mr. Z., is the mainstream media's lack of outrage about Berg's taped murder versus all that same media's hand-wringing and invective over the recent photos of alleged prisoner abuse at Abu Ghraib prison, which he views as a clear indication of the deluded, blame-America-first mentality of the U.S. press. It is an associated contrast between Americans' mortified response to the Abu Ghraib photos and reports of the Arab world's phlegmatic reaction to the Berg video that leads to his churn's climax, which is that we are plainly, unambiguously better than the Arab world—whereupon John Ziegler invites listeners to respond if they are so moved, repeats the special mnemonic KFI call-in number, and breaks for the :30 news and ads, on time to the second, as 'Mondo takes ISDN feed from Airwatch and the program's asso-

---

ISDN, in which the D stands for "Digital" is basically a phone line of very high quality and expense. ISDN is the main way that stations take feed for syndicated programs from companies like Infinity Broadcasting, Premiere Radio Networks, etc. KFI has its own News department and traffic reporters, but on nights and weekends it subscribes to an independent service called Airwatch that provides off-hour news and traffic for stations in the LA area. When, at :17 and :46 every hour, Mr. Z. intros a report from "Alan LaGreen in the KFI Traffic Center," it's really Alan LaGreen of Airwatch, who's doing ISDN traffic reports for different stations at different times all hour and has to be very careful to give the right call letters for the Traffic Center he's supposedly reporting from.

---

ciate producer and call screener, Vince Nicholas—twenty-six and hiply bald—pushes back from his console and raises both arms in congratulation, through the glass.

It goes without saying that there are all different kinds of stimulation. Depending on one's politics, sensitivities, and tastes in argumentation, it is not hard to think of objections to John Ziegler's climactic claim, or at least of some urgent requests for clarification. Like: Exactly what and whom does "the Arab world" refer to? And why are a few editorials and man-on-the-street interviews sufficient to represent the attitude and character of a whole diverse region? And why is al-Jazeera's showing of the Berg video so awful if Mr. Z. has just castigated the U.S. networks for *not* showing it? Plus, of course, what is "better" supposed to mean here? More moral? More diffident about our immorality? Is it not, in our own history, pretty easy to name some Berg-level atrocities committed by U.S. nationals, or agencies, or even governments, and approved by much of our populace? Or perhaps this: Leaving aside whether John Ziegler's assertions are true or coherent, is it even remotely helpful or productive to make huge, sweeping claims about some other region's/culture's inferiority to us? What possible effect can such remarks have except to incite hatred? Aren't they sort of irresponsible?

It is true that no one on either side of the studio's thick window expresses or even alludes to any of these objections. But this is not because Mr. Z.'s support staff is stupid, or hateful, or even necessarily on board with sweeping jingoistic claims. It is because they understand the particular codes and imperatives of large-market talk radio. The fact of the matter is that it is not John Ziegler's job to be responsible, or nuanced, or to think about whether his on-air comments are productive or dangerous, or cogent, or even defensible. That is not to say that the host would not defend his "we're better"—strenuously—or that he does not believe it's true. It is to say that he has exactly one on-air job, and that is to be stimulating. An obvious point, but it's one that's often overlooked by people who complain about propaganda, misinformation, and irrespon-

---

KFI management's explanation of "stimulating" is apposite, if a bit slippery. Following is an excerpted transcript of a May 25 Q & A with Ms. Robin Berto-lucci, the station's intelligent, highly successful, and sort of hypnotically intimidating Program Director. (The haphazard start is because the interviewing

> skills behind the Q parts are marginal; the excerpt gets more interesting as it goes along.)
>
> Q: Is there some compact way to describe KFI's programming philosophy?
>
> A: "What we call ourselves is 'More Stimulating Talk Radio.'"
>
> Q: Pretty much got that part already.
>
> A: "That is the slogan that we try to express every minute on the air. Of being stimulating. Being informative, being entertaining, being energetic, being dynamic.... The way we do it is a marriage of information and stimulating entertainment."
>
> Q: What exactly is it that makes information entertaining?
>
> A: "It's attitudinal, it's emotional."
>
> Q: Can you explain this attitudinal component?
>
> A: "I think 'stimulating' really sums it up. It's what we really try to do."
>
> Q: [strangled frustration noises]
>
> A: "Look, our station logo is in orange and black, and white—it's a stark, aggressive look. I think that typifies it. The attitude. A little in-your-face. We're not . . . stodgy."

sibility in commercial talk radio. Whatever else they are, the above-type objections to "We're better than the Arab world" are calls to accountability. They are the sort of criticisms one might make of, say, a journalist, someone whose job description includes being responsible about what he says in public. And KFI's John Ziegler is not a journalist—he is an entertainer. Or maybe it's better to say that he is part of a peculiar, modern, and very popular type of news industry, one that manages to enjoy the authority and influence of journalism without the stodgy constraints of fairness, objectivity, and responsibility that make trying to tell the truth such a drag for everyone involved. It is a frightening industry, though not for any of the simple reasons most critics give.

See, e.g., Mr. John Kobylt, of KFI's top-rated afternoon *John & Ken Show*, in a recent *LA Times* profile: "The truth is, we do everything for ratings. Yes, that's our job. I can show you the contract.... This is not *Meet the Press*. It's not *The Jim Lehrer News Hour*."

Or you could call it atavistic, a throwback. The truth is that what we think of as objectivity in journalism has been a standard since only the 1900s, and mainly in the United States. Have a look at some European dailies sometime.

✷ ✷ ✷

Distributed over two walls of KFI's broadcast studio, behind the monitors and clocks, are a dozen promotional KFI posters, all in the station's eye-catching Halloween colors against the Sweeper's bright white. On each poster, the word "stimulating" is both italicized and underscored. Except for the door and soundproof window, the entire studio is lined in acoustic tile with strange Pollockian patterns of tiny holes. Much of the tile is grayed and decaying, and the carpet's no color at all; KFI has been in this facility for nearly thirty years and will soon be moving out. Both the studio and Airmix are kept chilly because of all the electronics. The overhead lights are old inset fluorescents, the kind with the slight flutter to them; nothing casts any sort of shadow. On one of the studio walls is also pinned the special set of playing cards distributed for the invasion of Iraq, these with hand-drawn Xs over the faces of those Baathists captured or killed so far. The great L-shaped table that Mr. Z. sits at nearly fills the little room; it's got so many coats of brown paint on it that the tabletop looks slightly humped. At the L's base is another Shure microphone, used by Ken Chiampou of 3:00–7:00's *John & Ken*, its hinged stand now partly folded up so that the mike hangs like a wilted flower. The oddest thing about the studio is a strong scent of decaying bananas, as if many peels or even whole bananas were rotting in the room's wastebaskets, none of which look to have been emptied anytime recently. Mr. Ziegler, who has his ascetic side, drinks only bottled water in the studio, and certainly never snacks, so there is no way he is the source of the banana smell.

> KFI has large billboards at traffic nodes all over metro Los Angeles with the same general look and feel, although the billboards often carry both the Sweeper and extra tag phrases—"Raving Infomaniacs," "The Death of Ignorance," "The Straight Poop," and (against a military-camouflage background) "Intelligence Briefings."

> The Airmix room's analogue to the cards is a bumper sticker next to the producer's station: WHO WOULD THE FRENCH VOTE FOR?—AMERICANS FOR BUSH

> (He never leaves his chair during breaks, for example, not even to use the restroom.)

It is worth considering the strange media landscape in which political talk radio is a salient.

EDITORIAL ASIDE It's hard to understand Fox News tags like "Fair and Balanced," "No-Spin Zone," and "We Report, You Decide" as anything but dark jokes, ones that delight the channel's conservative audience precisely because their claims to objectivity so totally enrage liberals, whose own literal interpretation of the tag lines makes the left seem dim, humorless, and stodgy.

Never before have there been so many different national news sources— different now in terms of both medium and ideology. Major newspapers from anywhere are available online; there are the broadcast networks plus public TV, cable's CNN, Fox News, CNBC, et al., print and Web magazines, Internet bulletin boards, *The Daily Show,* e-mail newsletters, blogs. All this is well-known; it's part of the Media Environment we live in. But there are prices and ironies here. One is that the increasing control of U.S. mass media by a mere handful of corporations has—rather counterintuitively—created a situation of extreme fragmentation, a kaleidoscope of information options. Another is that the ever-increasing number of ideological news outlets creates precisely the kind of relativism that cultural conservatives decry, a kind of epistemic free-for-all in which "the truth" is wholly a matter of perspective and agenda. In some respects all this variety is probably good, productive of difference and dialogue and so on. But it can also be confusing and stressful for the average citizen. Short of signing on to a particular mass ideology and patronizing only those partisan news sources that ratify what you want to believe, it is increasingly hard to determine which sources to pay attention to and how exactly to distinguish real information from spin.

EDITORIAL ASIDE Of course, this is assuming one believes that information and spin are different things—and one of the dangers of partisan news's metastasis is the way it enables the conviction that the two aren't really distinct at all. Such a conviction, if it becomes endemic, alters democratic discourse from a "battle of ideas" to a battle of sales pitches for ideas (assuming, again, that one chooses to distinguish ideas from pitches, or actual guilt/innocence from lawyer's arguments, or binding commitments from the mere words "I promise," and so on and so forth).

This fragmentation and confusion have helped give rise to what's variously called the "meta-media" or "explaining industry." Under most classifications, this category includes media critics for news dailies, certain high-end magazines, panel shows like CNN's *Reliable Sources*, media-watch blogs like instapundit.com and talkingpointsmemo.com, and a large percentage of political talk radio. It is no accident that one of the signature lines Mr. Ziegler likes to deliver over his opening bumper music at :06 is ". . . the show where we take a look at the news of the day, we provide you the facts, and then we give you the truth." For this is how much of contemporary political talk radio understands its function: to explore the day's news in a depth and detail that other media do not, and to interpret, analyze, and explain that news.

Which all sounds great, except of course "explaining" the news really means editorializing, infusing the actual events of the day with the host's own opinions. And here is where the real controversy starts, because these opinions are, as just one person's opinions, exempt from strict journalistic standards of truthfulness, probity, etc., and yet they are often delivered by the talk-radio host not as opinions but as revealed truths, truths intentionally ignored or suppressed by a "mainstream press" that's "biased" in favor of liberal interests. This is, at any rate, the rhetorical template for Rush Limbaugh's program, on which most syndicated and large-market political talk radio is modeled, from ABC's Sean Hannity and Talk Radio Network's Laura Ingraham to G. G. Liddy, Rusty Humphries, Michael Medved, Mike Gallagher, Neal Boortz, Dennis Prager, and, in many respects, Mr. John Ziegler.

PURELY INFORMATIVE It's true that there are, in some large markets and even syndication, a few political talk-radio hosts who identify as moderate or liberal. The best known of these are probably Ed Schultz, Thom Hartmann, and Doug Stephan. But only a few—and only Stephan has anything close to a national audience. And the tribulations of Franken et al.'s Air America venture are well known. The point is that it is neither inaccurate nor unfair to say that today's political talk radio is, in general, overwhelmingly conservative.

(whose show is really only semi-political)

Quick sample intros: Mike Gallagher, a regular Fox News contributor whose program is syndicated by Salem Radio Network, has an upcoming book called *Surrounded by Idiots: Fighting Liberal Lunacy in America*. Neal Boortz, who's carried by Cox Radio Syndication and JRN, bills himself as "High Priest of the Church of the Painful Truth," and his recent ads in trade publications feature the quotation "How can we take airport security seriously until ethnic profiling is not only permitted, but *encouraged*?"

Mr. Z. identifies himself as a Libertarian, though he's not a registered member of the Libertarian Party, because he feels they "can't get their act together," which he does not seem to intend as a witticism.

KFI AM-640 carries Rush Limbaugh every weekday, 9:00 A.M. to noon, via live ISDN feed from Premiere Radio Networks, which is one of the dozen syndication networks that own talk-radio shows so popular that it's worth it for local stations to air them even though it costs the stations a portion of their spot load. The same goes for Dr. Laura

Spot load is the industry term for the number of minutes per hour given over to commercials. The point of the main-text sentence is that a certain percentage of the spots that run on KFI from 9:00 to noon are Rush/PRN commercials, and they are the ones who get paid by the advertisers. The exact percentages and distributions of local vs. syndicator's commercials are determined by what's called the "Clock," which is represented by a pie-shaped distribution chart that Ms. Bertolucci has on file but will show only a very quick glimpse of, since the spot-load apportionments for syndicated shows in major markets involve complex negotiations between the station and the syndicator, and KFI regards its syndicated Clocks as proprietary info—it doesn't want other stations to know what deals have been cut with PRN.

Schlessinger, who's based in southern California and used to broadcast her syndicated show from KFI until the mid-nineties, when Premiere

In White Star Productions' *History of Talk Radio* video, available at better libraries everywhere, there is footage of Dr. Laura doing her show right here at KFI, although she's at a mike in what's now the Airmix room—which, according to 'Mondo, used to be the studio, with what's now the studio serving as Airmix. (Why they switched rooms is unclear, but transferring all the gear must have been a serious hassle.) In the video, the little gray digital clock propped up counting seconds on Dr. Laura's desk is the same one that now counts seconds on the wall to Mr. Ziegler's upper left in the studio—i.e., it's the very same clock—which not only is strangely thrilling but also further testifies to KFI's thriftiness about capital expenses.

built its own LA facility and was able to offer Schlessinger more-sumptuous digs. Dr. Laura airs M-F from noon to 3:00 on KFI, though her shows are canned and there's no live feed. Besides 7:00–10:00 P.M.'s Phil Hendrie (another KFI host whose show went into national syndication, and who now has his own private dressing room and studio over at Premiere), the only other weekday syndication KFI uses is *Coast to Coast With George Noory*, which covers and analyzes news of the paranormal throughout the wee hours.

Whatever the social effects of talk radio or the partisan agendas of certain hosts, it is a fallacy that political talk radio is motivated by ideology. It is not. Political talk radio is a business, and it is motivated by revenue. The conservatism that dominates today's AM airwaves does so because it generates high Arbitron ratings, high ad rates, and maximum profits.

Radio has become a more lucrative business than most people know. Throughout most of the past decade, the industry's revenues have increased by more than 10 percent a year. The average cash-flow margin for major radio companies is 40 percent, compared with more like 15 percent for large TV networks; and the mean price paid for a radio station has gone from eight to more than thirteen times cash flow. Some of this extreme profitability, and thus the structure of the industry, is due to the 1996 Telecommunications Act, which allows radio companies to acquire up to eight stations in a

Clear Channel bought KFI—or rather the radio company that owned KFI—sometime around 2000. It's all a little fuzzy, because it appears that. Clear Channel actually bought, or absorbed, the radio company that had just bought KFI from another radio company, or something like that.

given market and to control as much as 35 percent of a market's total ad revenues. The emergence of huge, dominant radio conglomerates like Clear Channel and Infinity is a direct consequence of the '96 Act (which the FCC, aided by the very conservative D.C. Court of Appeals, has lately tried to make even more permissive). And these radio conglomerates enjoy not just substantial economies of scale but almost unprecedented degrees of business integration.

Example: Clear Channel Communications Inc. now owns KFI AM-640, plus two other AM stations and five FMs in the Los Angeles market. It also owns Premiere Radio Net-

(Which means that the negotiations between KFI and PRN over the terms of syndication for Rush, Dr. Laura, et al. are actually negotiations between two parts of the same company, which either helps explain or renders even more mysterious KFI's reticence about detailing the Clocks for its PRN shows.)

It turns out that one of the reasons its old Koreatown studios are such a latrine is that KFI's getting ready to move very soon to a gleaming new complex in Burbank that will house five of Clear Channel's stations and allow them to share a lot of cutting-edge technical equipment and software. Some of the reasons for the consolidation involve AM radio's complex, incremental move from analog to digital broadcast, a move that's a lot more economical if stations can be made to share equipment. The Burbank hub facility will also feature a new and improved mega-Prophet OS that all five stations can use and share files on, which for KFI means convenient real-time access to all sorts of new preloaded bumper music and sound effects and bites.

As the board op, 'Mondo Hernandez is also responsible for downloading and cueing up the sections of popular songs that intro the *John Ziegler Show* and background Mr. Z.'s voice when a new segment starts. Bumper music is, of course, a talk-radio convention: Rush Limbaugh has a franchise on The Pretenders, and Sean Hannity always uses that horrific Martina McBride "Let freedom ring/Let the guilty pay" song. Mr. Z. favors a whole rotating set of classic rock hooks, but his current favorites are Van Halen's "Right Now" and a certain jaunty part of the theme to *Pirates of the Caribbean*, because, according to 'Mondo, "they get John pumped."

N.B. Mr. Z. usually refers to himself as either "Zig" or "the Zigmeister," and has made a determined effort to get everybody at KFI to call him Zig, with only limited success so far.

works. It also owns the Airwatch subscription news/traffic service. And it designs and manufactures Prophet, KFI's operating system, which is state-of-the-art and much too expensive for most independent stations. All told, Clear Channel currently owns some one thousand two hundred radio stations nationwide, one of which happens to be Louisville, Kentucky's WHAS, the AM talk station from which John Ziegler was fired, amid spectacular gossip and controversy, in August of 2003. Which means that Mr. Ziegler now works in Los Angeles for the same company that just fired him in Louisville, such that his firing now appears—in retrospect, and considering the relative sizes of the Louisville and LA markets—to have been a promotion. All of which turns out to be a strange and revealing story about what a talk-radio host's life is like.

2

For obvious reasons, critics of political talk radio concern themselves mainly with the programs' content. Talk station management, on the other hand, tends to think of content as a subset of personality, of how stimulating a given host is. As for the hosts—ask Mr. Ziegler off-air what makes him good at his job, and he'll shrug glumly and say, "I'm not really all that talented. I've got passion, and I work really hard." Taken so for granted that nobody in the business seems aware of it is something that an outsider, sitting in Airmix and watching John Ziegler at the microphone, will notice right away. Hosting talk radio is an exotic, high-pressure gig that not many people are fit for, and being truly good at it requires skills so specialized that many of them don't have names.

> "Passion" is a big word in the industry, and John Ziegler uses the word in connection with himself a lot. It appears to mean roughly the same as what Ms. Bertolucci calls "edginess" or "attitude."

To appreciate these skills and some of the difficulties involved, you might wish to do an experiment. Try sitting alone in a room with a clock, turning on a tape recorder, and starting to speak into it. Speak about anything you want—with the proviso that your topic, and your opinions on it, must be of interest to some group of strangers who you imagine will be listening to the tape. Naturally, in order to be even minimally interesting, your remarks should be intelligible and their reasoning sequential—a listener will have to be able to follow the logic of what you're saying—which means that you will have to know enough about your topic to organize your statements in a coherent way. (But you cannot do much of this organizing beforehand; it has to occur at the same time you're speaking. Plus, ideally, what you're saying should be not just comprehensible and interesting but compelling, stimulating, which means that your remarks have to provoke and sustain some kind of emotional reaction in the

> Part of the answer to why conservative talk radio works so well might be that extreme conservatism provides a neat, clear, univocal template with which to organize one's opinions and responses to the world. The current term of approbation for this kind of template is "moral clarity."

> It is, of course, much less difficult to arouse genuine anger, indignation, and outrage in people than it is real joy, satisfaction, fellow feeling, etc. The latter are fragile and complex, and what excites them varies a great deal from person to person, whereas anger et al. are more primal, universal, and easy to stimulate (as implied by expressions like "He really pushes my buttons").

listeners, which in turn will require you to construct some kind of identifiable persona for yourself—your comments will need to strike the listener as coming from an actual human being, someone with a real

> This, too: Consider the special intimacy of talk radio. It's usually listened to solo—radio is the most solitary of broadcast media. And half-an-ear background-listening is much more common with music formats than with talk. This is a human being speaking to you, with a pro-caliber voice, eloquently and with passion, in what feels like a one-to-one; it doesn't take long before you start to feel you know him. Which is why it's often such a shock when you see a real host, his face—you discover you've had a
>
> > (as the industry is at pains to remind advertisers)
>
> picture of this person in your head without knowing it, and it's always wrong. This dissonant shock is one reason why Rush and Dr. Laura, even with their huge built-in audiences, did not fare well on TV.

personality and real feelings about whatever it is you're discussing. And it gets even trickier: You're trying to communicate in real time with someone you cannot see or hear responses from; and though you're communicating in speech, your remarks cannot have any of the fragmentary, repetitive, garbled qualities of real interhuman speech, or speech's ticcy unconscious umm's or you know's, or false starts or stutters or long pauses while you try to think of how to phrase what you want to say next. You're also, of course, denied the physical inflections that are so much a part of spoken English—the facial expressions, changes in posture, and symphony of little gestures that accompany and buttress real talking. Everything unspoken about you, your topic, and how you feel about it has to be conveyed through pitch, volume, tone, and pacing. The pacing is especially important: it can't be too slow, since that's low-energy and dull, but it can't be too rushed or it will sound like babbling. And so you have somehow to keep all these different imperatives and structures in mind at the same time, while also filling exactly, say, eleven minutes, with no dead air and no going over, such that at 10:46 you have wound things up neatly and are in a position to say, "KFI is the station with the

---

The exact-timing thing is actually a little less urgent for a host who's got the resources of Clear Channel behind him. This is because in KFI's Airmix room, nestled third from the bottom in one of the two eight-foot stacks of processing gear to the left of 'Mondo's mixing board, is an Akai DD1000 Magneto Optical Disk Recorder, known less formally as a "Cashbox." What this is is a sound compressor, which exploits the fact that even a live studio program is—because of the FCC-mandated seven-second delay—taped. Here is how 'Mondo, in exchange for certain vending-machine comestibles, explains the Cashbox: "All the shows are supposed to start at six past. But if they put more spots in the log, or say, like, if traffic goes long, now we're all of a sudden starting at seven past or something. The Cashbox can take a twenty-minute segment and turn it into a nineteen." It does this by using computerized sound-processing to eliminate pauses and periodically accelerate Mr. Z.'s delivery just a bit. The trick is that the Cashbox can compress sound so artfully that you don't hear the speed-up, at least not in a nineteen-for-twenty exchange ("You get down to eighteen it's risky, or down around seventeen you can definitely hear it"). So if things are running a little over, 'Mondo has to use the Cashbox—very deftly, via controls that look really complicated—in order to make sure that the Clock's adhered to and Airwatch breaks, promos, and ad spots

> all run as specified. A gathering suspicion as to why the Akai DD1000 is called the Cashbox occasions a Q: Does the station ever press 'Mondo or other board ops to use the Cashbox and compress shows in order to make room for additional ads? A: "Not really. What they'll do is just put an extra spot or two in the log, and then I've just got to do the best I can."

most frequent traffic reports. Alan LaGreen is in the KFI Traffic Center" (which, to be honest, Mr. Z. sometimes leaves himself only three or even two seconds for and has to say extremely fast, which he can always do without a flub). So then, ready: go.

> The only elocutionary problem Mr. Z. ever exhibits is a habit of confusing the words "censure" and "censor."

It's no joke. See for example the *John Ziegler Show*'s producer, Emiliano Limon, who broke in at KFI as a weekend overnight host before moving across the glass:

"What's amazing is that when you get new people who think that they can do a talk-radio program, you watch them for the first time. By three minutes into it, they have that look on their face like, 'Oh my God, I've got ten minutes left. What am I going to say?' And that's what happened to me a lot. So you end up talking about yourself [which, for complex philosophical reasons, the producer disapproves of], or you end up yammering." Emiliano is a large, very calm and competent man in his midthirties who either wears the same black *LA Times* T-shirt every day or owns a whole closetful of them. He was pulled off other duties to help launch KFI's experimental Live and Local evening show, an assignment that obviously involves working closely with Mr. Z., which Emiliano seems to accept as his karmic punishment for being so unflappable and easy to get along with. He laughs more than everyone else at KFI put together.

"I remember one time, I just broke after five minutes, I was just done, and they were going, 'Hey, what are you doing, you have another ten minutes!' And I was like, 'I don't know what else to say!' And that's what happens. For those people who think 'Oh, I could do talk radio,' well, there's more to it. A lot of people can't take it once they get that taste of, you know, 'Geez, I gotta fill all this time *and* sound interesting?'

"Then, as you keep on doing it over the days, there's something that becomes absolutely clear to you. You're not really acting on the radio. It's *you*. If no one really responds and the ratings aren't good, it means they don't like *you*." Which is worth keeping very much in mind.

An abiding question: Who exactly listens to political talk radio? Arbitron Inc. and some of its satellites can help measure how many are listening for how long and when, and they provide some rough age data and demographic specs. A lot of the rest is guesswork, and Program Directors don't like to talk about it.

From outside, though, one of the best clues to how a radio station understands its audience is spots. Which commercials it runs, and when, indicate how the station is pitching its listeners' tastes and receptivities to sponsors. In how often particular spots are repeated lie clues

> For instance, one has only to listen to *Coast to Coast With George Noory*'s ads for gold as a hedge against hyperinflation, special emergency radios you can hand-crank in case of extended power failure, miracle weight-loss formulas, online dating services, etc., to understand that KFI and the syndicator regard this show's audience as basically frightened, credulous, and desperate.
>
> (ad-wise, a lucrative triad indeed)

to the length of time the station thinks people are listening, how attentive it thinks they are, etc. Specific example: Just from its spot load, we can deduce that KFI trusts its audience to sit still for an extraordinary amount of advertising. An average hour of the *John Ziegler Show* consists of four program segments: :06–:17, :23–:30, :37–:46, and :53–:00, or thirty-four minutes of Mr. Z. actually talking. Since KFI's newscasts are never more than ninety seconds, and since quarterly traffic reports are always bracketed by "live-read" spots for Traffic Center sponsors, that makes each hour at least 40 percent ads; the percentage is higher if you count Sweepers for the station and promos for other KFI shows.

A live read is when a host or newsperson reads the ad copy himself on-air. They're sort of a radio tradition, but the degree to which KFI weaves live reads into its programming is a great leap forward for broadcast marketing. Live-read spots are more expensive for advertisers, especially the longer, more detailed ones read by the programs' hosts, since these ads (a) can sound at first like an actual talk segment and (b) draw on the personal appeal and credibility of the host. And the spots themselves are often clearly set up to exploit these features—see for instance John Kobylt's live read for LA's Cunning Dental Group during afternoons' *John & Ken*: "Have you noticed how bad the teeth are of all the contestants in these reality shows? I saw some of this the other day. Discolored, chipped, misshaped, misaligned, rotted-out teeth, missing teeth, not to mention the bleeding, oozing, pus-y gums. You go to Cunning Dental Group, they will take all your gross teeth and in one or two visits fix them and give you a bright shiny smile." Even more expensive than live reads are what's called "endorsements," which are when a host describes, in ecstatically favorable terms, his own personal experience with a product or service. Examples here include Phil Hendrie's weight loss on Cortislim, Kobylt's "better than 20-20" laser-surgery outcome with Saddleback Eye Center, and Mr. Bill Handel's frustrations with dial-up ISPs before discovering DSL extreme. These ads, which are KFI's most powerful device for exploiting the intimacy and trust of the listener-host relationship, also result in special "endorsement fees" paid directly to the host.

> (It's unclear how one spells the adjectival form of "pus," though it sounds okay on-air.)

> Handel, whose KFI show is an LA institution in morning drive, describes his program as "in-your-face, informational, with a lot of racial humor."

And this is the load just on a local program, one for which the Clock doesn't have to be split with a syndicator.

It's not that KFI's unaware of the dangers here. Station management reads its mail, and as Emiliano Limon puts it, "If there's one complaint listeners always have, it's the spot load." But the only important issue is whether all the complaints translate into actual listener behavior. KFI's spot load is an instance of the kind of multivariable maximization problem that M.B.A. programs thrive on. It is obviously in the station's financial interest to carry just as high a volume of ads as it can without hurting ratings—the moment listeners begin turning away from KFI because of too many commercials, the Arbitron numbers go down, the rates charged for ads have to be reduced, and profitability suffers. But anything more specific is, again, guesswork. When asked about management's thinking here, or whether there's any particular formula KFI

It's a little more complicated than that, really, because excessive spots can also affect ratings in less direct ways—mainly by lowering the quality of the programming. Industry analyst Michael Harrison, of *Talkers* magazine, complains that "The commercial breaks are so long today that it is hard for hosts to build upon where they left off. The whole audience could have changed. There is the tendency to go back to the beginning and re-set up the premise. It makes it very difficult to do what long-form programming is supposed to do."

uses to figure out how high a spot load the market will bear, Ms. Bertolucci will only smile and shrug as if pleasantly stumped: "We have more commercials than we've ever had, and our ratings are the best they've ever been."

SEMI-EDITORIAL Even in formal, on-record, and very PR-savvy interviews, the language of KFI management is filled with little unconscious bits of jargon— "inventory" for the total number of ad minutes available, "product" for a given program, or (a favorite) "to monetize," which means to extract ad revenue from a given show—that let one know exactly where KFI's priorities lie. Granted, the station is a business, and broadcasting is not charity work. But given how intimate and relationship-driven talk radio is, it's disheartening when management's only term for KFI's listeners, again and again, is "market."

How often a particular spot can run over and over before listeners just can't stand it anymore is something else no one will talk about, but the evidence suggests that KFI sees its audience as either very patient and tolerant or almost catatonically inattentive. Canned ads for local sponsors like Robbins Bros. Jewelers, Sit 'n Sleep Mattress, and the Power Auto Group play every couple hours, 24/7, until one knows every hitch and nuance. National saturation campaigns for products like Cortislim vary things somewhat by using both endorsements and canned spots. Pitches for caveat emptor–type nostrums like Avacor (for hair loss),

Enzyte ("For natural male enhancement!"), and Altovis ("Helps fight daily fatigue!") often repeat once an hour through the night. As of spring '04, though, the most frequent and concussive ads on KFI are for mortgage and home-refi companies—Green Light Financial, HMS Capital, Home Field Financial, Benchmark Lending. Over and over. Pacific Home Financial, U.S. Mortgage Capital, Crestline Funding, Advantix Lending. Reverse mortgages, negative amortization, adjustable rates,

---

CONSUMER ADVISORY As it happens, these two are products of Berkeley Premium Nutraceuticals, an Ohio company with annual sales of more than $100 million, as well as over 3,000 complaints to the BBB and the Attorney General's Office in its home state alone. Here's why. The radio ads say you can get a thirty-day free trial of Enzyte by calling a certain toll-free number. If you call, it turns out there's a $4.90 S&H charge for the free month's supply, which the lady on the phone wants you to put on your credit card. If you acquiesce, the company then starts shipping you more Enzyte every month and auto-billing your card for at least $35 each time, because it turns out that by taking the thirty-day trial you've somehow signed up for Berkeley's automatic-purchase program—which the operator neglected to mention. And calling Berkeley Nutraceuticals to get the automatic shipments and billings stopped doesn't much help; often they'll stop only if some kind of consumer agency sends a letter. It's the same with Altovis and its own "free trial." In short, the whole thing is one of those irksome, hassle-laden marketing schemes, and KFI runs dozens of spots per day for Berkeley products. The degree to which the station is legally responsible for an advertiser's business practices is, by FTC and FCC rules, nil. But it's hard not to see KFI's relationship with Berkeley as another indication of the station's true regard for its listeners.

FYI: Enzyte, which bills itself as a natural libido and virility enhancer (it also has all those "Smiling Bob & Grateful Wife" commercials on cable TV), contains tribulis terrestris, panax ginseng, ginko biloba, and a half dozen other innocuous herbal ingredients. The product costs Berkeley, in one pharmacologist's words, "nothing to make." But it's de facto legal to charge hundreds of dollars a year for it, and to advertise it as an OTC Viagra. The FDA doesn't regulate herbal meds unless people are actually falling over from taking them, and the Federal Trade Commission doesn't have anything like the staff to keep up with the advertising claims, so it's all basically an unregulated market.

(Calls to KFI's Sales department re consumers' amply documented problems with Enzyte and Altovis were, as the journalists say, not returned.)

APR, FICO . . . where did all these firms come from? What were these guys doing five years ago? Why is KFI's audience seen as so especially ripe and ready for refi? Betterloans.com, lendingtree.com, Union Bank of California, on and on and on.

Emiliano Limon's "It's *you*" seems true to an extent. But there is also the issue of persona, meaning the on-air personality that a host adopts in order to heighten the sense of a real person behind the mike. It is, after all, un-

(somewhat paradoxically)

likely that Rush Limbaugh always feels as jaunty and confident as he seems on the air, or that Howard Stern really is deeply fascinated by porn starlets every waking minute of the day. But a host's persona is not the same as outright acting. For the most part, it's probably more like the way we are all slightly different with some people than we are with others.

In some cases, though, the personas are more contrived and extreme. In the slot preceding Mr. Z.'s on KFI, for instance, is the *Phil Hendrie Show*, which is actually a cruel and complicated kind of meta-talk radio. What happens every night on this program is that Phil Hendrie brings on some wildly offensive guest—a man who's leaving his wife because she's had a mastectomy, a Little League coach who advocates corporal punishment of players, a retired colonel who claims that females' only proper place in the military is as domestics and concubines for the officers—and first-time or casual listeners will call in and

(who really is a gifted mimic)

argue with the guests and (not surprisingly) get very angry and upset. Except the whole thing's a put-on. The guests are fake, their different voices done by Hendrie with the aid of mike processing and a first-rate board op, and the show's real entertainment is the callers, who don't know it's all a gag—Hendrie's real audience, which is in on the joke, enjoys hearing these callers get more and more outraged and sputtery as the "guests" yank their chain. It's all a bit like the old *Candid Camera* if the joke perpetrated over and over on that show were convincing somebody that a loved one had just died.

So obviously Hendrie—whose show now draws an estimated one million listeners a week—lies on the outer frontier of radio persona.

A big part of John Ziegler's on-air persona, on the other hand, is that he doesn't have one. This may be just a function of all the time he's spent in the abattoir of small-market radio, but in Los Angeles it plays as a canny and sophisticated meta-radio move. Part of his January introduction to himself and his program is "The key to the John Ziegler Show is that I am almost completely real. Nearly every show begins with the credo 'This is the show where the host says what he believes and believes what he says.' I do not make up my opinions or exaggerate my stories simply to stir the best debate on that particular broadcast."

> Apparently, one reason why Hendrie's show was perfect for national syndication was that the wider dissemination gave Hendrie a much larger pool of uninitiated listeners to call in and entertain the initiated listeners.

Though Mr. Z. won't ever quite say so directly, his explicit I-have-no-persona persona helps to establish a contrast with weekday afternoons' John Kobylt, whose on-air voice is similar to Ziegler's in pitch and timbre. Kobylt and his sidekick Ken Chiampou have a hugely popular show

---

National talk-radio hosts like Limbaugh, Prager, Hendrie, Gallagher, et al. tend to have rich baritone radio voices that rarely peak, whereas today's KFI has opted for a local-host sound that's more like a slightly adenoidal second tenor. The voices of Kobylt, Bill Handel, Ken Chiampou, weekend host Wayne Resnick, and John Ziegler all share not only this tenor pitch but also a certain quality that is hard to describe except as sounding stressed, aggrieved, Type A: The Little Guy Who's Had It Up To Here. Kobylt's voice in particular has a consistently snarling, dyspeptic, fed-up quality—a perfect aural analogue to the way drivers' faces look in jammed traffic—whereas Mr. Ziegler's tends to rise and fall more, often hitting extreme upper registers of outraged disbelief. Off-air, Mr. Z.'s speaking voice is nearly an octave lower than it sounds on his program, which is a bit mysterious,

> (as in if you listen to an upset person say "I can't be*lieve* it!")

since 'Mondo denies doing anything special to the on-air voice except setting the default volume on the board's channel 7 a bit low because "John sort of likes to yell a lot." And Mr. Ziegler bristles at the suggestion that he, Kobylt, or Handel has anything like a high voice on the air: "It's just that we're passionate. Rush doesn't get all that passionate. You try being passionate and having a low voice."

based around finding stories and causes that will make white, middle-class Californians feel angry and disgusted, and then hammering away at these stories/causes day after day. Their personas are what the LA Times calls "brash" and Chiampou himself calls "rabid dogs," which latter KFI has developed into the promo line "The Junkyard Dogs of Talk Radio." What John & Ken really are is professional *oiks*. Their show is credited with helping jumpstart the '03 campaign to recall Governor Gray Davis, although they were equally disgusted by most of the candidates who wanted to replace him (q.v. Kobylt: "If there's anything I don't like more than politicians, it's those wormy little nerds who act as campaign han-

---

CONTAINS EDITORIAL ELEMENTS It should be conceded that there is at least one real and refreshing journalistic advantage that bloggers, fringe-cable newsmen, and most talk-radio hosts have over the mainstream media: they are neither the friends nor the peers of the public officials they cover. Why this is an advantage involves an issue that tends to get obscured by the endless fight over whether there's actually a "liberal bias" in the "elite" mainstream press. Whether one buys the bias thing or not, it is clear that leading media figures are part of a very different social and economic class than most of their audiences. See, e.g., a snippet of Eric Alterman's recent What Liberal Media?:

> No longer the working-class heroes of *The Front Page/His Gal Friday* lore, elite journalists in Washington and New York [and LA] are rock-solid members of the political and financial Establishment about whom they write. They dine at the same restaurants and take their vacations on the same Caribbean islands. . . . What's more, like the politicians, their jobs are not subject to export to China or Bangladesh.

This is why the really potent partisan label for the *NYT/Time*/network-level press is not "liberal media" but "elite media"—because the label's true.

(Except some of your more slippery right-wing commentators use "elitist media," which sounds similar but is really a far more loaded term.)

And talk radio is very deliberately not part of this elite media. With the exception of Limbaugh and maybe Hannity, these hosts are not stars, or millionaires, or sophisticates. And a large part of their on-air persona is that they are of and for their audience—the Little Guy—and against corrupt, incompetent pols and their "spokesholes," against smooth-talking lawyers and PC whiners and idiot bureaucrats, against illegal aliens clogging our highways and emergency rooms, paroled sex offenders living among us, punitive vehicle taxes, and stupid, self-righteous, agenda-laden laws against public smoking, SUV emissions, gun ownership, the right to watch the Nick Berg decapitation video over and over in slow motion, etc. In other words, the talk host's persona and appeal are deeply, totally populist, and if it's all somewhat fake—if John Kobylt can shift a little too easily from the apoplectic Little Guy of his segments to the smooth corporate shill of his live reads—then that's just life in the big city.

dlers and staff. . . . We just happened to on our own decide that Davis was a rotting stool that ought to be flushed"). In '02, they organized a parade of SUVs in Sacramento to protest stricter vehicle-emissions laws; this year they spend at least an hour a day attacking various government officials and their spokesholes for failing to enforce immigration laws and trying to bullshit the citizens about it; and so on. But the *John & Ken Show*'s real specialty is gruesome, high-profile California trials, which they often cover on-site, Kobylt eschewing all PC pussyfooting and legal niceties to speak his mind about defendants like 2002's David Westerfield and the current Scott Peterson, both "scumbags that are guilty as sin."

Besides legendary stunts like tossing broccoli at "vegetable-head" jurors for taking too long to find Westerfield guilty, Kobylt is maybe best known for shouting, "Come out, Scott! No one believes you! You can't hide!" at a window's silhouette as the *J & K Show* broadcast live from in front of Peterson's house, which scene got re-created in at least one recent TV movie about the Scott & Laci case.

The point is that John Kobylt broadcasts in an almost perpetual state of affronted rage; and, as more than one KFI staffer has ventured to observe off the record, it's unlikely that any middle-aged man could really go around this upset all the time and not drop dead. It's a persona, in other words, not exactly fabricated but certainly exaggerated . . . and of course it's also demagoguery of the most classic and unabashed sort.

But it makes for stimulating and profitable talk radio. As of Arbitron's winter '04 Book, KFI AM-640 has become the No. 1 talk station in the country, beating out New York's WABC in

The *John & Ken Show* pulls higher ratings in southern California than the syndicated Rush and Dr. Laura, which is pretty much unheard of.

These are measurement categories in Arbitron Inc.'s Radio Market Reports, which reports come out four times a year and are known in the industry as "Books." In essence, Cume is the total measure of all listeners, and AQH (for "Average Quarter Hour") represents the mean number of listeners in any given fifteen-minute period.

both Cume and AQH for the coveted 25-54 audience. KFI also now has the second highest market share of any radio station in Los Angeles, trailing only hip-hop giant KPWR. In just one year, KFI has gone from being the eighteenth to the seventh top-billing station in the country, which is part of why it received the 2003 News/Talk Station of the Year Award from *Radio and Records* magazine. Much of this recent success is attributed to Ms. Robin Bertolucci, the Program Director brought in from Denver shortly after Clear Channel acquired KFI, whom Mr. Z. describes as "a real superstar in the business right now." From all reports, Ms. Bertolucci has done everything from redesigning the station's ID and Sweeper and sound and overall in-your-face vibe to helping established hosts fine-tune their personas and create a distinctively KFI-ish style and 'tude for their shows.

Every Wednesday afternoon, Ms. Bertolucci meets with John Ziegler to review the previous week and chat about how the show's going. The Program Director's large private office is located just off the KFI prep room (where Mr. Z.'s own office is a small computer table with a homemade THIS AREA RESERVED FOR JOHN ZIEGLER taped to it). Ms. B. is soft-spoken, polite, unpretentious, and almost completely devoid of moving parts. Here is her on-record explanation of the Program Director's role w/r/t the *John Ziegler Show*:

"It's John's show. He's flying the airplane, a big 747. What I am, I'm the little person in the control tower. I have a different perspective—"

"I *have* no perspective!" Mr. Z. interrupts, with a loud laugh, from his seat before her desk.

"—which might be of value. Like, 'You may want to pull up because you're heading for a mountain.'" They both laugh. It's an outrageous bit of understatement: nine months ago John Ziegler's career was rubble, and Ms. B. is the only reason he's here, and she's every inch his boss, and he's nervous around her—which you can tell by the way he puts his long legs out and leans back in his chair with his hands in his slacks' pockets and yawns a lot and tries to look exaggeratedly relaxed.

> (On the other hand, he omits to wear his golf cap in her office, and his hair shows evidence of recent combing.)

The use of some esoteric technical slang occasions a brief Q & A on how exactly Arbitron works, while Mr. Z. joggles his sneaker impatiently. Then they go over the past week. Ms. B. gently chides the new host for not hitting the Greg Haidl trial harder,

> In truth, just about everyone at KFI except Ms. B. refers to Arbitron as "Arbitraryon." This is because it's 100 percent diary-based, and diary surveys are notoriously iffy, since a lot of subjects neglect to fill out their diaries in real time (especially when they're listening as they drive), tending instead to wait till the night before they're due and then trying to do them from memory. Plus it's widely held that certain ethnic minorities are chronically mis- or over-represented in metro LA's Books, evidently because Arbitron has a hard time recruiting these minorities as subjects, and when it lands a few it tends to stick with them week after week.

and for usually discussing the case in his show's second hour instead of the first. Her thrust: "It's a big story for us. It's got sex, it's got police, class issues, kids running amok, video, the courts, and who gets away with what. And it's in Orange County." When Mr. Ziegler (whose off-air method of showing annoyance or frustration is to sort of hang his head way over to one side) protests that both Bill Handel and John & Ken have already covered the story six ways from Sunday every day and there is no way for him to do anything fresh or stimulating with it, Ms. B. nods slowly and responds: "If we were KIIS-FM, and we had a new Christina Aguilera song, and they played it heavy on the morning show and the afternoon show, wouldn't you still play it on the evening show?" At which Mr. Z. sort of lolls his head from side to side several times—"All right. I see your point. All right."—and on tonight's (i.e., May 19's)

FOR THOSE OUTSIDE SOUTHERN CA Haidl, the teenage son of an Orange County Asst. Sheriff, is accused, together with some chums, of gang-raping an unconscious girl at a party two or three years ago. Rocket scientists all, the perps had videotaped the whole thing and then managed to lose the tape, which eventually found its way to the police.

program he does lead with and spend much of the first hour on the latest Haidl developments.

By way of post-meeting analysis, it is worth noting that a certain assumption behind Ms. B.'s Christina Aguilera analogy—namely, that a criminal trial is every bit as much an entertainment product as a Top 40 song—was not questioned or even blinked at by either participant. This is doubtless one reason for KFI's ratings éclat—the near total conflation of news and entertainment. It also explains why KFI's twice-hourly newscasts (which are always extremely short, and densely interwoven with station promos and live-read ads) concentrate so heavily on lurid, tabloidish stories. Post–Nick Berg, the station's newscasts in May and early June tend to lead with child-molestation charges against local clerics and teachers, revelations in the Peterson and Haidl trials, and developments in the Kobe Bryant and Michael Jackson cases. With respect to Ms. Bertolucci's on-record description of KFI's typical listener—"An information-seeking person that wants to know what's going on in the world and wants to be communicated to in an interesting, entertaining, stimulating sort of way"—it seems fair to observe that KFI provides a peculiar and very selective view of what's going on in the world.

Ms. B.'s description turns out to be loaded in a number of ways. The role of news and information versus personal and persona-driven stuff on the *John Ziegler Show*, for example, is a matter that Mr. Z. and his producer see very differently. Emiliano Limon, who's worked at the station for over a decade and believes he knows its audience, sees "two distinct eras at KFI. The first was the opinion-driven, personal, here's-my-take-on-things era. The second is the

[meaning for the station in its current talk format, which started sometime in the eighties. KFI itself has been on the air since 1922—the "FI" actually stands for "Farm Information."]

era we're in right now, putting the information first." Emiliano refers to polls he's seen indicating that most people in southern California get their news from local TV newscasts and Jay Leno's monologue on the *Tonight Show*. "We go on the presumption that the average driver, average listener, isn't reading the news the way we are. We read *everything*." In fact, this voracious news-reading is a big part of Emiliano's job. He is, like most talk-radio producers, a virtuoso on the Internet, and he combs through a daily list of sixty national papers, 'zines, and blogs, and he believes that his and KFI's main function is to provide "a kind of executive news summary" for busy listeners. In a separate Q & A, though, Mr. Ziegler's take on the idea of his show's providing news is wholly different: "We're trying to get away from that, actually. The original thought was that this would be mostly an informational show, and now

> Again, this sort of claim seems a little tough to reconcile with the actual news that KFI concentrates on, but—as Mr. Z. himself once pointedly observed during a Q & A— interviewing somebody is not the same as arguing with him over every last little thing.

> (with whom Emiliano, from all indications, does not enjoy a very chummy or simpatico relationship, although he's always a master of tact and circumspection on the subject of Mr. Z.)

> The upshot here is that there's a sort of triangular dissonance about the *John Ziegler Show* and how best to stimulate LA listeners. From all available evidence, Robin Bertolucci wants the program to be mainly info-driven (according to KFI's particular definition of info), but she wants the information heavily editorialized and infused with 'tude and in-your-face energy. Mr. Ziegler interprets this as the P.D.'s endorsing his talking a lot about himself, which Emiliano Limon views as an antiquated, small-market approach that is not going to be very interesting to people in Los Angeles, who tend to get more than their share of colorful personality and idiosyncratic opinion just in the course of their normal day. If Emiliano is right, then Mr. Z. may simply be too old-school and self-involved for KFI, or at least not yet aware of how different the appetites of a New York or LA market are from those of a Louisville or Raleigh.

we're trying to get a little more toward personality" . . . which, since Mr. Z. makes a point of not having a special on-air persona, means more stuff about himself, John Ziegler—his experiences, his résumé, his political and cultural outlook and overall philosophy of life.

3

If we're willing to disregard the complicating precedents of Joe Pyne and Alan Burke, then the origins of contemporary political talk radio can be traced to three phenomena of the 1980s.

(famous "confrontational" talk hosts of the sixties)

The first of these involved AM music stations' getting absolutely murdered by FM, which could broadcast music in stereo and allowed for much better fidelity on high and low notes. The human voice, on the other hand, is mid-range and doesn't require high fidelity. The eighties' proliferation of talk formats on the AM band also provided new careers for some music deejays—e.g., Don Imus, Morton Downey Jr.—whose chatty personas didn't fit well with FM's all-about-the-music ethos.

The second big factor was the repeal, late in Ronald Reagan's second term, of what was known as the Fairness Doctrine. This was a 1949 FCC rule designed to minimize any possible restrictions on free speech caused by limited access to broadcasting outlets. The idea was that, as one of the conditions for receiving an FCC broadcast license, a station had to "devote reasonable attention to the coverage of controversial issues of public importance," and consequently had to provide "reasonable, although not necessarily equal" opportunities for opposing sides to express their views. Because of the Fairness Doctrine, talk stations had to hire and program symmetrically: if you had a three-hour program whose host's politics were on one side of the ideological spectrum, you had to have another long-form program whose host more or less spoke for the other side. Weirdly enough, up through the mid-eighties it was usually the U.S. right that benefited most from the Doctrine. Pioneer talk syndicator Ed McLaughlin, who managed San Francisco's KGO in the 1960s, recalls that "I had more liberals on the air than I had conservatives or even moderates for that matter, and I had a hell of a time finding the other voice."

KGO happens to be the station where Ms. Robin Bertolucci, fresh out of Cal-Berkeley, first broke into talk radio.

The Fairness Doctrine's repeal was part of the sweeping deregulations of the Reagan era,

which aimed to liberate all sorts of industries from government interference and allow them to compete freely in the marketplace. The old,
Rooseveltian logic of the Doctrine had been that since the airwaves
belonged to everyone, a license to profit from those airwaves con-
ferred on the broadcast industry some special obligation to serve the
public interest. Commercial radio broadcasting was not, in other
words, originally conceived as just another for-profit industry; it was
supposed to meet a higher standard of social responsibility. After
1987, though, just another industry is pretty
much what radio became, and its only real | (except, obviously, for some
responsibility now is to attract and retain lis- | restrictions on naughty
teners in order to generate revenue. In other | language)
words, the sort of distinction explicitly drawn
by FCC Chairman Newton Minow in the 1960s—namely, that between "the public interest" and "merely what interests the public"—no
longer exists.

CONTAINS WHAT MIGHT BE PERCEIVED AS EDITORIAL ELEMENTS
It seems only fair and balanced to observe, from the imagined perspective of a
Neal Boortz or John Ziegler, that Minow's old distinction reflected exactly the sort
of controlling, condescending, nanny-state liberal attitude that makes government
regulation such a bad idea. For how and why does a federal bureaucrat like Newton
Minow get to decide what "the public interest" is? Why not respect the American
people enough to let the public itself decide what interests it? Of course, this sort of
objection depends on precisely the collapse of "the public interest" into "what
happens to interest the public" that liberals object to. For the distinction between
these two is *itself* liberal, as is the idea of a free press's and broadcast media's
special responsibilities—"liberal" in the sense of being rooted in a concern for the
common good over and above the preferences of individual citizens. The point is
that the debate over things like the Fairness Doctrine and the proper responsibility
of broadcasters quickly hits ideological bedrock on both sides.

DITTO (Which does indeed entail government's arrogating the power to decide
what that common good is, it's true. On the other hand, the idea is that at least
government officials are elected, or appointed by elected representatives, and
thus are somewhat accountable to the public they're deciding for. What appears
to drive liberals most crazy about the right's conflation of "common good"/
"public interest" with "what wins in the market" is the conviction that it's all a

scam, that what the deregulation of industries like broadcasting, health care, and energy really amounts to is the subordination of the public's interests to the financial interests of large corporations. Which is, of course, all part of a very deep, serious national argument about the role and duties of government that America's having with itself right now. It is an argument that's not being plumbed at much depth on political talk radio, though—at least not the more legitimate, non-wacko claims of some on the left [a neglect that then strengthens liberal suspicions that all these conservative talk hosts are just spokesholes for their corporate masters . . . and around and around it all goes].)

More or less on the heels of the Fairness Doctrine's repeal came the West Coast and then national syndication of *The Rush Limbaugh Show*

The crucial connection with the F.D.'s repeal was not Rush's show but that show's syndicatability. A station could now purchase and air three daily hours of Limbaugh without being committed to programming another three hours of Sierra Club or Urban League or something.

through Mr. McLaughlin's EFM Media. Limbaugh is the third great progenitor of today's political talk radio partly because he's a host of extraor-

EFM Media, named for Edward McLaughlin, was a sort of Old Testament patriarch of modern syndication, although Mr. McL. tended to charge subscribing stations cash instead of splitting the Clock, because he wanted a low spot load that would give Rush maximum air time to build his audience.

dinary, once-in-a-generation talent and charisma—bright, loquacious, witty, complexly authoritative—whose show's blend of news, entertainment, and partisan analysis became the model for legions of imitators. But he was also the first great promulgator of the Mainstream Media's Liberal Bias idea. This turned out to be a brilliantly effective rhetorical

In truth, Rush's disdain for the "liberal press" somewhat recalls good old Spiro Agnew's attacks on the Washington press corps (as in "nattering nabobs,"

> "hopeless, hysterical hypochondriacs," etc.), with the crucial difference being that Agnew's charges always came off as thuggish and pathetic *in that "liberal press,"* which at the time was the only vector for their transmission. Because of his own talent and the popularity of his show, Rush was able to move partisan distrust for the mainstream "liberal media" into the mainstream itself.

move, since the MMLB concept functioned simultaneously as a standard around which Rush's audience could rally, as an articulation of the need for right-wing (i.e., unbiased) media, and as a mechanism by which any criticism or refutation of conservative ideas could be dismissed (either as biased or as the product of indoctrination by biased media). Boiled way down, the MMLB thesis is able both to exploit and to perpetuate many conservatives' dissatisfaction with extant media sources— and it's this dissatisfaction that cements political talk radio's large and loyal audience.

> JUST CLEAR-EYED, DISPASSIONATE REASON Notwithstanding all sorts of interesting other explanations, the single biggest reason why left-wing talk-radio experiments like Air America or the Ed Schultz program are not likely to succeed, at least not on a national level, is that their potential audience is just not dissatisfied enough with today's mainstream news sources to feel that it has to patronize a special type of media to get the unbiased truth.

In the best Rush Limbaugh tradition, Mr. Ziegler takes pride in his on-air sense of humor. His media criticism is often laced with wisecracks, and he likes to leaven his show's political and cultural analyses with timely ad-lib gags, such as "It's maybe a good thing that Catholics and Muslims don't tend to marry. If they had a kid, he'd grow up and then, what, abuse some child and then blow him up?" And he has a penchant for comic maxims ("Fifty percent of all marriages are confirmed failures, while the other fifty percent end in divorce"; "The female figure is the greatest known evidence that there might be a God, but the female psyche is an indication that this God has a very sick sense of humor")

that he uses on the air and then catalogues as "Zieglerisms" on his KFI Web site.

Mr. Z. can also, when time and the demands of prep permit, go long-form. In his program's final hour for May 22, he delivers a mock commencement address to the Class of 2004, a piece of prepared sit-down comedy that is worth excerpting, verbatim, as a sort of keyhole into the professional psyche of Mr. John Ziegler:

> Class of 2004, congratulations on graduation. . . . I wish to let you in on a few secrets that those of you who are not completely brain-dead will eventually figure out on your own, but, if you listen to me, will save a lot of time and frustration. First of all, most of what you have been taught in your academic career is not true. I am not just talking about the details of history that have been distorted to promote the liberal agenda of academia. I am also referring to the big-picture lessons of life as well. The sad truth is that contrary to what most of you have been told, you *cannot* do or be anything you want.

Again, this is all better, and arguably funnier, when delivered aloud in Mr. Z.'s distinctive way.

EDITORIAL QUIBBLE It's unclear just when in college Mr. Z. thinks students are taught that they can do or be anything. A good part of what he considers academia's leftist agenda, after all, consists in teaching kids about social and economic stratification, inequalities, uneven playing fields—all (if conservatively disposed, please substitute "allegedly") the U.S. realities that actually limit possibilities for some people.

The vast majority of you . . . will be absolutely miserable in whatever career you choose or are forced to endure. You will most likely hate your boss because they will most likely be dumber than you think you are, and they will inevitably screw you at every chance they get. . . . The boss will not be the only stupid person you encounter in life. The vast majority of people are *much*, *much* dumber than you have ever been led to believe. Never forget this. And just like people are far dumber than you have been led to believe, they are also *far* more dishonest than anyone is seemingly willing to admit to you. If you have any doubt as to whether someone is telling you the truth, it is a safe bet to assume that they are lying to you.... Do not trust anyone unless you have some sort of significant leverage over him or her and they *know* that you have that leverage over them. Unless this condition exists, anyone—and I mean *anyone*—can and probably will stab you in the back.

That is about one sixth of the address, and for the most part it speaks for itself.

One of many intriguing things about Mr. Ziegler, though, is the contrast between his deep cynicism about backstabbing and the naked, seemingly self-destructive candor with which he'll discuss his life and career. This candor becomes almost paradoxical in Q & As with an

> The best guess re Mr. Z.'s brutal on-record frankness is that either (a) the host's on- and off-air personas really are identical, or (b) he regards speaking to a magazine correspondent as just one more part of his job, which is to express himself in a maximally stimulating way (there was a tape recorder out, after all).

outside correspondent, a stranger whom Mr. Z. has no particular reason to trust at those times when he winces after saying something and asks that it be struck from the record. As it happens, however, nearly all of what follows is from an autobiographical time-line volunteered by John Ziegler in late May '04 over a very large medium-rare steak. Especially interesting is the time-line's mixture of raw historical fact and passionate editorial opinion, which Mr. Z. blends so seamlessly that one really can believe he discerns no difference between them.

> (for a magazine, moreover, that pretty much everyone around KFI regards as a chattering-class organ of the most elitist liberal kind)

> (while both eating and watching a Lakers playoff game on a large-screen high-def TV, which latter was the only condition he placed on the interview)

1967–1989: Mr. John Ziegler grows up in suburban Philadelphia, the elder son of a financial manager and a homemaker. All kinds of unsummarizable evidence indicates that Mr. Z. and his mother are very close. In 1984, he is named High School Golfer of the Year by the *Bucks County Courier Times*. He's also a three-year golf letterman at Georgetown, where his liberal arts studies turn out to be "a great way to prepare for a life of being unemployed, which I've done quite a bit of."

1989–1995: Mr. Z.'s original career is in local TV sports. He works for stations in and around Washington DC, in Steubenville OH, and finally in Raleigh NC. Though sports news is what he's wanted to do ever since he was a little boy, he hates the jobs: "The whole world of sports and local news is so disgusting . . . local TV news is half a step above prostitution."

> (especially the one at Raleigh's WLFL Fox 22—"My boss there was the worst boss in the history of bosses")

1994–1995: Both personally and professionally, this period constitutes a dark night of the soul for John Ziegler. Summer '94: O. J. Simpson's ex-wife is brutally murdered. Fall '94: Mr. Ziegler's mother is killed in a car crash. Winter '95: During his sportscast, Mr. Z. makes "an incredibly tame joke about O. J. Simpson's lack of innocence" w/r/t his wife's murder, which draws some protest from Raleigh's black community. John Ziegler is eventually fired from WLFL because the station "caved in to Political Correctness." The whole nasty incident marks the start of (a) Mr. Z.'s deep, complex hatred for all things PC, and (b) "my history with O.J." He falls into a deep funk, decides to give up sports broadcasting, "pretty much gave up on life, actually." Mr. Z. spends his days watching the O. J. Simpson trial on cable television, often sitting through repeat broadcasts of the coverage late at night; and when O.J. is finally acquitted, "I was nearly suicidal." Two psychiatrist golf buddies talk him into going on antidepressants, but much of the time O.J. is still all Mr. Ziegler can think and talk about. "It got so bad—you'll find this funny—at one point I was so depressed that it was my goal, assuming that he'd

> ?!

be acquitted and that [O.J.'s] Riviera Country Club wouldn't have the guts to kick him out, that I was going to become a caddy at Riviera, knock him off, and see whether or not [a certain lawyer Mr. Z. also played golf with, whose name is here omitted] could get me off on jury nullification. That's how obsessed I was." The lawyer/golfer/friend's reaction to this plan is not described.

Late 1995: Mr. Z. decides to give life and broadcasting another shot. Figuring that "maybe my controversial nature would work better on talk radio," he takes a job as a weekend fill-in host for a station in Fuquay-Varina, NC—"the worst talk-radio station on the planet . . . to call the station owner a redneck was insulting to rednecks"—only to be abruptly fired when the station switches to an automated Christian-music format.

Early 1996: "I bought, actually *bought*, time on a Raleigh talk-radio station" in order to start "putting together a Tape," although Mr. Z. is good enough on the air that they soon put him on as a paid host. What happens, though, is that this station uses a certain programming consultant, whose name is being omitted—"a pretty big name in the industry, who [however] is a *snake*, and, I believe, extremely overrated—and he at first really took a shine to me, and then told me, *told me*, to do a show on how I got fired from the TV job, and I did the show," which evidently involves retelling the

> A Tape is sort of the radio/TV equivalent of an artist's portfolio.

> As Mr. Z. explains it, consultants work as freelance advisers to different stations' Program Directors—"They sort of give the P.D. a cover if he hires somebody and it doesn't work out."

original tame O.J. joke, after which the herpetic consultant stands idly by as the station informs Mr. Z. that "'We're done with you, no thank you,' which was another blow."

1996–1997: Another radio consultant recommends Mr. Z. for

(the whole story of which is very involved and takes up almost half a microcassette)

a job at WWTN, a Nashville talk station, where he hosts an evening show that makes good Book and is largely hassle-free for several months. Of his brief career at WWTN, the host now feels that "I kind of self-destructed there, actually, in retrospect. I got frustrated with management. I was right, but I was stupid as well." The trouble starts when Tiger Woods wins the 1997 Masters. As part of

(whom the host reveres—a standing gag on his KFI program is that Mr. Z. is a deacon in the First Church of Tiger Woods)

his commentary on the tournament, Mr. Z. posits on-air that Tiger constitutes living proof of the fact that "not all white people are racists." His supporting argument is that "no white person would ever think of Tiger as a nigger," because whites draw a mental distinction "between people who just happen to be black and people who act like niggers." His reason for broadcasting the actual word "nigger"? "This all goes back to O.J. I hated the fact that the media treated viewers and listeners like children by saying 'Mark Fuhrman used the N-word.' I despised that, and I think it gives the word too much power. Plus there's the whole hypocrisy of how black people can use it and white people can't. I was young and naive and thought I could stand on principle." As part of that principled stand, Mr. Z. soon redeploys the argument and the word in a discussion of boxer Mike Tyson, whereupon he is fired, "even though there very little listener reaction." As Mr. Z. understands it, the reason for his dismissal is that "a single black employee complained," and WWTN's parent, "a lily-white company," feared that it was "very vulnerable" to a discrimination lawsuit.

1998–1999: Mr. Z. works briefly as a morning fill-in at Nashville's WLAC, whose studios are right across the street from the station that just fired him. From there, he is hired to do overnights at WWDB, an FM talk station in Philadelphia, his hometown. There are again auspicious beginnings . . . "except my boss, [the PD who hired him], is completely unstable and ends up punching out a consultant, and gets fired. At that point I'm totally screwed—I have nobody who's got my back, and everybody's out to get me." Mr. Z. is suddenly fired to make room for syndicated raunchmeister Tom Leykis, then is quickly refired when listener complaints get Leykis's program taken off the air . . . then is re-

> For those unfamiliar with Tom Leykis: Imagine Howard Stern without the cleverness.

fired a week later when the station juggles its schedule again. Mr. Z. on his time at WWDB: "I should have sued those bastards."

Q: So what exactly is the point of a host's having a contract if the station can evidently just up and fire you whenever they feel like it?

A: "The only thing a contract's worth in radio is how much they're going to pay you when they fire you. And if they fire you 'For Cause,' then they don't have to pay you anything."

2000: John Ziegler moves over to WIP, a famous Philadelphia sports-talk station. "I hated it, but I did pretty well. I can do sports, obviously, and it was also a big political year." But there is both a general problem and a specific problem. The general problem is that "The boss there, [name omitted] is an evil, evil, evil, *evil* man. If God said, 'John, you get one person to kill for free,' this would be the man I would kill. And I would make it brutally painful." The specific problem arises when "Mike Tyson holds a press conference, and calls himself a nigger. And I can't resist—I mean, here I've gotten fired in the past for using the word in relation to a person who calls *himself* that now. I mean, my God. So I tell the story [of having used the word and gotten fired for it] on the air, but I do not use the N-word—I *spell* the N-word, every single time, to cover my ass, and to also make a point of the absurdity of the whole thing. And we get one, *one*, postcard, from a total lunatic black person— misspellings, just clearly a lunatic. And

> In the Q & A itself, Mr. Z. goes back and forth between actually using the N-word and merely referring to it as "the N-word," without apparent pattern or design.

[Mr. Z.'s boss at WIP] calls me in and says, 'John, I think you're a racist.' Now, first of all, *this guy* is a racist, I mean he is a *real* racist. I am anything but a racist, but to be called that by *him*

EDITORIAL OPINION This is obviously a high-voltage area to get into, but for what it's worth, John Ziegler does not appear to be a racist as "racist" is generally understood. What he is is more like very, very insensitive— although Mr. Z. himself would despise that description, if only because "insensitive" is now such a PC shibboleth. Actually, though, it is in the very passion of his objection to terms like "insensitive," "racist," and "the N-word" that his real problem lies. Like many other post-Limbaugh hosts, John Ziegler seems unable to differentiate between (1) cowardly, hypocritical acquiescence to the tyranny of Political Correctness and (2) judicious,

(just one person's opinion . . .)

compassionate caution about using words that cause pain to large groups of human beings, especially when there are several less upsetting words that can be used. Even though there is plenty of stuff for reasonable people to dislike about Political Correctness as a dogma, there is also something creepy about the brutal, self-righteous glee with which Mr. Z. and other conservative hosts defy all PC conventions. If it causes you real pain to hear or see something, and I make it a point to inflict that thing on you merely because I object to your reasons for finding it painful, then there's something wrong with my sense of proportion, or my recognition of your basic humanity, or both.

THIS, TOO (And let's be real: spelling out a painful word is no improvement. In some ways, it's worse than using the word outright, since spelling it could easily be seen as implying that the people who are upset by the word are also too dumb to spell it. What's puzzling here is that Mr. Ziegler seems much too bright and self-aware not to understand this.)

just made my blood boil. I mean, life's too short to be working overnights for this fucking bastard." A day or two later Mr. Z. is fired, For Cause, for spelling the N-word on-air.

Q: It sounds like you've got serious personal reasons for disliking Political Correctness.

A: "Oh my God, yes. My whole life has been ruined by it. I've lost relationships, I can't get married, I can't have kids, all because of Political Correctness. I can't put anybody else through the crap I've been through—I can't do it."

A corollary possibility: The reason why the world as interpreted by many hosts is one of such thoroughgoing selfishness and cynicism and fear is that these are qualities of the talk-radio industry they are part of, and they (like professionals everywhere) tend to see their industry as a reflection of the real world.

Mr. Z. explains that he's referring here to the constant moving around and apartment-hunting and public controversy caused by the firings. His sense of grievance and loss seems genuine. But one should also keep in mind how vital, for political talk hosts in general, is this sense of embattled persecution—by the leftist mainstream press, by slick Democratic operatives, by liberal lunatics and identity politics and PC and rampant cynical pandering. All of which provides the constant conflict required for good narrative and stimulating radio. Not, in John Ziegler's case, that any of his anger and self-pity is contrived—but they can be totally real and still function as parts of the skill set he brings to his job.

2001: While writing freelance columns for the *Philadelphia Inquirer* and *Philadelphia Daily News*, Mr. Ziegler also gets work at a small twenty-four-hour Comcast cable-TV network in Philly, where he's a writer and commentator on a prime-time issues-related talk show. Although Comcast is "an evil, evil, evil company, [which] created that network for the sole purpose of giving blow-jobs to politicians who vote on Comcast legislation," Mr. Z. discovers that "I'm actually really good at talk TV. I was the best thing that ever happened to this show. I actually ended up winning an Emmy, which is ironic." There are, however, serious and irresolvable problems with a female producer on the show, the full story of which you are going to be spared (mainly because of legal worries).

2002: John Ziegler is hired as the midmorning host at Clear Channel's WHAS in Louisville, which Arbitron lists as the fifty-fifth largest radio market in the U.S. According to a local paper, the host's "stormy, thirteen-month tenure in Louisville was punctuated by intrigue, outrage, controversy and litigation." According to John Ziegler, "The whole story would make a great movie—in fact, my whole life would make a great movie, but this in particular would make a great movie." Densely compressed synopsis: For several quarters, Mr. Z.'s program is a great success in Louisville. "I'm doing huge numbers—in one Book I got a fifteen share, which is ridiculous." He is also involved in a very public romance with one Darcie Divita, a former LA Lakers cheerleader who is part of a morning news show on the local Fox TV affiliate. The relationship is apparently Louisville's version of Ben & J.Lo, and its end is not amicable. In August '03, prompted by callers' questions on his regular "Ask John Anything" feature, Mr. Z. makes certain on-air comments about Ms. Divita's breasts, underwear, genital grooming, and libido. Part of the enduring controversy over John Ziegler's firing, which occurs a few days later, is exactly how much those comments and/or subsequent complaints from listeners and the Louisville media had to do with it. Mr. Z. has a

> Here, some of John Ziegler's specific remarks about Darcie Divita are being excised at his request. It turns out that Ms. Divita is suing both the host and WHAS—Mr. Z.'s deposition is scheduled for summer '04.

long list of reasons for believing that his P. D. was really just looking for an excuse to can him. As for all the complaints, Mr. Z. remains bitter and perplexed: (1) "The comments I made about Darcie's physical attributes were extremely positive in nature"; (2) "Darcie had, in the past, *volunteered* information about her cleavage on my program"; (3) "I've gone much further with other public figures without incident. . . . I mocked [Kentucky Governor] Paul Patton for his inability to bring Tina Conner to orgasm, [and] no one from management ever even mentioned it to me."

John Ziegler on why he thinks he was hired for the Live and Local job by KFI: "They needed somebody 'available.'" And on the corporate logic behind his hiring: "It's among the most bizarre things I've ever been

> (after what Ms. Bertolucci characterizes as "a really big search around the country")

> Mr. Z. explains the scare quotes around "available" as meaning that the experimental gig didn't offer the sort of compensation that could lure a large-market host away from another station. He describes his current KFI salary as "in the low six figures."

involved in. To simultaneously be fired by Clear Channel and negotiate termination in a market where I had immense value and be courted by the same company in a market where I had no current value is beyond explicable."

Mr. Z. on talk radio as a career: "This is a terrible business. I'd love to quit this business." On why, then, he accepted KFI's offer: "My current contract would be by far the toughest for them to fire me of anyplace I've been."

★ ★ ★

Compared with many talk-radio hosts, John Ziegler is unusually polite to on-air callers. Which is to say that he doesn't yell at them, call them names, or hang up while they're speaking, although he does get frustrated with some calls. But there are good and bad kinds of frustration, stimulation-wise. Hence the delicate art of call screening. The screener's little switchboard and computer console are here in the Airmix room, right up next to the studio window.

JZS Producer Emiliano Limon: "There are two types of callers. You've got your hard-core talk-radio callers, who just like hearing themselves on-air"—these listeners will sometimes vary the first names and home cities they give the screener, trying to disguise the fact that they've been calling in night after night—"and then there are the ones who just, for whatever reason, respond to the topic." Of these latter a certain percentage are wackos, but some wackos actually make good on-air callers. Assoc. prod. and screener Vince Nicholas: "The trick is knowing what kooks to get rid of and what to let through. People that are kooky on a particular issue—some of these Zig

> Vince (who is either a deep professional admirer or a titanic suck-up) states several times that John Ziegler is excellent with callers, dutifully referring to him each time as "Zig."

'Mondo Hernandez confirms on-record that Vince's screener voice sounds like someone talking around a huge bong hit.

likes; he can bust on them and have fun with them. He likes it."

Vince isn't rude or brusque with the callers he screens out; he simply becomes more and more laconic and stoned-sounding over the headset as the person rants on, and finally says, "Whoa, gotta go." Especially obnoxious and persistent callers can be placed on Hold at the screener's switchboard, locking up their phones until Vince decides to let them go. Those whom the screener lets through enter a different, computerized Hold system in which eight callers at a time can be kept queued up and waiting, each designated on Mr. Z.'s monitor by a different colored box displaying a first name, city, one-sentence summary of the caller's thesis, and the total time waiting. The host chooses, cafeteria-style, from this array.

In his selections, Mr. Z. has an observable preference for female callers. Emiliano's explanation: "Since political talk radio is so white male–driven, it's good to get female voices in there." It turns out that this is an industry convention; the roughly 50–50 gender mix of callers one hears on most talk radio is because screeners admit a much higher percentage of female callers to the system.

One of the last things that Emiliano Limon always does before air-time is to use the station's NexGen Audio Editing System to load various recorded sound bites from the day's broadcast news onto a Prophet file

NexGen (a Clear Channel product) displays a Richterish-looking sound wave, of which all different sizes of individual bits can be highlighted and erased in order to tighten the pacing and compress the sound bite. It's different from 'Mondo's Cashbox, which tightens things automatically according to pre-set specs; using NexGen requires true artistry. Emiliano knows the distinctive vocal wave patterns of George W. Bush, Bill O'Reilly, Sean Hannity, and certain others well enough that he can recognize them on the screen without any sound or ID. He is so good at using NexGen that he manages to make the whole high-stress Cut Sheet thing look dull.

that goes with the Cut Sheet. This is a numbered list of bites available for tonight's *John Ziegler Show*, of which both Mr. Z. and 'Mondo get a copy. Each bite must be precisely timed. It is an intricate, exacting process of editing and compilation, during which Mr. Z. often drums his fingers and looks pointedly at his watch as the producer ignores him and always very slowly and placidly edits and compresses and loads and has the Cut Sheet ready at the very last second. Emiliano is the sort of extremely chilled-out person who can seem to be leaning back at his station with his feet up on the Airmix table even when he isn't leaning back at all. He's wearing the *LA Times* shirt again. His own view on listener calls is that they are "overrated in talk radio," that they're rarely all that cogent or stimulating, but that hosts tend to be "overconcerned with taking calls and whether people are calling. Consider: This is the only type of live performance with absolutely no feedback from the audience. It's natural for the host to key in on the only real-time response he can get, which is the calls. It takes a long time with a host to get him to forget about the calls, to realize the calls have very little to do with the wider audience."

Vince, meanwhile, is busy at the screener's station. A lady with a heavy accent keeps calling in to say that she has vital information: a Czech newspaper has revealed that John Kerry is actually a Jew, that his grandfather changed his distinctively Jewish surname, and that this fact is being suppressed in the U.S. media and must be exposed. Vince finally tries putting her on punitive Hold, but her line's light goes out, which signifies that the lady has a cell phone and has disengaged by simply turning it off. Meaning that she can call back again as much as she likes, and that Vince is going to have to get actively rude. 'Mondo's great mild eyes rise from the board: "*Puto*, man, what's that about?" Vince, very flat and bored: "Kerry's a Jew." Emiliano: "Another big advent is the cell phone. Before cells

> 'Mondo and Vince clearly enjoy each other, exchanging "*puto*" and "*chilango*" with brotherly ease. When Vince takes a couple days off, it becomes difficult to get 'Mondo to say anything about anything, Doritos or no.

> Q: (based on seeing some awfully high minute-counts in some people's colored boxes on Vince's display): How long will callers wait to get on the air?
>
> Emiliano Limon: "We get some who'll wait for the whole show. [Laughs] If they're driving, what else do they have to do?"
>
> Q: If a drunk driver calls in, do you have to notify the police or something?
>
> A: "Well, this is why screening is tricky. You'll get, say, somebody calling in saying they're going to commit suicide—sometimes you have to refer the call. But sometimes you're getting pranked. Keep in mind, we're in an area with a lot of actors and actresses anxious to practice their craft. [Now his feet really are up on the table.] I remember we had Ross Perot call in one time, it sounded just like him, and actually he really was due to be on the show but not for an hour, and now he's calling saying he needs to be on right now because of a schedule change. Very convincing, sounded just like him, and I had to go, 'Uh, Mr. Perot, what's the name of your assistant press liaison?' Because I'd just talked to her a couple days prior. And he's [doing vocal impression]: 'Listen here, you all going to put me on the air or not?' And I'm: 'Umm, Mr. Perot, if you understand the question, please answer the question.' And he hangs up. [Laughs] But you would have sworn this was Ross Perot."

you got mostly homebound invalids calling in. [Laughs] Now you get the driving invalid."

4

Historically, the two greatest ratings periods ever for KFI AM-640 have been the Gray Davis gubernatorial recall and the O. J. Simpson trial. Now, in early June '04, the tenth anniversary of the Ron Goldman/Nicole Brown Simpson murders is approaching, and O. J. starts to pop up once again on the cultural radar. And Mr. John Ziegler happens to be more passionate about the O. J. Simpson thing than maybe any other

> Some of his personal reasons for this have been made clear. But the Simpson case also rings a lot of professional cherries for Mr. Ziegler as a host: sports, celebrity, race, racism, PC and the "race card," the legal profession, the U.S. justice system, sex, misogyny, miscegenation, and a lack of shame and personal accountability that Mr. Z. sees as just plain evil.

single issue, and feels that he "know[s] more about the case than anyone not directly involved," and is able to be almost unbearably stimulating about O. J. Simpson and the utter indubitability of his guilt. And the confluence of the murders' anniversary, the case's tabloid importance to the nation and business importance to KFI, and its deep personal resonance for Mr. Z. helps produce what at first looks like the absolute Monster talk-radio story of the month.

On June 3, in the third segment of the *John Ziegler Show*'s second hour, after lengthy discussions of the O.J. anniversary and the Michael

---

This annoys Alan LaGreen of Airwatch enough to cause him to snap at 'Mondo on an off-air channel (mainly because Alan LaGreen now ends up having to be the KFI Traffic Center during an interval in which he's supposed to be the Traffic Center for some country station); plus it pushes 'Mondo's skills with the Cashbox right to their limit in the hour's segment four.

Jackson case, Mr. Z. takes a phone call from one "Daryl in Temecula," an African-American gentleman who is "absolutely astounded they let a Klansman on the radio this time of night." The call, which lasts seven minutes and eighteen seconds and runs well over the :46 break, ends with John Ziegler's telling the audience, "That's as angry as I've ever gotten in the history of my career." And Vince Nicholas, looking awed and spent at his screener's station, pronounces the whole thing "some of the best talk radio I ever heard."

Some portions of the call are untranscribable because they consist mainly of Daryl and Mr. Z. trying to talk over each other. Daryl's core points appear to be (1) that Mr. Z. seems to spend all his time talking about black men like Kobe and O.J. and Michael Jackson—"Don't white people commit crimes?"—and (2) that O.J. was, after all, found innocent in a court of law, and yet Mr. Z. keeps "going on about 'He's guilty, he's guilty—'"

"He *is*," the host inserts.

Daryl: "He was acquitted, wasn't he?"

It turns out to be impossible, off the air, to Q & A Mr. Ziegler about his certainty re O.J.'s guilt. Bring up anything that might sound like reservations, and Mr. Z won't say a word—he'll angle his head way over to the side and look at you as if he can't tell whether you're trying to jerk him around or you're simply out of your mind.

It's different if you ask about O. J. Simpson *l'homme*, or about specific details of his psyche and marriage and lifestyle and golf game and horrible crimes. For instance, John Ziegler has a detailed and fairly plausible-sounding theory about O.J.'s motive for the murders, which boils down to Simpson's jealous rage over his ex-wife's having slept with Mr. Marcus Allen, a former Heisman Trophy winner and current (as of '94) NFL star. Mr. Z. can defend this theory with an unreproduceably long index of facts, names, and media citations, all of which you can ask him about if you keep your face and tone neutral and simply write down what he says without appearing to quibble or object or in any way question the host's authority on the subject.

(For instance, you cannot ask something like whether Ms. Simpson's liaison with Marcus Allen is a documented fact or just part of Mr. Z.'s theory—this will immediately terminate the Q & A.)

"That makes no difference as to whether or not he did it."

"O.J., Kobe: You just thrive on these black guys."

It is here that Mr. Z. begins to pick up steam. "Oh yeah, Daryl, right, I'm a racist. As a matter of fact, I often say, 'You know what? I just wish another black guy would commit a crime, because I hate black people so much.'"

Daryl: "I think you do have more to talk about on black guys. I think that's more '*news*'" . . . which actually would be kind of an interesting point to explore, or at least address; but Mr. Z. is now stimulated.

"As a matter of fact, Daryl, oftentimes when we go through who's committed the crimes, there are times when the white people who control the media, we get together and go, 'Oh, we can't talk about that one, because that was a white guy.' This is all a big conspiracy, Daryl. Except, to be serious for a second, Daryl, what really upsets me, assuming you're a black guy, is that you ought to be *ten* times more pissed off at O. J. Simpson than I am, because you know why?"

Daryl: "You can't tell me how I should feel. As a forty-year-old black man, I've seen racism for forty years."

Mr. Z. is starting to move his upper body back and forth excitedly in his chair. "I bet you have. I bet you have. And here's why you ought to be pissed off: Because, out of all the black guys who *deserved* to get a benefit of the doubt because of the history of racism which is real in this country, and which is insidious, the one guy—*the one guy*—who gets the benefit of all of that pain and suffering over a hundred years of history in this country is the one guy who deserves it less than anybody else, who sold his race out, who tried to talk white, who only had white friends, who had his ass

> In case memories of the trial have dimmed, Mr. Z. is referring here to the defense team's famous playing of the race card, the suggestion that the LAPD wanted to frame O.J. because he was a miscegenating black, etc.

> TINY EDITORIAL CORRECTION Umm, four hundred?

> John Ziegler is now screeching—except that's not quite the right word. Pitch and volume have both risen ('Mondo's at the channel 7 controls trying to forestall peaking), but his tone is meant to connote a mix of incredulity and outrage, with the same ragged edge to the stressed syllables as—no kidding—Jackson's and Sharpton's. Daryl of Temecula, meantime, has been silenced by the sheer passion of the host's soliloquy . . . and we should note that Daryl really has stopped speaking; it's not that Mr. Z. has turned off the volume on the caller's line (which is within his power, and which some talk-radio hosts do a lot, but Mr. Z. does not treat callers this way).

kissed all over the place because he decided he wasn't really a black guy, who was the first person in the history of this country ever accepted by white America, who was actually able to do commercial endorsements because he pretended to be white, and *that's the guy*? *That's the guy. That's the guy* who gets the benefit of that history, and that doesn't piss you off, *that doesn't piss you off?*" And then an abrupt decrescendo: "Daryl, I can assure you that the last thing I am is racist on this. This is the last guy who should benefit."

> (Mr. Z. means the first *black* person—he's now so impassioned he's skipping words. [It never once sounds like babbling, though.])

> (voice breaking a bit here)

And then June 4, the night following the Daryl interchange, turns out to be a climactic whirlwind of production challenges, logistical

EDITORIAL OPINION Again, it's nothing so simple as that he doth protest too much, but it would be less discomfiting if Mr. Z. didn't feel he could so totally assure Daryl of this—i.e., if Mr. Z. weren't so certain that his views are untainted by racism. Not to mention that the assurance resonates strangely against all the host's vented spleen about a black man's "selling out his race" by "pretending to be white." Not, again, that Mr. Z. wears a pointy hood—but he seems weirdly unconscious of the fact that Simpson's ostensible betrayal of his race is something that only a member of that race really has the right to get angry about. No? If a white person gets angry about a black person's "pretend-ing to be white," doesn't the anger come off far less as sympathy with the person's betrayed race than as antipathy for somebody who's trying to crash a party he doesn't belong at? (Or is Mr. Z. actually to be admired here for not giving a damn about how his anger comes off, for not buying into any of that it's-okay-for-a-black-person-to-say-it-but-not-okay-for-a-white-person stuff? And if so, why is it that his "selling out" complaints seem creepy and obtuse instead of admirable [although, of course, how his complaints "seem" might simply depend on the politics and sensitivities of the individual listener (such that the whole thing becomes not so much stimulating as exhausting)]?)

> Is it wimpy or white-guiltish to believe that we're all at least a little bit racist in some of our attitudes or beliefs, or at any rate that it's not impossible that we are?

> (Better than "the right" here might be "the rhetorical authority.")

brinksmanship, meta-media outrage, Simpsonian minutiae, and Monster-grade stimulation. As is SOP, it starts around 7:00 P.M. in KFI's large central prep room, which is where all the local hosts and their producers come in to prepare for their shows.

The prep room, which station management sometimes refers to as the production office, is more or less the nerve center of KFI, a large, complexly shaped space perimetered with battered little canted desks and hutches and two-drawer file cabinets supporting tabletops of com-

> The standard of professionalism in talk radio is one hour of prep for each hour on the air. But Mr. Ziegler, whose specialty in media criticism entails extra-massive daily consumption of Internet and cable news, professes to be "pretty much always prepping," at least during the times he's not asleep (3:00—10:00 A.M.) or playing golf (which since he's moved to LA he does just about every day, quite possibly by himself—all he'll say about it is "I have no life here").

posite planking. There are beat-up computers and pieces of sound equipment and funny Scotch-taped bits of office humor (e.g., pictures with staffers' heads Photoshopped onto tabloid celebrities' bodies). Like the studio and Air-mix, the prep room is also a D.P.H.-grade mess: half the overhead fluorescents are either out or flickering nauseously, and the gray carpet crunches underfoot, and the wastebaskets are all towering fire hazards, and many of the tabletops are piled with old books and newspapers. One window, which is hot to the touch, overlooks KFI's gated parking lot and security booth and the office of a Korean podiatrist across the street.

> There is also another large TV in the prep room, this one wired to a TiVo digital recording system so that anything from the day's cable news can be tagged, copied, and loaded into NexGen and prophet. The TV gets only one channel at a time, but apparently certain cable stuff can also be accessed on one of the prep-room computers by a producer who knows what he's doing.

Overall, the layout and myriad tactical functions of the prep room are too complicated to try to describe this late in the game. At one end, it gives on to the KFI newsroom, which is a whole galaxy unto itself. At the other, comparatively uncluttered end is a set of thick, distinguished-looking doors leading off into the offices of the Station Manager, Director of Marketing & Promotions Program Director and so on, with also a semi-attached former closet for the P.D.'s assistant, a very kindly and eccentric lady who's been at KFI for over twenty years and wears a high-tech headset that one begins, only over time, to suspect isn't really connected to anything.

> Examples of volumes pulled at random from the tabletops' clutter: Dwight Nichols's *God's Plans for Your Finances*, the Hoover Institution's *Education and Capitalism: How Overcoming Our Fear of Markets and Economics Can Improve America's Schools,* and Louis Barajas's *The Latino Journey to Financial Greatness.*

> (who's usually long gone by the time the *JZS* staff starts prepping)

There are three main challenges facing tonight's *John Ziegler Show.* One is that Emiliano Limon is off on certain personal business that he doesn't want described, and therefore Mr. Vince Nicholas is soloing as producer for the very first time. Another is that last night's on-air exchange with Daryl of Temecula is the type of intensely stimulating talk-radio event that cries out for repetition and commentary; Mr. Z. wants to rerun certain snippets of the call in a very precise order so that he can use them as jumping-off points for detailing his own "history with O.J." and explaining why he's so incandescently passionate about the case.

The third difficulty is that Simpson's big anniversary Q & A with Ms. Katie Couric is airing tonight on NBC's *Dateline*, and the cuts and discussions of the Daryl call are going to have to be interwoven with excerpts from what Mr. Z. refers to several times as "Katie's blowjob interview." An additional complication is that *Dateline* airs in Los Angeles from 8:00 to 10:00 p.m., and it has also now run teases for stories on the health hazards of the Atkins diet and the dangerously lax security in U.S. hotels. Assuming that *Dateline* waits and does the O.J. interview last (which it is clearly in the program's interests to do), then the interview's highlights will have to be recorded off TiVo, edited on NexGen, loaded onto Prophet, and queued up for the Cut Sheet all very quickly, since Mr. Z.'s opening segment starts at 10:06 and it's hard to fiddle with logistics once his show's under way.

> "You're going to need to kick some ass tonight, bud," Mr. Z. tells Vince as he highlights bites in a transcript of Daryl's call, eliciting something very close to a salute.

Thus Vince spends 7:00–8:00 working two side-by-side computers, trying simultaneously to assemble the cuts from last night's call, load an MSNBC interview with Nicole Brown Simpson's sister directly into NexCen, and track down a Web transcript of tonight's *Dateline* (which on the East Coast has already aired) so that he and Mr. Z. can choose and record bites from the Couric thing in real time. 'Mondo, who is back board-opping the ISDN feed of 7:00–10:00's *Phil Hendrie Show*, nevertheless comes in from Airmix several times to stand behind Vince at the terminals, ostensibly to see what's going on but really to lend moral support. 'Mondo's shadow takes up almost half the room's east wall.

John Ziegler, who is understandably quite keyed up, spends some of the pre-*Dateline* time standing around with an extremely pretty News-department intern named Kyra, watching the MSNBC exchange with half an eye while doing his trademark stress-relieving thing of holding two golf balls and trying to align the dimples so that one ball stays balanced atop the other. He is wearing a horizontally striped green-and-white golf

Nobody ever ribs Mr. Z. about the manual golf-ball thing vis-à-vis, say, Captain Queeg's famous ball bearings. It is not that he wouldn't get the allusion; Mr. Z. is just not the sort of person one kids around with this way. After one mid-May appearance on *Scarborough Country*, re some San Diego schoolteachers getting suspended for showing the Nick Berg decapitation video in class, a certain unnamed person had tried joshing around with him, in an offhand and light-hearted way, about a supposed very small facial tic that had kept appearing unbeknownst to John Ziegler whenever he'd used the phrase "wussification of America" on-camera; and Mr. Z. was, let's just say, unamused, and gave the person a look that chilled him to the marrow.

shirt, neatly pressed black shorts, and gleaming New Balance sneakers. He keeps saying that he cannot be*lieve* they're even giving Simpson air time. No one points out that his shock seems a bit naive given the business realities of network TV news, realities about which John Ziegler is normally very savvy and cynical. Kyra does venture to observe, quietly, that the Simpson thing draws even bigger ratings than today's Scott Peterson, who—

"Don't even compare the two," Mr. Z. cuts her off. "O.J.'s just in his own world in terms of arrogance."

The designated *JZS* intern, meanwhile, is at the prep room's *John & Ken Show* computer, working (in Vince's stead) on a comic review feature called "What Have We Learned This Week?," which is normally a Friday standard but which there may or may not be time for tonight. At 7:45 P.M. it is still 90° out, and smoggy. The windows' light makes people look greenish in the areas where the room's fluorescents are low. A large spread of takeout chicken sits uneaten and expensively

(negotiated ahead of time with Vince as the price for letting a mute, unobtrusive outside party observe tonight's prep)

'Mondo eventually starts taking plates of food back into Airmix with him.

(a UC-Irvine undergrad, name omitted)

congealing. Mr. Z.'s intern spends nearly an hour composing a mock poem to Ms. Amber Frey, the mistress to whom Scott Peterson evidently read romantic verse over the phone. The poem's final version, which is "Roses are red / Violets are blue / If I find out you're pregnant / I'll drown your ass too," takes such a long time because of confusions about the right conjugation of "to drown."

"And to top it off," Mr. Z. is telling Kyra as her smile becomes brittle and she starts trying to edge away, "to top it off, he leaves Nicole's body in a place where the most likely people to find it are his *children*. It's just

(meaning the Bundy Drive crime scene, which Mr. Z. has evidently walked every inch of)

a fluke that couple found her. I don't know if you've ever walked by there, but it's really dark at night, and they were in a, like [gesturing, one golf ball in each hand], cave formation out at the front."

Sure enough, *Dateline* runs the anti-Atkins story first. For reasons involving laser printers and a special editing room off the on-air news cubicle, there's suddenly a lot of running back and forth.

In Airmix, 'Mondo is eating Koo Koo Roo's chicken while watching Punk'd, an MTV show where friends of young celebrities collude with the producers to make the celebrities think they're in terrible legal trouble. 'Mondo is very careful about eating anywhere near the mixing board. It's always around 60° in this room. On the board's channel 6 and the overhead speakers, Phil Hendrie is pretending to mediate between apoplectic callers and a man who's filing sexual-harassment charges against female co-workers who've gotten breast implants. For unknown reasons, a waist-high pile of disconnected computer key-

> 'Mondo can neither confirm nor deny that these supposedly outraged uninitiated callers are maybe themselves fakes, just more disembodied voices that Hendrie and his staff are creating, and that maybe the real dupes are us, the initiated audience, for believing that the callers are genuine dupes. 'Mondo has not, he confesses, ever considered this possibility, but he agrees that it would constitute "a serious mind-fuck" for KFI listeners.

boards has appeared in the Airmix room's north corner, just across the wall from KFI's Imaging studio, whose door is always double-locked.

It is only right that John Ziegler gets the spot directly in front of the prep room's TV, with everyone else's office chairs sort of fanned out to either side behind him. Seated back on his tailbone with his legs out and ankles crossed, Mr. Z. is able simultaneously to watch *Dateline*'s are-you-in-danger-at-luxury-hotels segment, to hear and help rearrange Vince's cuts from the MSNBC exchange, and to highlight those parts of the O.J.–Katie Couric transcript that he wants to make absolutely sure to have Vince load from TiVo into Prophet when the greedy bastards at

---

(which Vince was able to find online, but which had to be specially reconfigured and printed in order to restore the original line breaks and transcript format of, this being one cause of all the running around between 8:00 and 8:30, as well as another reason why it took the *JZS* intern so long to finish his quatrain, which he is even now fidgeting in his chair and trying to decide on just the right moment to show to Mr. Z.)

Dateline finally air the interview. It must be said, too, that Vince is an impressive surprise as a producer. He's a veritable blur of all-business competence and technical savvy. There are none of Emiliano's stoic shrugs, sotto wisecracks, or passive-aggressive languor. Nor, tonight, is Vince's own slackerish stoner persona anywhere in view. It is the same type of change as when you put a fish back in the water and it seems to turn electric in your hand. Watching Vince and the host work so well as a team induces the night's first strange premonitory jolt: Emiliano's days are numbered.

> Sure enough, within just weeks Emiliano Limon will have left KFI for a job at New York's WCBS.

The broadcast studio is strange when no one's in here. Through the soundproof window, 'Mondo's head looks small and far away as he inclines over the spot log. It seems like a lonely, cloistered place in which to be passionate about the world. Mr. Z.'s padded host chair is old and lists slightly to port; it's the same chair that John Kobylt sits in, and morning drive's Bill Handel, and maybe even Dr. Laura back in the day. The studio wastebaskets have been emptied, but the banana scent still lingers. It might simply be that John and/or Ken eats a lot of bananas during afternoon drive. All the studio's monitors are on, though none is tuned to NBC. On the Fox News monitor up over the digital clock, Sean

> It is a medical common-place that bananas are good for ulcers.

Hannity and Susan Estrich are rerunning the Iowa Caucuses clip of Howard Dean screaming at the start of his concession speech. They play the scream over and over. Ms. Estrich is evidently filling in on *Hannity and Colmes.* "They have hatred for George W. Bush, but they don't have ideas," Sean Hannity says. "Where are the ideas on the left? Where is the thinking liberal?" Susan Estrich says, "I don't know. I don't have a full-time job on TV, so I can't tell you."

All multitasking ends when *Dateline*, after two teases and an extra-long spot break, finally commences the interview segment. It is Katie Couric and O. J. Simpson and Simpson's attor-

> Vince's broad back is now to the TV and everyone around it as he uploads real-time TiVo feed into NexGen and edits per his host's written specs.

ney in a living room that may or may not be real. One tends to forget how unusually, screen-fillingly large O.J.'s head is. Mr. Ziegler is now angled forward with his elbows on his knees and his fingers steepled just under his nose. Although he does, every so often, let loose with a "Katie Couric sucks!" or "Katie Couric should be fucking *shot!*," for the most part a person seated on the host's far flank has to watch his upper face—his right eye's and nostril's dilations—to discern when Mr. Z.'s reacting strongly or thinking about how he'll respond to some specific bit of Simpson's "socio-pathic BS" when it's his turn to talk.

It's odd: if you've spent some time watching Mr. Z. perform in the studio, you can predict just what he'll look like, how his head and arms will move and eyes fill with life as he says certain things that it's all but sure he'll say on-air tonight, such as "I have some very, very strong opinions about how this interview was conducted," and "Katie Couric is a disgrace to journalism everywhere," and that O.J.'s self-presentation was "delusional and arrogant beyond all belief," and that the original trial jury was "a collection of absolute nimrods," and that to believe in Simpson's innocence, as Ms. Couric says a poll shows some 70 percent of African Americans still do, "you have to be either crazy, deluded, or stupid—there are no other explanations."

All of this John Ziegler will and does say on his program—although what no one in the prep room can know is that a second-hour Airwatch flash on the imminent death of Ronald W. Reagan will cut short Mr. Z.'s analysis and require a total, on-the-fly change of both subject and mood.

(who is in so many ways the efficient cause, ideologically and statutorily, of today's partisan media, and whose passing will turn out to be June's true Monster . . .)

To be fair, though, there truly are some dubious, unsettling things about the *Dateline* interview,

The only bit of genuine fun is during the interview's first commercial break, when the opening ad is for Hertz—*Hertz*, of old O.J.-running-through-airports-spots fame—and Mr. Z. throws his head back and asks if he's really seeing what he's seeing. Even Vince turns around in his chair to look. Hertz's placement of an ad here is a brilliant, disgusting, unforgettable piece of metameta-media marketing. It's impossible not to laugh . . . and yet Mr. Z. doesn't. (Neither do the room's two interns, though that's only because they're too young to get the meta-reference.)

such as for instance that NBC has acceded to O. J. Simpson's "no editing" condition for appearing, which used to be an utter taboo for serious news organizations. Or that O.J. gets to sit there looking cheery and unguarded even though he has his lawyer almost in his lap; or that most of Katie Couric's questions turn out to be Larry King–size fluffballs; or that O. J. Simpson responds to one of her few substantive questions—about 1994's eerie, slow-motion Bronco chase and its bearing on how O.J.'s case is still perceived—by harping on the fact that the chase "never ever, in three trials that I had, it never came up," as if that had anything to do with whatever his behavior in the Bronco really signified (and at which nonanswer, and Ms. Couric's failure to press or follow up, Mr. Z. moans and smears his hand up and down over his face). Or that O.J.'s cheerful expression never changes when Katie Couric, leaning forward and speaking with a delicacy that's either decent or obscene, inquires whether his children ever ask him about the crime. And when someone in the arc

For instance, it's troubling that her delivery is that of someone who's choosing her words with great care, when clearly the words have already been chosen, the question scripted. Which would seem to mean she's acting.

EDITORIALIZING, OR JUST STATING THE OBVIOUS? Plus there's the creepy question of why O. J. Simpson is doing a murder-anniversary TV interview at all. What on earth does he stand to gain from sitting there on-camera and letting tens of millions of people search his big face for guilt or remorse? Why subject himself to America's ghoulish fascination? And make no mistake: it is fascinating. The interview and face are riveting television entertainment. It's almost impossible to look away, or not to feel that special kind of guilty excitement in the worst, most greedy and indecent parts of yourself. You can really feel it—this is why drivers slow down to gape at accidents, why reporters put mikes in the faces of bereaved relatives, why the Haidl gang-rape trial is a hit single that merits heavy play, why the cruelest forms of reality TV and tabloid news and talk radio generate such numbers. But that doesn't mean the fascination is good, or even feels good. Aren't there parts of ourselves that are just better left unfed? If it's true that there are, and that we sometimes choose what we wish we wouldn't, then there is a very serious unanswered question at the heart of KFI's Sweeper: "More *Stimulating*" of what?

of chairs around John Ziegler says, almost to himself, that the one pure thing to hope for here is that Simpson's kids believe he's innocent, Mr. Z. gives a snort of reply and states, very flatly, "They know, and he knows they know, that he did it." To which, in KFI's prep room, the best response would probably be compassion, empathy. Because one can almost feel it: what a bleak and merciless world this host lives in—believes, nay, knows for an absolute *fact* he lives in. I'll take doubt.

(It goes without saying that this is just one person's opinion.)

TALES OF THE TYRANT

Mark Bowden

★ ★ ★

SHAKHSUH (HIS PERSON)

Today is a day in the Grand Battle, the immortal Mother of All Battles. It is a glorious and a splendid day on the part of the self-respecting people of Iraq and their history, and it is the beginning of the great shame for those who ignited its fire on the other part. It is the first day on which the vast military phase of that battle started. Or rather, it is the first day of that battle, since Allah decreed that the Mother of All Battles continue till this day.

> —*Saddam Hussein, in a televised address to the Iraqi people,*
> *January 17, 2002*

The tyrant must steal sleep. He must vary the locations and times. He never sleeps in his palaces. He moves from secret bed to secret bed. Sleep and a fixed routine are among the few luxuries denied him. It is too dangerous to be predictable, and whenever he shuts his eyes, the nation drifts. His iron grip slackens. Plots congeal in the shadows. For those hours he must trust someone, and nothing is more dangerous to the tyrant than trust.

Saddam Hussein, the Anointed One, Glorious Leader, Direct De-scendant of the Prophet, President of Iraq, Chairman of its Revolution-ary Command Council, field marshal of its armies, doctor of its laws, and Great Uncle to all its peoples, rises at about three in the morning. He sleeps only four or five hours a night. When he rises, he swims. All his palaces and homes have pools. Water is a symbol of wealth and power in a desert country like Iraq, and Saddam splashes it everywhere—fountains and pools, indoor streams and waterfalls. It is a theme in all his buildings. His pools are tended scrupulously and tested hourly, more to keep the temperature and the chlorine and pH levels comfort-able than to detect some poison that might attack him through his pores, eyes, mouth, nose, ears, penis, or anus—although that worry is always there too.

He has a bad back, a slipped disk, and swimming helps. It also keeps him trim and fit. This satisfies his vanity, which is epic, but fit-ness is critical for other reasons. He is now sixty-five, an old man, but because his power is grounded in fear, not affection, he cannot be seen to age. The tyrant cannot afford to become stooped, frail, and gray. Weakness invites challenge, coup d'état. One can imagine Sad-dam urging himself through a fixed number of laps each morning, pushing to exceed the number he swam the previous year, as if time could be undone by effort and will. Death is an enemy he cannot defeat—only, perhaps, delay. So he works. He also dissembles. He dyes his gray hair black and avoids using his reading glasses in public. When he is to give a speech, his aides print it out in huge letters, just a few lines per page. Because his back problem forces him to walk with a slight limp, he avoids being seen or filmed walking more than a few steps.

He is long-limbed, with big, strong hands. In Iraq the size of a man still matters, and Saddam is impressive. At six feet two he towers over his shorter, plumper aides. He lacks natural grace but has ac-quired a certain elegance of manner, the way a country boy learns to match the right tie with the right suit. His weight fluctuates between about 210 and 220 pounds, but in his custom-tailored suits the girth isn't always easy to see. His paunch shows when he takes off his suit coat. Those who watch him carefully know he has a tendency to lose weight in times of crisis and to gain it rapidly when things are going well.

Fresh food is flown in for him twice a week—lobster, shrimp, and fish, lots of lean meat, plenty of dairy products. The shipments are sent first to his nuclear scientists, who X-ray them and test them for radiation and poison. The food is then prepared for him by European-trained chefs, who work under the supervision of al Himaya, Saddam's personal bodyguards. Each of his more than twenty palaces is fully staffed, and three meals a day are cooked for him at every one; security demands that palaces from which he is absent perform an elaborate pantomime each day, as if he were in residence. Saddam tries to regulate his diet, allotting servings and portions the way he counts out the laps in his pools. For a big man he usually eats little, picking at his meals, often leaving half the food on his plate. Sometimes he eats dinner at restaurants in Baghdad, and when he does, his security staff invades the kitchen, demanding that the pots and pans, dishware, and utensils be well scrubbed, but otherwise interfering little. Saddam appreciates the culinary arts. He prefers fish to meat, and eats a lot of fresh fruits and vegetables. He likes wine with his meals, though he is hardly an oenophile; his wine of choice is Mateus rosé. But even though he indulges only in moderation, he is careful not to let anyone outside his most trusted circle of family and aides see him drinking. Alcohol is forbidden by Islam, and in public Saddam is a dutiful son of the faith.

He has a tattoo on his right hand, three dark-blue dots in a line near the wrist. These are given to village children when they are only five or six years old, a sign of their rural, tribal roots. Girls are often marked on their chins, forehead, or cheeks (as was Saddam's mother). For those who, like Saddam, move to the cities and come up in life, the tattoos are a sign of humble origin, and some later have them removed, or fade them with bleach until they almost disappear. Saddam's have faded, but apparently just from age; although he claims descent from the prophet Muhammad, he has never disguised his humble birth.

The President-for-life spends long hours every day in his office—whichever office he and his security minders select. He meets with his ministers and generals, solicits their opinions, and keeps his own counsel. He steals short naps during the day. He will abruptly leave a meeting, shut himself off in a side room, and return refreshed a half hour later. Those who meet with the President have no such luxury. They must stay awake and alert at all times. In 1986, during the Iran-Iraq War, Saddam caught Lieutenant General Aladin al-Janabi dozing during a meeting. He stripped the general of his rank and threw him out of the army. It was years before al-Janabi was able to win back his position and favor.

Saddam's desk is always immaculate. Reports from his various department heads are stacked neatly, each a detailed accounting of recent accomplishments and spending topped by an executive summary. Usually he reads only the summaries, but he selects some reports for closer examination. No one knows which will be chosen for scrutiny. If the details of the full report tell a story different from the summary, or if Saddam is confused, he will summon the department head. At these meetings Saddam is always polite and calm. He rarely raises his voice. He enjoys showing off a mastery of every aspect of his realm, from crop rotation to nuclear fission. But these meetings can be terrifying when he uses them to cajole, upbraid, or interrogate his subordinates. Often he arranges a surprise visit to some lower-level office or laboratory or factory—although, given the security preparations necessary, word of his visits outraces his arrival. Much of what he sees from his offices and on his "surprise" inspections is doctored and full of lies. Saddam has been fed unrealistic information for so long that his expectations are now also uniformly unrealistic. His bureaucrats scheme mightily to maintain the illusions. So Saddam usually sees only what those around him want him to see, which is, by definition, what he wants to see. A stupid man in this position would believe he had created a perfect world. But Saddam is not stupid. He knows he is being deceived, and he complains about it.

He reads voraciously—on subjects from physics to romance—and has broad interests. He has a particular passion for Arabic history and military history. He likes books about great men, and he admires Winston Churchill, whose famous political career is matched by his prodigious literary output. Saddam has literary aspirations himself. He employs ghostwriters to keep up a ceaseless flow of speeches, articles, and books of history and philosophy; his oeuvre includes fiction as well. In recent years he appears to have written and published two romantic fables, *Zabibah and the King* and *The Fortified Castle*; a third, as-yet-untitled work of fiction is due out soon. Before publishing the books Saddam distributes them quietly to professional writers in Iraq for comments and suggestions. No one dares to be candid—the writing is said to be woefully amateurish, marred by a stern pedantic strain—but everyone tries to be helpful, sending him gentle suggestions for minor improvements. The first two novels were published under a rough Arabic equivalent of "Anonymous" that translates as "Written by He Who Wrote It," but the new book may bear Saddam's name.

Saddam likes to watch TV, monitoring the Iraqi stations he controls and also CNN, Sky, al Jazeera, and the BBC. He enjoys movies, particularly those involving intrigue, assassination, and conspiracy—*The Day of the Jackal*, *The Conversation*, *Enemy of the State*. Because he has not traveled extensively, such movies inform his ideas about the world and feed his inclination to believe broad conspiracy theories. To him the world is a puzzle that only fools accept at face value. He also appreciates movies with more literary themes. Two of his favorites are *The Godfather* series and *The Old Man and the Sea*.

Saddam can be charming and has a sense of humor about himself. "He told a hilarious story on television," says Khidhir Hamza, a scientist who worked on Iraq's nuclear-weapons project before escaping to the West. "He is an excellent storyteller, the kind who acts out the story with gestures and facial expressions. He described how he had once found himself behind enemy lines in the war with Iran. He had been traveling along the front lines, paying surprise visits, when the Iranian line launched an offensive and effectively cut off his position. The Iranians, of course, had no idea that Saddam was there. The way he told the story, it wasn't boastful or self-congratulatory. He didn't claim to have fought his way out. He said he was scared. Of the troops at his position, he said, 'They just left me!' He repeated 'Just left me!' in a way that was humorous. Then he described how he hid with his pistol, watching the action until his own forces retook the position and he was again on safe ground. 'What can a pistol do in the middle of battle?' he asked. It was charming, extremely charming."

General Wafic Samarai, who served as Saddam's chief of intelligence during the eight-year Iran-Iraq War (and who, after falling out of favor in the wake of the Persian Gulf War, walked for thirty hours through the rugged north of Iraq to escape the country), concurs: "It is pleasant to sit and talk to him. He is serious, and meetings with him can get tense, but you don't get intimidated unless he wants to intimidate you. When he asks for your opinion, he listens very carefully and doesn't interrupt. Likewise, he gets irritated if you interrupt him. 'Let me finish!' he will say sharply."

Saddam has been advised by his doctors to walk at least two hours a day. He rarely manages that much time, but he breaks up his days with strolls. He used to take these walks in public, swooping down with his entourage on neighborhoods in Baghdad, his bodyguards clearing sidewalks and streets as the tyrant passed. Anyone who approached him unsolicited was beaten nearly to death. But now it is too dangerous to walk in public—and the limp must not be seen. So Saddam makes no more unscripted public appearances. He limps freely behind the high walls and patrolled fences of his vast estates. Often he walks with a gun, hunting deer or rabbit in his private preserves. He is an excellent shot.

Saddam has been married for nearly forty years. His wife, Sajida, is his first cousin on his mother's side and the daughter of Khairallah Tulfah, Saddam's uncle and first political mentor. Sajida has borne him two sons and three daughters, and remains loyal to him, but he has long had relationships with other women. Stories circulate about his nightly selecting of young virgins for his bed, like the Sultan Shahryar in *The Thousand and One Nights*, about his having fathered a child with a longtime mistress, and even about his having killed one young woman after a kinky tryst. It is hard to sort the truth from the lies. So many people, in and out of Iraq, hate Saddam that any disgraceful or embarrassing rumor is likely to be embraced, believed, repeated, and written down in the Western press as truth. Those who know him best scoff at the wildest of these tales.

"Saddam has personal relationships with women, but these stories of rape and murder are lies," Samarai says. "He is not that kind of person. He is very careful about himself in everything he does. He is fastidious and very proper, and never wants to give the wrong impression. But he is occasionally attracted to other women, and he has formed relationships with them. They are not the kind of women who would ever talk about him."

Saddam is a loner by nature, and power increases isolation. A young man without power or money is completely free. He has nothing, but he also has everything. He can travel, he can drift. He can make new acquaintances every day, and try to soak up the infinite variety of life. He can seduce and be seduced, start an enterprise and abandon it, join an army or flee a nation, fight to preserve an existing system or plot a revolution. He can reinvent himself daily, according to the discoveries he makes about the world and himself. But if he prospers through the choices he makes, if he acquires a wife, children, wealth, land, and power, his options gradually and inevitably diminish. Responsibility and commitment limit his moves. One might think that the most powerful man has the most choices, but in reality he has the fewest. Too much depends on his every move. The tyrant's choices are the narrowest of all. His life—the nation!—hangs in the balance. He can no longer drift or explore, join or flee. He cannot reinvent himself, because so many others depend on him—and he, in turn, must depend on so many others. He stops learning, because he is walled in by fortresses and palaces, by generals and ministers who rarely dare to tell him what he doesn't wish to hear. Power gradually shuts the tyrant off from the world. Everything comes to him second- or thirdhand. He is deceived daily. He becomes ignorant of his land, his people, even his own family. He exists, finally, only to preserve his wealth and power, to build his legacy. Survival becomes his one over-riding passion. So he regulates his diet, tests his food for poison, exercises behind well-patrolled walls, trusts no one, and tries to control everything.

Major Sabah Khalifa Khodada, a career officer in the Iraqi army, was summoned from his duties as assistant to the commander of a terrorist training camp on January 1, 1996, for an important meeting. It was nighttime. He drove to his command center at Alswayra, southwest of Baghdad, where he and some other military officers were told to strip to their underwear. They removed their clothing, watches, and rings, and handed over their wallets. The clothing was then laundered, sterilized, and X-rayed. Each of the officers, in his underwear, was searched and passed through a metal detector. Each was instructed to wash his hands in a disinfecting permanganate solution.

They then dressed and were transported in buses with blackened windows, so that they could not see where they were going. They were driven for a half hour or more, and then were searched again as they filed off. They had arrived at an official-looking building, Khodada did not know where. After a time they were taken into a meeting room and seated at a large round table. Then they were told that they were to be given a great honor: the President himself would be meeting with them. They were instructed not to talk, just to listen. When Saddam entered, they were to rise and show him respect. They were not to approach or touch him. For all but his closest aides, the protocol for meeting with the dictator is simple. He dictates.

"Don't interrupt," they were told. "Don't ask questions or make any requests."

Each man was given a pad of paper and a pencil, and instructed to take notes. Tea in a small glass cup was placed before each man and at the empty seat at the head of the table.

When Saddam appeared, they all rose. He stood before his chair and smiled at them. Wearing his military uniform, decorated with medals and gold epaulets, he looked fit, impressive, and self-assured. When he sat, everyone sat. Saddam did not reach for his tea, so the others in the room didn't touch theirs. He told Khodada and the others that they were the best men in the nation, the most trusted and able. That was why they had been selected to meet with him and to work at the terrorist camps where warriors were being trained to strike back at America. The United States, he said, because of its reckless treatment of Arab nations and the Arab people, was a necessary target for revenge and destruction. American aggression must be stopped in order for Iraq to rebuild and to resume leadership of the Arab world. Saddam talked for almost two hours. Khodada could sense the great hatred in him, the anger over what America had done to his ambitions and to Iraq. Saddam blamed the United States for all the poverty, backwardness, and suffering in his country.

Khodada took notes. He glanced around the room. Few of the others, he concluded, were buying what Saddam told them. These were battle-hardened men of experience from all over the nation. Most had fought in the war with Iran and the Persian Gulf War. They had few illusions about Saddam, his regime, or the troubles of their country. They coped daily with real problems in cities and military camps all over Iraq. They could have told Saddam a lot. But nothing would pass from them to the tyrant. Not one word, not one microorganism.

The meeting had been designed to allow communication in only one direction, and even in this it failed. Saddam's speech was meaningless to his listeners. Khodada despised him, and suspected that others in the room did too. The major knew he was no coward, but, like many of the other military men there, he was filled with fear. He was afraid to make a wrong move, afraid he might accidentally draw attention to himself, do something unscripted. He was grateful that he felt no urge to sneeze, sniffle, or cough.

When the meeting was over, Saddam simply left the room. The teacups had not been touched. The men were then returned to the buses and driven back to Alswayra, from which they drove back to their camps or homes. The meeting with Saddam had meant nothing. The notes they had been ordered to take were worthless. It was as if they had briefly visited a fantasy zone with no connection to their own world.

They had stepped into the world of the tyrant.

TUMOOH (AMBITION)

The Iraqis knew that they had the potential, but they did not know how to muster up that potential. Their rulers did not take the responsibility on the basis of that potential. The leader and the guide who was able to put that potential on its right course had not yet emerged from amongst them. Even when some had discovered that potential, they did not know how to deal with it. Nor did they direct it where it should be directed so as to enable it to evolve into an effective act that could make life pulsate and fill hearts with happiness.

—*Saddam Hussein, in a speech to the Iraqi people, July 17, 2000*

In Saddam's village, al-Awja, just east of Tikrit, in north-central Iraq, his clan lived in houses made of mud bricks and flat, mud-covered wooden roofs. The land is dry, and families eke out a living growing wheat and vegetables. Saddam's clan was called al-Khatab, and they were known to be violent and clever. Some viewed them as con men and thieves, recalls Salah Omar al-Ali, who grew up in Tikrit and came to know Saddam well in later life. Those who still support Saddam may see him as Saladinesque, as a great pan-Arab leader; his enemies may see him as Stalinesque, a cruel dictator; but to al-Ali, Saddam will always be just an al-Khatab, acting out a family pattern on a much, much larger stage.

Al-Ali fixed tea for me in his home in suburban London last January. He is elegant, frail, gray, and pale, a man of quiet dignity and impeccable manners who gestures delicately with long-fingered hands as he speaks. He was the Information Minister of Iraq when, in 1969, Saddam (the real power in the ruling party), in part to demonstrate his displeasure over Arab defeats in the Six-Day War, announced that a Zionist plot had been discovered and publicly hanged fourteen alleged plotters, among them nine Iraqi Jews; their bodies were left hanging in Baghdad's Liberation Square for more than a day. Al-Ali defended this atrocity in his own country and to the rest of the world. Today he is just one of many exiled or expatriated former Iraqi government officials, an old Socialist who served the revolutionary pan-Arab Baath Party and Saddam until running afoul of the Great Uncle. Al-Ali would have one believe that his conscience drove him into exile, but one suspects he has fretted little in his life about human rights. He showed me the faded dot tattoos on his hand which might have been put there by the same Tikriti who gave Saddam his.

Although al-Ali was familiar with the al-Khatab family, he did not meet Saddam himself until the midsixties, when they were both Socialist revolutionaries plotting to overthrow the tottering government of General Abd al-Rahman Arif. Saddam was a tall, thin young man with a thick mop of curly black hair. He had recently escaped from prison, after being caught in a failed attempt to assassinate Arif's predecessor. The attempt, the arrest, the imprisonment, had all added to Saddam's revolutionary luster. He was an impressive combination: not just a tough capable of commanding respect from the thugs who did the Baath Party's dirty work, but also well-read, articulate, and seemingly open-minded; a man of action who also understood policy; a natural leader who could steer Iraq into a new era. Al-Ali met the young fugitive at a café near Baghdad University. Saddam arrived in a Volkswagen Beetle and stepped out in a well-cut gray suit. These were exciting times for both men. The intoxicating aroma of change was in the air, and prospects for their party were good. Saddam was pleased to meet a fellow Tikriti. "He listened to me for a long time," al-Ali recalled. "We discussed the party's plans, how to organize nationally. The issues were complicated, but it was clear that he understood them very well. He was serious, and took a number of my suggestions. I was impressed with him."

The party seized control in 1968, and Saddam immediately became the real power behind his cousin Ahmad Hassan al-Bakr, the president and chairman of the new Revolutionary Command Council. Al-Ali was a member of that council. He was responsible for the north-central part of Iraq, including his home village. It was in Tikrit that he started to see Saddam's larger plan unfold. Saddam's relatives in al-Awja were throwing their newly ascendant kinsman's name around, seizing farms, ordering people off their land. That was how things worked in the villages. If a family was lucky, it produced a strongman, a patriarch, who by guile, strength, or violence accumulated riches for his clan. Saddam was now a strongman, and his family was moving to claim the spoils. This was all ancient stuff. The Baath philosophy was far more egalitarian. It emphasized working with Arabs in other countries to rebuild the entire region, sharing property and wealth, seeking a better life for all. In this political climate Saddam's family was a throwback. The local party chiefs complained bitterly, and al-Ali took their complaints to his powerful young friend. "It's a small problem," Saddam said. "These are simple people. They don't understand our larger aims. I'll take care of it." Two, three, four times al-Ali went to Saddam, because the problem didn't go away. Every time it was the same: "I'll take care of it."

It finally occurred to al-Ali that the al-Khatab family was doing exactly what Saddam wanted them to do. This seemingly modern, educated young villager was not primarily interested in helping the party achieve its idealistic aims; rather, he was using the party to help him achieve his. Suddenly al-Ali saw that the polish, the fine suits, the urbane tastes, the civilized manner, and the Socialist rhetoric were a pose. The real story of Saddam was right there in the tattoo on his right hand. He was a true son of Tikrit, a clever al-Khatab, and he was now much more than the patriarch of his clan.

Saddam's rise through the ranks may have been slow and deceitful, but when he moved to seize power, he did so very openly. He had been serving as vice-chairman of the Revolutionary Command Council, and as Vice President of Iraq, and he planned to step formally into the top positions. Some of the party leadership, including men who had been close to Saddam for years, had other ideas. Rather than just hand him the reins, they had begun advocating a party election. So Saddam took action. He staged his ascendancy like theater.

On July 18, 1979, he invited all the members of the Revolutionary Command Council and hundreds of other party leaders to a conference hall in Baghdad. He had a video camera running in the back of the hall to record the event for posterity. Wearing his military uniform, he walked slowly to the lectern and stood behind two microphones, gesturing with a big cigar. His body and broad face seemed weighted down with sadness. There had been a betrayal, he said. A Syrian plot. There were traitors among them. Then Saddam took a seat, and Muhyi Abd al-Hussein Mashhadi, the secretary-general of the Command Council, appeared from behind a curtain to confess his own involvement in the putsch. He had been secretly arrested and tortured days before; now he spilled out dates, times, and places where the plotters had met. Then he started naming names. As he fingered members of the audience one by one, armed guards grabbed the accused and escorted them from the hall. When one man shouted that he was innocent, Saddam shouted back, *"Itla! Itla!"*—"Get out! Get out!" (Weeks later, after secret trials, Saddam had the mouths of the accused taped shut so that they could utter no troublesome last words before their firing squads.) When all of the sixty "traitors" had been removed, Saddam again took the podium and wiped tears from his eyes as he repeated the names of those who had betrayed him. Some in the audience, too, were crying—perhaps out of fear. This chilling performance had the desired effect. Everyone in the hall now understood exactly how things would work in Iraq from that day forward. The audience rose and began clapping, first in small groups and finally as one. The session ended with cheers and laughter. The remaining "leaders"—about three hundred in all—left the hall shaken, grateful to have avoided the fate of their colleagues, and certain that one man now controlled the destiny of their entire nation. Videotapes of the purge were circulated throughout the country.

It was what the world would come to see as classic Saddam. He tends to commit his crimes in public, cloaking them in patriotism and in effect turning his witnesses into accomplices. The purge that day reportedly resulted in the executions of a third of the Command Council. (Mashhadi's performance didn't spare him; he, too, was executed.) During the next few weeks scores of other "traitors" were shot, including government officials, military officers, and people turned in by ordinary citizens who responded to a hotline phone number broadcast on Iraqi TV. Some Council members say that Saddam ordered members of the party's inner circle to participate in this bloodbath.

While he served as vice-chairman, from 1968 to 1979, the party's goals had seemed to be Saddam's own. That was a relatively good period for Iraq, thanks to Saddam's blunt effectiveness as an administrator. He orchestrated a Draconian nationwide literacy project. Reading programs were set up in every city and village, and failure to attend was punishable by three years in jail. Men, women, and children attended these compulsory classes, and hundreds of thousands of illiterate Iraqis learned to read. UNESCO gave Saddam an award. There were also ambitious drives to build schools, roads, public housing, and hospitals. Iraq created one of the best public-health systems in the Middle East. There was admiration in the West during those years, for Saddam's accomplishments if not for his methods. After the Islamic fundamentalist revolution in Iran, and the seizure of the U.S. embassy in Tehran in 1979, Saddam seemed to be the best hope for secular modernization in the region.

Today all these programs are a distant memory. Within two years of his seizing full power, Saddam's ambitions turned to conquest, and his defeats have ruined the nation. His old party allies in exile now see his support for the social-welfare programs as an elaborate deception. The broad ambitions for the Iraqi people were the party's, they say. As long as he needed the party, Saddam made its programs his own. But his single, overriding goal throughout was to establish his own rule.

"In the beginning the Baath Party was made up of the intellectual elite of our generation," says Hamed al-Jubouri, a former Command Council member who now lives in London. "There were many professors, physicians, economists, and historians—really the nation's elite. Saddam was charming and impressive. He appeared to be totally different from what we learned he was afterward. He took all of us in. We supported him because he seemed uniquely capable of controlling a difficult country like Iraq, a difficult people like our people. We wondered about him. How could such a young man, born in the countryside north of Baghdad, become such a capable leader? He seemed both intellectual and practical. But he was hiding his real self. For years he did this, building his power quietly, charming everyone, hiding his true instincts. He has a great ability to hide his intentions; it may be his greatest skill. I remember his son Uday said one time, 'My father's right shirt pocket doesn't know what is in his left shirt pocket.'"

What does Saddam want? By all accounts, he is not interested in money. This is not the case with other members of his family. His wife, Sajida, is known to have gone on million-dollar shopping sprees in New York and London, back in the days of Saddam's good relations with the West. Uday drives expensive cars and wears custom-tailored suits of his own design. Saddam himself isn't a hedonist; he lives a well-regulated, somewhat abstemious existence. He seems far more interested in fame than in money, desiring above all to be admired, remembered, and re-vered. A nineteen-volume official biography is mandatory reading for Iraqi government officials, and Saddam has also commissioned a six-hour film about his life, called *The Long Days*, which was edited by Ter-ence Young, best known for directing three James Bond films. Saddam told his official biographer that he isn't interested in what people think of him today, only in what they will think of him in five hundred years. The root of Saddam's bloody, single-minded pursuit of power appears to be simple vanity.

But what extremes of vanity compel a man to jail or execute all who criticize or oppose him? To erect giant statues of himself to adorn the public spaces of his country? To commission romantic portraits, some of them twenty feet high, portraying the nation's Great Uncle as a des-ert horseman, a wheat-cutting peasant, or a construction worker carry-ing bags of cement? To have the nation's television, radio, film, and print devoted to celebrating his every word and deed? Can ego alone explain such displays? Might it be the opposite? What colossal insecurity and self-loathing would demand such compensation?

The sheer scale of the tyrant's deeds mocks psychoanalysis. What begins with ego and ambition becomes a political movement. Saddam embodies first the party and then the nation. Others conspire in this process in order to further their own ambitions, selfless as well as self-ish. Then the tyrant turns on them. His cult of self becomes more than a political strategy. Repetition of his image in heroic or paternal poses, repetition of his name, his slogans, his virtues, and his accomplish-ments, seeks to make his power seem inevitable, unchallengeable. Fi-nally he is praised not out of affection or admiration but out of obligation. One *must* praise him.

Saad al-Bazzaz was summoned to meet with Saddam in 1989. He was then the editor of Baghdad's largest daily newspaper and the head of the ministry that oversees all of Iraq's TV and radio programming.

Al-Bazzaz took the phone call in his office. "The President wants to ask you something," Saddam's secretary said.

Al-Bazzaz thought nothing of it. He is a short, round, garrulous man with thinning hair and big glasses. He had known Saddam for years and had always been in good odor. The first time Saddam had asked to meet him had been more than fifteen years earlier, when Saddam was vice-chairman of the Revolutionary Command Council. The Baath Party was generating a lot of excitement, and Saddam was its rising star. At the time, al-Bazzaz was a twenty-five-year-old writer who had just published his first collection of short stories and had also written articles for Baghdad newspapers. That first summons from Saddam had been a surprise. Why would the vice-chairman want to meet with him? Al-Bazzaz had a low opinion of political officials, but as soon as they met, this one struck him as different. Saddam told al-Bazzaz that he had read some of his articles and was impressed by them. He said he knew of his book of short stories and had heard they were very good. The young writer was flattered. Saddam asked him what writers he admired, and after listening to al-Bazzaz, told him, "When I was in prison, I read all of Ernest Hemingway's novels. I particularly like *The Old Man and the Sea*." Al-Bazzaz thought, *This is something new for Iraq—a politician who reads real literature.* Saddam peppered him with questions at that meeting and listened with rapt attention. This, too, al-Bazzaz thought was extraordinary.

By 1989 much had changed. Saddam's regime had long since abandoned the party's early, idealistic aims, and al-Bazzaz no longer saw the dictator as an open-minded man of learning and refinement. But he had prospered personally under Saddam's reign. His growing government responsibilities left him no time to write, but he had become an important man in Iraq. He saw himself as someone who advanced the cause of artists and journalists, as a force for liberalization in the country. Since the end of the war with Iran, the previous year, there had been talk of loosening controls on the media and the arts in Iraq, and al-Bazzaz had lobbied quietly in favor of this. But he wasn't one to press too hard, so he had no worries as he drove the several miles from his office to the Tashreeya area of Baghdad, near the old Cabinet Building, where an emissary from the President met him and instructed him to leave his car. The emissary drove al-Bazzaz in silence to a large villa nearby. Inside, guards searched him and showed him to a sofa, where he waited for half an hour as people came and went from the President's office. When it was his turn, he was handed a pad and a pencil, reminded to speak only if Saddam asked a direct question, and then ushered in. It was noon. Saddam was wearing a military uniform. Staying seated behind his desk, Saddam did not approach al-Bazzaz or even offer to shake his hand.

"How are you?" the President asked.

"Fine," al-Bazzaz replied. "I am here to listen to your instructions."

Saddam complained about an Egyptian comedy show that had been airing on one of the TV channels: "It is silly, and we shouldn't show it to our people." Al-Bazzaz made a note. Then Saddam brought up something else. It was the practice for poems and songs written in praise of him to be aired daily on TV. In recent weeks al-Bazzaz had urged his producers to be more selective. Most of the work was amateurish—ridiculous doggerel written by unskilled poets. His staff was happy to oblige. Paeans to the President were still aired every day, but not as many since al-Bazzaz had changed the policy.

"I understand," Saddam said, "that you are not allowing some of the songs that carry my name to be broadcast."

Al-Bazzaz was stunned, and suddenly frightened. "Mr. President," he said, "we still broadcast the songs, but I have stopped some of them because they are so poorly written. They are rubbish."

"Look," Saddam said, abruptly stern, "you are not a judge, Saad."

"Yes. I am not a judge."

"How can you prevent people from expressing their feelings toward me?"

Al-Bazzaz feared that he was going to be taken away and shot. He felt the blood drain from his face, and his heart pounded heavily. The editor said nothing. The pencil shook in his hand. Saddam had not even raised his voice.

"No, no, no. You are not the judge of these things," Saddam reiterated.

Al-Bazzaz kept repeating, "Yes, sir," and frantically wrote down every word the President said. Saddam then talked about the movement for more freedoms in the press and the arts. "There will be no loosening of controls," he said.

"Yes, sir."

"Okay, fine. Now it is all clear to you?"

"Yes, sir."

With that Saddam dismissed al-Bazzaz. The editor had sweated through his shirt and sport coat. He was driven back to the Cabinet Building, and then drove himself back to the office, where he immediately rescinded his earlier policy. That evening a full broadcast of the poems and songs dedicated to Saddam resumed.

HADAFUH (HIS GOAL)

You are the fountain of willpower and the wellspring of life, the essence of earth, the sabers of demise, the pupil of the eye, and the twitch of the eyelid. A people like you cannot but be, with God's help. So be as you are, and as we are determined to be. Let all cowards, piggish people, traitors, and betrayers be debased.

—Saddam Hussein, addressing the Iraqi people, July 17, 2001

Iraq is a land of antiquity. It is called the Land of Two Rivers (the Tigris and the Euphrates); the land of Sumerian kings, Mesopotamia, and Babylon; one of the cradles of civilization. Walking the streets of Baghdad gives one a sense of continuity with things long past, of unity with the great sweep of history. Renovating and maintaining the old palaces is an ongoing project in the city. By decree, one of every ten bricks laid in the renovation of an ancient palace is now stamped either with the name Saddam Hussein or with an eight-pointed star (a point for each letter of his name spelled in Arabic).

In 1987 Entifadh Qanbar was assigned to work on the restoration of the Baghdad Palace, which had once been called al-Zuhoor, or the Flowers Palace. Built in the 1930s for King Ghazi, it is relatively small and very pretty; English in style, it once featured an elaborate evergreen maze. Qanbar is an engineer by training, a short, fit, dark-haired man with olive skin. After earning his degree he served a compulsory term in the army, which turned out to be a five-year stint, and survived the mandatory one-month tour on the front lines in the war with Iran.

Work on the palace had stalled some years earlier, when the British consultant for the project refused to come to Baghdad because of the war. One of Qanbar's first jobs was to supervise construction of a high and ornate brick wall around the palace grounds. Qanbar is a perfectionist, and because the wall was to be decorative as well as functional, he took care with the placement of each brick. An elaborate gate had already been built facing the main road, but Qanbar had not yet built the portions of the wall on either side of it, because the renovation of the palace itself was unfinished, and that way large construction equipment could roll on and off the property without danger of damaging the gate.

One afternoon at about five, as he was preparing to close down work for the day, Qanbar saw a black Mercedes with curtained windows and custom-built running boards pull up to the site. He knew immediately who was in it. Ordinary Iraqis were not allowed to drive such fancy cars. Cars like this one were driven exclusively by al Himaya, Saddam's bodyguards.

The doors opened and several guards stepped out. All of them wore dark-green uniforms, black berets, and zippered boots of reddish-brown leather. They had big moustaches like Saddam's, and carried Kalashnikovs. To the frightened Qanbar, they seemed robotic, without human feelings.

The bodyguards often visited the work site to watch and make trouble. Once, after new concrete had been poured and smoothed, some of them jumped into it, stomping through the patch in their red boots to make sure that no bomb or listening device was hidden there. Another time a workman opened a pack of cigarettes and a bit of foil wrapping fluttered down into the newly poured concrete. One of the guards caught a glimpse of something metallic and reacted as if someone had thrown a hand grenade. Several of them leaped into the concrete and retrieved the scrap. Angered to discover what it was, and to have been made to look foolish, they dragged the offending worker aside and beat him with their weapons. "I have worked all my life!" he cried. They took him away, and he did not return. So the sudden arrival of a black Mercedes was a frightening thing.

"Who is the engineer here?" the chief guard asked. He spoke with the gruff Tikriti accent of his boss. Qanbar stepped up and identified himself. One of the guards wrote down his name. It is a terrible thing to have al Himaya write down your name. In a country ruled by fear, the best way to survive is to draw as little attention to yourself as possible. To be invisible. Even success can be dangerous, because it makes you stand out. It makes other people jealous and suspicious. It makes you enemies who might, if the opportunity presents itself, bring your name to the attention of the police. For the state to have your name for any reason other than the most conventional ones—school, driver's license, military service—is always dangerous. The actions of the state are entirely unpredictable, and they can take away your career, your freedom, your life. Qanbar's heart sank and his mouth went dry.

"Our Great Uncle just passed by," the chief guard began. "And he said, 'Why is this gate installed when the two walls around it are not built?'"

Qanbar nervously explained that the walls were special, ornamental, and that his crew was saving them for last because of the heavy equipment coming and going. "We want to keep it a clean construction," he said.

"Our Great Uncle is going to pass by again tonight," said the guard. "When he does, it must be finished."

Qanbar was dumbfounded. "How can I do it?" he protested.

"I don't know," said the guard. "But if you don't do it, you will be in trouble." Then he said something that revealed exactly how serious the danger was: "And if you don't do it, we will be in trouble. How can we help?"

There was nothing to do but try. Qanbar dispatched Saddam's men to help round up every member of his crew as fast as they could—those who were not scheduled to work as well as those who had already gone home. Two hundred workers were quickly assembled. They set up floodlights. Some of the guards came back with trucks that had machine guns mounted on top. They parked alongside the work site and set up chairs, watching and urging more speed as the workers mixed mortar and threw down line after line of bricks.

The crew finished at nine-thirty. They had completed in four hours a job that would ordinarily have taken a week. Terror had driven them to work faster and harder than they believed possible. Qanbar and his men were exhausted. An hour later they were still cleaning up the site when the black Mercedes drove up again. The chief guard stepped out. "Our Uncle just passed by, and he thanks you," he said.

Walls define the tyrant's world. They keep his enemies out, but they also block him off from the people he rules. In time he can no longer see out. He loses touch with what is real and what is unreal, what is possible and what is not—or, as in the case of Qanbar and the wall, what is just barely possible. His ideas of what his power can accomplish, and of his own importance, bleed into fantasy.

★ ★ ★

Each time Saddam has escaped death—when he survived, with a minor wound to his leg, a failed attempt in 1959 to assassinate Iraqi President Abd al-Karim Qasim; when he avoided the ultimate punishment in 1964 for his part in a failed Baath Party uprising; when he survived being trapped behind Iranian lines in the Iran-Iraq War; when he survived attempted coups d'état; when he survived America's smart-bombing campaign against Baghdad, in 1991; when he survived the nationwide revolt after the Gulf War—it has strengthened his conviction that his path is divinely inspired and that greatness is his destiny. Because his worldview is essentially tribal and patriarchal, destiny means blood. So he has ordered genealogists to construct a plausible family tree linking him to Fatima, the daughter of the prophet Muhammad. (This ancestry is an honor he shares, perhaps, with everyone in the hated West. Saddam sees the prophet less as the bearer of divine revelation than as a political precursor—a great leader who unified the Arab peoples and inspired a flowering of Arab power and culture. The concocted link of bloodlines to Muhammad is symbolized by a six hundred-page hand-lettered copy of the Koran that was written with Saddam's own blood, which he donated a pint at a time over three years. It is now on display in a Baghdad museum.

If Saddam has a religion, it is a belief in the superiority of Arab history and culture, a tradition that he is convinced will rise up again and rattle the world. His imperial view of the grandeur that was Arabia is romantic, replete with fanciful visions of great palaces and wise and powerful sultans and caliphs. His notion of history has nothing to do with progress, with the advance of knowledge, with the evolution of individual rights and liberties, with any of the things that matter most to Western civilization. It has to do simply with power. To Saddam, the present global domination by the West, particularly the United States, is just a phase. America is infidel and inferior. It lacks the rich ancient heritage of Iraq and other Arab states. Its place at the summit of the world powers is just a historical quirk, an aberration, a consequence of its having acquired technological advantages. It cannot endure.

In a speech this past January 17, the eleventh anniversary of the start of the Gulf War, Saddam explained, "The Americans have not yet established a civilization, in the deep and comprehensive sense we give to civilization. What they have established is a metropolis of force.... Some people, perhaps including Arabs and plenty of Muslims and more than these in the wide world ... considered the ascent of the U.S. to the summit as the last scene in the world picture, after which there will be no more summits and no one will try to ascend and sit comfortably there. They considered it the end of the world as they hoped for, or as their scared souls suggested it to them."

Arabia, which Saddam sees as the wellspring of civilization, will one day own that summit again. When that day comes, whether in his lifetime or a century or even five centuries hence, his name will rank with those of the great men in history. Saddam sees himself as an established member of the pantheon of great men—conquerors, prophets, kings and presidents, scholars, poets, scientists. It doesn't matter if he understands their contributions and ideas. It matters only that they are the ones history has remembered and honored for their accomplishments.

In a book titled *Saddam's Bombmaker* (2000), Khidhir Hamza, the nuclear scientist, remembers his first encounter with Saddam, when the future dictator was still nominally the vice-chairman. A large new computer had just been installed in Hamza's lab, and Saddam came sweeping through for a look. He showed little interest in the computer; his attention was drawn instead to a lineup of pictures that Hamza had tacked to the wall, each of a famous scientist, from Copernicus to Einstein. The pictures had been torn from magazines.

"What are those?" Saddam asked.

"Sir, those are the greatest scientists in history," Hamza told him.

Then, as Hamza remembers it, Saddam became angry. "What an insult this is! All these great men, these great scientists! You don't have enough respect for these great men to frame their pictures? You can't honor them better than this?"

To Hamza, the outburst was irrational; the anger was out of all proportion. Hamza interpreted it as Saddam's way of testing him, of putting him in his place. But Saddam seemed somehow *personally* offended. To understand his tantrum one must understand the kinship he feels with the great men of history, with history itself. Lack of reverence for an image of Copernicus might suggest a lack of reverence for Saddam.

✳ ✳ ✳

In what sense does Saddam see himself as a great man? Saad al-Bazzaz, who defected in 1992, has thought a lot about this question, during his time as a newspaper editor and TV producer in Baghdad, and in the years since, as the publisher of an Arabic newspaper in London.

"I need a piece of paper and a pen," he told me recently in the lobby of Claridge's Hotel. He flattened the paper out on a coffee table and tested the pen. Then he drew a line down the center. "You must understand, the daily behavior is just the result of the mentality," he explained. "Most people would say that the main conflict in Iraqi society is sectarian, between the Sunni and the Shia Muslims. But the big gap has nothing to do with religion. It is between the mentality of the villages and the mentality of the cities."

"Okay. Here is a village." On the right half of the page al-Bazzaz wrote a *V* and beneath it he drew a collection of separate small squares. "These are houses or tents," he said. "Notice there are spaces between them. This is because in the villages each family has its own house, and each house is sometimes several miles from the next one. They are self-contained. They grow their own food and make their own clothes. Those who grow up in the villages are frightened of everything. There is no real law enforcement or civil society. Each family is frightened of each other, and all of them are frightened of outsiders. This is the tribal mind. The only loyalty they know is to their own family, or to their own village. Each of the families is ruled by a patriarch, and the village is ruled by the strongest of them. This loyalty to tribe comes before everything. There are no values beyond power. You can lie, cheat, steal, even kill, and it is okay so long as you are a loyal son of the village or the tribe. Politics for these people is a bloody game, and it is all about getting or holding power."

Al-Bazzaz wrote the word "city" atop the left half of the page. Beneath it he drew a line of adjacent squares. Below that he drew another line, and another. "In the city the old tribal ties are left behind. Everyone lives close together. The state is a big part of everyone's life. They work at jobs and buy their food and clothing at markets and in stores. There are laws, police, courts, and schools. People in the city lose their fear of outsiders and take an interest in foreign things. Life in the city depends on cooperation, on sophisticated social networks. Mutual self-interest defines public policy. You can't get anything done without cooperating with others, so politics in the city becomes the art of compromise and partnership. The highest goal of politics becomes cooperation, community, and keeping the peace. By definition, politics in the city becomes nonviolent. The backbone of urban politics isn't blood, it's law."

In al-Bazzaz's view, Saddam embodies the tribal mentality. "He is the ultimate Iraqi patriarch, the village leader who has seized a nation," he explained. "Because he has come so far, he feels anointed by destiny. Everything he does is, by definition, the right thing to do. He has been chosen by Heaven to lead. Often in his life he has been saved by God, and each escape makes him more certain of his destiny. In recent years, in his speeches, he has begun using passages and phrases from the Koran, speaking the words as if they are his own. In the Koran, Allah says, 'If you thank me, I will give you more.' In the early nineties Saddam was on TV, presenting awards to military officers, and he said, 'If you thank me, I will give you more.' He no longer believes he is a normal person. Dialogue with him is impossible because of this. He can't understand why journalists should be allowed to criticize him. How can they criticize the father of the tribe? This is something unacceptable in his mind. To him, strength is everything. To allow criticism or differences of opinion, to negotiate or compromise, to accede to the rule of law or to due process—these are signs of weakness."

Saddam is, of course, not alone in admiring *The Godfather* series. They are obvious movies for him to like (they were also a favorite of the Colombian cocaine tycoon Pablo Escobar). On the surface it is a classic patriarchal tale. Don Vito Corleone builds his criminal empire from nothing, motivated in the main by love for his family. He sees that the world around him is vicious and corrupt, so he outdoes the world at its own cruelty and preys upon its vices, creating an apparent refuge of wealth and safety for himself and his own. We are drawn to his single-mindedness, subtle intelligence, and steadfast loyalty to an ancient code of honor in a changing world—no matter how unforgiving that code seems by modern standards. The Godfather suffers greatly but dies playing happily in the garden with his grandson, arguably a successful man. The deeper meaning of the films, however, apparently evades Saddam. *The Godfather* saga is more the story of Michael Corleone than of his father, and the film's message is not a happy one. Michael's obsessive loyalty to his father and to his family, to the ancient code of honor, leads him to destroy the very things it is designed to protect. In the end Michael's family is torn by tragedy and hatred. He orders his own brother killed, choosing loyalty to code over loyalty to family. Michael becomes a tragic figure, isolated and unloved, ensnared by his own power. He is a lot like Saddam.

In Saddam's other favorite movie, *The Old Man and the Sea*, the old man, played by Spencer Tracy, hooks a great fish and fights alone in his skiff to haul it in. It is easy to see why Saddam would be stirred by the image of a lone fisherman, surrounded by a great ocean, struggling to land this impossible fish. "I will show him what a man can do and what a man endures," the old man says. In the end he succeeds, but the fish is too large for the dinghy and is devoured by sharks before the trophy can be displayed. The old man returns to his hut with cut and bleeding hands, exhausted but happy in the knowledge that he has prevailed. It would be easy for Saddam to see himself in that old man.

Or is he the fish? In the movie it leaps like a fantasy from the water—a splendid, wild, dangerous thing, magnificent in its size and strength. It is hooked, but it refuses to accept its fate. "Never have I had such a strong fish, or one that acted so strangely," the old man proclaims. Later he says, "There is no panic in his fight." Saddam believes that he is a great natural leader, the likes of which his world has not seen in thirteen centuries. Perhaps he will fail in the struggle during his lifetime, but he is convinced that his courage and vision will fire a legend that will burn brightly in a future Arab-centered world.

Even as Saddam rhapsodizes over the rich history of Arabia, he concedes the Western world's clear superiority in two things. The first is weapons technology—hence his tireless efforts to import advanced military hardware and to develop weapons of mass destruction. The second is the art of acquiring and holding power. He has become a student of one of the most tyrannical leaders in history: Joseph Stalin.

Saïd Aburish's biography, *Saddam Hussein: The Politics of Revenge* (2000), tells of a meeting in 1979 between Saddam and the Kurdish politician Mahmoud Othman. It was an early-morning meeting, and Saddam received Othman in a small office in one of his palaces. It looked to Othman as if Saddam had slept in the office the night before. There was a small cot in the corner, and the President received him wearing a bathrobe.

Next to the bed, Othman recalled, were "over twelve pairs of expensive shoes. And the rest of the office was nothing but a small library of books about one man, Stalin. One could say he went to bed with the Russian dictator."

In the villages of Iraq the patriarch has only one goal: to expand and defend his family's power. It is the only thing of value in the wide, treacherous world. When Saddam assumed full power, there were still Iraqi intellectuals who had hopes for him. They initially accepted his tyranny as inevitable, perhaps even as a necessary bridge to a more inclusive government, and believed, as did many in the West, that his outlook was essentially modern. In this they were gradually disappointed.

In September of 1979 Saddam attended a conference of unaligned nations in Cuba, where he formed a friendship with Fidel Castro, who still keeps him supplied with cigars. Saddam came to the gathering with Salah Omar al-Ali, who was then the Iraqi ambassador to the United Nations, a post he had accepted after a long period of living abroad as an ambassador. Together Saddam and al-Ali had a meeting with the new Foreign Minister of Iran. Four years earlier Saddam had made a surprise concession to the soon-to-be-deposed Shah, reaching an agreement on navigation in the Shatt-al-Arab, a sixty-mile strait formed by the confluence of the Tigris and Euphrates rivers as they flow into the Persian Gulf. Both countries had long claimed the strait. In 1979, with the Shah roaming the world in search of cancer treatment, and power in the hands of the Ayatollah Khomeini (whom Saddam had unceremoniously booted out of Iraq the year before), relations between the two countries were again strained, and the waters of the Shatt-al-Arab were a potential flash point. Both countries still claimed ownership of two small islands in the strait, which were then controlled by Iran.

But al-Ali was surprised by the tone of the discussions in Cuba. The Iranian representatives were especially agreeable, and Saddam seemed to be in an excellent mood. After the meeting al-Ali strolled with Saddam in a garden outside the meeting hall. They sat on a bench as Saddam lit a big cigar.

"Well, Salah, I see you are thinking of something," Saddam said. "What are you thinking about?"

"I am thinking about the meeting we just had, Mr. President. I am very happy. I'm very happy that these small problems will be solved. I'm so happy that they took advantage of this chance to meet with you and not one of your ministers, because with you being here we can avoid another problem with them. We are neighbors. We are poor people. We don't need another war. We need to rebuild our countries, not tear them down."

Saddam was silent for a moment, drawing thoughtfully on his cigar. "Salah, how long have you been a diplomat now?" he asked.

"About ten years."

"Do you realize, Salah, how much you have changed?"

"How, Mr. President?"

"How should we solve our problems with Iran? Iran took our lands. They are controlling the Shatt-al-Arab, our big river. How can meetings and discussions solve a problem like this? Do you know why they decided to meet with us here, Salah? They are weak is why they are talking with us. If they were strong there would be no need to talk. So this gives us an opportunity, an opportunity that only comes along once in a century. We have an opportunity here to recapture our territories and regain control of our river."

That was when al-Ali realized that Saddam had just been playing with the Iranians, and that Iraq was going to go to war. Saddam had no interest in diplomacy. To him, statecraft was just a game whose object was to outmaneuver one's enemies. Someone like al-Ali was there to maintain a pretense, to help size up the situation, to look for openings, and to lull foes into a false sense of security. Within a year the Iran-Iraq War began.

It ended horrifically, eight years later, with hundreds of thousands of Iranians and Iraqis dead. To a visitor in Baghdad the year after the war ended, it seemed that every other man on the street was missing a limb. The country had been devastated. The war had cost Iraq billions. Saddam claimed to have regained control of the Shatt-al-Arab. Despite the huge losses, he was giddy with victory. By 1987 his army, swelled by compulsory service and modern Western armaments, was the fourth largest in the world. He had an arsenal of Scud missiles, a sophisticated nuclear-weapons program under way, and deadly chemical and biological weapons in development. He immediately began planning more conquest.

Saddam's invasion of Kuwait, in August of 1990, was one of the great military miscalculations of modern history. It was a product of grandiosity. Emboldened by his "victory" over Iran, Saddam had begun to plan other improbable undertakings. He announced that he was going to build a world-class subway system for Baghdad, a multibillion-dollar project, and then proclaimed that he would construct a state-of-the-art nationwide rail system along with it. Ground was never broken for either venture. Saddam didn't have the money. One thing he did have, however, was an army of more than a million idle soldiers— easily enough men to overrun the neighboring state of Kuwait, with its rich oil deposits. He gambled that the world would not care, and he was wrong. Three days after Saddam's takeover of the tiny kingdom President George H. W. Bush announced, "This will not stand," and immediately began assembling one of the largest military forces ever in the region.

Through the end of 1990 and into 1991 Ismail Hussain waited in the Kuwaiti desert for the American counterattack. He is a short, stocky man, a singer, musician, and songwriter. The whole time he was forced to wear a uniform, he knew that he did not belong in one. Although some of the men in his unit were good soldiers, none of them thought they belonged in Kuwait. They hoped that they would not have to fight. Everyone knew that the United States had more soldiers, more supplies, and better weapons. Surely Saddam would reach an agreement to save face, and his troops would be able to withdraw peacefully. They waited and waited for this to happen, and when word came that they were actually going to fight, Hussain decided that he was already dead. There was no hope: he foresaw death everywhere. If you went toward the American lines, they would shoot you. If you stayed in the open, they would blow you up. If you dug a hole and buried yourself, American bunker-buster bombs would stir your remains with the sand. If you ran, your own commanders would kill you—because they would be killed if their men fled. If a man was killed running away, his coffin would be marked with the word "*jaban*," or "coward." His memory would be disgraced, his family shunned. There would be no pension for them from the state, no secondary school for his children. "*Jaban*" was a mark that would stain the family for generations. There was no escaping it. Some things are worse than staying with your friends and waiting to die. Hussain's unit manned an anti-aircraft gun. He never even saw the American fighter jet that took off his leg.

It was apparent to everyone in the Iraqi military, from conscripts like Hussain to Saddam's top generals, that they could not stand up against such force. Saddam, however, didn't see it that way. Al-Bazzaz remembers being shocked by this. "We had the most horrible meeting on January 14, 1991, just two days before the allied offensive," he told me. "Saddam had just met with the UN Secretary General, who had come at the final hour to try to negotiate a peaceful resolution. They had been in a meeting for more than two and a half hours, so hopes were running high that some resolution had been reached. Instead Saddam stepped out to address us, and it was clear he was going to miss this last opportunity. He told us, 'Don't be afraid. I see the gates of Jerusalem open before me.' I thought, *What is this shit?* Baghdad was about to be hit with this terrible firestorm, and he's talking to us about visions of liberating Palestine?"

Wafic Samarai was in a particularly difficult position. How does one function as chief of intelligence for a tyrant who does not wish to hear the truth? On the one hand, if you tell him the truth and it contradicts his sense of infallibility, you are in trouble. On the other, if you tell him only what he wants to hear, time will inevitably expose your lies and you will be in trouble.

Samarai was a lifelong military officer. He had advised Saddam throughout the long war with Iran, and he had seen him develop a fairly sophisticated understanding of military terminology, weaponry, strategy, and tactics. But Saddam's vision was clouded by a strong propensity for wishful thinking—the downfall of many an amateur general. If Saddam wanted something to happen, he believed he could will it to happen. Samarai kept up a steady stream of intelligence reports as the United States and its allies assembled an army of nearly a million soldiers in Kuwait, with airpower far beyond anything the Iraqis could muster, with artillery, missiles, tanks, and other armored vehicles decades more advanced than Iraq's arsenal. The Americans didn't hide these weapons. They wanted Saddam to understand exactly what he was up against.

Yet Saddam refused to be intimidated. He had a plan, which he outlined to Samarai and his other generals in a meeting in Basra weeks before the American offensive started. He proposed capturing U.S. soldiers and tying them up around Iraqi tanks, using them as human shields. "The Americans will never fire on their own soldiers," he said triumphantly, as if such squeamishness was a fatal flaw. It was understood that he would have no such compunction. In the fighting, he vowed, thousands of enemy prisoners would be taken for this purpose. Then his troops would roll unopposed into eastern Saudi Arabia, forcing the allies to back down. This was his plan, anyway.

Samarai knew that this was nothing more than a hallucination. How were the Iraqis supposed to capture thousands of American soldiers? No one could approach the American positions, especially in force, without being discovered and killed. Even if it could be done, the very idea of using soldiers as human shields was repulsive, against all laws and international agreements. Who knew how the Americans would respond to such an act? Might they bomb Baghdad with a nuclear weapon? Saddam's plan was preposterous. But none of the generals, including Samarai, said a word. They all nodded dutifully and took notes. To question the Great Uncle's grand strategy would have meant to admit doubt, timidity, and cowardice. It might also have meant demotion or death.

Still, as chief of intelligence, Samarai felt compelled to tell Saddam the truth. Late in the afternoon of January 14 the general reported for a meeting in Saddam's office in the Republican Palace. Dressed in a well-cut black suit, the President was behind his desk. Samarai swallowed hard and delivered his grim assessment. It would be very difficult to stand fast against the assault that was coming. No enemy soldiers had been captured, and it was unlikely that any would be. There was no defense against the number and variety of weapons arrayed against Iraq's troops. Saddam had refused all previous military advice to withdraw the bulk of his forces from Kuwait and move them back across the Iraqi border, where they might be more effective. Now they were so thinly strung out across the desert that there was little to stop the Americans from advancing straight to Baghdad itself. Samarai had detailed evidence to back up his views—photographs, news reports, numbers. The Iraqis could expect nothing more than swift defeat, and the threat that Iran would take advantage of their weakness by invading from the north.

Saddam listened patiently to this litany of pending disaster. "Are these your personal opinions or are they facts?" he asked. Samarai had presented many facts in his report, but he conceded that some of what he was offering was educated conjecture.

"I will now tell you my opinion," Saddam said calmly, confidently. "Iran will never interfere. Our forces will put up more of a fight than you think. They can dig bunkers and withstand America's aerial attacks. They will fight for a long time, and there will be many casualties on both sides. Only we are willing to accept casualties; the Americans are not. The American people are weak. They would not accept the losses of large numbers of their soldiers."

Samarai was flabbergasted. But he felt he had done his duty. Saddam would not be able to complain later that his chief intelligence officer had misled him. The two men sat in silence for a few moments. Samarai could feel the looming American threat like a great weight pressing on his shoulders. There was nothing to be done. To Samarai's surprise, Saddam did not seem angry with him for delivering this bad news. In fact, he acted appreciative that Samarai had given it to him straight. "I trust you, and that's your opinion," he said. "You are a trustworthy person, an honorable person."

Heavy aerial attacks began three days later. Five weeks after that, on February 24, the ground offensive began, and Saddam's troops promptly surrendered or fled. Thousands were pinned at a place called Mutla Ridge as they tried to cross back into Iraq; most were incinerated in their vehicles. Iran did not invade, but otherwise the war unfolded precisely as Samarai had predicted.

In the days after this rout Samarai was again summoned to meet with Saddam. The President was working out of a secret office. He had been moving from house to house in the Baghdad suburbs, commandeering homes at random in order to avoid sleeping where American smart bombs might hit. Still, Samarai found him looking not just unfazed but oddly buoyed by all the excitement.

"What is your evaluation, general?" Saddam asked.

"I think this is the biggest defeat in military history," Samarai said.

"How can you say that?"

"This is bigger than the defeat at Khorramshahr [one of the worst Iraqi losses in the war with Iran, with Iraqi casualties in the tens of thousands]."

Saddam didn't say anything at first. Samarai knew the President wasn't stupid. He surely had seen what everyone else had seen—his troops surrendering en masse, the slaughter at Mutla Ridge, the grinding devastation of the U.S. bombing campaign. But even if Saddam agreed with the general's assessment, he could not bring himself to say so. In the past, as at Khorramshahr, the generals could always be blamed for defeat. Military people would be accused of sabotage, betrayal, incompetence, or cowardice. There would be arrests and executions, after which Saddam could comfortably harbor the illusion that he had rooted out the cause of failure. But this time the reasons for defeat rested squarely with him, and this, of course, was something he could never admit. "That's your opinion," he said curtly, and left it at that.

Defeated militarily, Saddam has in the years since responded with even wilder schemes and dreams, articulated in his typically confused, jargon-laden, quasi-messianic rhetoric. "On this basis, and along the same central concepts and their genuine constants, together with the required revolutionary compatibility and continuous renewal in styles, means, concepts, potentials, and methods of treatment and behavior, the proud and loyal people of Iraq and their valiant armed forces will win victory in the final results of the immortal Mother of All Battles," he declared in a televised address to the Iraqi people in August of last year. "With them and through them, good Arabs will win victory. Their victory will be splendid, immortal, immaculate, with brilliance that no interference can overshadow. In our hearts and souls as in the hearts and souls of the high-minded, glorious Iraqi women and high-spirited Iraqi men, victory is absolute conviction, Allah willing. The picking of its final fruit, in accordance with its description which all the world will point to, is a matter of time whose manner and last and final hour will be determined by the Merciful Allah. And Allah is the greatest!"

To help Allah along, Saddam had already started secret programs to develop nuclear, chemical, and biological weapons.

QASWAH (CRUELTY)

The flood has reached its climax and after the destruction, terror, murder, and sacrilege practiced by the aggressive, terrorist, and criminal Zionist entity, together with its tyrannical ally, the United States, have come to a head against our brothers and our faithful struggling people in plundered Palestine. If evil achieves its objectives there, Allah forbid, its gluttony for more will increase and it will afflict our people and other parts of our wide homeland too.

—Saddam Hussein, in a televised address to the Iraqi people,
December 15, 2001

In the early 1980s a midlevel Iraqi bureaucrat who worked in the Housing Ministry in Baghdad saw several of his colleagues accused by Saddam's regime of accepting bribes. The accusations, he believes, were probably true. "There was petty corruption in our department," he says. The accused were all sentenced to die.

"All of us in the office were ordered to attend the hanging," says the former bureaucrat, who now lives in London. "I decided I wasn't going to go, but when my friends found out my plans, they called me and urged me to reconsider, warning that my refusal could turn suspicion on me." So he went. He and the others from his office were led into a prison courtyard, where they watched as their colleagues and friends, with whom they had worked for years, with whose children their children played, with whom they had attended parties and picnics, were marched out with sacks tied over their heads. They watched and listened as the accused begged, wept, and protested their innocence from beneath the sacks. One by one they were hanged. The bureaucrat decided then and there to leave Iraq.

"I could not live in a country where such a thing takes place," he says. "It is wrong to accept bribes, and those who do it should be punished by being sent to jail. But to hang them? And to order their friends and colleagues to come watch? No one who has witnessed such cruelty would willingly stay and continue to work under such conditions."

Cruelty is the tyrant's art. He studies and embraces it. His rule is based on fear, but fear is not enough to stop everyone. Some men and women have great courage. They are willing to brave death to oppose him. But the tyrant has ways of countering even this. Among those who do not fear death, some fear torture, disgrace, or humiliation. And even those who do not fear these things for themselves may fear them for their fathers, mothers, brothers, sisters, wives, and children. The tyrant uses all these tools. He commands not just acts of cruelty but cruel spectacle. So we have Saddam hanging the fourteen alleged Zionist plotters in 1969 in a public square and leaving their dangling bodies on display. So we have Saddam videotaping the purge in the Baghdad conference hall and sending the tape to members of his organization throughout the nation. So we have top party leaders forced to witness and even to participate in the executions of their colleagues. When Saddam cracks down on Shia clerics, he executes not just the mullahs but also their families. Pain and humiliation and death become public theater. Ultimately, guilt or innocence doesn't matter, because there is no law or value beyond the tyrant's will; if he wants someone arrested, tortured, tried, and executed, that is sufficient. The exercise not only serves as warning, punishment, or purge but also advertises to his subjects, his enemies, and his potential rivals that he is strong. Compassion, fairness, concern for due process or the law, are all signs of indecision. Indecision means weakness. Cruelty asserts strength.

Among the Zulu, tyrants are said to be "full of blood." According to one estimate, in the third and fourth years of Saddam's formal rule (1981 and 1982) more than three thousand Iraqis were executed. Saddam's horrors over the more than thirty years of his informal and formal rule will someday warrant a museum and archives. But lost among the most outrageous atrocities are smaller acts that shed light on his personality. Tahir Yahya was the Prime Minister of Iraq when the Baath Party took power in 1968. It is said that in 1964, when Saddam was in prison, Yahya had arranged for a personal meeting and tried to coerce him into turning against the Baathists and cooperating with the regime. Yahya had served Iraq as a military officer his whole adult life and had at one time even been a prominent member of the Baath Party, one of Saddam's superiors. But he had earned Saddam's enduring scorn. After seizing power, Saddam had Yahya, a well-educated man whose sophistication he resented, confined to prison. On his orders Yahya was assigned to push a wheelbarrow from cell to cell, collecting the prisoners' slop buckets. He would call out "Rubbish! Rubbish!" The former Prime Minister's humiliation was a source of delight to Saddam until the day Yahya died, in prison. He still likes to tell the story, chuckling over the words "Rubbish! Rubbish!"

In another case Lieutenant General Omar al-Hazzaa was overheard speaking ill of the Great Uncle in 1990. He was not just sentenced to death. Saddam ordered that prior to his execution his tongue be cut out; for good measure, he also executed al-Hazzaa's son, Farouq. Al-Hazzaa's homes were bulldozed, and his wife and other children left on the street.

Saddam is realistic about the brutal reprisals that would be unleashed should he ever lose his grip on power. In their book *Out of the Ashes* (1999), Andrew and Patrick Cockburn tell of a family that complained to Saddam that one of their members had been unjustly executed. He was unapologetic, and told them, "Do not think you will get revenge. If you ever have the chance, by the time you get to us there will not be a sliver of flesh left on our bodies." In other words, if he ever becomes vulnerable, his enemies will quickly devour him.

Even if Saddam is right that greatness is his destiny, his legend will be colored by cruelty. It is something he sees as regrettable, perhaps, but necessary—a trait that defines his stature. A lesser man would lack the stomach for it. His son Uday once boasted to a childhood playmate that he and his brother, Qusay, had been taken to prisons by their father to witness torture and executions—to toughen them up for "the difficult tasks ahead," he said.

Yet no man is without contradictions. Even Saddam has been known to grieve over his excesses. Some who saw him cry at the lectern during the 1979 purge dismiss it as a performance, but Saddam has a history of bursting into tears. In the wave of executions following his formal assumption of power, according to Saïd Aburish's biography, he locked himself in his bedroom for two days and emerged with eyes red and swollen from weeping. Aburish reports that Saddam then paid a brazen though apparently sincere condolence call on the family of Adnan Hamdani, the executed official who had been closest to him during the previous decade. He expressed not remorse—the execution was *necessary*—but sadness. He told Hamdani's widow apologetically that "national considerations" must outweigh personal ones. So on occasion, at least, Saddam the person laments what Saddam the tyrant must do. During the Civil War, Abraham Lincoln drew a sharp distinction between what he personally would do—abolish slavery—and what his office required him to do: uphold the Constitution and the Union. Saddam ought to feel no such conflict; by definition, the interests of the state are his own. But he does.

The conflict between his personal priorities and his presidential ones has been particularly painful in his own family. Two of his sons-in-law, the brothers Saddam and Hussein Kamel, fled to Jordan and spilled state secrets—about biological, chemical, and nuclear-weapons programs—before inexplicably returning to Iraq and their deaths. Uday Hussein, Saddam's eldest son, is by all reports a sadistic criminal, if not completely mad. He is a tall, dark-skinned, well-built man of thirty-seven, who in his narcissism and willfulness is almost a caricature of his father. Uday has all his father's brutal instincts and, apparently, none of his discipline. He is a flamboyant drunk, and famous for designing his own wild apparel. Photographs show him wearing enormous bow ties and suits in colors to match his luxury cars, including a bright-red one with white stripes, and one that is half red, half white. Some of his suit jackets have a lapel on one side but not the other.

Ismail Hussain, the hapless Iraqi soldier who lost his leg in the Kuwaiti desert, attracted Uday's attention as a singer after the war. He became the First Son's favorite performer and was invited to sing at the huge parties Uday threw every Monday and Thursday night. The parties were often held at a palace, which Saddam built, on an island in the Tigris near Baghdad. The opulence was eye-popping. All the door handles and fixtures in the palace were made of gold.

"At the parties," says Ismail, who now lives in Toronto, "I would be performing, and Uday would climb up on the stage with a machine gun and start shooting it at the ceiling. Everyone would drop down, terrified. I was used to being around weapons, bigger weapons than Uday's Kalashnikov, so I would just keep on singing. Sometimes at these parties there would be dozens of women and only five or six men. Uday insists that everyone get drunk with him. He would interrupt my performance, get up on stage with a big glass of Cognac for himself and one for me. He would insist that I drink all of it with him. When he gets really drunk, out come the guns. His friends are all terrified of him, because he can have them imprisoned or killed. I saw him once get angry with one of his friends. He kicked the man in the ass so hard that his boot flew off. The man ran over and retrieved the boot and then tried to put it back on Uday's foot, with Uday cursing him all the while."

Uday's blessing paves the way for a singer like Ismail to perform regularly on Iraqi television. For this service Uday demands a kickback, and he can unmake a star as quickly as he can make one. The same is true in sports. Raed Ahmed was an Olympic weightlifter who carried the Iraqi flag during the opening ceremonies of the Atlanta games in 1996. "Uday was head of the Olympic Committee, and all sports in Iraq," Ahmed told me early this year, in his home in a suburb of Detroit. "During training camp he would closely monitor all the athletes, keeping in touch with the trainers and pushing them to push the athletes harder. If he's unhappy with the results, he will throw the trainers and even the athletes into a prison he keeps inside the Olympic Committee building. If you make a promise of a certain result and fail to achieve it in competition, then the punishment is a special prison where they torture people. Some of the athletes started to quit when Uday took over, including many who were the best in their sports. They just decided it was not worth it. Others, like me, loved their sports, and success can be a stepping-stone in Iraq to better things, like a nice car, a nice home, a career. I always managed to avoid being punished. I was careful never to promise anything that I couldn't deliver. I would always say that there was a strong possibility that I would be beaten. Then, when I won, Uday was so happy."

Ahmed sat like a giant in his small living room, his shoulders nearly as wide as the back of the couch. The world of Saddam and Uday now strikes him as a bizarre wonderland, an entire nation hostage to the whims of a tyrant and his crazy son. "When I defected, Uday was very angry," he said. "He visited my family and questioned them. 'Why would Ahmed do such a thing?' he asked. 'He was always rewarded by me.' But Uday is despised."

Saddam tolerated Uday's excesses—his drunken parties, his private jail in the Olympic Committee headquarters—until Uday murdered one of the Great Uncle's top aides at a party in 1988. Uday immediately tried to commit suicide with sleeping pills. According to the Cockburns, "As his stomach was being pumped out, Saddam arrived in the emergency room, pushed the doctors aside, and hit Uday in the face, shouting: 'Your blood will flow like my friend's!'" His father softened, and the murder was ruled an accident. Uday spent four months in custody and then four months with an uncle in Geneva before he was picked up by the Swiss police for carrying a concealed weapon and asked to leave the country. Back in Baghdad, in 1996, he became the target of an assassination attempt. He was hit by eight bullets and is now paralyzed from the waist down. His behavior has presumably disqualified him from succeeding his father. Saddam has made a show in recent years of grooming Qusay, a quieter, more disciplined and dutiful heir.

But the shooting of Uday was a warning to Saddam. Reportedly, a small group of well-educated Iraqi dissidents—none of whom has ever been apprehended, despite thousands of arrests and interrogations—carried it out. The would-be assassins are rumored to be associated with the family of General Omar al-Hazzaa, the officer whose tongue was cut out before he and his son were executed. This may be true; but there is no shortage of aggrieved parties in Iraq.

As Saddam approaches his sixty-sixth birthday, his enemies are numerous, strong, and determined. He celebrated the 1992 electoral defeat of George Bush by firing a gun from a palace balcony. Ten years later a new President Bush is in the White House, with a new national mission to remove Saddam. So the walls that protect the tyrant grow higher and higher. His dreams of pan-Arabia and his historical role in it grow ever more fanciful. In his clearer moments Saddam must know that even if he manages to hang on to power for the remainder of his life, the chances of his fathering a dynasty are slim. As he retreats to his secret bed each night, sitting up to watch a favorite movie on TV or to read one of his history books, he must know it will end badly for him. Any man who reads as much as he does, and who studies the dictators of modern history, knows that in the end they are all toppled and disdained.

"His aim is to be leader of Iraq forever, for as long as he lives," Samarai says. "This is a difficult task, even without the United States targeting you. The Iraqis are a divided and ruthless people. It is one of the most difficult nations in the world to govern. To accomplish his own rule, Saddam has shed so much blood. If his aim is for his power to be transferred to his family after his death, I think this is far into the realm of wishful thinking. But I think he lost touch with reality in that sense long ago."

This, ultimately, is why Saddam will fail. His cruelty has created great waves of hatred and fear, and it has also isolated him. He is out of step. His speeches today play like a broken record. They no longer resonate even in the Arab world, where he is despised by secular liberals and Muslim conservatives alike. In Iraq itself he is universally hated. He blames the crippling of the state on UN sanctions and U.S. hostility, but

Iraqis understand that he is the cause of it. "Whenever he would start in blaming the Americans for this and that, for everything, we would look at each other and roll our eyes," says Sabah Khalifa Khodada, the former Iraqi major who was stripped and decontaminated for a meeting with the Great Uncle. The forces that protect him know this too—they do not live full-time behind the walls. Their loyalty is governed by fear and self-interest, and will tilt decisively if and when an alternative appears. The key to ending Saddam's tyranny is to present such an alternative. It will not be easy. Saddam will never give up. Overthrowing him will almost certainly mean killing him. He guards his hold on the state as he guards his own life. There is no panic in his fight.

But for all the surrounding threats, Saddam sees himself as an immortal figure. Nothing could be more illustrative of this than the plot of his first novel, *Zabibah and the King*. Set in a mythical Arabian past, it is a simple fable about a lonely king, trapped behind the high walls of his palace. He feels cut off from his subjects, so he sets out on occasion to mingle. On one such outing, to a rural village, the king is struck by the beauty of the young Zabibah. She is married to a brutish husband, but the king summons her to his palace, where her rustic ways are at first scorned by the sophisticated courtiers. In time Zabibah's sweet simplicity and virtue charm the court and win the king's heart— although their relationship remains chaste. Questioning his own stern methods, the king is reassured by Zabibah, who tells him, "The people need strict measures so that they can feel protected by this strictness." But dark forces invade the kingdom. Infidel outsiders pillage and destroy the village, aided by Zabibah's jealous and humiliated husband, who rapes her. (The outrage occurs on January 17, the day in 1991 when the United States and allied powers began aerial attacks on Iraq.) Zabibah is later killed; the king defeats his enemy and slays Zabibah's husband. He then experiments with giving his people more freedoms, but they fall to fighting among themselves. Their squabbles are interrupted by the good king's death and their realization of his greatness and importance. The martyred Zabibah's sage advice reminds them: the people need strict measures.

And so Saddam champions the simple virtues of a glorious Arab past, and dreams that his kingdom, though universally scorned and defiled, will rise again and triumph. Like the good king, he is vital in a way that will not be fully understood until he is gone. Only then will we all study the words and deeds of this magnificent, defiant soul. He awaits his moment of triumph in a distant, glorious future that mirrors a distant, glorious past.

LOSING THE WAR

Lee Sandlin

★ ★ ★

Man is a bubble, and all the world is a storm.

—*Jeremy Taylor,* Holy Dying *(1651)*

My father owned a gorgeous porcelain tiger about half the size of a house cat. He kept it on a shelf in our family den, where for years when I was a kid it roared down at us. It's roaring at me again as I write this: it stands on a shelf in my study. My father hadn't got it because he was fond of tigers or because he had any interest in nature. He'd bought it in Korea, where he'd been a bomber pilot during the Korean war; his squadron had been called the Flying Tigers.

My father didn't like telling war stories. He'd accumulated fistfuls of medals over there, and he kept them stashed in an anonymous little plush case at the back of his closet, where they went unseen for decades. That was all part of the past, and he had no use for the past. He used to wave off any question I asked about the world before I was born, irritatedly dismissing it as if all of that were self-evidently too shabby and quaint to interest a modern kid like me. "It was a long time ago," he'd always tell me, which was as much as to say, "It's meaningless now."

And yet every night, whenever he'd sit down in his easy chair, he'd be confronted by the tiger glaring at him. What did he think about when he saw it? I don't know, because he wouldn't say. Whatever patina of private associations the tiger had for him is gone for good.

That's the common fate of mementos. No matter what their occasion was, they sooner or later slip free and are lost in a generic blur: a Day at the Carnival, a Triumph at the State Finals, a Summer Vacation, My First Love. It's particularly true, I think, of the mementos of soldiers, because nobody other than a soldier remembers the details of any war once it's safely over. What really happened in Korea? I don't have the slightest idea; war just isn't an experience I'm up on. I was barely young enough to miss the Vietnam draft, and I'm old enough now that the only way I could figure in a future war is as a victim.

People my age and younger who've grown up in the American heartland can't help but take for granted that war is unnatural. We think of the limitless peace around us as the baseline condition of life. All my life I've heard people say "war is insanity" in tones of dramatic insight and final wisdom.

But there've been places and times where people have thought of war as the given and peace the perversion. The Greeks of Homer's time, for instance, saw war as the one enduring constant underlying the petty affairs of humanity, as routine and all-consuming as the cycle of the seasons: grim and squalid in many ways, but still the essential time when the motives and powers of the gods are most manifest. To the Greeks, peace was nothing but a fluke, an irrelevance, an arbitrary delay brought on when bad weather forced the spring campaign to be canceled, or a back-room deal kept the troops at home until after harvest time. Any of Homer's heroes would see the peaceful life of the average American as some bizarre aberration, like a garden mysteriously cultivated for decades on the slopes of an avalanche-haunted mountain.

Out of idle curiosity, I've been asking friends, people my age and younger, what they know about war—war stories they've heard from their families, facts they've learned in school, stray images that might have stuck with them from old TV documentaries. I wasn't interested in fine points of strategy, but the key events, the biggest moments, the things people at the time had thought would live on as long as there was anybody around to remember the past. To give everybody a big enough target I asked about World War II.

I figured people had to know the basics—World War II isn't exactly easy to miss. It was the largest war ever fought, the largest single event in history. Other than the black death of the Middle Ages, it's the worst thing we know of that has ever happened to the human race. Its after-effects surround us in countless intertwining ways: all sorts of techno-logical commonplaces, from computers to radar to nuclear power, date back to some secret World War II military project or another; the most efficient military systems became the model for the bureaucratic struc-tures of postwar white-collar corporations; even the current landscape of America owes its existence to the war, since the fantastic profusion of suburban development that began in the late 1940s was essentially underwritten by the federal government as one vast World War II vet-erans' benefit. (Before the war there were three suburban shopping centers in the United States; ten years after it ended there were three thousand.)

Then too, World War II has been a dominant force in the American popular imagination. In the mid-1960s, when my own consumption of pop culture was at its peak, the war was the only thing my friends and I thought about. We devoured World War II comic books like Sgt. Fury and Sgt. Rock; we watched World War II TV shows like *Hogan's Heroes* and *The Rat Patrol*; our rooms overflowed with World War II hobby kits, with half-assembled, glue-encrusted panzers and Spitfires and Zeroes. I think I had the world's largest collection of torn and mangled World War II decal insignia. We all had toy boxes stuffed with World War II armaments—with toy pistols and molded plastic rifles and alarmingly realistic rubber hand grenades. We refought World War II battles daily and went out on our campaigns so overloaded with gear we looked like ferocious porcupines. Decades after it was over the war was still expand-ing and dissipating in our minds, like the vapor trails of an immense explosion.

So what did the people I asked know about the war? Nobody could tell me the first thing about it. Once they got past who won they almost drew a blank. All they knew were those big totemic names—Pearl Harbor, D-day, Auschwitz, Hiroshima—whose unfathomable reaches of experience had been boiled down to an abstract atrocity. The rest was gone. Kasserine, Leyte Gulf, Corregidor, Falaise, the Ardennes didn't provoke a glimmer of recognition; they might as well have been off-ramps on some exotic interstate. I started getting the creepy feeling that the war had actually happened a thousand years ago, and so it was forgivable if people were a little vague on the difference between the Normandy invasion and the Norman Conquest and couldn't say offhand whether the boats sailed from France to England or the other way around.

What had happened, for instance, at one of the war's biggest battles, the Battle of Midway? It was in the Pacific, there was something about aircraft carriers. Wasn't there a movie about it, one of those Hollywood all-star behemoths in which a lot of admirals look worried while pushing toy ships around a map? (*Midway*, released in 1976 and starring Glenn Ford, Charlton Heston, and—inevitably—Henry Fonda.) A couple of people were even surprised to hear that Midway Airport was named after the battle, though they'd walked past the ugly commemorative sculpture in the concourse so many times. All in all, this was a dispiriting exercise. The astonishing events of that morning, the "fatal five minutes" on which the war and the fate of the world hung, had been reduced to a plaque nobody reads, at an airport with a vaguely puzzling name, midway between Chicago and nowhere at all.

Is it that the war was fifty years ago and nobody cares anymore what happened before this week? Maybe so, but I think what my little survey really demonstrates is how vast the gap is between the experience of war and the experience of peace. One of the persistent themes in the best writing about the war—I'm thinking particularly of Paul Fussell's brilliant polemic *Wartime: Understanding and Behavior in the Second World War*—is that nobody back home has ever known much about what it was like on the battlefield. From the beginning, the actual circumstances of World War II were smothered in countless lies, evasions, and distortions, like a wrecked landscape smoothed by a blizzard. People all along have preferred the movie version: the tense border crossing where the flint-eyed SS guards check the forged papers; the despondent high-level briefing where the junior staff officer pipes up with the crazy plan that just might work; the cheerful POWs running rings around the Nazi commandant; the soldier dying gently in a sunlit jungle glade, surrounded by a platoon of teary-eyed buddies. The truth behind these clichés was never forgotten—because nobody except the soldiers ever learned it in the first place.

I think my own childhood image was typical. For me, the war was essentially a metaphysical struggle: America versus the Nazis, all over the world and throughout time. I couldn't have told you anything about its real circumstances; those didn't interest me. The historical war was just a lot of silent newsreel footage of soldiers trudging, artillery pumping, buildings collapsing, and boats bumping ashore—fodder for dull school movies and the duller TV documentaries I was reduced to watching on weekend afternoons when our neighborhood campaigns were rained out. I think I was an adult before I fully grasped that Guadalcanal wasn't a battle over a canal; I'd always fondly pictured furious soldiers fighting over immense locks and reservoirs somewhere where they had canals—Holland maybe, or Panama.

Granted, children always get the child's version of war. But the child's version is the only one readily available. It's no problem of course, if you have sufficient archaeological patience, to root out a more complicated form of historical truth; bookstores offer everything from thumpingly vast general surveys to war-gaming tactical analyses of diversionary skirmishes to maniacally detailed collector's encyclopedias about tank treads. The best academic histories—such as Gerhard L. Weinberg's extraordinary *A World at Arms: A Global History of World War II*—document and analyze in-depth aspects of the war that even the most fanatical buff may not have heard of before: the campaigns along the Indian border, for instance, or the diplomatic maneuvering about Turkish neutrality. But reading almost all of them, one has the sense that some essential truth is still not being disclosed. It's as though the experience of war fits the old definition of poetry: war is the thing that gets lost in translation.

When I was taking my survey a friend told me that he was sitting with his father, a veteran of the European campaign, watching a TV special on the fiftieth anniversary of D-day. My friend suddenly had the impulse to ask a question that had never occurred to him in his entire adult life: "What was it really like to be in a battle?"

His father opened his mouth to answer—and then his jaw worked, his face reddened, and, without saying a word, he got up and walked out of the room. That's the truth about the war: the sense that what happened over there simply can't be told in the language of peace.

But is it really impossible to get across that barrier, even in imagination?

One somnolent Sunday in Chicago the hush of an old brownstone apartment building was disturbed by a woman running down the hallway knocking on doors. Everybody came out to see what she wanted. At first they couldn't make out why she was so excited. More and more people emerged from their apartments to find out what the fuss was about. It was December 1941, and the woman was asking everybody if they were listening to the radio.

My mother told me that story when I asked her what she remembered about the war. This is the sort of story everybody who was around in those days could tell; it was a defining moment in their lives, the way the Kennedy assassination would be for a later generation—where they were when they learned that the Japanese had attacked Pearl Harbor.

So great was the shock of that moment that even now Americans think of Pearl Harbor as the real beginning of World War II. Maybe it's a sign of how invincibly provincial we are, how instinctual is our certainty that the war, like every other big event in the world, was something that happened mainly to us. The truth was that by December 1941 the rest of the world had had enough of the war to last the millennium.

In any orthodox history you can find the standard autopsy of the causes. Germany was falling apart after the decades of social and economic chaos that followed its defeat in World War I. Japan's growing dependence on foreigners to keep its industrializing economy going was leading to widespread and deepening feelings of humiliated anger and outraged national pride. In both countries extremely racist and xenophobic parties had come to power and begun an explosive military expansion: throughout the 1930s the Germans and Japanese built up huge new armies and navies, amassed vast stockpiles of new armaments, and made lots and lots of demands and threats.

All of this is true enough, yet there's something faintly bogus and overly rationalized about it. The approaching war didn't seem like a political or economic event; it was more like a collective anxiety attack. Throughout the '30s people around the world came to share an unshakable dread about the future, a conviction that countless grave international crises were escalating out of control, a panicked sense that everything was coming unhinged and that they could do nothing to stop it. The feeling was caught perfectly by W. H. Auden, writing in 1935:

> *From the narrow window of my fourth-floor room*
> *I smoke into the night, and watch the lights*
> *Stretch in the harbor. In the houses*
> *The little pianos are closed, and a clock strikes.*
> *And all sway forward on the dangerous flood*
> *Of history, that never sleeps or dies,*
> *And, held one moment, burns the hand.*

For instance, in China—to take one arbitrary starting point—a war had been going on since 1931. This was a nagging turmoil at the edge of the world's consciousness, a problem that couldn't be understood, resolved, or successfully ignored. When the Japanese army invaded the city of Nanking in December 1937 they killed tens of thousands of Chinese civilians—some say hundreds of thousands—in the space of a couple of weeks. It was one of the worst orgies of indiscriminate violence in modern times, and as the news of it spread around the world everybody began saying that Nanking would be remembered forever, just as the Spanish civil war's Guernica (the first town to be bombed from airplanes) would be: shorthand landmarks for our century's most horrible atrocities.

But that just shows how little anybody really understood what was happening to the world. Nobody outside of China remembered Nanking a couple years later when the German Reich began its stunning expansion through Europe. The Wehrmacht stampeded whole armies before it with its terrifyingly brutal new style of tank attack (the European press called it "blitzkrieg," and the name stuck), and rumors immediately began circulating of appalling crimes committed in the occupied territories—wholesale deportations and systematic massacres, like a vast mechanized replay of the Mongol invasions. A story solemnly made the rounds of the world's newspapers that storks migrating from Holland to South Africa had been found with messages taped to their legs that read, "Help us! The Nazis are killing us all!"

It was in September 1939, in the wake of the German invasion of Poland, that the phrase "the Second World War" began turning up in newspapers and government speeches. The name was a kind of despairing admission that nobody knew how long the war would go on or how far the fighting would spread. Over the next two years the news arrived almost daily that battles had broken out in places that only weeks before had seemed like safe havens. By the time of Pearl Harbor the war had erupted in Norway and Mongolia, on Crete and in the Dutch East Indies; the Italian Army had marched on Egypt, and the German army was pushing into the outskirts of Moscow; there had been savage fighting in Finland north of the Arctic Circle and sea battles off the coast of Argentina. The United States was one of the last secluded places left on earth.

But the depths of that seclusion were still profound. This is one of the things about America in those days that's hardest for us to imagine now: how impossibly far away people thought the problems of the world were. It's not just that there was no TV, and thus no live satellite feed from the current crisis zone. America didn't even have a decent road system back then. Any long trip across the country was a fearsomely ambitious undertaking—and foreign travel was as fanciful as an opium dream. It wasn't unusual for them to spend every moment of their lives within walking distance of the place where they were born.

They weren't wholly oblivious. But the news they got of the outside world came in through newspapers and radio—which is to say, through words, not images. This imposed even more distance on events that were already as remote as the dust storms of Mars. Their sense of heedlessness wasn't helped by the style of journalism reporters practiced in those days, which was heavy on local color and very light on analysis. The war as it appeared in the American press was a gorgeous tapestry of romance and swashbuckling adventure—frenzied Nazi rallies, weird religious rites in Japan, hairbreadth escapes on overcrowded trains teetering along mountain ravines, nights sleeping in haystacks in the backcountry of France after the fall of Paris, journeys in remotest Yugoslavia where the reporter "spent hours watching the army, with its wagons, horses, and guns, file past the minareted village in the moonlight." (I'm quoting, here and elsewhere, from the Library of America's excellent anthology *Reporting World War II: American Journalism 1938–1946*.) It convinced people that the war was just a lot of foreigners going exotically crazy—nothing for Americans to bother their heads about.

Still, by early 1941 most Americans had come to understand that they couldn't stay unscathed forever. Even in the most remote towns of the heartland, people had some hint of the world's collective terrors: by then the local schoolteacher or minister had come back from a European trip still shaken by the sight of a Nazi book burning, or a neighbor had received a letter—battered, heavily postmarked, and exotically stamped—from a long-forgotten cousin, pleading for help getting out of the old country. A Gallup poll taken in the summer of 1941 showed that a large majority of respondents agreed that America was bound to be drawn into the war eventually; a slightly smaller majority even agreed that it was more important to stop the Nazis than to stay neutral. (Japan wasn't mentioned; even then nobody thought of Japan as a likely enemy.)

Yet "eventually drawn in" really meant "not now." That was what routinely stunned travelers returning to America from the war zones, even late in 1941: how unworried everybody in America seemed. Crowds still swarmed heedlessly on undamaged streets; city skylines still blazed at night, like massed homing beacons for enemy bombers. But if you'd even mentioned the possibility of an air raid out loud, you'd have been laughed at. *New Yorker* reporter A. J. Liebling wrote a piece that summer about coming back to Manhattan after the fall of France and discovering just how impossible it was to get his friends to take the thought of war seriously: "They said soothingly that probably you had had a lot of painful experiences, and if you just took a few grains of nembutol so you would get one good night's sleep, and then go out to the horse races twice, you would be your old sweet self again. It was like the dream in which you yell at people and they don't hear you."

It all changed of course, with a knock on the door, that weekend day in December.

There's a phrase people sometimes use about a nation's collective reaction to events like Pearl Harbor—war fever. We don't know what a true war fever feels like today, since nothing in our recent history compares with it; even a popular war like the Gulf War was preceded by months of solemn debate and a narrow vote in Congress approving military action. World War II came to America like an epidemic from overseas. Immediately after Pearl Harbor, recruitment offices all over America swarmed with long lines of enlistees; flags and patriotic posters popped up on every street and store window; wild and hysterical cheers greeted the national anthem at every rally and concert and sporting event. Overnight the war was the only subject of conversation in the country; it was the only subject of the movies you could see at the local theater (Blondie and Dagwood were absorbed into the war effort in *Blondie for Victory*; Sherlock Holmes came out of retirement to chase Nazi spies in *Sherlock Holmes in Washington*). War was the only acceptable motif in advertising: for years after Pearl Harbor every manufacturer of spark plugs and orange juice routinely proclaimed that its product was essential to an Allied victory.

In an earlier time poet Rupert Brooke had written that people hurried into war out of the moral griminess of civilian life "like swimmers into cleanness leaping." In World War II the leap was perfect, complete, and profound. To the end there were none of the signs of disaffection we've come to expect from Americans over the course of a long war: no peace rallies, no antiescalation petition drives, no moves in Congress for compromise or a negotiated settlement. Men who appeared able-bodied found themselves harassed on the street by strangers demanding to know why they weren't in uniform; baseball players who hadn't yet enlisted, godlike figures like DiMaggio and Williams, were loudly booed by the hometown crowd when they came out on the field.

Why? You'd have a hard time figuring out the answer from reading the nation's press. From the beginning the issues of the war were discussed only in the dreariest of platitudes. "America is the symbol for freedom," *Life* magazine patiently explained to its readers—as though there might have been some confusion about whether the other side was the symbol for freedom. But *Life* firmly refused to be drawn into a debate about what "freedom" might mean: "Freedom is more than a set of rules, or a set of principles. Freedom is a free man. It is a package. But it is God's package."

End of discussion. Hard to believe anybody was moved to go to war by such tripe, but it was typical. When they're consumed by war fever, people don't need considered rationales for the use of military force; they don't even bother with the appearance of logic. As it happened, a purely cynical and cold-blooded calculation of the world crisis could have suggested to Americans that they could easily have stayed out. There were no treaties compelling the nation into the war, no overwhelming strategic or economic pressures; it was self-sufficient in food and raw materials, and it was geographically impregnable. Neither the Japanese nor the Germans would ever have been able to mount an invasion—and, in fact, neither ever seriously considered the possibility; Hitler at his most expansive still thought any transoceanic war was a century away. But when the Germans and Japanese looked across the ocean at America, what they saw was a nation of weaklings and cowards, with no honor or fighting spirit. One of the reasons behind the Japanese attack on Pearl Harbor—apart from the obvious military necessity of taking out the American fleet so that the Japanese military could conquer the western Pacific unopposed—was the unshakable conviction that Americans would collectively fold at the first sign of trouble; one big, nasty attack would be enough to get a negotiated settlement, on whatever terms the Japanese would care to name. In the same way Hitler and his inner circle were blithely sure that America would go to any lengths to stay out of the fight. Hitler's catastrophic decision to declare war on America three days after Pearl Harbor was made almost in passing, as a diplomatic courtesy to the Japanese. To the end he professed himself baffled that America was in the war at all; he would have thought that if Americans really wanted to fight, they'd join with him against their traditional enemies, the British. But evidently they were too much under the thumb of Roosevelt—whom Hitler was positive was a Jew named Rosenfeldt, part of the same evil cabal that controlled Stalin.

As fanciful as that was, it shows the average wartime grasp of the real motives of the enemy. It was at least on a par with the American Left's conviction that Hitler was an irrelevant puppet in the hands of the world's leading industrialists. Throughout the war all sides regarded one another with blank incomprehension.

Millions of young men poured into the military—and most everybody not signing up was hiring on at some new war-related industry. (The American economy grew by almost half during the war; unemployment was wiped out, and skilled workers were in such short supply that wages began a steep upward spiral.) But it was the soldiers who became the natural focus of the nation's sentimental refusal to wonder about what it was doing, as though they were a kind of collective vector for war fever. In the press and the popular imagination the whole American military was merged into one archetypical meta-soldier: the singular emblem of the mass noun "our boys." This soldier was decent, soft-spoken, down-to-earth, and polite; he was shrewd, but he was honest; he was clever, but he wasn't an intellectual. When asked what the war was all about he would scratch his head and slowly drawl that he guessed the Jerries and Japs had started this fight and they had to get what was coming to them. When asked what he himself most wanted to have happen he'd look sincere and say softly that he wanted to get the job done and go home.

In one of his pieces for the *New Yorker* A. J. Liebling caught the soldier's style in a single word. He describes how he found a typical American soldier passing time before a battle by reading *Candide*—which (Liebling carefully noted) he said was by some "fellow" named Voltaire. There it is: the soldier has never heard of Voltaire but is smart enough to read a good book if he wants to. Liebling evidently never met a soldier who'd read Voltaire before the war—much less read him in French. Our boys weren't bothering their heads with culture or history when they were out there in foreign parts; they were going to win the war and come back untouched.

As the war darkened over the years, the figure of the soldier eventually darkened as well. In magazine illustrations later in the war—where a soldier contemplated the memory of breakfast cereal or reflected on how rubber cement saved his platoon—he looked a little wearier and his face was harder, his jaw not always clean-shaven, his eyes more nakedly homesick. But his soft-spoken manner was unruffled—though in feature stories and ad copy from around 1943 on he'd sometimes coyly admit to having fudged his birth date on his enlistment forms. The reason did him nothing but credit, of course. He had to make sure he got overseas and into combat "before it was all over."

You'd think nobody would have had to worry about that: after the first flush of enthusiasm everybody knew the war wasn't going to be over for a long while. But at the same time, people in America remained consistently vague about what the real status of the war was—how soon victory would come, what our boys were going through. The ordinary sources of information were closed, and not just because the news was sanitized by the government. Draftees in those days didn't get to serve out a specified time and then go home—at which point they could tell everybody their war stories. They were in "for the duration"—that is, until the war ended or they were killed. They were swallowed up by the service and were gone, for months and then years, with only a fitful stream of officially censored letters fluttering back from the remoteness of the world to say that everything was still OK. New recruits in the later years of the war were going in essentially as innocent of the realities of combat as enlistees had been before Pearl Harbor.

Caught up in the glory of being soldiers, they soon invented a ritual to be performed as soon as they were fitted with their new uniforms. They'd rush out to photographers' studios and document the occasion for their proud families. The mantels and nightstands of America were strewn with these relics—soldiers posed with quiet dignity against a studio backdrop, half turning to face the camera with an expression both grave and proud. Some guys couldn't help clowning and left photos that baffle people to this day: foreheads furrowed, jaws clenched, eyes fixed and furious—tinted by the studio not ordinary pink but a belligerent orange rose, like a Halloween mask. When you see these photos now, they look like antique novelty items from carnivals, or illustrations for *Ripley's Believe It or Not: "The Angriest Soldier in the World."* We don't remember the pride behind them, the innocence, the mysterious and happy ferocity—the warning to all enemies of just how tough the American soldier would be when he got into the war.

"You folks at home must be disappointed at what happened to our American troops in Tunisia. So are we over here." That was how wire-service reporter Ernie Pyle began a dispatch in February 1943. A few days before, at Kasserine Pass, in the desolate mountain ranges fringing the Sahara, American troops had had their first major encounter with the Germans. The Americans had been undertrained and overconfident; confronted by the ferocity of an artillery barrage, they'd panicked and run. Pyle sounds like he was breaking the news that the hometown swim team had lost at the state finals.

That was pretty bold by the standards of the time. From the beginning of the war any little setback like Kasserine had been veiled in impenetrable layers of vague regret and consolatory wisdom. "No one here has the slightest doubt that the Germans will be thrown out of Tunisia," Pyle goes on to say almost immediately. "It is simply in the cards." That was a lucky thing, because right then there was no compelling military reason to expect an Allied victory. Pyle then adds this remarkable bit to the mythology of "our boys": "As for the soldiers themselves, you need feel no shame nor concern about their ability. I have seen them in battle and afterwards, and there is nothing wrong with the common American soldier. His fighting spirit is good. His morale is OK. The deeper he gets into a fight the more of a fighting man he becomes."

Which is as much as to say that the actual result of the battle shouldn't be allowed to dent the myth. This is where the falsification of the war began—not in the movies and not in government propaganda, but in the simple refusal of reporters in the field to describe honestly what they were seeing.

American soldiers early on grew accustomed to the idea that the truth of their experience wasn't going to be told to the folks back home. They knew the score: despite the drone of triumph surrounding their every deed, the American entry into the war was a gory fiasco.

The military had been caught wholly unprepared and was rushing troops into battle all over the world with a minimum of training and a maximum of chaos. To this day, if you ask any veteran for war stories, what you're likely to hear first is some appalling epic of American military incompetence. Every unit rapidly accumulated its share of grim legends. There was the arrogant lieutenant fresh out of officer school who was assigned to lead troops into battle and turned coward under fire or was fatally befuddled by ambiguous orders. There was the murderous stupidity of a supply clerk up the line who contemptuously mishandled an urgent request for emergency provisions—on Guadalcanal, for instance, desperately needed drinking water arrived in used oil drums nobody had thought to wash out first. And there was the almost daily occurrence of the routine patrol turned into a nightmare by friendly fire. Friendly fire was a worse problem in World War II than in any other American war before or since. American troops on the ground were so frequently bombed by their own planes that they were known to shoot back with their heaviest guns.

The folks at home learned none of this. The news was being censored of course: American reporters in the field, like those of every combatant nation, had to submit all stories for official clearance, and reporters who tried to describe the war honestly would quickly find their stories going unapproved and their press credentials in doubt. But the First Amendment was still in force back home; unlike the newspapers of the Axis, which were wholly given over to government-enforced fantasies of imminent global triumph, American newspapers were still free, at least in theory, to publish whatever they liked. Some of them did so: *The Library of America's Reporting World War II* anthology contains reasonably honest and critical pieces from major newspapers and magazines on conditions in the internment camps, on the lack of enthusiasm for the war in African American ghettos, and on the institutionalized racism of the military. But when it came to what was happening on the battlefields themselves the unbreakable silence closed in.

Part of it was the deep reluctance of the American military to approve stories that suggested—as A. J. Liebling put it—that American soldiers might "die in an undignified way." Part of it was simple patriotism: the reporters were under no obligation to be neutral; they wanted America to win and weren't going to risk hurting home-front morale by writing honestly of the terror and desperation of the battlefield.

But there was another reason as well: a kind of psychological block. There was something essential about the battlefield that reporters didn't tell the folks back home. They weren't being censored exactly; they probably could have published it if they'd wanted to. They just didn't know how. In any anthology of wartime journalism (it happens constantly in *Reporting World War II*), you can find instances of reporters coming up against the fundamental truth of the war and being unable to say what it was. Instead they resorted to a curious verbal tic, almost an involuntary distress signal, to mark the place where their verbal abilities left off and the incommunicable reality of what they were witnessing began.

Here's a typical example, from Ernie Pyle's Tunisian reporting: "One of our half-tracks, full of ammunition, was livid red, with flames leaping and swaying. Every few seconds one of the shells would go off, and the projectile would tear into the sky with a weird *whang-zing* sort of noise."

That seems unexceptionable enough. Like most of what Pyle sent in over the wire, it has a striking visual vigor and simplicity, down to the comic-book sound effects—put a grinning American soldier in the foreground, and you've got a perfect Norman Rockwell war poster. But compare it with this, from John Hersey's reporting of the Guadalcanal campaign for *Life* magazine: "But weirdest of all was the sound of our artillery shells passing overhead. At this angle, probably just about under the zenith of their trajectory, they gave off a soft, fluttery sound, like a man blowing through a keyhole."

This seems to be out of another universe of literary style: compared with Pyle's report, this is a sinuously Jamesian prose poem. But it has an unexpected point of resemblance. Hersey, like Pyle, calls the sound of a shell in flight "weird."

That word and its cognates recur countless times in American war reporting. The war was weird. Or it was haunted, or spectral, or uncanny, or supernatural. Battle zones were eerie, bomb craters were unearthly, even diplomatic conferences were strange and unreal. Here's an elaborate example, from Edward R. Murrow's famous radio broadcasts from London during the German air raids of September 1940. Murrow was standing on a rooftop at night, looking out on a blacked-out roofscape lit up by flashes of antiaircraft fire and distant swarming searchlights. His eye was caught by an odd detail: "Out of one window there waves something that looks like a white bedsheet, a window curtain swinging free in this night breeze. It looks as though it were being shaken by a ghost. There are a great many ghosts around these buildings in London."

It's worth following the implicit logic here in some detail. There's an obvious meaning you would expect Murrow to find in the sight of a white sheet waving in the middle of an air raid: it's a flag of surrender, a pathetic gesture of submission made to the unseen forces thundering across the night skies overhead. But that's exactly what Murrow doesn't say. There was a straightforward reason: he was passionately pro-British and wasn't about to suggest that anybody in London was about to surrender—even metaphorically. But then what did the sheet look like? Now we get to that short-circuit: another reason it didn't look like a white flag was that a white flag was something you'd see in a battle—and this wasn't like a battle. It was much too strange for that. It was more like a haunted house: some kind of border zone where the barriers between this world and the next were dissolving, and ghosts came fluttering up out of nothingness. It was certainly not a place where the traditional language of warfare had any meaning. As Murrow himself put it directly: "There are no words to describe the thing that is happening."

So what was this "thing" these reporters were seeing? Is there any way for us now to get a sense of what they were seeing?

There was a battle soon after Pearl Harbor that may, better than any other, define just what was so strange about the war. Unlike most of the war's battles, it was contained within a narrow enough area that it can be visualized clearly, yet its consequences were so large and mysterious that they rippled throughout the entire world for years afterward. It happens that no American reporters were around to witness it directly, but it has been amply documented even so. From survivors' accounts, and from a small library of academic and military histories, ranging in scope and style from Walter Lord's epic *Miracle at Midway* to John Keegan's brilliant tactical analysis in *The Price of Admiralty: The Evolution of Naval Warfare*, it's possible to work out with some precision just what happened in the open waters of the Pacific off Midway Island at 10:25 a.m. local time on June 4, 1942.

In the months after Pearl Harbor the driving aim of Japanese strategy was to capture a string of islands running the length of the western Pacific and fortify them against an American counterattack. This defensive perimeter would set the boundaries of their new empire—or, as they called it, the "Greater Asia Coprosperity Sphere." Midway Island, the westernmost of the Hawaiian Islands, was one of the last links they needed to complete the chain. They sent an enormous fleet, the heart of the Japanese navy, to do the job: four enormous aircraft carriers, together with a whole galaxy of escort ships. On June 4 the attack force arrived at Midway, where they found a smaller American fleet waiting for them.

Or so the history-book version normally runs. But the sailors on board the Japanese fleet saw things differently. They didn't meet any American ships on June 4. That day, as on all the other days of their voyage, they saw nothing from horizon to horizon but the immensity of the Pacific. Somewhere beyond the horizon line, shortly after dawn, Japanese pilots from the carriers had discovered the presence of the American fleet, but for the Japanese sailors, the only indications of anything unusual that morning were two brief flyovers by American fighter squadrons. Both had made ineffectual attacks and flown off again. Coming on toward 10:30 a.m., with no further sign of enemy activity anywhere near, the commanders ordered the crews on the aircraft carriers to prepare for the final assault on the island, which wasn't yet visible on the horizon.

That was when a squadron of American dive-bombers came out of the clouds overhead. They'd gotten lost earlier that morning and were trying to make their way back to base. In the empty ocean below they spotted a fading wake—one of the Japanese escort ships had been diverted from the convoy to drop a depth charge on a suspected American submarine. The squadron followed it just to see where it might lead. A few minutes later they cleared a cloud deck and discovered themselves directly above the single largest "target of opportunity," as the military saying goes, that any American bomber had ever been offered.

When we try to imagine what happened next we're likely to get an image out of *Star Wars*—daring attack planes, as graceful as swallows, darting among the ponderously churning cannon of some behemoth of a *Death Star*. But the sci-fi trappings of *Star Wars* disguise an archaic and sluggish idea of battle. What happened instead was this: the American squadron commander gave the order to attack, the planes came hurtling down from around twelve thousand feet and released their bombs, and then they pulled out of their dives and were gone. That was all. Most of the Japanese sailors didn't even see them.

The aircraft carriers were in a frenzy just then. Dozens of planes were being refueled and rearmed on the hangar decks, and elevators were raising them to the flight decks, where other planes were already revving up for takeoff. The noise was deafening, and the warning sirens were inaudible. Only the sudden, shattering bass thunder of the big guns going off underneath the bedlam alerted the sailors that anything was wrong. That was when they looked up. By then the planes were already soaring out of sight, and the black blobs of the bombs were already descending from the brilliant sky in a languorous glide.

One bomb fell on the flight deck of the *Akagi*, the flagship of the fleet, and exploded amidships near the elevator. The concussion wave of the blast roared through the open shaft to the hangar deck below, where it detonated a stack of torpedoes. The explosion that followed was so powerful it ruptured the flight deck; a fireball flashed like a volcano through the blast crater and swallowed up the midsection of the ship. Sailors were killed instantly by the fierce heat, by hydrostatic shock from the concussion wave, by flying shards of steel; they were hurled overboard unconscious and drowned. The sailors in the engine room were killed by flames drawn through the ventilating system. Two hundred died in all. Then came more explosions rumbling up from belowdecks as the fuel reserves ignited. That was when the captain, still frozen in shock and disbelief, collected his wits sufficiently to recognize that the ship had to be abandoned.

Meanwhile another carrier, the *Kaga*, was hit by a bomb that exploded directly on the hangar deck. The deck was strewn with live artillery shells, and open fuel lines snaked everywhere. Within seconds, explosions were going off in cascading chain reactions, and uncontrollable fuel fires were breaking out all along the length of the ship. Eight hundred sailors died. On the flight deck a fuel truck exploded and began shooting wide fans of ignited fuel in all directions; the captain and the rest of the senior officers, watching in horror from the bridge, were caught in the spray, and they all burned to death.

Less than five minutes had passed since the American planes had first appeared overhead. The *Akagi* and the *Kaga* were breaking up. Billowing columns of smoke towered above the horizon line. These attracted another American bomber squadron, which immediately launched an attack on a third aircraft carrier, the *Soryu*. These bombs were less effective—they set off fuel fires all over the ship, but the desperate crew managed to get them under control. Still, the *Soryu* was so badly damaged it was helpless. Shortly afterward it was targeted by an American submarine (the same one the escort ship had earlier tried to drop a depth charge on). American subs in those days were a byword for military ineffectiveness; they were notorious for their faulty and unpredictable torpedoes. But the crew of this particular sub had a large stationary target to fire at point-blank. The *Soryu* was blasted apart by repeated direct hits. Seven hundred sailors died.

The last of the carriers, the *Hiryu*, managed to escape untouched, but later that afternoon it was located and attacked by another flight of American bombers. One bomb set off an explosion so strong it blew the elevator assembly into the bridge. More than four hundred died, and the crippled ship had to be scuttled a few hours later to keep it from being captured.

Now there was nothing left of the Japanese attack force except a scattering of escort ships and the planes still in the air. The pilots were the final casualties of the battle; with the aircraft carriers gone, and with Midway still in American hands, they had nowhere to land. They were doomed to circle helplessly above the sinking debris, the floating bodies, and the burning oil slicks until their fuel ran out.

This was the Battle of Midway. As John Keegan writes, it was "the most stunning and decisive blow in the history of naval warfare." Its consequences were instant, permanent, and devastating. It gutted Japan's navy and broke its strategy for the Pacific war. The Japanese would never complete their perimeter around their new empire; instead they were thrown back on the defensive, against an increasingly large and better-organized American force, which grew surgingly confident after its spectacular victory. After Midway, as the Japanese scrambled to rebuild their shattered fleet, the Americans went on the attack. In August 1942 they began landing a marine force on the small island of Guadalcanal (it's in the Solomons, near New Guinea) and inexorably forced a breach in the perimeter in the southern Pacific. From there American forces began fanning out into the outer reaches of the empire, cutting supply lines and isolating the strongest garrisons. From Midway till the end of the war the Japanese didn't win a single substantial engagement against the Americans. They had "lost the initiative," as the bland military saying goes, and they never got it back.

But it seems somehow paltry and wrong to call what happened at Midway a "battle." It had nothing to do with battles the way they were pictured in the popular imagination. There were no last-gasp gestures of transcendent heroism, no brilliant counterstrategies that saved the day. It was more like an industrial accident. It was a clash not between armies, but between TNT and ignited petroleum and drop-forged steel. The thousands who died there weren't warriors but bystanders— the workers at the factory who happened to draw the shift when the boiler exploded.

This was exactly what the witnesses to the war were finding so impossible to believe. The cliché in those days was that World War I had destroyed the old romantic notions about battle—after the slaughter in the trenches of Europe, it was said, nobody would ever again rhapsodize about the chivalry of jousting knights or the grandeur of a sword-waving cavalry charge. The reporters going out to cover World War II had prepared themselves to see battles that were mechanized, anonymous, and horrible. But they weren't prepared, not really. World War I had been a generation earlier, and the military industries of the great powers hadn't stopped their drive for innovation. The combatant nations of World War II were supplying their forces with armaments of such dramatically increased power they made those of World War I obsolete. The reporters got out into the war and discovered a scale of mass destruction so inhuman that cynicism and disillusionment seemed just as irrelevant as the sentimental pieties of the home front.

What were they supposed to say about what they were seeing? At Kasserine American soldiers were blown apart into shreds of flesh scattered among the smoking ruins of exploded tanks. Ernie Pyle called this "disappointing." Well, why not? There were no other words to describe the thing that had happened there. The truth was, the only language that seemed to register the appalling strangeness of the war was supernatural: the ghost story where nightmarish powers erupt out of nothingness, the glimpse into the occult void where human beings would be destroyed by unearthly forces they couldn't hope to comprehend. Even the most routine event of the war, the firing of an artillery shell, seemed somehow uncanny. The launch of a shell and its explosive arrival were so far apart in space and time you could hardly believe they were part of the same event, and for those in the middle there was only the creepy whisper of its passage, from nowhere to nowhere, like a rip in the fabric of causality.

Even the military powers themselves, which had spent so many years planning for the war, which had built up titanic armies and commissioned the factories to churn out wave after wave of advanced weaponry— even they didn't understand the furies they were unleashing. That's what had caused the disaster at Midway. Aircraft carriers were the most powerful ships ever to set sail; they were so large and strongly built they sometimes seemed to their crews not to be ships at all, but floating cities of metal, floating industrial districts delivering destruction to their enemies on the other side of the world. But nobody had stopped to consider just how vulnerable they'd be in a combat zone. Midway was the first major naval battle involving aircraft carriers, and in those few minutes the sailors on board suddenly realized the fundamental defect in their design. For all its appearance of self-sufficiency and invulnerability, an aircraft carrier really was an immense oilcan stuffed with explosives, floating in the middle of an inhospitable ocean.

In the obsolete days of naval warfare Midway would have been different. An old-fashioned attack fleet would have been carrying less-powerful explosives and far less fuel (and the American planes wouldn't have been equipped with such large bombs); its ships could probably have survived the attack at Midway with only moderate damage. But the Japanese carrier attack force was on the hair trigger of total catastrophe—ready not only to self-destruct in an instant, but to cause a vast, unpredictable, and wholly uncontrollable wave of secondary disasters. It took only a couple of fluke hits to trigger the cataclysm; the Japanese empire was lost at Midway in five unlucky minutes.

There's another military phrase: "in harm's way." That's what everybody assumes going to war means—putting yourself in danger. But the truth is that for most soldiers war is no more inherently dangerous than any other line of work. Modern warfare has grown so complicated and requires such immense movements of men and materiel over so vast an expanse of territory that an ever-increasing proportion of every army is given over to supply, tactical support, and logistics. Only about one in five of the soldiers who took part in World War II was in a combat unit (by the time of Vietnam the ratio in the American armed forces was down to around one in seven). The rest were construction workers, accountants, drivers, technicians, cooks, file clerks, repairmen, warehouse managers—the war was essentially a self-contained economic system that swelled up out of nothing and covered the globe.

For most soldiers the dominant memory they had of the war was of that vast structure arching up unimaginably high overhead. It's no coincidence that two of the most widely read and memorable American novels of the war, Joseph Heller's *Catch-22* and Thomas Pynchon's *Gravity's Rainbow*, are almost wholly about the cosmic scale of the American military's corporate bureaucracy and mention Hitler and the Nazis only in passing. Actual combat could seem like almost an incidental side product of the immense project of military industrialization. A battle for most soldiers was something that happened up the road, or on the fogbound islands edging the horizon, or in the silhouettes of remote hilltops lit up at night by silent flickering, which they mistook at first for summer lightning. And when reporters traveled through the vast territories under military occupation looking for some evidence of real fighting, what they were more likely to find instead was a scene like what Martha Gellhorn, covering the war for *Collier's*, discovered in the depths of the Italian countryside: "The road signs were fantastic. . . . The routes themselves, renamed for this operation, were marked with the symbols of their names, a painted animal or a painted object. There were the code numbers of every outfit, road warnings—bridge blown, crater mines, bad bends—indications of first-aid posts, gasoline dumps, repair stations, prisoner-of-war cages, and finally a marvelous Polish sign urging the troops to notice that this was a malarial area: this sign was a large green death's-head with a mosquito sitting on it."

That was the war: omnipresent, weedlike tendrils of contingency and code spreading over a landscape where the battle had long since passed.

It was much the same in the United States. The bureaucracy of war became an overpowering presence in people's lives, even though the reality of battle was impossibly remote. Prices were controlled by war-related government departments, nonessential nonmilitary construction required a nightmare of paperwork, food and gas were rationed—any long-distance car travel that wasn't for war business meant a special hearing before a ration board, and almost every train snaking through the depths of the heartland had been commandeered for classified military transport. The necessities of war even broke up the conventional proprieties of marriage: the universal inevitability of military service meant that young couples got married quickly, sometimes at first meeting—and often only so the women could get the military paycheck and the ration stamps.

The war was the single dominant fact in the world, saturating every radio show and newspaper. Every pennant race was described on the sports pages in the metaphor of battle; every car wreck and hotel fire was compared to the air raids that everyone was still expecting to hit the blacked-out cities on the coasts.

But who was controlling the growth of this fantastic edifice? Nobody could say. People who went to Washington during those years found a desperately overcrowded town caught up in a kind of diffuse bureaucratic riot. New agencies and administrations overflowed from labyrinthine warrens of temporary office space. People came to expect that the simplest problem would lead to hours or days of wandering down featureless corridors, passing door after closed door spattered by uncrackable alphabetic codes: OPA, OWI, OSS. Nor could you expect any help or sympathy once you found the right office: if the swarms of new government workers weren't focused on the latest crisis in the Pacific, they were distracted by the hopeless task of finding an apartment or a boarding house or a cot in a spare room. Either way, they didn't give a damn about solving your little squabble about petroleum rationing.

It might have been some consolation to know that people around the world were stuck with exactly the same problems—particularly people on the enemy side. There was a myth (it still persists) that the Nazi state was a model of efficiency; the truth was that it was a bureaucratic shambles. The military functioned well—Hitler gave it a blank check—but civilian life was made a misery by countless competing agencies and new ministries, all claiming absolute power over every detail of German life. Any task, from getting repairs in an apartment building to requisitioning office equipment, required running a gauntlet of contradictory regulations. One historian later described Nazi Germany as "authoritarian anarchy."

But then everything about the war was ad hoc and provisional. The British set up secret installations in country estates; Stalin had his supreme military headquarters in a commandeered Moscow subway station. Nobody cared about making the system logical, because everything only needed to happen once. Every battle was unrepeatable, every campaign was a special case. The people who were actually making the decisions in the war—for the most part, senior staff officers and civil service workers who hid behind anonymous doors and unsigned briefing papers—lurched from one improvisation to the next, with no sense of how much the limitless powers they were mustering were remaking the world.

But there was one constant. From the summer of 1942 on, the whole Allied war effort, the immensity of its armies and its industries, were focused on a single overriding goal: the destruction of the German army in Europe. Allied strategists had concluded that the global structure of the Axis would fall apart if the main military strength of the German Reich could be broken. But that task looked to be unimaginably difficult. It meant building up an overwhelmingly large army of their own, somehow getting it on the ground in Europe and confronting the German army at point-blank range. How could this possibly be accomplished? The plan was worked out at endless briefings and diplomatic meetings and strategy sessions held during the first half of 1942. The Soviet Red Army would have to break through the Russian front and move into Germany from the east. Meanwhile, a new Allied army would get across the English Channel and land in France, and the two armies would converge on Berlin.

The plan set the true clock time of the war. No matter what the surface play of battle was in Africa or the South Seas, the underlying dynamic never changed: every hour, every day the Allies were preparing for the invasion of Europe. They were stockpiling thousands of landing craft, tens of thousands of tanks, millions upon millions of rifles and mortars and howitzers, oceans of bullets and bombs and artillery shells—the united power of the American and Russian economies was slowly building up a military force large enough to overrun a continent. The sheer bulk of the armaments involved would have been unimaginable a few years earlier. One number may suggest the scale. Before the war began the entire German *Luftwaffe* consisted of four thousand planes; by the time of the Normandy invasion American factories were turning out four thousand new planes every two weeks.

The plan was so ambitious that even with this torrential flow of war production it would take years before the Allies were ready. The original target date for the invasion was the spring of 1943—but as that date approached the Allies realized they weren't prepared to attempt it. So it was put off until the late spring of 1944. But what would happen in the meanwhile? A worldwide holding action. The Red Army would have to hang on to its positions in Russia, the Americans would go on inching their way into the Japanese empire, and the Allies everywhere would commit their forces to campaigns designed only to keep the Axis from expanding further. In the years between Pearl Harbor and the Normandy invasion the war around the world grew progressively larger, more diffuse, less conclusive, and massively more chaotic.

Those were desperate years. The storm center then was in Russia, where the German army was hurling attack after overwhelming attack at the Soviet lines. To this day, most Russians think World War II was something that happened primarily in their country and the battles everywhere else in the world were a sideshow. In August 1943, for instance, in the hilly countryside around the town of Kursk (about two hundred miles south of Moscow), the German and Soviet armies collided in an uncontrolled slaughter: more than four million men and thousands of tanks desperately maneuvered through miles of densely packed minefields and horizon-filling networks of artillery fire. It may have been the single largest battle fought in human history, and it ended—like all the battles on the eastern front—in a draw.

The American military, meanwhile, was conducting campaigns that to this day are almost impossible to understand or justify. What was the point, for instance, of the Allied invasion of Italy in the summer of 1943? None of the reporters who covered it could figure it out. It was poorly planned and incompetently commanded, and its ultimate goal seemed preposterous: even if it had gone perfectly, it would have left a large army in northern Tuscany faced with the impossible task of getting across the Alps. Most baffling of all, Allied commanders up the line didn't even seem to care whether it worked perfectly—or at all. One reporter, Eric Sevareid, watched it go on for eighteen months of brutal stalemate and wrote an essay for *The Nation* (it's the angriest and most honest piece in the whole of *Reporting World War II*) suggesting that its only real purpose was "to lay waste and impoverish for many years the major part of Italy."

Somewhere in the bureaucratic stratosphere, of course, there were people who did know the justification for it and for everything else the Allies were doing. They just didn't want to tell anybody what those reasons were. The Italian invasion, as it happened, was the result of a complicated attempt to appease the Russians, who were increasingly doubtful that their allies were serious about taking on Germany. It was intended as an expedient compromise—a direct confrontation with the Axis, in an area where defeat wouldn't be fatal. In other words, there was no compelling military logic behind it; it was just an arbitrary way of marking time while the buildup for the real invasion went on.

No wonder American combat troops in those years started calling themselves "G.I. Joe." Reporters passed the term back home as a charming bit of sentimentality; they didn't know, or chose to ignore, that it was really a despairing joke—"G.I." for "general issue," a mass-produced unit of basic military hardware. The soldiers knew the score: for all the halos of glory they were being heaped with in the press, they were nothing more than anonymous, interchangeable items in the limitless inventory of the war. No "politician" (as they called any noncombatant decision maker) gave a damn what they were going through; you'd never find one of them getting anywhere near an actual battle. But for the soldiers who had to go into them, the combat zones were proving to be more horrible than their darkest imaginings.

"The infantryman hates shells more than anything else," Bill Mauldin wrote about the front lines in Italy. His phrasing makes it sound like the men were expressing an aesthetic preference, like a choice among distasteful rations. But "shells" weren't a few rounds of artillery floating in at odd intervals. They were deafening, unrelenting, maddening, terrifying. One fortified American position in the Pacific recorded being hit in a single day by sixteen thousand shells. In the middle of an artillery barrage, hardened veterans would hug each other and sob helplessly. Men caught in a direct hit were unraveled by the blast, blown apart into shards of flying skeleton that would maim or kill anyone nearby. Afterward the survivors would sometimes discover one of their buddies so badly mangled they couldn't understand how he could still be breathing; all they could do was give him the largest dose of morphine they dared and write an "M" for "morphine" on his forehead in his own blood, so that nobody else who found him would give him a second, fatal dose. (One soldier marked with that "M" was Bob Dole, wounded in Italy in 1945; he wasn't released from the hospital until 1948.) Commanders came to prefer leading green troops into combat, because the veterans were far more scared. They knew what was coming.

There was the brassy, metallic twang of the small 50mm knee mortar shells as little puffs of dirty smoke appeared thickly around us. The 81mm and 90mm mortar shells crashed and banged all along the ridge. The whiz-bang of the high-velocity 47mm gun's shells (also an antitank gun) was on us with its explosion as soon as we heard it. . . . The slower screaming, whining sound of the 75mm artillery shells seemed the most abundant. Then there was the roar and rumble of the huge enemy 150mm howitzer shell, and the *ka-boom* of its explosion. The bursting radius of these big shells was of awesome proportions. Added to all this noise was the swishing and fluttering overhead of our own supporting artillery fire. Our shells could be heard bursting out across the ridge over enemy positions.

The noise of small-arms fire from both sides resulted in a chaotic bedlam of racket and confusion.

This is from a memoir by Eugene B. Sledge, a marine who fought in the Pacific. It was issued by the marines' own printing house, with prefaces by a couple of brigadier generals. That might lead it to be discounted as the usual party-line war-memoir whitewash, especially since Sledge does try to put the best possible spin on everything the marines did in the Pacific, finding excuses for every act of grotesque cruelty and softening the routine drone of daily barbarism. He even claims that marines said things like "all fouled up" and "when the stuff hits the fan." (To be fair, Sledge is an unusually kindhearted man, who records with great satisfaction the rescue of Okinawan ponies trapped in the combat zone.) But notice the connoisseurlike precision in this passage, the sense shared by writer and readers that each shell in a barrage sounds its own distinct note of lethality. And one may notice too that Sledge's whole memoir is free of reporters' words like "occult" and "eerie" and "ghostly." The adjectives that occur most often are "insane," "hellish," and "unendurable."

The major campaign Sledge fought in was Okinawa, which took place toward the end of the war. It was expected to be quick: one more island recaptured from a defeated enemy. But the Japanese withdrew deep into Okinawa's lush interior, where the rains and the dense foliage made the few roads impassable. The marines had to bring their supplies in on foot—carrying mortars and shells, water and food on their backs across miles of ravine-cut hills. Often they were so exhausted they couldn't move when the enemy attacked. The battle lines, as so often happened in the war, soon froze in place. The quick campaign lasted for months.

Conditions on the front rapidly deteriorated. Soldiers were trapped in their foxholes by barrages that went on for days at a time. They were stupefied by the unbroken roar of the explosions and reduced to sick misery by the incessant rain and deepening mud. They had to use discarded grenade cans for latrines, then empty the contents into the mud outside their foxholes. The rain washed everything into the ravines; the urine and feces mixed with the blood and the shreds of rotting flesh blown by the shell bursts from the hundreds of unburied bodies scattered everywhere. The smell was so intolerable it took an act of supreme will for the soldiers to choke down their rations each day. Sledge calls it "an environment so degrading I believed we had been flung into hell's own cesspool."

He writes, "If a Marine slipped and slid down the back slope of the muddy ridge, he was apt to reach the bottom vomiting. I saw more than one man lose his footing and slip and slide all the way to the bottom only to stand up horror-stricken as he watched in disbelief while fat maggots tumbled out of his muddy dungaree pockets, cartridge belt, legging lacings, and the like. Then he and a buddy would shake or scrape them away with a piece of ammo box or a knife blade."

The soldiers began to crack. As Sledge writes, "It is too preposterous to think that men could actually live and fight for days and nights on end under such terrible conditions and not be driven insane." He catalogs the forms the insanity took: "from a state of dull detachment seemingly unaware of their surroundings, to quiet sobbing, or all the way to wild screaming and shouting." Sledge himself began having hallucinations that the dead bodies were rising at night. "They got up slowly out of their waterlogged craters or off the mud and, with stooped shoulders and dragging feet, wandered around aimlessly, their lips moving as though trying to tell me something." It was a relief to shake himself alert and find the corpses decomposing in their accustomed spots.

The casualty figures from Okinawa were a demonstration that even at the end of the war the military bureaucracies of the combatant nations hadn't yet learned, or didn't care, what the combat zones were routinely doing to the soldiers who fought in them. Around one hundred thousand Japanese soldiers died on Okinawa—a few hundred were captured, mostly those who were too badly wounded to commit suicide. About one hundred thousand of the native inhabitants of the island died as well. Almost eight thousand Americans were killed or missing; almost thirty-two thousand were wounded. And there were more than twenty-six thousand "neuropsychiatric" casualties—more than a third of the American casualties in the Okinawa combat zone were soldiers who were driven insane.

Long after the war John Keegan, who'd been evacuated with his family from London to the quiet depths of the English countryside, recalled a particular night when he was ten years old. "The sky over our house began to fill with the sound of aircraft, which swelled until it overflowed the darkness from edge to edge. Its first tremors had taken my parents into the garden, and as the roar grew I followed and stood between them to gaze awestruck at the constellations of red, green and yellow lights which rode across the heavens and streamed southward towards the sea. . . . It seemed as if every aircraft in the world was in flight, as wave after wave followed without intermission."

It was the night of June 5, 1944. Twelve thousand planes were rising from airfields all across England and roaring into the darkness over Europe. The next day Keegan's family listened as the BBC repeated over and over an austere news bulletin: "Early this morning units of the Allied armies began landing on the coast of France."

The Allied Expeditionary Force was on the ground in Europe at last. The great invasion had achieved its first goal. The decisive battle unfolded in the middle of August. The Germans launched a major offensive to break apart the Allied armies and force them back toward the English Channel. Twenty German divisions raced forward into the Allied lines in the wooded countryside south of the small town of Falaise. It was a large-scale version of the blitzkrieg attack that had terrorized and stampeded whole armies in the early days of the war. But the Allies were expecting the blitzkrieg, and they'd had years to work out the correct tactical response. The "Falaise pocket," they called it afterward. The Allied army allowed the forward wedge of panzers to penetrate the lines, then made a flanking attack and encircled them from the rear. Then Allied barrages opened up from all sides, and massed air force squadrons swept overhead and bombed at will. The Germans were trapped in the pocket for more than a week. Their best panzer divisions were torn to pieces. More than two hundred thousand German soldiers were killed, wounded, or captured. Only a death stand by a lone division of Hitler Youth held open a gap in the rapidly tightening lines long enough for the remnants of the forces to make a frantic escape.

That was the end of the greatest myth of the war: the invincibility of the German army. Overnight the blitzkrieg had been made obsolete. It was now just another classroom exercise at the world's military schools, an object lesson in the dangers of leaving your flanks exposed.

Meanwhile, more than a thousand miles to the east, the Red Army was launching its own big offensive. Two weeks after the first wave of Allied invaders came ashore at Normandy a gigantic Soviet force crashed down on the German positions in Belorussia. The German soldiers there were already exhausted, their supplies were chronically low, and their faith in their cause was dwindling—the result of having spent three years in a nightmarish stalemate with an enemy their commanders had too often told them was on the verge of surrender. The overwhelming attack caught them completely by surprise, and they were routed. Within weeks the battle line that had been writhing across the immensity of Russia for the last three years was torn apart; hundreds of thousands of German soldiers were falling back to the west, and the Red Army was pouring by the millions through the disintegrating front.

So that was the result of the Allies' grand invasion plan: after all those years of delays and equivocations and false hopes and murderously bungled diversions it had in the end gone just the way it was supposed to. The Allies had confronted the most fearsome army in history and had broken it in battle. The Greater Reich was falling apart, its troops in retreat all across Europe. And with Germany gone, Japan couldn't hope to stand up to the world alone. The war was won.

As the news of the victories in Europe spread, a mood of jubilation broke out among the Allied nations. For the first time newspapers in America and Britain predicted the imminent surrender of the Axis. People made bets about whether the war could last till Labor Day, Thanksgiving at the latest. In anticipation of the end, the American government announced that food and gas rationing were being suspended. The word was everywhere: our boys will be home by Christmas.

Every day the war persisted after that became a puzzle, and then an agony. As Martha Gellhorn wrote that September, "It is awful to die when you know the war is won anyhow. . . . Every man dead is a greater sorrow because the end of all this tragic dying is so near." But how near? Into the fall, news continued to arrive of battles and large-scale counterattacks all over Europe. Meanwhile, the Allied forces in the Pacific were just beginning to position themselves for the invasion of the Philippines, with their ultimate goal, the Japanese home islands, still thousands of miles away. And no rumors were circulating, on or off the record, of Axis offers of surrender. The war was won, but it was mysteriously accelerating into fresh violence by the day.

The Allied commanders in northern Europe were still sure that victory was within reach. It was true that German forces were fighting everywhere with savage tenacity. But the Allied hold on the continent was daily growing stronger, the networks of resupply and reinforcement were jelling, and the battle lines were pushing inexorably toward the old borders of Germany. And yet the Allies still hadn't crossed the Rhine. By the beginning of winter their armies were only beginning to move through eastern France and Belgium, gradually unfolding, like a river slipping past a rock, around the immense forests of the Ardennes. And that was where, in the middle of December, they met what one reporter on the scene called "the most frightening, unbelievable experience of the war."

The German army had been building up its strongest forces for a counterattack. For months in the remote wooded valleys of the Ardennes—the last surviving old-growth forests in Europe—hidden from Allied reconnaissance flights by the dense tree cover and the perpetual fog of late autumn, thousands of tanks and hundreds of thousands of troops had been massing. The Allies suspected nothing; their lines along the western fringes of the Ardennes were lightly manned and casually patrolled. No one in the command hierarchy even realized what was happening when the first reports began filtering in on December 16 of mysterious movements in the deep reaches of the forests. Then Allied forward positions began receiving furious barrages. German tank battalions came rumbling out of the snow-buried valleys to shatter the thin Allied lines. Gradually the Allied commanders began to understand that the German army had come roaring forward with a major new offensive.

The weeks that followed were a nightmare. German divisions broke through all along the front in Belgium and northern France. Allied positions were wiped out, and the troops fell back in panic. As the German forces advanced west the weather turned foul, and Allied troops trying to pull together new lines found themselves baffled by heavy snows that buried the roads and obliterated the few landmarks. The fog and snowstorms shrouding the interior of the forests made reconnaissance and bombardment behind the lines impossible. The troops on the ground were left to wander through the interminable woods or hole up in the charred wreckage of evacuated villages while the storms worsened, the temperature dropped, and blizzard winds reduced visibility to zero. Everywhere, in uncertain vistas of ground fog, among the countless tapered pillars of snow-heavy pine trees, they saw sinister movement: endless lines of advancing German soldiers, wraithlike in their white winter camouflage gear; thundering herds of tanks; booming artillery pieces scattering torrents of snow and slush; and mist dissolving in swirls around the burning hulks of trucks left behind as the long, straggling convoys of Allied soldiers retreated.

The troops called it the Battle of the Bulge, after the way the front bulged so alarmingly to the west. It's counted in the history books as an Allied victory. The way the story is usually told, after a brief period when the Allies were forced to pull back they reorganized and by the middle of January had recaptured all the territory they'd lost. The invasion of Germany was staved off for only a few negligible weeks. But for a lot of people, soldiers and civilians, the Battle of the Bulge was the moment they finally lost hope. The size and ferocity of the attack meant that the

Germans had no intention of ever giving up. The war was simply going to go on, from horror to horror, into the indefinite future. The year of the great Allied victories wouldn't end with tender holiday homecomings or triumphant parades, but with Americans soldiers dying by the thousands in the snowbound forests of Europe.

Back when the forest still stretched in an unbroken expanse from Scandinavia to the Urals, the Vikings who inhabited its northernmost reaches wrote down their own stories about war. Their legends may have been garish fantasies—cursed rings and enchanted gold and dragon slayers and the fall of the realm of the gods—but when they wrote about battle, they were unsparingly exact. Their sagas still offer the subtlest and most rigorous accounts of the unique psychology of combat. The anonymous authors knew that the experience of being on a battlefield is fundamentally different from everything else in life. It simply can't be described with ordinary words, so they devised a specialized Old Norse vocabulary to handle it. Some of their terms will do perfectly well for a world war fought a thousand years later.

The Vikings knew, for instance, that prolonged exposure to combat can goad some men into a state of uncontrolled psychic fury. They might be the most placid men in the world in peacetime, but on the battlefield they begin to act with the most inexplicable and gratuitous cruelty. They become convinced that they're invincible, above all rules and restraints, literally transformed into supermen or werewolves. The Vikings called such men "berserkers." World War II was filled with instances of ordinary soldiers giving in to berserker behavior. In battle after battle soldiers on all sides were observed killing wantonly and indiscriminately, defying all orders to stop, in a kind of collective blood rage. The Axis powers actually sanctioned and encouraged berserkers among their troops, but they were found in every army, even among those that emphasized discipline and humane conduct. American marines in the Pacific became notorious for their berserker mentality, particularly their profound lack of interest in taking prisoners. Eugene Sledge once saw a marine in a classic berserker state urinating into the open mouth of a dead Japanese soldier.

Another Viking term was "fey." People now understand it to mean effeminate. Previously it meant odd, and before that uncanny, fairylike. That was back when fairyland was the most sinister place people could imagine. The Old Norse word meant "doomed." It was used to refer to an eerie mood that would come over people in battle, a kind of transcendent despair. The state was described vividly by an American reporter, Tom Lea, in the midst of the desperate Battle of Peleliu in the South Pacific. He felt something inside of himself, some instinctive psychic urge to keep himself alive, finally collapse at the sight of one more dead soldier in the ruins of a tropical jungle: "He seemed so quiet and empty and past all the small things a man could love or hate. I suddenly knew I no longer had to defend my beating heart against the stillness of death. There was no defense."

There was no defense—that's fey. People go through battle willing the bullet to miss, the shelling to stop, the heart to go on beating—and then they feel something in their soul surrender, and they give in to everything they've been most afraid of. It's like a glimpse of eternity. Whether the battle is lost or won, it will never end; it has wholly taken over the soul. Sometimes men say afterward that the most terrifying moment of any battle is seeing a fey look on the faces of the soldiers standing next to them.

But the fey becomes accessible to civilians in a war too—if the war goes on long enough and its psychic effects become sufficiently pervasive. World War II went on so long that both soldiers and civilians began to think of feyness as a universal condition. They surrendered to that eternity of dread: the inevitable, shattering resumption of an artillery barrage; the implacable cruelty of an occupying army; the panic, never to be overcome despite a thousand false alarms, at an unexpected knock on the door, or a telegram, or the sight out the front window of an unfamiliar car pulling to a halt. They got so used to the war they reached a state of acquiescence, certain they wouldn't stop being scared until they were dead.

It was in a fey mood that, in the depths of the German invasion,

Russian literary scholar Mikhail Bakhtin took the only copy of his life's work, a study of Goethe, and ripped it up, page by page and day by day, for that unobtainable commodity, cigarette paper. It was because fey-ness poisons ordinary life that British writer Walter de la Mare could in 1943 begin a poem about the English countryside with the line "No, they are only birds" and not bother to say what he'd first thought they were. Everyone knew; they had learned the reflex of sudden terror, fol-lowed by infinite relief, triggered by the sight of small black forms mov-ing quickly against a bright sky.

Feyness might also explain the deepest mystery of the war: why the surrender everybody expected never came. The Germans and Japanese refused to surrender even though they knew the war was lost.

It's possible to quibble about the exact point at which the war was decided: Midway, Stalingrad, Falaise, Okinawa. In one sense, of course, the Axis never had any real hope of winning, because their whole strat-egy depended on a hopelessly idealized assessment of their chances. In effect, they'd convinced themselves that they were bound to win because their enemies would never fight back. The Americans would surrender after Pearl Harbor, the Soviet Union would crumble as soon as German troops crossed the border—the whole world would bow down before their inherent racial superiority. But by some unmistakable point—the autumn of 1942 at the latest—they should have understood that they'd been wrong and that their prospects for long-term victory were inexora-bly zeroing out. They still had the economic and military strength to sustain their armies in the field indefinitely, no matter how grim the strategic situation became, but by any rational calculation of the odds, they should have begun hinting through backwater diplomatic channels that they were willing to negotiate a cease-fire. Neither Germany nor Japan ever did so. Not until the last days of the war did either govern-ment even begin to consider the possibility of a negotiated settlement—not until they had absolutely nothing left to negotiate with.

But then, that's the point. A rational calculation of the odds is a calcu-lation by the logic of peace. War has a different logic. A kind of vast fey-ness can infect a military bureaucracy when it's losing a war, a collective slippage of the sense of objective truth in the face of approaching disaster. In the later years of World War II the bureaucracies of the Axis—partially in Germany, almost wholly in Japan—gave up any pretense of realism about their situation. Their armies were fighting all over the world with desperate berserker fury, savagely contesting every inch of terrain, hurling countless suicide raids against Allied battalions (kamikaze attacks on American ships at Okinawa came in waves of a hundred planes at a time)—while the bureaucrats behind the lines gradually retreated into a dreamy paper war where they were on the brink of a triumphant reversal of fortune.

They had the evidence. Officers in the field, unable to face or admit the imminence of defeat, routinely submitted false reports up the chain of command. Commanders up the line were increasingly prone to believe them, or to pretend to believe them. And so, as the final catastrophe approached, strategists in both Berlin and Tokyo could be heard solemnly discussing the immense weight of paper that documented the latest round of imaginary victories, the long-overrun positions that they still claimed to hold, and the Allied armies and fleets that had just been conclusively destroyed—even though the real-world Allied equivalents had crashed through the lines and were advancing toward the homeland.

Not everybody succumbed to these fantasies. But another, even stronger pressure worked against those who understood how hopeless the situation really was: they knew that defeat meant accountability.

The consequences of the Axis commitment to total war were becoming inescapable. This was particularly true in Germany; the Japanese people never learned much about the appalling behavior of their armies. But the real purpose of the concentration camps had seeped through the Nazi bureaucracy and into Germany's civilian world through a million rumors and confessions. Tens of thousands of people were directly involved in the administration of the camp system; countless others knew or had guessed the truth. All of them had a reasonably good idea what would happen to them if they were ever forced to answer for what they'd done.

So while their colleagues fell into daydreams of imminent victory, the few remaining rational men of the Axis bureaucracy grew just as convinced that surrender to the Allies on any terms was tantamount to suicide. As far as they were concerned, every additional day the war lasted—no matter how pointless, no matter how phantasmal the hope of victory, no matter how desperate and horrible the conditions on the battlefield—was another day of judgment successfully deferred.

This is the dreadful logic that comes to control a lot of wars. (The American Civil War is another example.) The losers prolong their agony as much as possible, because they're convinced the alternative is worse. Meanwhile the winners, who might earlier have accepted a compromise peace, become so maddened by the refusal of their enemies to stop fighting that they see no reason to settle for anything less than absolute victory. In this sense the later course of World War II was typical: it kept on escalating, no matter what the strategic situation was, and it grew progressively more violent and uncontrollable long after the outcome was a foregone conclusion. The difference was that no other war had ever had such deep reserves of violence to draw upon.

The Vikings would have understood it anyway. They didn't have a word for the prolongation of war long past any rational goal—they just knew that's what always happened. It's the subject of their longest and greatest saga, the *Brennu-Njáls Saga*, or *The Saga of Njal Burned Alive*. The saga describes a trivial feud in backcountry Iceland that keeps escalating for reasons nobody can understand or resolve until it engulfs the whole of northern Europe. Provocation after fresh provocation, peace conference after failed peace conference, it has its own momentum, like a hurricane of carnage. The wise and farseeing hero Njal, who has never met the original feuders and has no idea what their quarrel was about, ultimately meets his appalling death (the Vikings thought there was nothing worse than being burned alive) as part of a chain of ever-larger catastrophes that he can tell is building but is helpless to stop—a fate that seems in the end to be as inevitable as it is inexplicable.

For the Vikings, this was the essence of war: it's a mystery that comes out of nowhere and grows for reasons nobody can control, until it shakes the whole world apart.

From the fall of 1944, the Allies at last acknowledged that, despite the decisive battles of the previous summer, the Axis was never going to surrender. That was when the Allies changed their strategy. They set out to make an Axis surrender irrelevant.

From that winter into the next spring the civilians of Germany and Japan were helpless before a new Allied campaign of systematic aerial bombardment. The air forces and air defense systems of the Axis were in ruins by then. Allied planes flew where they pleased, day or night— five hundred at a time, then one thousand at a time, indiscriminately dumping avalanches of bombs on every city and town in Axis territory that had a military installation or a railroad yard or a factory. By the end of the winter most of Germany's industrial base had been bombed repeatedly in saturation attacks; by the end of the following spring Allied firebombing raids had burned more than 60 percent of Japan's urban surface area to the ground.

There was no precedent even in this war for destruction on so ferocious a scale. It was the largest berserker rage in history. The Allies routinely dropped incendiary bombs in such great numbers that they created firestorms in cities throughout the Axis countries. These weren't simply large fires. A true firestorm is a freak event, where a large central core of flame heats up explosively to more than one thousand five hundred degrees, and everything within it goes up by spontaneous combustion—buildings erupt, the water boils out of rivers and canals, and the asphalt in the pavement ignites. Immense intake vortices spring up around the core and begin sucking in oxygen from the surrounding atmosphere at hurricane speeds. The Allied raids reduced cities in minutes to miles of smoldering debris. Hundreds of thousands of people were killed—about 20 percent of them children. Tens of thousands suffocated, because in the area around a firestorm there's no oxygen left to breathe.

Tens of millions of Germans and Japanese were driven from the wreckage of their homes to join the hundreds of millions of people already flooding the roads of Europe and Asia. They were seen everywhere. "DPs," they were called, displaced persons: interminable lines of refugees in an anonymous stream. Not everyone joined the stampede, but those who stayed to protect their homes learned that their worst fears had been wholly justified. The Red Army murdered more than a million civilians in the eastern provinces of Germany as it marched toward Berlin.

Meanwhile the crimes the Axis had so long fought to conceal were coming to light. Every day brought news of some large-scale atrocity. When the three-year siege of Leningrad was at last broken, it was learned that more than a million people had died of starvation; they'd killed their house pets for food, and before the end there were pervasive rumors of cannibalism. The collapse of the Japanese empire revealed famine throughout China; more than ten million people in provinces once controlled by the Japanese were dying or dead. And in April 1945 the line of German defenses finally shrank back far enough that the death camps were discovered by Allied troops. "A crime beyond the imagination of man," the first news reports called it. People who thought they'd been permanently numbed to horror found they were wrong.

But by then the Holocaust seemed almost lost in the universal destruction. The deaths are still being counted. In the decades after the war it was believed that between fifteen million and twenty million people had died in the war, but historians now believe the real number was at least three times higher, and some recent estimates (based on studies of newly declassified archives in Russia and China) put the total at close to seventy-five million. The extent of the material damage was incalculable. The civilian economies of Europe and Asia were a shambles. Most industries not related to war production had been shut down or destroyed outright. Basic commodities were unobtainable, even on the black market. Roads and bridges throughout two continents had been blown up, ports had been wrecked, and commercial shipping had stopped. The submarine war had sent rivers of oil into the ocean—a torrent that made the great postwar spills look like irrelevant trickles;

oil from torpedoed tankers was washing up on beaches all over the world.

Whenever people talk about the meaning of history somebody brings up that old bromide from Santayana, "Those who do not remember the past are condemned to repeat it." But that's nonsense. The circumstances that created an event like World War II couldn't be duplicated no matter how many millennia of amnesia intervened.

Besides, even if we did want to follow Santayana's advice and remember the war, how could we do it? Too much of its detail and complexity is already gone, even at this narrow distance. As Thomas Browne wrote, "There is no antidote to the opium of time." There are warehouses of secret wartime documents still scattered in nondescript factory districts all over the world—stacks of debriefings from some nameless Pacific island that fifty years ago was swallowed up in an artillery barrage. No one will ever unearth them all and produce a final accounting of the war—any more than the world will finally achieve justice for the war's innumerable, officially sanctioned crimes. Oblivion has always been the most trustworthy guardian of classified files.

But there is another and simpler reason the war has been forgotten: people wanted to forget it. It had gone on for so many years, had destroyed so much, had killed so many—most U.S. casualties were in the final year of fighting. When it came to an end, people were glad to be rid of everything about it. That was what surprised commentators about the public reaction in America and Europe when the news broke that Germany and then Japan had at last surrendered. In the wild celebrations that followed nobody crowed, "Our enemies are destroyed." Nobody even yelled, "We've won." What they all said instead was, "The war is over."

That was the message that flashed around the world in the summer of 1945: the war is over, the war is over. Huge cheering crowds greeted the announcement in cities across America and Europe. A spectacular clamor of church bells rang out across the heartland. Wails of car horns and sirens soared up from isolated desert towns.

But a mysterious letdown awaited as well. Even amid the endless parades, the night-long parties, and the prolonged and tearful home-comings, the veterans discovered the first signs of impatience when they tried to tell of the horrors they'd endured, the first delicate hints from their families that nobody cared about those grisly things, the gentle message that the world was different now and whatever they'd done in the war didn't matter anymore. It was no doubt just what Noah had had to endure from his descendants, muttering at the edge of ear-shot that the flood was no big deal—if he hadn't built the ark, somebody else would have, because the Lord himself had promised that the world would always be saved by somebody.

In his memoirs Eugene Sledge recorded that he eventually stopped trying to tell the folks back home what had happened to him on Oki-nawa. Even among veterans, he writes, "we did not talk of such things. They were too horrible and obscene." And what was the point of recall-ing them anyway? The next generation would just see the stories as the product of some pardonable desire to exaggerate, of an old-fogy insis-tence that things had been much rougher back when the teller was young. Sledge himself had a hard time seeing that the things he'd been through meant anything now. He went back to Alabama after the war and returned to the college he'd dropped out of to enlist; ultimately he got his graduate degree and became a professor of biology and a re-spected ornithologist. His life continued on that track as though the war had never happened. The only problem was that he was having nightmares. Forty years later it still had the power to wake him in a blind panic—he was back on Okinawa, and orders were about to come through that would return him to the front.

How many such visions troubled the peace of the new American suburbs? In the decades after the war ended there probably wasn't a sin-gle night in which thousands of men across America didn't wake up sweating in terror—the patrol was about to set out again, the first alarms were arriving from the sentinels, the barrage was about to resume. Sometimes only those who remember the past are condemned to repeat it.

In the mid-1960s, when my friends and I were out infiltrating Nazi strongholds along the mossy stillness of an apartment-building gangway, charging phantom Nip battalions in the green depths of a park, executing daring flanking attacks against the *Wehrmacht* among the weed towers and cinder paths of the commuter railway corridor, I never stopped to wonder what it must have sounded like to the veterans of the war to hear us at our games. All through those elm-shaded mazes of old brownstone and white clapboard our voices shrilly rang out with "Nazi!" and "Japs!" and "Look out! Jerries attacking!" Maybe they were relieved when we finally outgrew the game and went on to fight wars against space monsters.

It's been decades since I've heard kids choosing up sides between the Allies and the Axis. Sometimes I wonder whether anybody ever did after my friends and I stopped. Maybe nobody followed our secret paths through dank apartment basements or worried if the old shuttered house on the next street harbored a Nazi spy ring. But evidently the war was already fading out around us as we played. We never suspected it, but we were the last defenders of Evanston.

Is it possible to say precisely when a war ends? When I was a kid there was a version of the bogeyman legend that we repeated to one another constantly, in tones of delicious dread. Hitler had survived the wreck of Germany and was still alive on a South American plantation, plotting his revenge against the world. Even as we played at recess and argued about our favorite TV shows, we worried that he was lurking out there, maybe right outside the school's fences, waiting for a chance to snatch at young Allied warriors. But there was a point—unrecorded, unknown, but still undeniable—when even this tottering ghost of the führer became too old and weak to trouble the sleep of the world any longer. The rumor died, and took the last terrors of the war with it.

War ends at the moment when peace permanently wins out. Not when the articles of surrender are signed or the last shot is fired, but when the last shout of a sidewalk battle fades, when the next generation starts to wonder whether the whole thing ever really happened. World War II ended as war always ends—by trailing off into nothingness and doubt.

This is excerpted from a much longer story that originally appeared in the *Chicago Reader*, March 7 and March 14, 1997. The full text is on the author's Web site, www.leesandlin.com.

THE HOSTESS DIARIES: MY YEAR AT A HOT SPOT

Coco Henson Scales

It is near midnight and I am standing at the door of the restaurant with Kevin, the bouncer, patiently waiting for customers, so that I can turn them away.

"Who are you here with?" I ask a man holding a woman's hand.

"Just us," he says. Couples are usually passive, pleading. I look them up and down. I look past them and around them, even if there is no one else there. I bite my bottom lip as if I am genuinely worried for them. "I don't know," I say pensively.

If they are meek and I am bored, I will let them in. But if they become agitated, I turn away, or—even better—pick the group behind them. Either way, my ego is going to get a boost.

I have been working at Hue, a Vietnamese restaurant and lounge in the West Village, since shortly after it opened last summer. From the beginning it was a hit with a young, fast crowd because of one of its owners, Karim Amatullah. He has been in the nightlife business for years, starting as a promoter and most recently as an owner of Halo. So many celebrities have been coming that we have grown selective. Once, Chad Lowe's assistant called and asked if he could have a table in the next hour. "Sorry," I said, "we're all booked."

"Really? That's a shame because his wife, Academy Award–winner Hilary Swank, is very hungry."

"Ah, yes, something just opened up," I say.

Celebrities and models are my least favorite customers. They never want to pay and they demand constant attention. The models wear jeans or a jean skirt with heels and a white T-shirt. Drunken skeletons, they stand outside smoking and talking in foreign accents. They don't tip, but if they aren't here, the men who do won't stay, so we cater to models. I don't bother learning their names. I call them all darling.

One night Karim, the owner—a short, bald man with perfect posture, who has the habit of looking people in the eye a little longer than is comfortable—waves me over. "Star Jones is coming tonight," he says. "I want you to take care of her. Where will you put her?"

At Hue there are two floors—a bar at street level and, one flight down, restaurant seating, a lounge and an inner sanctum known as the suite because it has king-size beds for sitting or lying. I tell Karim I will give Star Jones one of the beds.

"Fine," he says, patting my head, which makes me both happy and uncomfortable; I don't want him to feel my tracks of fake hair. I dash upstairs to tell Kevin on the door that Star Jones is coming.

He shrugs. For an hour I run up and down the stairs to the front door, thinking she must have arrived. Then I see Kevin holding her at the door and hear her dressing him down.

"I do not like your attitude," she tells Kevin, who is well over two hundred pounds and dressed in a black suit—a good-looking baby giant. Star is in full makeup with a long wavy wig. Short and chubby, she is with a tall man with curly hair, wearing gold MC Hammer-ish glasses. I recognize him as Al Scales Reynolds, a banker who is Star's fiancé (and no relation to me). He is wearing a diamond pinky ring.

"I'm sorry," I interrupt. "Please come inside."

"No!" says Star, backing up. "I don't think I want to. I don't like the way I've been treated."

Here we go, I think. Now someone else's ego is looking for a boost.

"I'm sorry," I say. "It's his job to stop everyone at the door. Please come in, let me buy you a drink."

"He has a terrible attitude," Star says. "I am a guest, invited by Karim. I do not have to come here."

"No, you don't," I say. "But I'm so glad you did." I wince, thinking that sounds sarcastic. "He's sorry," I say. She and her fiancé step in cautiously, and I lead them down to the VIP room. She laughs when she sees the beds, and the two of them climb onto one. He orders two Passion Cosmos—*girly drinks*, I think. I run to the bar and tell Liza, a server, that Star has just sat down in her section.

Liza sighs. "Is she paying?" she asks. I frown at such a silly question.

A few minutes later, I check on the happy couple. Fully clothed, Star is on her hands and knees on the bed, laughing. Her fiancé is behind her, hands around her waist, mimicking a sex act. In front of the other customers in the room, he then flips her over and climbs on top of her. I stare, mortified.

After two rounds of drinks, they are ready to leave. I watch curiously as they ask for the check and Liza tells them politely it is on Karim. "Oh, wow, thank you," Star says. "I'm sorry, I would tip you but I don't have my wallet," she tells Liza.

"Oh, no problem," Liza says, clasping her hands in prayer. "God will provide."

Star smiles as her eyes look to the ceiling. "Yes," she says. "He will."

I *never* aspired to be a nightclub hostess. I wanted to be a waitress. I had heard of waitresses making nice money, and, really, how hard could it be? After a string of low-level office jobs, I was burnt out working eighty frenzied hours a week or worse, forty boring hours. Jobs I was hired for because I looked attractive but would later be fired from because I wasn't "detail oriented" or punctual. At twenty-six, I felt old.

So I quit my latest office job and interviewed at restaurants, even though I had no experience. At Hue, the third place I tried, a manager quizzed, "What kind of wine would you recommend with a beef entree?"

"Something light," I said. "You know, beef is heavy so something light." I smiled, pleased with my answer. He smiled back and said, "Maybe you can start as a hostess and then pick up some waitressing shifts."

It turns out I like working at a restaurant very much. I like dealing with people, making them happy, being with them on their date or their birthday. I tilt my head to the side and nod at customers, particularly when giving bad news. "Yeah, it's going to be about a half hour before your table is ready," I say. Head-tilt, nod, no smile.

Initially I am too nice. I am nodding and apologizing to everyone who is unhappy, but then they feel free to keep complaining. They all want to speak with the manager, who demands I become tougher. This is unnatural for me, particularly because I often agree with the customers. They did have poor service. Waiters forgot their orders or ignored them. Why is the wait so long? Good question. Because one of the owners or a celebrity arrived with eight friends and needed a table. There are too many reservations in the books.

"Stop apologizing so much," the manager insists.

Slowly, I grow thicker skinned. About a month after I start, on a crowded Saturday, a dark-haired young man wants a table for himself and five friends. They don't have a reservation and don't want to wait. I tell him it will be "about an hour," which really means two. After consulting with his friends, he peels off a one-hundred-dollar bill and slips it to me in a handshake. I am surprised—no one has offered me a bribe before—but I give him the next available table. The hostesses all divide the money, and when he and his group leave, we wave to them, smiling.

I like this business of people paying for tables, and I begin to go out of my way for customers, hoping for a reward.

In the lounge there is "bottle service" only. At first, I am too embarrassed to ask what this means, and when I learn that customers have to buy a whole bottle of vodka or rum for three hundred dollars rather than single cocktails, I am shocked. But soon I learn to push those bottles.

Karim likes to keep the tables turning. He surveys the room, eyes fixing on a table of men without dates. "Turn the lights down right there," he tells me, without pointing. "Right away." I dash to the dimmer and run back to his side. "How many bottles do they have?" he asks. I have no idea. "Three," I say.

"Get them another one," he orders. "Or drop the check." He shakes his head at the men and walks through the room. From his years in the club business, he knows everyone—celebrities, models, socialites. People stop him every few feet to shake his hand. He greets them all but smiles only for the models.

Other times, we are less subtle about urging customers to leave. On a cold night around Halloween, Monica Lewinsky and a friend are deep in conversation downstairs when Liza approaches them. "Hi, I hate to bother you," she says.

I can see Monica look up and break into a pretty smile—her face is pale, if overly made-up, like someone who has come from a television appearance. She seems to think Liza wants an autograph. But the waitress tells her she might want to leave the restaurant.

The big smile fades. Liza explains: Chelsea Clinton and her boyfriend, Ian Klaus, are upstairs having a drink.

"Oh my God!" Monica says loud enough to hear halfway across the room. "Why won't these people leave me alone?" she whines, and stands straight up.

The woman she is with asks: "What's going on? What happened?"

"Chelsea Clinton is here," Monica says. "We've got to leave through the back." Her friend's eyes widen.

Liza says she doesn't mean right this moment, just whenever they're ready. But as her friend pulls on a scarf and hat, Monica shimmies past the other tables. She is curvy and walks with a bounce. The rest of the waiters collect at the service station, trying not to stare.

"Monica is walking out," I tell Kevin over the walkie-talkie. "We'll escort her through the rear exit." But instead she heads toward the stairs that lead to the main bar—where Chelsea is having her cocktail.

"Excuse me," Liza calls out. "Moni— . . . Ms. Lewinsky!" Other diners look up or self-consciously study their plates. Monica whips around, and Liza, who has long curly hair and ornate tattoos on her legs, signals her to come back down the stairs. "This way," she says quickly. She seems to be biting her lip in embarrassment.

Monica storms back down, and the waitress escorts the two women through the lounge, toward a glowing exit sign, me following behind. The lounge is closed tonight, and furniture is pushed aside and the carpet filthy. I feel embarrassed and want to apologize to Monica. At the end of a passage leading up and back out to Charles Street, Liza pushes open the door. Cold wind blasts us all.

"I can't seeeee," Monica cries, her voice like a hurt kitten's. A motion-activated light has not yet come on. Liza flaps her arms like a stork to trigger the light. Finally it goes on. "See?" she says, consolingly. "That's much better."

"There we go," she says, extending her arm out the door.

Monica turns and smiles. "Thank you," she says.

"Thank you for coming," Liza says, somewhat absurdly.

We watch to see that she steps off the property and then dash back in and upstairs to the bar, where we break into laughter and jump around holding each other. I have no idea why we are so excited.

The next morning, the *Daily News* reports that Chelsea Clinton and Ian Klaus haven't been out together in weeks and suggests they have broken up.

★ ★ ★

My shift begins at 6:00 and ends at 2:00 a.m. I am not allowed to sit and am reprimanded for leaning on the wall. My legs hurt almost all the time from standing in heels. I begin to take baths instead of showers, just to sit. The other staffers, who wear sensible flats, tease me for insisting on heels.

Every day, I spend over an hour getting dressed. I hate to wear the same thing twice, and I spend nearly every cent I make on clothing. My rent is always late. But people compliment me on the way I look, and I glow with the attention. One day my bosses tell me that I am being promoted to host of the VIP lounge, in charge of guarding the door and managing the waitresses.

Shortly after I begin the new job, Karim tells me: "You wear too much black. No one can see you in black. You have to stick out, wear brighter colors. And be sexy, damn it."

Greg, the bartender, echoes the message. "You're the peacock," he says. "You've got to stick out."

I spend my next paychecks buying yellow, orange and white outfits, trying to chose sexier pieces. My skirts are not much longer than a belt, so I have to be careful to never actually bend over. When I pass through the kitchen, the cooks mumble, "Diablo." I smile and wave. I often trip or fall staring at my reflection in the steel hood of the stove.

Karim is fanatical about making the lounge an oasis of rail-thin, beautiful women. He drills me about the kind of clientele he wants and doesn't want. If people are unattractive, I must seat them in corners or turn down the lights so as not to draw attention to them. I make sure the servers know to bring their orders quickly so they are not tempted to walk around.

One night a manager tells me that Naomi Campbell will be giving a party in the lounge. We have all heard the stories about her—how she hits a restaurant like a hurricane—and when she appears later that night she is wearing a white fur coat over a white minidress with gold heels. Her very perfect, very long brown legs and arms are shining, and in my life I do not remember seeing a woman more beautiful.

I offer to check her coat, picturing the stark white fur with fish sauce and rum spilled on it.

She looks at me wildly, her eyes hugely open. She nods her head in quick jerking movements. Yes? No? She's not speaking. She lifts her hands above her head, fingers spread apart, and does a quick shaking dance. She towers over me, her waist-length hair swinging. I smile and move to take her coat from the chair she has draped it over when she grabs my shoulder.

"Where are you taking that?" she says in her light English accent.

"I'm going to check your coat," I say. Didn't we just cover this?

"Yes. Oh God, I need a drink," Naomi says. "I need a drink, give-me-a-drink-I-need-one-please!" Her voice is a cross between a loud scream and a pleading demand.

"Yes-well-what-do-you-want?!" I reply. Her style of speech is contagious.

"I want a pink one," she squeals.

I literally run to the bar. But I realize I don't know what to ask for. I search for Ariana, our best waitress, who is good at memorizing customers' drink orders. Maybe Naomi has some special blend. Ariana doesn't know, and I look around the room and realize Naomi wants a Passion Cosmo, several of which are being passed around and which are indeed pink. I pluck one from the waitress's tray and find Naomi ducking into the back suite with the beds, which is empty. She is alone there when I deliver her drink, and she looks at me perplexed.

"Here's the drink you asked for," I say.

"You're beautiful and nice," she says.

"Thanks," I say, frowning.

"I want to eat dinner in this room, away from everyone else," she says with her arms spread wide. "What's for dinner?" she asks.

"Um, whatever is on the menu," I say, wondering for a moment if that is rude.

"I want fish," Naomi says, sticking out her bottom lip like a child asking for candy.

We have cod. Good, she says. She likes cod. She wants her friend Norma, part of the entourage in the lounge, to come sit with her while she eats. Okay, I'll get Norma. I am beginning to feel like a mother tending to a needy toddler.

Later that night, after Naomi leaves and we are closing up, I tell Karim all about her behavior. He shakes his head. "Man, she is crazy as hell," he says. "She'll start screaming—yelling at people for a drink at the top of her lungs.

"And that's during dinner," he says, laughing.

"Hey, she did that tonight," I tell him. I add that she looked beautiful, perfect in fact, in a fur coat and short dress, all white.

Karim shrugs. "She wore the exact same thing the last time she was here," he says.

One cold night I am working the lounge when a waitress grabs me by the arm. "A guy wants to talk to you," she says.

I assume it's a complaint.

"This guy," the waitress says, pulling me toward a tall, heavy-set man. He is clasping his hands and leaning his head to one side in a pleading gesture. He is going to ask me if I will let his friends in, I see.

"I'm expecting Jenna and Barbara Bush in about half an hour," he says. "They're going to arrive with several of their friends, but they're not going to stay long, they're just going to have a few drinks and leave. Is this OK?"

My first response is surprise—Barbara Bush is coming here? Jenna I would expect, but not her grandmother. Jenna's antics in bars have been well publicized, and it does not seem unusual to me that she would pass through our door, or any door for that matter where there is a party. But Barbara Bush? She's got to be eighty.

"Yes, the twins. Barbara and Jenna," the man responds quickly. Of course. I feel embarrassed that I know only the one daughter's name.

"They're just going to come for a little while and have a few drinks," the advance man says. I am agitated because the lounge is bottle-service only, and serving cocktails is more work for the bartender and waitress, for less money. "How many are you expecting?" I ask. I let my irritation show.

"I don't know. Maybe . . . eight?"

"What?" I say indignantly, throwing up my hands.

"Please," he responds. "They're already on their way. Please." *Yes, begging is good*, I think. In lieu of money, I accept pleading. I fold my arms. "I don't know," I say.

"Please." He's on to my game and sticks out his lower lip playfully.

"Yeah, all right," I say, bored now. I suppose it can't hurt to have the

Bush daughters here. Not twenty minutes later, I see him leading a dozen people inside.

I rush to meet them and he introduces me. "Barbara, this is Coco."

I smile and Barbara Bush smiles wider. "Hi! How are you?" she says in a very loud voice. She immediately wraps her arms around me. "Oh my God," she says enthusiastically, "I love your shirt. Guys, look at her shirt." I am wearing a black turtleneck. Her friends look and nod approvingly. She surveys the room and steps very close to my face. For a minute I think she is going to kiss me. "Oh my God, this place is cool!" she shouts. "How long has it been here?" Even though the music is loud, her voice is much more forceful than needed to be heard.

"Since August," I say.

"It's so nice!" she says, adding, "You have pretty eyes."

I look around and spot Ariana and grab her arm. "Make sure that you give them a round on us," I tell her. "And, um, Barbara is a bit of a close-talker if you know what I mean."

"Oh yeah?" Ariana says. That is all she ever says. I could confess all my sins to her, tell her I slaughtered my entire family and she would respond, "Oh yeah?" I am irritated that Ariana doesn't share my excitement about the Bush girls being in the house, and so I snap, "I see empty glasses on the tables."

From behind me I hear a loud voice. "Thank you, this is great, really." I turn around and there is Barbara, drink in hand, so close that if I just thrust my lips out a little we would touch. She is smiling widely, and I smile, too. Her friendliness and lack of pretense make it impossible not to like her.

"I love this song!" Barbara exclaims, grabbing my wrists and starting to wave my arms around. She throws her shoulders back and grinds her hips. It is the part of the evening when the DJ goes old school with Guns N' Roses. For people who work here every night, this is the saddest point.

Fifteen minutes later, I step outside to make sure the entrance is swept, and there I see Barbara bent over, hands on her knees, out on the sidewalk. "Are you all right?" I ask. Please, I think, don't let me see her throw up.

She spits on the pavement. "Yeah, I just needed some fresh air," she says. She stands and I see her forehead is damp with sweat. It must be twenty degrees out, and windy. I want to go back into the warm restaurant, but I stay with her.

I massage her back for a moment. Finally she lets out a loud burp, mumbles, "Excuse me," and returns inside.

A few moments later she and everyone in her entourage are leaving. As they file out, it seems odd to me that the president's daughters are not accompanied by Secret Service agents. I have not noticed anyone in black suits with ear pieces or carrying walkie-talkies. Where were Barbara's minders when she was nearly sick outside? I ask Kevin, standing watch at the door, if he noticed anyone.

"They're supposed to stay undercover, blend in," he says.

"Oh," I say. It seems obvious.

"Do you want to be a Secret Service officer?" I ask, imagining that is the pinnacle of the security field.

He looks at me as if I am an idiot. "I'm in school for accounting," he says.

★ ★ ★

Spring comes, and I have a new job: working outside as a doorkeeper. From 10:00 p.m. until 4:00 a.m., I am on my feet.

Kevin and I spend the time waiting and talking. He calls his girlfriend or checks on his car. We wave to the neighbors we recognize and their pets. With so much time together, we end up repeating the same stories over and over. "Did I tell you about this pedicure I got?" I ask him. "They clipped my toenails too short. I am so mad."

"Yeah, you already told me that," he says. "Why don't you sue for pain and suffering?"

It is quiet. We are not doing much business anymore. Some nights, only a few of the tables in the lounge are taken. Maybe it is the weather, or maybe everyone is over at Marquee and the other new clubs that have opened. This has made Karim, the owner, testy.

Karim still makes me nervous. When he talks to me, I have the habit of stuttering or speed-talking, using way too many words. Kevin, though, does not fear him. As the restaurant has lost some of its magic, he has begun expressing his sarcasm. When we see Karim pulling his truck into the garage, Kevin announces, "Daddy's home."

The models he is with tonight are very young and very beautiful. "Those looked way young, didn't they?" I say to Kevin after they have gone inside.

"Yeah, but Karim can still pour vodka into their sippy cups," he says.

A few minutes later, Karim comes out to look around at the crowd, but there is only Kevin and me. Kevin starts waving his arms frantically and jumping around. "Karim, over here! Karim, I'm over here, man!"

Karim scowls. I cannot hold my laughter. Karim gives us a list of people he's expecting, but it's irrelevant because I'm letting everyone in. We're empty.

In mid-June, I give him my notice, telling him I will leave the restaurant at the end of the month. I don't know what I'm going to do next. I am considering auditioning for parts, or going back to school, anything. Working as a hostess or a door person is not a career.

"But you just learned how to do your job," Karim says, shaking his head. He shrugs his shoulders and walks away from me.

MY REPUBLICAN JOURNEY

Dan Savage

★ ★ ★

This is excerpted from a series of three stories that originally ran in *The Stranger*, Seattle's weekly alternative paper, over the course of the 1996 presidential elections. That year, Pat Buchanan won the New Hampshire primary, on a platform of economic populism and culture war. This was familiar territory for Buchanan. He'd run on the same issues four years before, culminating famously in his keynote speech on the opening night of the 1992 Republican National Convention, where he declared "there is a religious war going on in our country for the soul of America."

Buchanan kept with these themes in New Hampshire in the weeks before this series started to run, pledging to uphold "eternal truths that do not change from the Old and New Testament." Homosexuality, in his view, was "anti-biblical and amoral." He was also on record saying things like "Homosexuality is not a civil right. Its rise almost always is accompanied, as in the Weimar Republic, with a decay of society and a collapse of its basic cinder block, the family." He'd also declared that AIDS was payback against gays: "They have declared war upon nature, and now nature is exacting an awful retribution."

Two weeks after Buchanan won the 1996 New Hampshire primary, Savage decided he could not sit on the sidelines any longer, and showed up at his first neighborhood Republican meeting.

PART ONE

"Your job as a Republican Precinct Committee Officer is an extremely important one. In many respects, you are the Republican Party within your neighborhood."

Hello, my name is Dan Savage and I am the Republican Party in my neighborhood. I am the Republican Precinct Committee Officer for Precinct 1846 in the 43rd District. If you have any questions about the Republican Party, our platform, or any of our candidates, feel free to give me a call here at work.

You're probably wondering two things. First, if I'm serious. I am. Second, how a commie-pinko drag fag sex-advice columnist with a fourteen-year-old boyfriend (kidding) managed to find a home in the hate-mongering, gay-bashing Republican Party?

Well, let me tell you something, pal: the Republican Party is a big tent, a huge tent. There were no ideological litmus tests at the Republican Party caucuses I attended last Tuesday night. I didn't even have to produce a voter registration card or a picture ID: a measure of the respect the Republican Party has for the rights of the individual. I just walked through the door, signed on the dotted line (Dan Savage "certifies that he/she considers himself/herself Republican"), and that was it. Who knew going over to the dark side could be so simple?

What prompted my conversion? Why would someone who's never once voted Republican on a local or national ticket, someone who voted for Walter Mondale and would do so again, join the Republican Party? Well, the Republican presidential primaries, specifically the early successes of fellow Irish Catholic Pat Buchanan, got me thinking about my childhood.

When I was beginning to drift away from the Catholic Church, out of disgust with our holy mother's hypocrisy, sexism, and homophobia, my biological mother implored me to keep the faith. "If everyone who isn't an asshole leaves the church," my momma told me, "the church will be just a bunch of assholes."

In my mother's opinion, the best way to change an oppressive, backward, socially malevolent institution such as the Catholic Church is from the inside. Well, after listening to Pat Buchanan's victory speech the night of the New Hampshire primary, it occurred to me that maybe the same goes for the Republican Party. If progressives joined the GOP, perhaps we could temper its social Neanderthalism.

Pat Buchanan's "culture war" conservatism helped cost the Republicans the White House in '92. A little moderation, a few cooler heads, and we could save the Republicans from themselves, and in the process perhaps save ourselves from the Republicans.

So I called the King County Republican Central Committee, found out the location of the caucuses in the 43rd, and went. The first shock was the location: my caucus was at Seattle Central Community College, steps from my apartment and smack-dab in the middle of Seattle's gay community. I know there are gay Republicans in Seattle—I've beat up enough of them—but I thought Republicans gay and straight would at least have the courtesy to meet the hell off Capitol Hill. But there they were, bold as brass, at Pine and Broadway.

The second shock of the evening was the tremendously diverse group of Hill Republicans in the room. There were old white people, young white people, tall white people, short white people, male white people, female white people, skinny white people, fat white people, socially maladapted white people, and white people with a full complement of social skills. There were, of course, a few of those troubling gay white people. That the Republican Party is a collection of homogenous, flat-earth motherfuckers is obviously a lie of the sneaky liberal media elite.

While waiting for the voting to begin, we were treated to a few videos: a Bob Dole video with a lot of smiling white people in it, and a Lamar Alexander video with a lot of beaming white people in it. Then we watched videos touting Republican candidates for governor: Pam Roach, Jim Waldo, Norm Maleng, Ellen Craswell.

Then came the third shock of the evening. Since I was the only person from my precinct (the 43rd District is divided up into a hundred or so precincts), and these were the precinct caucuses, I was automatically appointed my precinct's committee officer. And guess what? Precinct committee officers get to be delegates to the County Republican Convention on May 11 at Seattle Pacific University. According to the woman I spoke with at the King County Republican Committee office, since I'm the 1846's PCO, I don't have to stand for election as a delegate. I'm "automatically a delegate." I'm in. They're stuck with me, and there ain't nothing they can do about it. I feel so . . . empowered.

Before we got down to voting, or "indicating our preferences," for president and governor, all us white people filled out a survey. According to a letter from Reed M. Davis, chairman of the King County Republican Party, this survey would "provide guidance to our Platform Committee on many key issues." It seemed to me the questions were written in such a way as to indicate exactly what the Platform Committee thought about these issues, and we, the Republican rank and file, were only there to rubber-stamp the platform folks' foregone conclusions.

The nice young man running the caucus read all the survey questions aloud ("Should law-abiding citizens be prohibited from owning firearms?" "Do you agree with Republican-led efforts to require parental notification before a minor can have an abortion?"), and did very well, only stumbling slightly when the time came to read questions concerning "special rights" to the caucus participants. "Should the state of Washington recognize same-sex marriages?"

Now, as I said before, there were about a half dozen gay men in the room. None of them blanched at the loaded, leading question about gay marriage; none leapt up exclaiming, "Wait a minute! You're exploiting people's fear and hatred of homosexuals for short-term political gain! I won't stand for it!" That didn't happen. My fellow gay Republicans, like me, filled out the form in silence. Which, the last time I checked, equaled death.

Doing my part to pull the Republican Party to the left, I gave opposite answers from the ones the survey's authors hoped to get. I voted yes on gay marriage, no on parental notification, yes on gun control, and so on.

You're probably curious as to who I voted for. For president: Pat Buchanan. For governor: Ellen Craswell—a scary Christian conservative with Ronald Reagan's throat, Nancy Reagan's hairdo, and Frances Farmer's post-lobotomy joie de vivre.

Wait a minute: Didn't I join the GOP to pull the party to the left, to change it (for the better) from within? Why then did I vote for the most conservative candidates? Well, I have this theory: The scarier and more conservative the Republican nominees, the better the Democrats will do in the fall. And the better the Demos do, the sooner the Repubs will realize their "social" conservatism is a losing game. Then they'll give up the gay-bashing, immigrant-bashing, female-bashing, race-baiting bullshit.

See, back when I was a Democrat, I wanted the Demos to win 'cause, well, I was a Democrat. Now that I'm a Republican, I want the Demos to win because it's in the long-term best interests of the Republican Party.

Well, I've got to go doorbelling now, one of my "primary responsibilities" as the 1846's Republican PCO. I'll let you know how the King County convention goes. In the meantime, why not join me here in the GOP's big tent? Washington State's Presidential Primaries are coming up on Tuesday, March 26. Since Bill Clinton has the Democratic nomination wrapped up, why not vote in the Republican primary? Go to your polling place, ask for a Republican ballot, and vote for Buchanan and Craswell: it's the right thing to do.

PART TWO

Last month I joined the Republican Party and wrote a little article about it. Due to the dearth of Republicans on Capitol Hill, I wound up an automatic delegate to the King County Republican Convention. But then the Republicans did a stoopid thing: they told a reporter from the

Seattle Times I'd filled out the wrong forms, and I wasn't going to be a delegate—not now, not never. They weren't going to seat me. By the time the Republicans realized they'd made a simple clerical error, that I'd filled out the right forms and was in fact, a delegate, it was too late. KVI, KIRO, KING-TV, KOMO-TV, CBS, NPR, the *Seattle Times*, the *Seattle Post-Intelligencer*, the AP wire, and United Press International all picked up the story: "Republican Party Attempts to Toss Out Drag Queen Delegate!"

A couple of weeks after I'd traveled over to the Dark Side, Daniel Mead Smith, Chair of the 43rd, wrote me a letter. "I think you will be surprised that the 'hate-mongering, gay-bashing, neo-fascist Republican Party' does not exist in the 43rd," Smith wrote. "I invite you to come to one of our meetings and see for yourself." Last Saturday, I went to one of Smith's meetings to see for myself: the 43rd District Republican Caucus. This caucus was the second in a series of Republican events crowding my calendar this spring and summer: precinct caucus, district caucus, county convention, state convention, and (keeping my fingers crossed) the National Republican Convention this August in San Diego.

I arrived at the Montlake Community Center for the 1996 43rd District Republican Caucus at 8:00 a.m. I paid my five dollars, signed in, grabbed a seat, and waited for the work to begin: we were here to elect delegates to the State Republican Convention coming up Memorial Day weekend, and vote on nonbinding resolutions. While waiting for the action to start, I was treated to a tape loop of Ellen Craswell, Republican candidate for governor, stating and restating her opposition to gun control, gay rights, and "moral decay." A nice older lady and her husband sat down next to me, and I was helping her with some forms when she asked me what I did for a living. "I'm a writer." "What do you write?" she pressed. "A sex advice column."

"Oh," she said, smiling at me sweetly, "you're that person."

The caucus began with a prayer—we asked God to guide us in selecting delegates—and then we were ready to pledge allegiance to the flag. Only trouble was, no one brought a flag. I thought about suggesting we pledge allegiance to the fag—hey, that's me!—but I didn't want to be disruptive.

Someone found some red, white, and blue bunting in the back room, tossed it over an easel, and we pledged allegiance to that. The easel was needed post-pledge, so the red, white, and blue bunting to which we had just pledged our allegiance was tossed on the floor.

We had to elect delegates before we could get to the resolutions. I won't bore you with the *Robert's Rules of Order* stuff, or the impossibly convoluted process by which the eighty of us in the cramped, steeple-roofed, fluorescent-lit room elected seventeen delegates to the State Republican Convention. Suffice it to say it was crushingly dull. To entertain us while we waited for the ballots to be counted—four times—Republican Party activists and candidates gave little speeches. Some of these speeches were pure fantasy: one woman read a prepared speech about the United Nations working in concert with abortionists to take over the country.

The other recurring fantasy had to do with us "re-taking" the 43rd for the Republican Party. One man reminisced about the time, not too long ago, that the 43rd was a solidly Republican district: "We can make this district Republican again, just like it was when I joined the party twenty-five years ago. All we have to do is get out there and doorbell, and identify the voters in this district who are sympathetic to our issues!" Again and again, pretty much the same speech, and usually the same guy: the 43rd could be a Republican haven again if only we got out the vote.

Heart pounding, I stuck my hand in the air. "Have any of you been out of the house, or walked down Broadway, in the last twenty-five years?" I asked, standing and looking around at the toughest crowd I've probably ever played. The 43rd District, I pointed out, had gone gay all of a sudden. So long as the Republican Party was identified with homophobes and anti-gay bigot-activists, the Republican Party could kiss the 43rd District good-bye.

When I sat down, a different little old lady, one sitting behind me, pointed out that she knew a very nice gay couple in the Republican Party, so she—and by extension, the party—was not homophobic, and I was wrong: "The party isn't against gay people, that's just a false impression you have."

Gee, I wonder where I could've picked up that false impression? Maybe Jesse Helms; Bob Dornan; Bob "$1,000" Dole; anti-gay-rights rallies during the primaries attended by all the Republican presidential hopefuls (even "moderate" Lamar Alexander); Pat Robertson; Ralph Reed; Newt Gingrich; Linda Smith; Ellen Craswell; Spokane County Coroner Dexter Amend; the Washington State Legislature; the Christian Coalition; "Family Values Forever—Gay Rights Never!"; Jerry Falwell; anti-gay-rights planks in local, state, and national Republican Party platforms; the Gay Agenda videotape; and Lon Mabon. Or maybe it's the Republican Party's sponsorship of anti-gay-rights initiatives, anti-gay adoption laws, anti-same-sex marriage bills, Republican support for the ban on queers in the military, Republican opposition to gay and lesbian civil-rights legislation, Republican-led attacks on queer art, safe sex information for gay men, "mean" lesbians, etc., etc., etc.

During a break, an attractive middle-aged man approached me. He was a little angry. "I was offended by you forcing me to take responsibility for Jesse Helms"—as if the Republican Party isn't responsible for Jesse Helms.

Another man took me aside during a break to let me know that the gay-bashing within the Republican Party wasn't "for real," it was only to "get out the vote, and motivate the front lines." Well, then—I guess that makes it okay. I'm happy to be vilified and scapegoated and denied my civil rights, so long as it motivates people to go to the polls! Disenfranchisement is a small price to pay to increase voter turnout. I'm sure Asian Americans feel the same way I do, so let's resurrect the Yellow Peril, shall we? It's for the best.

There was a table off to one side with bad store-bought doughnuts, worse coffee, and a bowl for "honor system" donations to cover the expense of providing delicious Hostess products. The room was ugly and cramped and hard to move through without brushing past my fellow delegates.

Unfortunately, when it came time to vote, my fellow precinct delegates did not elect me a delegate to the state convention. I made the first cut—there were four rounds of voting—but failed in the second. But in a consolation round, I was elected an alternate delegate: I can go to the state convention, but I won't be allowed to speak, unless quite a few of the elected delegates fail to show.

With the delegate selection out of the way, it was resolution time! One resolution, which called on the party not to have prayers before beginning business "since not all Republicans are Christians" failed. Another calling for single-sex academies passed. Then the caucus chair recited my resolution. He had a hard time with my handwriting, and I admit that my resolution was not very elegantly written, but I wrote it on the fly:

> Be it resolved that we, the Republicans of the 43rd District, call on the Republican Party, its candidates, and officials, to chart a pro-family course that does not resort to scapegoating gay and lesbian Americans. Further, that we recognize the fundamental human rights of gay and lesbian individuals; the respect for the rights of the individual at the foundation of Republican values demands no less of us.
>
> As Republican residents of the 43rd District of Washington State, we recognize our special responsibility to defend the rights of our gay and lesbian friends and neighbors. We reject elements on the fringe of our party who would exploit fear and hatred of gay and lesbian citizens for short-term political gain.

After this was read and duly seconded, I was allowed to speak for five minutes. I quoted from District Chair Smith's letter, the part about the 43rd not being a home for gay-bashers and hate-mongers, and then threw my lavender gauntlet: Was Smith, I asked, telling me the truth? Did hate-mongers and gay-bashers "exist" in the 43rd District Republican

Party, or didn't they? Was the 43rd District Republican Party homophobic, or Were 43rd District Republicans willing to "recognize the fundamental rights of Gay and Lesbian individuals," or not? I was curious, I said, and wanted to see the issue put to a vote.

Well, that got people going: one woman wanted to know why she should support gay people, since gay people didn't support her when her home was burned down by arsonists. The arsonists weren't gay or anything, but where were gay people when she needed them? Another pointed out that some had broken the windows of Republican Party headquarters—so who's oppressing whom? And another person reacted violently to being labeled "homophobic": "Just because you're opposed to gay rights does not mean you're homophobic."

Funny how nobody likes to be called homophobic, especially homophobes.

During the Civil Rights Movement, I'm sure people opposed to integration, the Fourteenth Amendment, and racially mixed marriages resented being labeled "racist," but that's what they were. And that's what opponents of gay and lesbian civil-rights legislation, marriage rights, adoption rights, and the rest of it are: homophobes, whether they have the courage to admit it or not.

Debate ended, the time came to vote, and my resolution passed. It was a voice vote, so I can't tell you exactly how the room shook out, but it sounded like roughly 60 percent in favor and about 40 percent opposed. You could've knocked me over with a Craswell video.

Oddly enough, no other pro-queer resolutions were introduced, even though this was the 43rd District caucus, and the 43rd District is a hotbed of "Log Cabin Club" gay Republican activism. Yet I saw no other out gay person that morning—I was all alone—and there were, so far as I could tell, no other gay men in the room. So much for all that "changing the Party from the inside" rhetoric gay Republicans are always throwing around.

If being a "Gay Republican" is about working within the party to change it, then where were the 43rd's Gay Republicans when it came time to vote on and speak in favor of a pro-gay-rights initiative? Or, hey: maybe being a "Gay Republican" isn't about changing the Grand Old Party at all, from the inside or the outside. Maybe it's about what we've always suspected it's about: self-hatred. Instead of drinking or drugging or fucking themselves to death, like other gay men dying of their internalized homophobia, Gay Republicans have opted to vote themselves to death.

Since I'm just an alternate delegate, I can't speak at the State Convention, so maybe I'll go in drag—the right outfit speaks volumes. In the meantime, there's the County Convention May 11. I'm a full-fledged delegate at that one, and I will have the opportunity to address the floor and introduce resolutions like the one the 43rd District Republican Party passed last Saturday. Wish me luck: I have the sneaking feeling I'll be on my own again.

PART THREE

A few weeks later the big day arrived, the King County Republican Convention. My first major party function. Hats, speeches, amendments. I bounded out of bed at 7:00 a.m.—ugh—and ran to meet my new friend Steve at the QFC on Broadway. Steve attended his precinct caucuses way back in March with the intention of getting himself elected a delegate to the county and state Republican conventions. Like me he joined the party out of a sincere desire to move the GOP to the center. Kindred spirits, we decided to attend the county convention together.

The doors opened at 7:30 a.m. After the crowd settled down, a preacher read an alarming opening invocation, which pretty much set the tone for what was to come. Please forgive our leaders for endorsing perversion, and God deliver us from spineless compromise. Then we bellowed the pledge of allegiance to the flag of the United States of America.

I slipped up to the merchandise tables on the second floor, where I bought myself a red, white, and blue *Craswell for Governor* hat. It must have been fate. On the way back down from the merchandise tables, I ran smack-dab into Ellen Craswell herself.

I said hello, and, looking very serious in my little red, white, and blue hat, asked, "What are we going to do about the homosexual problem, Ms. Craswell? What is the final solution to all this homosexual nonsense?"

"So long as they stay inside," Ellen Craswell confided in me. "But when they organize and demand special rights, we must oppose them. We can't give special rights to something that is an abomination in the eyes of God."

Now, Ellen didn't seem interested in elaborating on just what it is we are supposed to stay inside of—the closet, our apartments, the priesthood—so I said good-bye, promising to vote for her in the primary. You see, the better Ellen does in the primary, the better the Democratic candidate for governor will do in the fall.

I made it back to the convention floor just in time for the opening of debate on the party platform. The King County Republican platform is a document drawn up by committee that lays out what the King County Republican party stands for. And here's the beautiful part.

Delegates are allowed to propose amendments. Once an amendment is proposed the amendment's sponsor is allowed to speak, followed by a few people in favor, a few opposed . . . after that, the sponsor gets another minute or so to address the floor. I was a delegate. I had amendments. And so, I would get to address the delegation. Over and over again. And, as amendments are time-consuming, determined delegates can grind the convention to a halt.

The first section we were to vote on was the Preamble, in which we acknowledged God to be our Creator and the family as the foundation of our culture. We embraced free markets, recognized that tax and regulatory burdens are a threat to our freedoms, yadda yadda yadda.

Before we could vote on the Preamble, and it hadn't occured to me to amend the Preamble, a delegate proposed that a line be addded, stating that the party was open to all who accept its basic principles, regardless of race, religion, sex, or national origin. After debate the first resolution of the day passed by a distressingly narrow margin.

Race, creed, sex, national origin . . . something was missing. Steve approached the microphone and proposed that the just-passed amendment also be amended to include the words *sexual orientation*. Well, Steve's amendment was soundly defeated, by a voice vote that, though untabulated, sounded to me like 1,589 to 11.

Then the Liberty section was up for a vote. I dashed to a microphone, wearing my Ellen Craswell hat, and proposed this amendment:

> As respect for the rights of the individual are the bedrock of Republican values, the King County Republican party hereby recognizes the fundamental human rights of gay and lesbian citizens. We reject elements on the fringe of the Republican party that would exploit fear and hatred of gay and lesbian American citizens for short-term political gain.

Through the shouting I pointed out that we King County Republicans can't have it both ways. We can't say in one breath that we oppose discrimination and with our next breath support discrimination against gay and lesbian American citizens. So let's vote on it. Do we, the Republicans of King County, recognize the fundamental rights of gay and lesbian American citizens, or do we not?

We do not.

After some heated debate, and the names I was called—pervert, sodomite, Democrat—my amendment was voted down. After my amendment failed, a woman in a Craswell hat approached me. "Why are you wearing that hat?" she briskly inquired.

"Because I'm for Craswell."

"You know where she stands on gay things, don't you?"

Having recently had a conversation with Ellen herself, I most certainly did. "But I'm not"—I smilingly informed my new friend and fellow Craswell supporter—"a single-issue voter."

Try to imagine now that you are a homophobic Republican jerkoff, which might be a triple redundancy, at your county convention. You came for the speeches, an anti-Clinton T-shirt for your collection, and a hot dog. This is what you do for fun, whoohoo, but these three guys keep introducing pro-gay-rights amendments, moving to have anti-gay amendments struck, and generally messing with your afternoon. You didn't come to the convention to defend your party's homophobia, and you certainly didn't come expecting to listen to gay men giving speeches all day long. Who are these guys? And why is that one wearing a Craswell hat? OK, you're this person, what do you do? You get mad. Very, very mad.

One delegate decided to get even. In what can only be described as a David Lynch moment, a palsied delegate staggered up to the microphone and proposed a change in the rules. No further discussion of homosexuality allowed. His resolution needed a two-thirds majority to pass, because it was a rules change, not a simple amendment. And pass it did, to hoots and hollers and cheers.

But we had yet to vote on the education section, which contained a plank about homosexuality. When we got to education, all hell broke loose. *Robert's Rules of Order* fetishists leapt to their feet insisting that the anti-gay plank in the legislation would have to be struck. If we can't discuss homosexuality, we can't vote on it, for voting is a discussion. Uh-oh, we were talking about homosexuality again. People were booing, shouting, oh the humanity.

The chair, bringing the room to order, calmly ruled that the no-further-discussion resolution applied only to pro-gay discussion. We could discuss homosexuality if we wanted, he said, but only if we weren't saying anything nice about it.

And the convention limped to a close, most of the day having been wasted debating gay rights, gay marriage, what makes people gay, and my hat.

WHAT I LEARNED

Here's what I learned about Republicans that weekend. They don't like homos very much. They certainly don't like having to talk about us, and they certainly like listening to us even less. But they do like beating up on us in their platforms. So, King County Republicans, I'll make you a deal. Leave us out of your platform in '98, the next convention cycle, and I'll stay away from your convention. But, if we're in the platform, I intend to return.

POWER STEER

Michael Pollan

✯ ✯ ✯

Garden City, Kansas, missed out on the suburban building boom of the postwar years. What it got instead were sprawling subdivisions of cattle. These feedlots—the nation's first—began rising on the high plains of western Kansas in the '50s, and by now developments catering to cows are far more common here than developments catering to people.

You'll be speeding down one of Finney County's ramrod roads when the empty, dun-colored prairie suddenly turns black and geometric, an urban grid of steel-fenced rectangles as far as the eye can see—which in Kansas is really far. I say "suddenly," but in fact a swiftly intensifying odor (an aroma whose Proustian echoes are more bus-station-men's-room than cow-in-the-country) heralds the approach of a feedlot for more than a mile. Then it's upon you: Poky Feeders, population thirty-seven thousand. Cattle pens stretch to the horizon, each one home to 150 animals standing dully or lying around in a grayish mud that it eventually dawns on you isn't mud at all. The pens line a network of unpaved roads that loop around vast waste lagoons on their way to the feedlot's beating heart: a chugging, silvery feed mill that soars like an industrial cathedral over this teeming metropolis of meat.

I traveled to Poky early in January with the slightly improbable notion of visiting one particular resident: a young black steer that I'd met in the fall on a ranch in Vale, South Dakota. The steer, in fact, belonged to me. I'd purchased him as an eight-month-old calf from the Blair brothers, Ed and Rich, for $598. I was paying Poky Feeders $1.60 a day for his room, board and meds and hoped to sell him at a profit after he was fattened.

My interest in the steer was not strictly financial, however, or even gustatory, though I plan to retrieve some steaks from the Kansas packing plant where No. 534, as he is known, has an appointment with the stunner in June. No, my primary interest in this animal was educational. I wanted to find out how a modern, industrial steak is produced in America these days, from insemination to slaughter.

Eating meat, something I have always enjoyed doing, has become problematic in recent years. Though beef consumption spiked upward during the flush '90s, the longer-term trend is down, and many people will tell you they no longer eat the stuff. Inevitably they'll bring up mad cow disease (and the accompanying revelation that industrial agriculture has transformed these ruminants into carnivores—indeed, into cannibals). They might mention their concerns about E. coli contamination or antibiotics in the feed. Then there are the many environmental problems, like groundwater pollution, associated with "concentrated animal feeding operations." (The word "farm" no longer applies.) And of course there are questions of animal welfare. How are we treating the animals we eat while they're alive, and then how humanely are we "dispatching" them, to borrow an industry euphemism?

Meat-eating has always been a messy business, shadowed by the shame of killing and, since Upton Sinclair's writing of *The Jungle*, by questions about what we're really eating when we eat meat. Forgetting, or willed ignorance, is the preferred strategy of many beef eaters, a strategy abetted by the industry. (What grocery-store item is more silent about its origins than a shrink-wrapped steak?) Yet I recently began to feel that ignorance was no longer tenable. If I was going to continue to eat red meat, then I owed it to myself, as well as to the animals, to take more responsibility for the invisible but crucial transaction between ourselves and the animals we eat. I'd try to own it, in other words.

So this is the biography of my cow.

The Blair brothers ranch occupies 11,500 acres of short-grass prairie a few miles outside Sturgis, South Dakota, directly in the shadow of Bear Butte. In November, when I visited, the turf forms a luxuriant pelt of grass oscillating yellow and gold in the constant wind and sprinkled with perambulating black dots: Angus cows and calves grazing.

Ed and Rich Blair run what's called a "cow-calf" operation, the first stage of beef production, and the stage least changed by the modern industrialization of meat. While the pork and chicken industries have consolidated the entire life cycles of those animals under a single roof, beef cattle are still born on thousands of independently owned ranches. Although four giant meatpacking companies (Tyson's subsidiary IBP, Monfort, Excel and National) now slaughter and market more than 80 percent of the beef cattle born in this country, that concentration represents the narrow end of a funnel that starts out as wide as the Great Plains.

The Blairs have been in the cattle business for four generations. Although there are new wrinkles to the process—artificial insemination to improve genetics, for example—producing beef calves goes pretty much as it always has, just faster. Calving season begins in late winter, a succession of subzero nights spent yanking breeched babies out of their bellowing mothers. In April comes the first spring roundup to work the newborn calves (branding, vaccination, castration); then more roundups in early summer to inseminate the cows (fifteen-dollar mail-order straws of elite bull semen have pretty much put the resident stud out of work); and weaning in the fall. If all goes well, your herd of 850 cattle has increased to 1,600 by the end of the year.

My steer spent his first six months in these lush pastures alongside his mother, No. 9,534. His father was a registered Angus named GAR Precision 1,680, a bull distinguished by the size and marbling of his offspring's rib-eye steaks. Born last March 13 in a birthing shed across the road, No. 534 was turned out on pasture with his mother as soon as the eighty-pound calf stood up and began nursing. After a few weeks, the calf began supplementing his mother's milk by nibbling on a salad bar of mostly native grasses: western wheatgrass, little bluestem, green needle-grass.

Apart from the trauma of the April day when he was branded and castrated, you could easily imagine No. 534 looking back on those six months grazing at his mother's side as the good old days—if, that is, cows do look back. ("They do not know what is meant by yesterday or today," Friedrich Nietzsche wrote, with a note of envy, of grazing cattle, "fettered to the moment and its pleasure or displeasure, and thus neither melancholy or bored." Nietzsche clearly had never seen a feedlot.) It may be foolish to presume to know what a cow experiences, yet we can say that a cow grazing on grass is at least doing what he has been splendidly molded by evolution to do. Which isn't a bad definition of animal happiness. Eating grass, however, is something that, after October, my steer would never do again.

Although the modern cattle industry all but ignores it, the reciprocal relationship between cows and grass is one of nature's underappreciated wonders. For the grasses, the cow maintains their habitat by preventing trees and shrubs from gaining a foothold; the animal also spreads grass seed, planting it with its hoofs and fertilizing it. In exchange for these services, the grasses offer the ruminants a plentiful, exclusive meal. For cows, sheep and other grazers have the unique ability to convert grass—which single-stomached creatures like us can't digest—into high-quality protein. They can do this because they possess a rumen, a forty-five-gallon fermentation tank in which a resident population of bacteria turns grass into metabolically useful organic acids and protein.

This is an excellent system for all concerned: for the grasses, for the animals and for us. What's more, growing meat on grass can make superb ecological sense: so long as the rancher practices rotational grazing, it is a sustainable, solar-powered system for producing food on land too arid or hilly to grow anything else.

So if this system is so ideal, why is it that my cow hasn't tasted a blade of grass since October? Speed, in a word. Cows raised on grass simply take longer to reach slaughter weight than cows raised on a richer diet, and the modern meat industry has devoted itself to shortening a beef calf's allotted time on earth. "In my grandfather's day, steers were four or five years old at slaughter," explained Rich Blair, who, at forty-five, is the younger of the brothers by four years. "In the fifties, when my father was ranching, it was two or three. Now we get there at fourteen to sixteen months." Fast food indeed. What gets a beef calf from eighty to one thousand two hundred pounds in fourteen months are enormous quantities of corn, protein supplements—and drugs, including growth hormones. These "efficiencies," all of which come at a price, have transformed raising cattle into a high-volume, low-margin business. Not everybody is convinced that this is progress. "Hell," Ed Blair told me, "my dad made more money on two hundred and fifty head than we do on eight hundred and fifty."

Weaning marks the fateful moment when the natural, evolutionary logic represented by a ruminant grazing on grass bumps up against the industrial logic that, with stunning speed, turns that animal into a box of beef. This industrial logic is rational and even irresistible—after all, it has succeeded in transforming beef from a luxury item into everyday fare for millions of people. And yet the farther you follow it, the more likely you are to wonder if that rational logic might not also be completely insane.

In early October, a few weeks before I met him, No. 534 was weaned from his mother. Weaning is perhaps the most traumatic time on a ranch for animals and ranchers alike; cows separated from their calves will mope and bellow for days, and the calves themselves, stressed by the change in circumstance and diet, are prone to get sick.

On many ranches, weaned calves go directly from the pasture to the sale barn, where they're sold at auction, by the pound, to feedlots. The Blairs prefer to own their steers straight through to slaughter and to keep them on the ranch for a couple of months of "backgrounding" before sending them on the five-hundred-mile trip to Poky Feeders. Think of backgrounding as prep school for feedlot life: the animals are confined in a pen, "bunk broken"—taught to eat from a trough—and gradually accustomed to eating a new, unnatural diet of grain. (Grazing cows encounter only tiny amounts of grain, in the form of grass seeds.)

It was in the backgrounding pen that I first met No. 534 on an unseasonably warm afternoon in November. I'd told the Blairs I wanted to follow one of their steers through the life cycle; Ed, forty-nine, suggested I might as well buy a steer, as a way to really understand the daunting economics of modern ranching. Ed and Rich told me what to look for: a broad, straight back and thick hindquarters. Basically, you want a strong frame on which to hang a lot of meat. I was also looking for a memorable face in this Black Angus sea, one that would stand out in the feedlot crowd. Almost as soon as I started surveying the ninety or so steers in the pen, No. 534 moseyed up to the railing and made eye contact. He had a wide, stout frame and was brockle-faced—he had three distinctive white blazes. If not for those markings, Ed said, No. 534 might have been spared castration and sold as a bull; he was that good-looking. But the white blazes indicate the presence of Hereford blood, rendering him ineligible for life as an Angus stud. Tough break.

Rich said he would calculate the total amount I owed the next time No. 534 got weighed but that the price would be $98 a hundredweight for an animal of this quality. He would then bill me for all expenses (feed, shots, etc.) and, beginning in January, start passing on the weekly "hotel charges" from Poky Feeders. In June we'd find out from the packing plant how well my investment had panned out: I would receive a payment for No. 534 based on his carcass weight, plus a premium if he earned a USDA grade of choice or prime. "And if you're worried about the cattle market," Rich said jokingly, referring to its post–September 11 slide, "I can sell you an option too." Option insurance has become increasingly popular among cattlemen in the wake of mad cow and foot-and-mouth disease.

Rich handles the marketing end of the business out of an office in Sturgis, where he also trades commodities. In fact you'd never guess from Rich's unlined, indoorsy face and golfish attire that he was a rancher. Ed, by contrast, spends his days on the ranch and better looks the part, with his well-creased visage, crinkly cowboy eyes and ever-present plug of tobacco. His cap carries the same prairie-flat slogan I'd spotted on the ranch's roadside sign: Beef: It's What's for Dinner.

My second morning on the ranch, I helped Troy Hadrick, Ed's son-in-law and a ranch hand, feed the steers in the backgrounding pen. A thickly muscled post of a man, Hadrick is twenty-five and wears a tall black cowboy hat perpetually crowned by a pair of mirrored Oakley sunglasses. He studied animal science at South Dakota State and is up on the latest university thinking on cattle nutrition, reproduction and medicine. Hadrick seems to relish everything to do with ranching, from calving to wielding the artificial-insemination syringe.

Hadrick and I squeezed into the heated cab of a huge swivel-hipped tractor hooked up to a feed mixer: basically, a dump truck with a giant screw through the middle to blend ingredients. First stop was a hopper filled with Rumensin, a powerful antibiotic that No. 534 will consume with his feed every day for the rest of his life. Calves have no need of regular medication while on grass, but as soon as they're placed in the backgrounding pen, they're apt to get sick. Why? The stress of weaning is a factor, but the main culprit is the feed. The shift to a "hot ration" of grain can so disturb the cow's digestive process—its rumen, in particular—that it can kill the animal if not managed carefully and accompanied by antibiotics.

After we'd scooped the ingredients into the hopper and turned on the mixer, Hadrick deftly sidled the tractor alongside the pen and flipped a switch to release a dusty tan stream of feed in a long, even line. No. 534 was one of the first animals to belly up to the rail for breakfast. He was heftier than his pen mates and, I decided, sparkier too. That morning, Hadrick and I gave each calf six pounds of corn mixed with seven pounds of ground alfalfa hay and a quarter-pound of Rumensin. Soon after my visit, this ration would be cranked up to fourteen pounds of corn and six pounds of hay—and added two and a half pounds every day to No. 534.

While I was on the ranch, I didn't talk to No. 534, pet him or other-wise try to form a connection. I also decided not to give him a name, even though my son proposed a pretty good one after seeing a snap-shot. ("Night") My intention, after all, is to send this animal to slaughter and then eat some of him. No. 534 is not a pet, and I certainly don't want to end up with an ox in my backyard because I suddenly got sentimental.

As fall turned into winter, Hadrick sent me regular e-mail messages apprising me of my steer's progress. On November 13 he weighed 650 pounds; by Christmas he was up to 798, making him the seventh-heaviest steer in his pen, an achievement in which I, idiotically, took a measure of pride. Between November 13 and January 4, the day he boarded the truck for Kansas, No. 534 put away 706 pounds of corn and 336 pounds of alfalfa hay, bringing his total living expenses for that period to $61.13. I was into this deal now for $659.

Hadrick's e-mail updates grew chattier as time went on, cracking a window on the rancher's life and outlook. I was especially struck by his relationship to the animals, how it manages to be at once intimate and unsentimental. One day Hadrick is tenderly nursing a newborn at 3:00 a.m., the next he's "having a big prairie oyster feed" after castrating a pen of bull calves.

Hadrick wrote empathetically about weaning ("It's like packing up and leaving the house when you are eighteen and knowing you will never see your parents again") and with restrained indignation about "animal activists and city people" who don't understand the first thing about a rancher's relationship to his cattle. Which, as Hadrick put it, is simply this: "If we don't take care of these animals, they won't take care of us."

"Everyone hears about the bad stuff," Hadrick wrote, "but they don't ever see you give CPR to a newborn calf that was born backward or bringing them into your house and trying to warm them up on your kitchen floor because they were born on a minus-twenty-degree night. Those are the kinds of things ranchers will do for their livestock. They take precedence over most everything in your life. Sorry for the sermon."

To travel from the ranch to the feedlot, as No. 534 and I both did (in separate vehicles) the first week in January, feels a lot like going from the country to the big city. Indeed, a cattle feedlot is a kind of city, populated by as many as one hundred thousand animals. It is very much a premodern city, however—crowded, filthy and stinking, with open sewers, unpaved roads and choking air.

The urbanization of the world's livestock is a fairly recent historical development, so it makes a certain sense that cow towns like Poky Feeders would recall human cities several centuries ago. As in fourteenth-century London, the metropolitan digestion remains vividly on display: the foodstuffs coming in, the waste streaming out. Similarly, there is the crowding together of recent arrivals from who knows where, combined with a lack of modern sanitation. This combination has always been a recipe for disease; the only reason contemporary animal cities aren't as plague-ridden as their medieval counterparts is a single historical anomaly: the modern antibiotic.

I spent the better part of a day walking around Poky Feeders, trying to understand how its various parts fit together. In any city, it's easy to lose track of nature—of the connections between various species and the land on which everything ultimately depends. The feedlot's eco-system, I could see, revolves around corn. But its food chain doesn't end there, because the corn itself grows somewhere else, where it is impli-cated in a whole other set of ecological relationships. Growing the vast quantities of corn used to feed livestock in this country takes vast quan-tities of chemical fertilizer, which in turn takes vast quantities of oil—1.2 gallons for every bushel. So the modern feedlot is really a city floating on a sea of oil.

I started my tour at the feed mill, the yard's thundering hub, where three meals a day for thirty-seven thousand animals are designed and mixed by computer. A million pounds of feed passes through the mill each day. Every hour of every day, a tractor-trailer pulls up to disgorge another twenty-five tons of corn. Around the other side of the mill, tanker trucks back up to silo-shaped tanks, into which they pump thousands of gallons of liquefied fat and protein supplement. In a shed attached to the mill sit vats of liquid vitamins and synthetic estrogen;

next to these are pallets stacked with fifty-pound sacks of Rumensin and tylosin, another antibiotic. Along with alfalfa hay and corn silage for roughage, all these ingredients are blended and then piped into the dump trucks that keep Poky's eight and a half miles of trough filled.

The feed mill's great din is made by two giant steel rollers turning against each other twelve hours a day, crushing steamed corn kernels into flakes. This was the only feed ingredient I tasted, and it wasn't half bad; not as crisp as Kellogg's, but with a cornier flavor. I passed, however, on the protein supplement, a sticky brown goop consisting of molasses and urea.

Corn is a mainstay of livestock diets because there is no other feed quite as cheap or plentiful: thanks to federal subsidies and ever-growing surpluses, the price of corn ($2.25 a bushel) is fifty cents less than the cost of growing it. The rise of the modern factory farm is a direct result of these surpluses, which soared in the years following World War II, when petrochemical fertilizers came into widespread use. Ever since, the USDA's policy has been to help farmers dispose of surplus corn by passing as much of it as possible through the digestive tracts of food animals, converting it into protein. Compared with grass or hay, corn is a compact and portable foodstuff, making it possible to feed tens of thousands of animals on small plots of land. Without cheap corn, the modern urbanization of livestock would probably never have occurred.

We have come to think of "corn-fed" as some kind of old-fashioned virtue; we shouldn't. Granted, a corn-fed cow develops well-marbled flesh, giving it a taste and texture American consumers have learned to like. Yet this meat is demonstrably less healthy to eat, since it contains more saturated fat. A recent study in *The European Journal of Clinical Nutrition* found that the meat of grass-fed livestock not only had substantially less fat than grain-fed meat but that the type of fats found in grass-fed meat were much healthier. (Grass-fed meat has more omega-3 fatty acids and fewer omega-6, which is believed to promote heart disease; it also contains betacarotine and CLA, another "good" fat.) A growing body of research suggests that many of the health problems associated with eating beef are really problems with corn-fed beef.

In the same way ruminants have not evolved to eat grain, humans may not be well adapted to eating grain-fed animals. Yet the USDA's grading system continues to reward marbling—that is, intermuscular fat—and thus the feeding of corn to cows.

The economic logic behind corn is unassailable, and on a factory farm, there is no other kind. Calories are calories, and corn is the cheapest, most convenient source of calories. Of course the identical industrial logic—protein is protein—led to the feeding of rendered cow parts back to cows, a practice the FDA banned in 1997 after scientists realized it was spreading mad cow disease.

Make that mostly banned. The FDA's rules against feeding ruminant protein to ruminants make exceptions for "blood products" (even though they contain protein) and fat. Indeed, my steer has probably dined on beef tallow recycled from the very slaughterhouse he's heading to in June. "Fat is fat," the feedlot manager shrugged when I raised an eyebrow.

FDA rules still permit feedlots to feed nonruminant animal protein to cows. (Feather meal is an accepted cattle feed, as are pig and fish protein and chicken manure.) Some public-health advocates worry that since the bovine meat and bonemeal that cows used to eat is now being fed to chickens, pigs and fish, infectious prions could find their way back into cattle when they eat the protein of the animals that have been eating them. To close this biological loophole, the FDA is now considering tightening its feed rules.

Until mad cow disease, remarkably few people in the cattle business, let alone the general public, comprehended the strange semicircular food chain that industrial agriculture had devised for cattle (and, in turn, for us). When I mentioned to Rich Blair that I'd been surprised to learn that cows were eating cows, he said, "To tell the truth, it was kind of a shock to me too." Yet even today, ranchers don't ask many questions about feedlot menus. Not that the answers are so easy to come by. When I asked Poky's feedlot manager what exactly was in the protein supplement, he couldn't say. "When we buy supplement, the supplier says it's 40 percent protein, but they don't specify beyond that." When I called the supplier, it wouldn't divulge all its "proprietary ingredients" but promised that animal parts weren't among them. Protein is pretty much still protein.

Compared with ground-up cow bones, corn seems positively wholesome. Yet it wreaks considerable havoc on bovine digestion. During my day at Poky, I spent an hour or two driving around the yard with Dr. Mel Metzen, the staff veterinarian. Metzen, a 1997 graduate of Kansas State's vet school, oversees a team of eight cowboys who spend their days riding the yard, spotting sick cows and bringing them in for treatment. A great many of their health problems can be traced to their diet. "They're made to eat forage," Metzen said, "and we're making them eat grain."

Perhaps the most serious thing that can go wrong with a ruminant on corn is feedlot bloat. The rumen is always producing copious amounts of gas, which is normally expelled by belching during rumination. But when the diet contains too much starch and too little roughage, rumination all but stops, and a layer of foamy slime that can trap gas forms in the rumen. The rumen inflates like a balloon, pressing against the animal's lungs. Unless action is promptly taken to relieve the pressure (usually by forcing a hose down the animal's esophagus), the cow suffocates.

A corn diet can also give a cow acidosis. Unlike that in our own highly acidic stomachs, the normal pH of a rumen is neutral. Corn makes it unnaturally acidic, however, causing a kind of bovine heartburn, which in some cases can kill the animal but usually just makes it sick. Acidotic animals go off their feed, pant and salivate excessively, paw at their bellies and eat dirt. The condition can lead to diarrhea, ulcers, bloat, liver disease and a general weakening of the immune system that leaves the animal vulnerable to everything from pneumonia to feedlot polio.

Cows rarely live on feedlot diets for more than six months, which might be about as much as their digestive systems can tolerate. "I don't know how long you could feed this ration before you'd see problems," Metzen said; another vet said that a sustained feedlot diet would eventually "blow out their livers" and kill them. As the acids eat away at the rumen wall, bacteria enter the bloodstream and collect in the liver. More than 13 percent of feedlot cattle are found at slaughter to have abscessed livers.

What keeps a feedlot animal healthy—or healthy enough—are antibiotics. Rumensin inhibits gas production in the rumen, helping to prevent bloat; tylosin reduces the incidence of liver infection. Most of the antibiotics sold in America end up in animal feed—a practice that, it is now generally acknowledged, leads directly to the evolution of new antibiotic-resistant "superbugs." In the debate over the use of antibiotics in agriculture, a distinction is usually made between clinical and nonclinical uses. Public-health advocates don't object to treating sick animals with antibiotics; they just don't want to see the drugs lose their efficacy because factory farms are feeding them to healthy animals to promote growth. But the use of antibiotics in feedlot cattle confounds this distinction. Here the drugs are plainly being used to treat sick animals, yet the animals probably wouldn't be sick if not for what we feed them.

I asked Metzen what would happen if antibiotics were banned from cattle feed. "We just couldn't feed them as hard," he said. "Or we'd have a higher death loss." (Less than 3 percent of cattle die on the feedlot.) The price of beef would rise, he said, since the whole system would have to slow down.

"Hell, if you gave them lots of grass and space," he concluded dryly, "I wouldn't have a job."

Before heading over to Pen 43 for my reunion with No. 534, I stopped by the shed where recent arrivals receive their hormone implants. The calves are funneled into a chute, herded along by a ranch hand wielding an electric prod, then clutched in a restrainer just long enough for another hand to inject a slow-release pellet of Revlar, a synthetic estrogen, in the back of the ear. The Blairs' pen had not yet been implanted, and I was still struggling with the decision of whether to forgo what is virtually a universal practice in the cattle industry in the United States. (It has been banned in the European Union.)

American regulators permit hormone implants on the grounds that no risk to human health has been proved, even though measurable hormone residues do turn up in the meat we eat. These contribute to the buildup of estrogenic compounds in the environment, which some scientists believe may explain falling sperm counts and premature maturation in girls. Recent studies have also found elevated levels of synthetic growth hormones in feedlot wastes; these persistent chemicals eventually wind up in the waterways downstream of feedlots, where scientists have found fish exhibiting abnormal sex characteristics.

The FDA is opening an inquiry into the problem, but for now, implanting hormones in beef cattle is legal and financially irresistible: an implant costs $1.50 and adds between forty and fifty pounds to the weight of a steer at slaughter, for a return of at least $25. That could easily make the difference between profit and loss on my investment in No. 534. Thinking like a parent, I like the idea of feeding my son hamburgers free of synthetic hormones. But thinking like a cattleman, there was really no decision to make.

I asked Rich Blair what he thought. "I'd love to give up hormones," he said. "If the consumer said, We don't want hormones, we'd stop in a second. The cattle could get along better without them. But the market signal's not there, and as long as my competitor's doing it, I've got to do it, too."

Around lunchtime, Metzen and I finally arrived at No. 534's pen. My first impression was that my steer had landed himself a decent piece of real estate. The pen is far enough from the feed mill to be fairly quiet, and it has a water view—of what I initially thought was a reservoir, until I noticed the brown scum. The pen itself is surprisingly spacious, slightly bigger than a basketball court, with a concrete feed bunk out front and a freshwater trough in the back. I climbed over the railing and joined the ninety steers, which, en masse, retreated a few steps, then paused.

I had on the same carrot-colored sweater I'd worn to the ranch in South Dakota, hoping to jog my steer's memory. Way off in the back, I spotted him—those three white blazes. As I gingerly stepped toward him, the quietly shuffling mass of black cowhide between us parted, and there No. 534 and I stood, staring dumbly at each other. Glint of recognition? None whatsoever. I told myself not to take it personally. No. 534 had been bred for his marbling, after all, not his intellect.

I don't know enough about the emotional life of cows to say with any confidence if No. 534 was miserable, bored or melancholy, but I would not say he looked happy. I noticed that his eyes looked a little bloodshot. Some animals are irritated by the fecal dust that floats in the feedlot air; maybe that explained the sullen gaze with which he fixed me. Unhappy or not, though, No. 534 had clearly been eating well. My animal had put on a couple hundred pounds since we'd last met, and he looked it: thicker across the shoulders and round as a barrel through the middle. He carried himself more like a steer now than a calf, even though he was still less than a year old. Metzen complimented me on his size and conformation. "That's a handsome-looking beef you've got there." (Aw, shucks.)

Staring at No. 534, I could picture the white lines of the butcher's chart dissecting his black hide: rump roast, flank steak, standing rib, brisket. One way of looking at No. 534—the industrial way—was as an efficient machine for turning feed corn into beef. Every day between now and his slaughter date in June, No. 534 will convert thirty-two pounds of feed (twenty-five of them corn) into another three and a half pounds of flesh. Poky is indeed a factory, transforming cheap raw materials into a less-cheap finished product, as fast as bovinely possible.

Yet the factory metaphor obscures as much as it reveals about the creature that stood before me. For this steer was not a machine in a factory but an animal in a web of relationships that link him to certain other animals, plants and microbes, as well as to the earth. And one of those other animals is us. The unnaturally rich diet of corn that has compromised No. 534's health is fattening his flesh in a way that in turn may compromise the health of the humans who will eat him. The antibiotics he's consuming with his corn were at that very moment selecting, in his gut and wherever else in the environment they wind up, for bacteria that could someday infect us and resist the drugs we depend on. We inhabit the same microbial ecosystem as the animals we eat, and whatever happens to it also happens to us.

I thought about the deep pile of manure that No. 534 and I were standing in. We don't know much about the hormones in it—where they will end up or what they might do once they get there—but we do know something about the bacteria. One particularly lethal bug most probably resided in the manure beneath my feet. Escherichia coli 0157 is a relatively new strain of a common intestinal bacteria (it was first isolated in the 1980s) that is common in feedlot cattle, more than half of whom carry it in their guts. Ingesting as few as ten of these microbes can cause a fatal infection in a human.

Most of the microbes that reside in the gut of a cow and find their way into our food get killed off by the acids in our stomachs, since they originally adapted to live in a neutral-pH environment. But the digestive tract of the modern feedlot cow is closer in acidity to our own, and in this new, man-made environment acid-resistant strains of E. coli have developed that can survive our stomach acids—and go on to kill us. By acidifying a cow's gut with corn, we have broken down one of our food chain's barriers to infection. Yet this process can be reversed: James Russell, a USDA microbiologist, has discovered that switching a cow's diet from corn to hay in the final days before slaughter reduces the population of E. coli 0157 in its manure by as much as 70 percent. Such a change, however, is considered wildly impractical by the cattle industry.

So much comes back to corn, this cheap feed that turns out in so many ways to be not cheap at all. While I stood in No. 534's pen, a dump truck pulled up alongside the feed bunk and released a golden stream of feed. The animals stepped up to the bunk for their lunch. The $1.60 a day I'm paying for three giant meals is a bargain only by the narrowest of calculations. It doesn't take into account, for example, the cost to the public health of antibiotic resistance or food poisoning by E. coli or all the environmental costs associated with industrial corn.

For if you follow the corn from this bunk back to the fields where it grows, you will find an eighty-million-acre monoculture that consumes more chemical herbicide and fertilizer than any other crop. Keep going and you can trace the nitrogen runoff from that crop all the way down the Mississippi into the Gulf of Mexico, where it has created (if that is the right word) a twelve-thousand-square-mile "dead zone."

But you can go farther still, and follow the fertilizer needed to grow that corn all the way to the oil fields of the Persian Gulf. No. 534 started life as part of a food chain that derived all its energy from the sun; now that corn constitutes such an important link in his food chain, he is the product of an industrial system powered by fossil fuel. (And in turn, defended by the military—another uncounted cost of "cheap" food.) I asked David Pimentel, a Cornell ecologist who specializes in agriculture and energy, if it might be possible to calculate precisely how much oil it will take to grow my steer to slaughter weight. Assuming No. 534 continues to eat 25 pounds of corn a day and reaches a weight of 1,250 pounds, he will have consumed in his lifetime roughly 284 gallons of oil. We have succeeded in industrializing the beef calf, transforming what was once a solar-powered ruminant into the very last thing we need: another fossil-fuel machine.

Sometime in June, No. 534 will be ready for slaughter. Though only fourteen months old, my steer will weigh more than one thousand two hundred pounds and will move with the lumbering deliberateness of the obese. One morning, a cattle trailer from the National Beef plant in Liberal, Kansas, will pull in to Poky Feeders, drop a ramp and load No. 534 along with thirty-five of his pen mates.

The one-hundred-mile trip south to Liberal is a straight shot on Route 83, a two-lane highway on which most of the traffic consists of speeding tractor-trailers carrying either cattle or corn. The National Beef plant is a sprawling gray-and-white complex in a neighborhood of trailer homes and tiny houses a notch up from shanties. These are, presumably, the homes of the Mexican and Asian immigrants who make up a large portion of the plant's workforce. The meat business has made southwestern Kansas an unexpectedly diverse corner of the country.

A few hours after their arrival in the holding pens outside the factory, a plant worker will open a gate and herd No. 534 and his pen mates into an alley that makes a couple of turns before narrowing down to a single-file chute. The chute becomes a ramp that leads the animals up to a second-story platform and then disappears through a blue door.

That door is as close to the kill floor as the plant managers were prepared to let me go. I could see whatever I wanted to farther on—the cold room where carcasses are graded, the food-safety lab, the fabrication room where the carcasses are broken down into cuts—on the condition that I didn't take pictures or talk to employees. But the stunning, bleeding and evisceration process was off-limits to a journalist, even a cattleman-journalist like myself.

What I know about what happens on the far side of the blue door comes mostly from Temple Grandin, who has been on the other side and, in fact, helped to design it. Grandin, an assistant professor of animal science at Colorado State, is one of the most influential people in the United States cattle industry. She has devoted herself to making cattle slaughter less stressful and therefore more humane by designing an ingenious series of cattle restraints, chutes, ramps and stunning systems. Grandin is autistic, a condition she says has allowed her to see the world from the cow's point of view. The industry has embraced Grandin's work because animals under stress are not only more difficult to handle but also less valuable: panicked cows produce a surge of adrenaline that turns their meat dark and unappetizing. "Dark cutters," as they're called, sell at a deep discount.

Grandin designed the double-rail conveyor system in use at the National Beef plant; she has also audited the plant's killing process for McDonald's. Stories about cattle "waking up" after stunning only to be skinned alive prompted McDonald's to audit its suppliers in a program that is credited with substantial improvements since its inception in 1999. Grandin says that in cattle slaughter "there is the pre-McDonald's era and the post-McDonald's era—it's night and day."

Grandin recently described to me what will happen to No. 534 after he passes through the blue door. "The animal goes into the chute single file," she began. "The sides are high enough so all he sees is the butt of the animal in front of him. As he walks through the chute, he passes over a metal bar, with his feet on either side. While he's straddling the bar, the ramp begins to decline at a twenty-five-degree angle, and before he knows it, his feet are off the ground and he's being carried along on a conveyor belt. We put in a false floor so he can't look down and see he's off the ground. That would panic him."

Listening to Grandin's rather clinical account, I couldn't help wondering what No. 534 would be feeling as he approached his end. Would he have any inkling—a scent of blood, a sound of terror from up the line—that this was no ordinary day?

Grandin anticipated my question: "Does the animal know it's going to get slaughtered? I used to wonder that. So I watched them, going into the squeeze chute on the feedlot, getting their shots and going up the ramp at a slaughter plant. No difference. If they knew they were going to die, you'd see much more agitated behavior."

"Anyway, the conveyor is moving along at roughly the speed of a moving sidewalk. On a catwalk above stands the stunner. The stunner has a pneumatic-powered 'gun' that fires a steel bolt about seven inches long and the diameter of a fat pencil. He leans over and puts it smack in the middle of the forehead. When it's done correctly, it will kill the animal on the first shot."

For a plant to pass a McDonald's audit, the stunner needs to render animals "insensible" on the first shot 95 percent of the time. A second shot is allowed, but should that one fail, the plant flunks. At the line speeds at which meatpacking plants in the United States operate—390 animals are slaughtered every hour at National, which is not unusual— mistakes would seem inevitable, but Grandin insists that only rarely does the process break down.

"After the animal is shot while he's riding along, a worker wraps a chain around his foot and hooks it to an overhead trolley. Hanging upside down by one leg, he's carried by the trolley into the bleeding area, where the bleeder cuts his throat. Animal rights people say they're cutting live animals, but that's because there's a lot of reflex kicking." This is one of the reasons a job at a slaughter plant is the most dangerous in America. "What I look for is, Is the head dead? It should be flopping like a rag, with the tongue hanging out. He'd better not be trying to hold it up—then you've got a live one on the rail." Just in case, Grandin said, "they have another hand stunner in the bleed area."

Much of what happens next—the de-hiding of the animal, the tying off of its rectum before evisceration—is designed to keep the animal's feces from coming into contact with its meat. This is by no means easy to do, not when the animals enter the kill floor smeared with manure and 390 of them are eviscerated every hour. (Partly for this reason, European plants operate at much slower line speeds.) But since that manure is apt to contain lethal pathogens like E. coli 0157, and since the process of grinding together hamburger from hundreds of different carcasses can easily spread those pathogens across millions of burgers, packing plants now spend millions on "food safety"—which is to say, on the problem of manure in meat.

Most of these efforts are reactive: it's accepted that the animals will enter the kill floor caked with feedlot manure that has been rendered lethal by the feedlot diet. Rather than try to alter that diet or keep the animals from living in their waste or slow the line speed—all changes regarded as impractical—the industry focuses on disinfecting the manure that will inevitably find its way into the meat. This is the purpose of irradiation (which the industry prefers to call "cold pasteurization"). It is also the reason that carcasses pass through a hot steam cabinet and get sprayed with an antimicrobial solution before being hung in the cooler at the National Beef plant.

It wasn't until after the carcasses emerged from the cooler, thirty-six hours later, that I was allowed to catch up with them, in the grading room. I entered a huge arctic space resembling a monstrous dry cleaner's, with a seemingly endless overhead track conveying thousands of red-and-white carcasses. I quickly learned that you had to move smartly through this room or else be tackled by a 350-pound side of beef. The carcasses felt cool to the touch, no longer animals but meat.

Two by two, the sides of beef traveled swiftly down the rails, six pairs every minute, to a station where two workers—one wielding a small power saw, the other a long knife—made a single six-inch cut between the twelfth and thirteenth ribs, opening a window on the meat inside.

The carcasses continued on to another station, where a USDA inspector holding a round blue stamp glanced at the exposed rib eye and stamped the carcass's creamy white fat once, twice or—very rarely—three times: select, choice, prime.

For the Blair brothers, and for me, this is the moment of truth, for that stamp will determine exactly how much the packing plant will pay for each animal and whether the fourteen months of effort and expense will yield a profit.

Unless the cattle market collapses between now and June (always a worry these days), I stand to make a modest profit on No. 534. In February, the feedlot took a sonogram of his rib eye and ran the data through a computer program. The projections are encouraging: a live slaughter weight of 1,250, a carcass weight of 787 pounds and a grade at the upper end of choice, making him eligible to be sold at a premium as Certified Angus Beef. Based on the June futures price, No. 534 should be worth $944. (Should he grade prime, that would add another $75.)

I paid $598 for No. 534 in November; his living expenses since then come to $61 on the ranch and $258 for 160 days at the feedlot (including implant), for a total investment of $917, leaving a profit of $27. It's a razor-thin margin, and it could easily vanish should the price of corn rise or No. 534 fail to make the predicted weight or grade—say, if he gets sick and goes off his feed. Without the corn, without the antibiotics, without the hormone implant, my brief career as a cattleman would end in failure.

The Blairs and I are doing better than most. According to Cattle-Fax, a market-research firm, the return on an animal coming out of a feedlot has averaged just three dollars per head over the last twenty years.

"Some pens you make money, some pens you lose," Rich Blair said when I called to commiserate. "You try to average it out over time, limit the losses and hopefully make a little profit." He reminded me that a lot of ranchers are in the business "for emotional reasons—you can't be in it just for the money."

Now you tell me.

The manager of the packing plant has offered to pull a box of steaks from No. 534 before his carcass disappears into the trackless stream of commodity beef fanning out to America's supermarkets and restaurants this June. From what I can see, the Blair brothers, with the help of Poky Feeders, are producing meat as good as any you can find in an American supermarket. And yet there's no reason to think this steak will taste any different from the other high-end industrial meat I've ever eaten.

While waiting for my box of meat to arrive from Kansas, I've explored some alternatives to the industrial product. Nowadays you can find hormone-and antibiotic-free beef as well as organic beef, fed only grain grown without chemicals. This meat, which is often quite good, is typically produced using more grass and less grain (and so makes for healthier animals). Yet it doesn't fundamentally challenge the corn-feedlot system, and I'm not sure that an "organic feedlot" isn't, ecologically speaking, an oxymoron. What I really wanted to taste is the sort of preindustrial beef my grandparents ate—from animals that have lived most of their full-length lives on grass.

Eventually I found a farmer in the Hudson Valley who sold me a quarter of a grass-fed Angus steer that is now occupying most of my freezer. I also found ranchers selling grass-fed beef on the Web; Eatwild.com is a clearinghouse of information on grass-fed livestock, which is emerging as one of the livelier movements in sustainable agriculture.

I discovered that grass-fed meat is more expensive than supermarket beef. Whatever else you can say about industrial beef, it is remarkably cheap, and any argument for changing the system runs smack into the industry's populist arguments. Put the animals back on grass, it is said, and prices will soar; it takes too long to raise beef on grass, and there's not enough grass to raise them on, since the Western range lands aren't big enough to sustain America's one hundred million head of cattle. And besides, Americans have learned to love cornfed beef. Feedlot meat is also more consistent in both taste and supply and can be harvested twelve months a year. (Grass-fed cattle tend to be harvested in the fall, since they stop gaining weight over the winter, when the grasses go dormant.)

All of this is true. The economic logic behind the feedlot system is hard to refute. And yet so is the ecological logic behind a ruminant grazing on grass. Think what would happen if we restored a portion of the Corn Belt to the tall grass prairie it once was and grazed cattle on it. No more petrochemical fertilizer, no more herbicide, no more nitrogen runoff. Yes, beef would probably be more expensive than it is now, but would that necessarily be a bad thing? Eating beef every day might not be such a smart idea anyway—for our health, for the environment. And how cheap, really, is cheap feedlot beef? Not cheap at all, when you add in the invisible costs: of antibiotic resistance, environmental degradation, heart disease, E. coli poisoning, corn subsidies, imported oil and so on. All these are costs that grass-fed beef does not incur.

So how does grass-fed beef taste? Uneven, just as you might expect the meat of a nonindustrial animal to taste. One grass-fed tenderloin from Argentina that I sampled turned out to be the best steak I've ever eaten. But unless the meat is carefully aged, grass-fed beef can be tougher than feedlot beef—not surprisingly, since a grazing animal, which moves around in search of its food, develops more muscle and less fat. Yet even when the meat was tougher, its flavor, to my mind, was much more interesting. And specific, for the taste of every grass-fed animal is inflected by the place where it lived. Maybe it's just my imagination, but nowadays when I eat a feedlot steak, I can taste the corn and the fat, and I can see the view from No. 534's pen. I can't taste the oil, obviously, or the drugs, yet now I know they're there.

A considerably different picture comes to mind while chewing (and, OK, chewing) a grass-fed steak: a picture of a cow outside in a pasture eating the grass that has eaten the sunlight. Meat-eating may have become an act riddled with moral and ethical ambiguities, but eating a steak at the end of a short, primordial food chain comprising nothing more than ruminants and grass and light is something I'm happy to do and defend. We are what we eat, it is often said, but of course that's only part of the story. We are what what we eat eats too.

FORTUNE'S SMILE:
WORLD SERIES OF POKER

James McManus

★ ★ ★

BETTING BIG AT THE WORLD SERIES OF POKER

I flew in on American Airlines, the nickname for two pocket aces, and I take that as a very good sign. I've got my poker books, sunglasses, and lucky hats, including the White Sox cap I got married in. My room at Binion's Horseshoe overlooks downtown Las Vegas's dolorous, last-gasp attempt to keep up with the billion-dollar resorts five miles south on the Strip, which in the last few years have siphoned off most of the city's thirty-four million annual tourists with pixilated facsimiles of Paris and Bellagio, Imperial Rome and Renaissance Venice—all the more reason to be happily ensconced way up here at the Horseshoe. Even better this evening is that the 2000 World Series of Poker is in full swing downstairs. Tomorrow, with a $4,000 stake, I'm going to try to win a seat in the million-dollar championship event, due to begin in five days.

I ain't superstitious, as Willie Dixon once sang, but my second daughter, Beatrice, was conceived in Bellagio, Italy, so my lucky hats include a sun visor sporting the logo of the local version. I've also been playing poker for thirty-nine years now, everything from penny-ante family games in the Bronx to $80 to $160 hold'em at the Bellagio, but never at anything close to this level. The championship event costs $10,000 to enter, and always draws the top two or three hundred pros in the world. I'm good, but not that good. I was taught by my uncle and grandfather, both named Tom Madden, then got schooled in caddy shacks by guys with names like Doc and Tennessee. My current home game in Chicago involves day-traders, attorneys, a transit-systems planner, and a pizza delivery man. It's a game that I fare pretty well in, but I still have no reason to doubt T. J. Cloutier, the former Canadian Football League tight end who is now one of poker's best players, when he says, "The World Series is a conglomeration of local champions. There's Joe Blow from Iowa who's the champion in his game at home; hundreds of local champions like him come to Vegas to play the World Series. But it's like the difference in going from playing high-school football to college football: It's a big step up."

To reduce the long odds that I'll only embarrass myself, I've spent the last year practicing on a computer while studying the four poker bibles: *Cloutier's Championship No-Limit and Pot-Limit Hold'em*, cowritten with Tom McEvoy, the 1983 world champion; David Sklansky's seminal *Theory of Poker and Hold'em Poker for Advanced Players*, the latter cowritten with Mason Malmuth; and Doyle Brunson's *Super/System: A Course in Power Poker*, cowritten with (among others) Sklansky, Chip Reese, and Bobby Baldwin, the 1978 champion and currently president of the Bellagio—which is good luck right there, I figure, as I switch on the light in the bathroom. These little yellow horseshoes on the shampoo and soap might help, too.

The crowded main tournament area has forty-five oval poker tables, each surrounded by ten or eleven chairs. The size of a grammar-school gym, the room has an eighteen-foot ceiling fitted with cameras and monitors but not quite enough ventilation for the number of players who smoke. Posters along the walls give results from previous events, including a color photograph of each winner. There's precious little else in the way of adornment, no music besides the droning announcements of poker activity and locust-like clacking of chips. Shangri-la!

The $3,000 no-limit hold'em event starts tomorrow at noon, so that's when I'll play my first satellite—while the best two or three hundred players are otherwise engaged. Before I go to bed, though, I need to take a few notes on the action. In satellites for the Big One, ten people pay $1,000 apiece and play a winner-take-all freeze-out. Which will make me a 9 to 1 underdog tomorrow, assuming I'm evenly matched with my adversaries, and of course I will not be. But a night's sleep and diluted competition will give me the best, or least bad, chance of winning.

Most of the satellites have $300 buy-ins and generate a seat in tomorrow's event, but one table along the near rail is reserved for $1,000 action. A harried blond floorperson with a microphone—her nametag says CAROL—is trying to fill the next one. "Just one more seat, players! Chance to win a seat in the Big One. . . ." Nine hopefuls already have chips stacked in front of them, along with their Walkmans and water bottles, ashtrays and fans. As Fyodor Mikhailovich confessed to his second bride, Anna Grigoryevna, who'd conquered his heart while taking down *The Gambler* in shorthand: "Once I hear the clatter of the chips, I almost go into convulsions. Hear hear!" Down I sit, forking over $1,015, the $15 being the juice. Tired schmired. Once I receive my own $1,000 stack of green ($25) and brown ($100) chips and the dealer starts shuffling, I've never felt any more ready.

Hold'em involves nine or ten players receiving two facedown cards each (called "the pocket"), followed by three faceup shared or "community" cards ("the flop"), a fourth community card ("the turn" or "fourth street"), and a fifth community card ("the river" or "fifth street").[1] Two rotating antes called "blinds," small and large, initiate a round of betting before the flop, with a round of betting after the flop, after fourth street, and after fifth street. Starting at $25 and $50, the blinds double every twenty minutes. Since the game is no-limit, a player may bet anything from $50 up to all his chips at any point in the sequence. No-limit action seldom reaches a showdown on fifth street, where, if it did, the best five-card poker hand wins. Most often,

---

1. A guide to poker hands and terms is on pages 453–454.

an intimidating wager before or just after the flop gets no callers, and the bettor receives the whole pot.

Things get much trickier when factoring in your position. Acting last from the dealer's button (which rotates hand by hand) is the strongest position, since you see everyone else's action before deciding whether to fold, call, or raise, and can therefore get away with playing slightly weaker hands; whereas only big pairs, ace-king, or suited connecting face cards (Q♦ J♦, for example) are likely to make money played from an early position. As early shades clockwise into middle, then late position, the valences of wagering assert themselves and less savvy players get soundly outmaneuvered.

My satellite rivals are mostly middle-aged guys of all stripes: the anxious, the collected, the pocky, the sleek; ex-beatniks, ex-jocks, and ex-hippies. So I feel right at home on all counts. Although one of us will stroll off with everyone else's money, the table has a friendly, if not quite munificent, vibe. When someone gets edged at the showdown, the usual response is, "Good hand." We also tip the cocktail waitress for one another. None of this fools me, however.

A gray-haired Vietnamese woman in round mirrored shades has taken the lead, winning three of the first eleven pots. Doing less well is the toothless varmint in seat one, just to the left of the dealer. His scraggly beard starts high on his cheekbones and covers his Adam's apple, with scalp hair of similar aspect, the entire gnarled package tentatively winched together by a powder-blue UNLV cap. Yours truly sports poker face, titanium shades, and Bellagio visor but still hasn't entered one pot. Him too scared.

Most of my no-limit experience is on Masque's World Series of Poker program and Bob Wilson's Tournament Texas Hold'em. By playing hundreds of thousands of hands (and winning three virtual tournaments), I've sharpened my card sense and money-management skills, and developed a not-bad sense of no-limit wagering rhythms. Yet computer play affords no opportunity to read faces and body language for "tells," and may actually diminish the mental, fiscal, and physical stamina required for live-action poker. The $1,015 I'm risking is real, with 9 to 1 odds that

I'll lose every cent. I can't sit here with T.J. and Brunson and Sklansky open in my lap, thumbing an index or two for advice about playing an unsuited ace-jack.* The main thing I need here is feel, and for this, books and computers can't help much. Right now the pot has been raised by the muscular Arab in the salt-stained tortoiseshell Wayfarers, not Masque's "Player #4." What is Stains thinking that I'm thinking that he's thinking? Is his visceral aplomb all an act? The only things I'm sure of is that he wants my money more than Player #4 ever could and that he's already knocked out Madame Ho. But if I can't look into his eyes, at least I can observe how hard his lungs are working. If I've tuned him in right, I can feel it.

Right now from middle position I'm playing A♦ J♥, having called Stains's $200 preflop raise. The flop has come ace, five, king—all of spades. With flushes abroad, there's a bet and three calls ahead of me. That no one has raised makes my pot odds about 12 to 1, with my shot at a full house a lot worse than one in thirteen. But I call, God knows why, and fourth street comes up J♠, giving me aces and jacks. After Stains bets another $200, two hands get folded, but the guy on the button re-raises. Two other calls on my right, then a fold, then . . . the next thing I know the dealer is staring at me. So is Stains. So is the Pakistani guy to his left. With only four outs (the two remaining aces and jacks), folding aces-up makes me groan with irrational pride, but when the dealer turns over J♣, I no longer have a good feeling.

I need to take a piss about now, but I hold it, and the poker gods deem fit to reward me. Fifteen hands go by in which I can do no wrong. I win six good-sized pots, three in a row toward the end, using check-raises, semi-bluffs, traps—the whole works. By midnight I have $4,900, almost half the chips on the table. The slender Pakistani guy, who's named Hasan Habib, has roughly $2,700; a big, bearded guy named Tom Jacobs about $2,400.

With the blinds at $400 and $800, Jacobs moves all-in on the third

---

* In a poker tournament one plays hundreds of hands a day; the hands discussed in this article have been reconstructed as accurately as I and others can recall.

hand we play. Habib calls, turning over two sevens. (In heads-up action, when one player goes all-in usually both expose their hole cards since no more betting is possible.) When Jacobs flips over A-10, Habib becomes an 11 to 9 favorite, and I get to watch the do-or-die "race" from the sideline: J-J-3, followed by a trey, then a deuce. I'm down to one adversary. The only problem is that it's Hasan Habib, who finished second last month at the World Poker Open no-limit event down in Tunica, Mississippi. And he now has me slightly outchipped.

We fence for a half-dozen hands, neither of us willing to call preflop bets, before I discover a pair of queens peering back up between my thumbs. Betting first, I can try to trap Hasan by (1) merely calling his big blind, (2) putting in a modest raise, or (3) moving all-in, hoping that he (a) calls, and (b) doesn't have aces or kings. I decide to try door number three. And he calls, then puts the frighteners on me by turning over K♦ and ... 10♦. When the board fails to improve either of our hands, the dealer yells, "Winner on table 64!" Yawning yet flabbergasted, I sit back and try to relax. Carol takes my name and address, then issues a printed receipt for $10,001, the last buck being the token entry fee. *Event 25*, it says, *World Championship, 5/15/2000*, and assigns me to Table 53, Seat 6. I'm in.

Besides drawing record numbers of entries, the 2000 WSOP, I've discovered, has already produced a few of what might be called cultural achievements. The $1,500 seven-stud bracelet, along with the $135,975 first prize, went to Jerri Thomas, a forty-one-year-old from Cincinnati who had given birth only three months earlier. She and her husband, Harry, are now only the second married couple with a WSOP bracelet apiece. The following event, limit Omaha, was won by Ivo Donev, a former chess pro from Austria who'd spent the past two years reading Sklansky and McEvoy and practicing on Wilson software.

A week ago, on May 4, Jennifer Harman won the no-limit deuce-to-seven event. Because of its steep degree of difficulty, the event drew only thirty entrants, but the deuce (in which the lowest hand wins) is the title poker professionals covet almost as much as the Big One. No satellites get played for it, so only by putting up $5,000 can the cockiest, best-bankrolled players compete. Harman is a blond, thirty-twoish, dog-crazy gamine who plays high-stakes lowball games every night with the likes of Brunson, Chip Reese, and Annie Duke, but she'd never played no-limit deuce. Neither had Duke, for that matter, but that didn't faze either of them. They took a ten-minute lesson from Howard Lederer, Duke's brother, and ten hours later Harman had the bracelet and $146,250. And then, on May 5, Phillip Ivey took home the Omaha bracelet, defeating Thomas "Amarillo Slim" Preston with a series of fifth-street miracles at the final table, coming back from a 5 to 1 chip deficit. In thirty years of World Series play, during which he's won four bracelets, Slim had never lost at a final table. Playing out of Atlantic City, the twenty-three-year-old Ivey has been on the tournament circuit for less than six months but is now the only African American with a WSOP bracelet.

The World Series of Poker (and tournament poker in general) was invented by Benny Binion in the spring of 1970. He simply invited a few of his high-rolling cronies to compete among themselves and then vote for the best all-around player; the winner, Johnny Moss, received a small trophy and whatever money he'd earned at the table. The current freeze-out structure, which continues until one player has all the chips, was instated in 1971, and Moss won again, this time taking home $30,000. The next year's winner, Amarillo Slim, won $80,000, wrote a book, and went on the talk-show circuit, boosting the public's interest in tourna-ment poker. By the time Brunson became the second repeat champion in 1977, first prize had quadrupled to $340,000. It was up to $700,000 by 1988, the second year Johnny Chan won. From 1991 until last year, first prize was an even $1 million, with the number of entries and total prize money steadily climbing. Last year's championship event drew 393 en-tries, with second place paying a record $768,625.

Almost from the WSOP's inception, the total prize money awarded has dwarfed the purses of Wimbledon, the Masters, and the Kentucky Derby. There are now twenty-four preliminary events. The buy-in to the Big One remains $10,000, but these days the majority of players gain entry by winning satellites or super-satellites, mini-tournaments de-signed to democratize the competition; they are also thought to be the most legitimate route in, since they reward poker skill instead of deep pockets, though the two often work hand in hand.

T minus seventy minutes, and counting. After half an hour of lazy backstroke in the rooftop pool, I open my Cloutier and start cramming for my first big exam since I was an undergrad twenty-seven years ago. I'm reviewing all twelve of T.J.'s practice hands, poring over underlined phrases to see if I've absorbed the logic of his analyses. "Cardinal rule number one in no-limit hold'em is: If you limp with aces, you will never get broke with aces." And this, on the luck factor: "You can set up all the plays in the world, you can play perfectly on a hand, and you can still lose. And there's nothing that you can do about it." The rest of his advice I've tried to reduce to four memorizable aphorisms.

1. Don't call big bets; fold or raise.

2. Avoid trouble hands like K♦ Q♣, K♥ J♣, or any ace with a kicker smaller than a king in the first four positions.

3. Don't always steal-raise in obvious bluffing positions (the small blind, the button), and play big hands (even A♦ A♣) slowly from them.

4. Drawing hands are death.

This last one means: Don't risk your tournament life chasing big pairs with small ones or medium suited connectors, as is often correct in a limit game. You'd win a big pot if you filled your straight or flush, but aggressive no-limit players make you pay too high a price to draw against them. Mistakes in no-limit tend to be costlier by an order of magnitude, and the chips that you lose in a tournament can't be replenished by digging into your pocket. Amen.

Furious satellite action is still under way as I arrive in the tournament area just before noon, with the overflow crowd getting denser by the second. Judging from their faces, a few of these hombres have been playing all night. Dealers raise the betting levels every three minutes instead of every twenty, eliminating players tout de suite but reducing the caliber of poker to little better than all-in crapshoots. Railbirds are six or eight deep, clapping and whistling when their hombre survives, as four camera crews roam the aisles. One guy they're focusing on is tournament director Bob Thompson, a silver-haired cowboy with a dulcet basso drawl. With his big jaw and narrow-eyed gaze, he effortlessly personifies the American West, Texas hold'em in particular. And that's what we came here to play: cowboy poker. Thompson runs the floor with his son, Robert, and Tom Elias; his daughter, Cathi Wood, coordinates the administration. Her fact sheet says that if five hundred entrants sign up, nine players more than the usual thirty-six will be paid; first place will pay $1.5 million, second will pay almost $900,000, and all other payouts will escalate. Her father just announced that last year's record of 393 has been shattered, then pointed to the line of new entrants with ten grand in their pocket still snaking three-players thick out the door. Clearly no cards will be in the air for a spell.

In the meantime, Puggy Pearson, the 1973 champion, holds court in a gold-and-lemon silk Genghis Khan outfit, including a crown with tasseled earflaps to go with his broad smile, eponymous pug nose, and Abe Lincoln mustacheless beard. Elsewhere I see little black dresses, tuxedos, and a short, wild-eyed black guy in a cloth airman's helmet hung with a dozen pink or yellow rabbit's feet. The leading sartorial choice, though, is Poker Practical: baseball cap, sunglasses, sateen casino jacket. Among so many corn-fed middle-aged guys in goatees and Levi's, Slim still looks clear-eyed and rangy at seventy-seven, bedecked in pressed khaki trousers, platinum belt buckle, mother-of-pearl buttons on his crisp cowboy shirt.

However unlikely this sounds, the World Series of Poker has evolved from its good-old-boy roots into a stronghold of, yes, functional multiculturalism, proving, if nothing else, that there is such a thing. The field is an ecumenical crazy quilt of players from twenty-three countries on all six inhabited continents, among them Scotty Nguyen (the goldbedecked 1998 champion) from Saigon, Hasan Habib from Karachi, and, from Pamplona, a Carlos Fuentes. Any all-name team would also have to include Tab Thiptinnakon, Jesus Ferguson, Exxon Feyznia, David Plastik, Chip Jett, Spring Cheong, Sam Grizzle, Lin Poon Wang, and

Huckleberry Seed, the 1996 champion. Among toned jocks like Seed and Layne Flack and Daniel Negreanu we have equal numbers of the obese and the skeletal, plus plenty of folks who are youthful or ancient, wheelchair-bound or in dance shoes. Evangelical Christians are competing with Larry Flynt, CEOs and dot-com millionaires against call girls and poker dealers, gay men and lesbians, cowgirls and golfers and artists, black poker professionals and Jewish physicians, Jewish pros and black docs, at least one Aramaic scholar, and several Vietnamese boat people. All told our number is 512, breaking last year's record by 119 and bringing the purse to a staggering $5.12 million.

I fail to recognize any stars at my table, cause enough for slightly less pessimism. After showing our receipts, we each receive a stack of $10,000 in chips: one orange five-thousand, three white-and-royal-blue "dimes," two black-and-yellow five-hundreds, and seven slate-colored "ones" topped by a dozen green "quarters." The cards finally go in the air at 1:35, with the blinds at $25 and $50, no antes. Our dealer flicks out a card apiece to determine who starts on the button—and, with the sad-eyed king of spades, that would be *moi*. On the first hand, I look down and find A♣ 6♣. No less than five limp in front of me; i.e., they call the big blind by tossing $50 each into the pot, trying to get a cheap look at the flop. Not on *moi*'s watch! I make it $250 to go, get no callers, and, with $10,325, take the lead.

Not for long, of course. I start playing far too impulsively, overriding my own blueprint by entering pots with small pairs, K♥ J♦, or 5♥ 4♥, getting smoked. Is someone else pushing my chips in or making my mouth say, "Let's raise it"? The main person making me pay is an un-fearsome cowpoke five seats to my right. Wearing the same puzzled grin, he rakes in pot after pot. The worst hammering comes when I turn an overset of queens—make three queens on fourth street, that is, with no higher card on the board—and bet $2,000. Henrik calls. Even when I fail to improve on fifth street, I feel that six titties, or three queens, are worth another $2,000, a foolish amount at this stage. My logic is that if I could only get Henrik to call—I'd put him on two little pairs—I'd be back up to even: lesson learned, tabula rasa, ready to start playing solid.

But not only does the little shit call me, he shows me a seven-high straight.

By the first fifteen-minute break at 3:35 I'm down to $2,200 and change. I skulk up to my room and call my wife, Jennifer, in St. Louis. I give her the ball-crushing news, and she sighs. What I need is a kiss and a head rub, she says, but all she can provide is a suggestion to page through my brag book, the 4-by-6 photo album with pictures of our girls and my two other children. "Just keep it in your pocket and think about us." It's truly a sorry idea, but since I don't have a better one I take the book with me downstairs. My goal all along has been to go to bed tonight still alive, and it looks like I'm not gonna make it. Yet I have absolutely zero reason to be surprised by this turn of events. Competing against inspired professionals, I'm not even heeding my pedigreed battle plan. Entering this event was an act of mind-bending hubris, so the only surprise is that I still have some chips to my name.

As we're sitting back down to the tables, word comes that Harman, Ivey, Seed, and Flack have already bitten the dust. So that's something. But have I "beaten" these people? Not really, since we only have to take on eight players at a time. What I've done is outlast them. I should therefore be thrilled to be stroking my orange-free stack while Geraldo yucks it up for the cameras.

The players I'm sitting with couldn't care less. All they want is to eliminate me and one another. But not me! Because as soon as I put the brag book next to my chips and open it to the page on which Jennifer reads *The Little Mouse, The Red Ripe Strawberry,* and *The Big Hungry Bear* to our daughter Beatrice, my pocket cards start to get better. I manage to steal a few blinds, then take down a decent-sized pot when two pairs hold up over kings. More important, I've persuaded myself at long last to fold all my trouble hands. With my new leather ass and my talismans, I manage to hang around until the nine o'clock dinner break, when I've scratched my way up to $16,450. I dash to my room, call Jennifer again in St. Louis, and brag. And she lets me.

Back at the poker table, I grab myself by the collar and demand that

I wait for big hands in all but the last three positions; and I listen. But escalating blinds and a stretch of cold cards grind my stack down to $13,825 by midnight. We're still at Level 4, anteing $25 a hand with $100 and $200 blinds. Down to $11,700, I can't wait forever for a hand. With the blinds at $200 to $400 and $50 antes, it's costing me $1,050 a round just to sit here and fold all my rags. But finally, one off the button, I peek between my knuckles and discover J♥ J♦. Ooh la la. Raising to $1,000, I get three callers, and the flop comes K-J-8 rainbow. Even with the over-card (king) and all these damn callers, I bet $1,500. Seat seven folds, but the Japanese yuppie in seat eight makes it $3,000. Then the shaved head in one cold-calls both bets. Jesus Christ! It's gonna cost me every last chip to keep playing this hand, and without the mortal nuts (at this point, a "set" of three kings) I'm petrified of set over set; even worse are the obvious straight draws. Yet if I don't get my chips in with this hand, when am I going to? Never, I decide, as I call, then watch fourth street come a darling, a beautissimous, a sideways-infinity 8, providing my first full house of the day—in two days, actually. I nudge the rest of my chips ten inches forward. "All-in." Japan meditates on his options for a minute, then folds, flashing two queens in disgust. Sayonara! Shaved Head, however, smooth-calls me. Since I'm all-in, no further betting is possible, so we both turn over our hole cards. His are 10♣ 9♣, not the cowboys or the other two eights, so it's over: Any straight he might make will still lose to jacks full of eights—a full house. The pot comes to $36,900. Stacking it next to my brag book, I'd love nothing better than to trudge off to bed, but we still have fifty-two minutes left at Level 5. I order hot chocolate and sit tight, once folding pocket sevens from middle position even though no one had raised yet. Me solid!

Bob Thompson calls a halt to our march at nine after two. Sheets are passed around with places to record our chip count. Mine comes to $35,325. Tom Elias recounts them, signs my sheet, stuffs chips and sheet into a Ziploc bag, staples it shut. Done. Still alive. It's too late to call my wife, but my rush while it lasted—one hand!—has gladdened my heart as much as any sonnet or fuck or narcotic or shot glass of silver Patron, as much as any three of those things, though it still takes 150mg of Tra-zodone washed down by room-service Cabernet to finally fall off, I'm so wired. . . .

Tuesday morning, after thirty-six laps in the pool, a fast shower, room-service oatmeal and OJ, all in the service of tuning my nerves, muscles, and glucose, I arrive back downstairs to the sunlit fact of my name on page one of the five-page, single-spaced leader board. Two hundred fourteen still have chips, and my $35,325 is good for thirty-eighth place. With par at $23,933, this puts me in pretty good shape, though Mehul Chaudhari, the leader, has me almost tripled with $92,500. My satellite rivals, Hasan and Tom, are in fifth and sixteenth, respectively. Rising star Kathy Liebert is seventh, T.J. nineteenth, Noel Furlong right above me in thirty-sixth. Bunched near the middle are Hayden, Duke, Enright, and Erik Seidel, runner-up to Chan in 1988. All of these folks are my heroes.

By the end of today we'll have to lose 169 more of us, but every survivor will be guaranteed at least $15,000. Am I ready for this? Maybe not. My first big mistake is walking pocket kings, failing to protect them by raising in hopes of building a pot, then getting caught by a straight on the river. Exactly when, I have to wonder, did I become a person on whom everything is lost? This game is designed to blast draws from the battlefield, imbecile! Down to $28,000, I resolve, for the umpteenth time, to play solid poker—to stay out of pots until I find what Sklansky calls the Group 1 or 2 hands (aces or kings down through suited K-Q), then attack. For the next ninety minutes, it works. I also manage, from later positions, to slip into a few unraised pots with suited connectors, two of which turn into flushes. Bottom line? Ninety-eight grand. If I hadn't wasted a call with A♦ 3♣ on the previous hand, I'd now have the magic one large.

After dinner I get moved to seat two of a table with Hasan in seat one, J. J. Bortner in three, Kathy Liebert in four, Mickey Appleman in six, and Daniel Negreanu in eight. Scary, but also more fun. Bortner keeps a plastic baby rattler coiled atop her stacks that she's quite fond of shoving toward the pot, snake and all. Appleman is one of the game's veteran pros and melancholy philosophers. He used to work with alcoholics in Harlem, but he's been on the pro-poker circuit for twenty-five years now. He's wearing a white Massada baseball cap over his ash-blond Groucho Marx moptop, and losing. The goateed Negreanu is whippet thin under his Sharks jersey and www.ultimatebet.com hat. Fresh off a win at the U.S. Poker Championship, he's brimming with humor and confidence. "Let's be honest here," he tells Hasan, after a flop comes off A♣ 7♠ 7♥. "You've got the seven. Why walk it?" As Hasan tries to keep a straight face, Daniel grabs a dozen orange chips, winds up like he's getting ready to throw a left hook, and wings the chips into the pot, which he goes on to win with A♦ 10♣.

With sixty players left, I'm back down to $82,000, so I play extratight for a stretch, waiting for a monster I can sic on these big shots. The leaders are Duke, Liebert, Habib, and a guy called Captain Tom Franklin, all with around a quarter of a million in chips. With the blinds at $1,500–$3,000 and $500 antes, it's costing me nine grand per round. So the last thing I'm in the mood for is a photo op, but here, as the cameras shark in, we have Slim standing up behind Liebert, holding a butcher knife to his throat. Turns out that back in 1972 Slim reportedly threatened to cut his throat if a woman ever won the tournament. (What he said was that he'd do it if a particular woman won, but the misquote makes much better copy.) I'm sure Kathy wants to concentrate on poker, but she's being a pretty good sport, though I'd be smiling, too, if I had big straight white teeth and $270,000 in front of me.

With a dozen eliminations to go till we reach forty-five, I basically hang around for two hours, actively avoiding confrontations. Doesn't work. By the time we're down to forty-seven, I have only $36,000 left, almost exactly where I started the day. But if I can only survive two more ousters, I'll not only be good for $15,000 but will be on a freeroll for the $1.5 million.

At this stage we're forced to play hand for hand, holding up the next shuffle until all six tables complete the previous hand, this to keep short stacks from stalling. My table is already a terrifying convocation, but when the player in the eight seat goes out, he's replaced by—oh, shit—T. J. Cloutier. It gets worse. More than content to just sit here and wait, I somehow get forced into a series of make-or-break jousts. The first comes when, one off the button, I find A♣ J♥. T.J. has already raised it to $5,000, and both the tanned, blond cowboy in nine and Hasan have folded. Don't call big bets, I remind myself. Fold or raise. Yet I'm also aware that strong players target weak players, especially when the pressure is on, and my guess is that this is what T.J. is up to. I call. Jerry, the mustachioed Latin dealer, raps the felt, turns the flop: A♦ 9♣ 6♥. T.J. stares at me, checking. If he's got a bigger ace I am cooked, ditto for A-9 or A-6, but with top pair and a decent kicker I still have to bet $20,000, having put him on an ace with a medium kicker. I meet his warm glare for a second or two, then study the smoke-marbled distance. I must appear terribly frightened, however, because T.J. moves in with alacrity. His stack is smaller than mine, but only by three or four thousand. I call.

Now it's old T.J. who don't look so happy. "I think you've got me outkicked," he growls hoarsely, then exhales a yard-long plume of smoke as I show him A♣ J♥. He makes me wait while snuffing his Salem, then turns over . . . A♥ 10♠! My heart hurdles four of my ribs.

The turn is 9♦, giving both T.J. and me aces up, with my J♥ still outkicking his 10♠. Only a ten will beat me, I figure; any other card comes on fifth street, I win. Instead of going out two off the money, I'm a 44 to 3 favorite not only to win a big pot but to punch out the number one badass. Jerry raps the felt, turns over . . . an ace. Whew! The crowd around us gasps, and I hear Liebert say, "Oh my God!" With so much hot blood in my head, I'm able to parse neither the buzz of commentary nor the looks on the other seven players. All I know is that T.J. is grinning. Even after Jerry announces, "Split pot," and is echoed by dozens of railbirds, it takes me a moment to fathom that we both just made aces full of nines. Jerry shoves me my measly half-share of the chips. I try to restack them by color, but my fingers don't work very well.

For the next thirty minutes, Liebert keeps the table pretty much under control, maneuvering her $300,000 stack like Rommel in a short desert war, blitzkrieging our antes and blinds, setting us all-in when we draw. Down to forty-six we are still hand for hand, and sometimes the suspensions last eight or ten minutes. When I try to stand up, the tendons in my legs yank me forward. As I hobble into the men's room, Jesus Ferguson is manning a urinal in his trademark unreadable getup: full beard and yard-long auburn locks under black cowboy hat slung low over wraparound shades. "Still have chips?" he asks cordially. Sort of, I tell him. What about you? "I guess I'm still doing all right. Hey, good luck." Heading out after washing our hands, I notice that his feet are adorned with elegant little black dancer's shoes. Strange! Before I sit back down, I try to survey the other five tables. Jacobs and Duke have big stacks, though Liebert still rules the whole tournament. The tiniest stacks are at my table, where Appleman is down to $4,500. Another round of blinds and he's through.

Three hands later I flop two pair in a heads-up pot with Hasan and get elated all over again—until Hasan sets me all-in. The two diamonds on board are what scares me. If he makes his flush while I fail to improve, it'll be me going out instead of Appleman, and in the worst of all possible places. I've put Hasan on a flush draw and inferred that he's semi-bluffing before his own hand gets made—or does not. Only a fool wouldn't do so with those scary-looking diamonds out there, and Hasan is no fool. So I call. And my sevens and sixes hold up, doubling me through to $78,000.

During the next break I notice that Andy Glazer, the *Detroit Free Press* gaming columnist, is talking to Jesus. When I introduce myself and ask for a cigarette, it turns out that neither of them smokes. I tell Ferguson that I'm shocked: in spite of the dance shoes, he looks like a Marlboro Man all the way. In fact, he's a gentle-voiced, day-trading wonk with a new Ph.D. in computer science from UCLA who happens to love ballroom dancing; the outfit is "just for disguise." Does he prefer to be called Jesus or Chris? "Both." Both? "Either one. I like them both the same." Helpful! Andy now suggests that I might want to slow down at this point. I tell him that the last thing I want is to keep mixing it up, but the table's not giving me much choice. "Plus my hand keeps grabbing the chips and tossing them into—"

"Almost as though you've been hypnotized."

"Ri-i-ight . . ."

"We understand perfectly," says Jesus.

With me on the button and Liebert in the big blind, Appleman folds one more hand, leaving him with barely enough to post the next blind. The next player, Roman Abinsay, pushes his entire $10,500 into the pot. Appleman, of course, desperately wants someone to knock out Abinsay, in forty-sixth place, but no one ahead of me can call; neither can I, with 7♠ 4♦. Which leaves it up to Liebert to play sheriff, especially since she already has $3,500 invested in the pot. And that's what she does, calling and turning over K♣ Q♦. Appleman's long face never once changes expression, even when Abinsay turns over . . . aces. Liebert sighs. The flop comes Q♠ 7♥ 3♥, leaving her dead to either of the two remaining queens. The turn comes a seven, apparently helping neither of them. When a king comes on fifth street, some overexcited railbirds start chirping that we're done for the night, and I'd love to believe them. But another quick look at the board makes it clear what Liebert already knows: that kings and queens loses to aces and whatever pair.

On we play. I'm more determined than ever to stay on the sidelines. Even when under the gun I find aces, I think about mucking them, but it's too easy to imagine kicking myself fifteen minutes from now, let alone fifteen years. Deciding to walk them, I bet "only" $10,000 and get called by the cowboy. When the flop comes J♠ 4♥ 2♠, I bet $12,000 more, expecting to win a nice pot then and there, though with part of me hoping he'll raise. When he smooth-calls again, it finally dawns on me that I may well be trapped by three jacks. Fourth street is 5♥, giving me an inside straight draw to go with my aces. I can't put the cowboy on anything higher than jacks, since he wouldn't have called $24,000 with A-3. I almost prefer he has jacks as my right hand picks up fifteen blue chips, breaking them down into three piles . . . and Cowboy smooth-calls me again! Thank God the river card is 3♠, backdooring me into a wheel (giving me, in other words, an unexpected five-high straight on the final two cards). No way is Cowboy holding 6-3, and since the board hasn't paired, he couldn't have filled his three jacks. I check, hoping he'll at least represent the 6-3 and I can raise him all-in. He had me trapped back there on the flop and the turn, but now I believe I have him. When he shows me two pocket jacks, I turn over one ace for the wheel, and then, for good measure, the other one, which Cowboy doesn't seem to appreciate.

All of a sudden I have almost $200,000, second at this table only to Liebert's four large. I'm reminding myself to avoid her, in fact, when, back on the button again, I find A♦ Q♠. When it gets checked around to me, I raise it to $12,000. After Bortner folds, who else but Liebert re-raises to $24,000. She does this, of course, with an absolute minimum of anima. Zero. She could care less, she couldn't care less: take your pick. Assuming again that the big-time pros want to push me around, but failing for the dozenth time to heed T.J.'s advice about raising or folding, I call.

The flop of 2♠ 7♣ Q♣ bails me out, in a way. Because when Kathy, the reraiser, taps a slender pink finger to check, I catch a faint whiff of check-raise. As the odor becomes more insistent, my overmatched brain seizes up—*chcheckcheckch*—but my thumb and middle finger somehow manage to bet $20,000 without even pausing to consult with their boss. Kathy stares me down through my polarized lenses like some chick laser surgeon zinging my capillaries. Do they smoke? Do they twitch? I don't know. The hand I'd put her on was a medium pair, but now I ain't so sure—not that I was sure in the first place, though I doubt she reraised me preflop with Q-2 or Q-7. Whatever queen she's playing I've got her tied or outkicked, but what if she's slow-playing two of them? After weighing and squeezing her miniature blue-and-white soccer ball for over a minute, she cuts out a stack of fifteen orange chips, fondling them as though ready to move them forward, all the while watching me closely. *Zzzt . . . zzzzzzt . . .* I stare away from the table for ten or twelve seconds, then pointedly look back at her. I like her a lot, and she knows that.

When she finally mucks, I flash her my Q♠ in what I hope will be taken as a comradely gesture. "Show one, show all," Abinsay demands. I pick up both my cards from the edge of the muck and flip them over. Kathy nods twice but doesn't look happy. She also makes a point of sliding her own cards facedown toward the dealer.

Two hands later, after T.J. has raised to $10,000, I find an eminently foldable A♠ 5♥, but I can't shake the feeling that my new favorite author wants to pilfer our antes and blinds. The longer I think about it the more convinced I become, so I call. My heart thumps out signals visible all over my body—fingers, neck, pupils, complexion—of how nervous I am, so I try to persuade myself that they can also be read as elation, as in, "Yes! I'm finally gonna get T.J.'s chips!" I camouflage my relief when the flop comes A♦ 3♦ 2♣, giving me an inside straight draw to go with top pair and pitiful kicker. When T.J. raps his fist on the table I'm convinced I'll be check-raised, but even if he comes back over the top of me I've got enough chips to survive. I pluck two pink $10,000 chips from the top of one stack and toss them forward. Take that!

Now it's T.J. who's staring me down, an altogether more visceral experience than my face-off with Kathy. While there's nothing overt about it, the man comfortably embodies a lethal threat, even from the seated position. If it happens to suit him, he can reach across the table and rupture key vertebrae with his bare hand, and everyone sitting here understands this down in our helical enzymes—my helical enzymes, at least, not to mention my looping and straight ones. Doing my best to meet his jagged scrutiny, I decide not to taunt him about his run-on sentences or the stench from his Salems. The best way to take care of that is to break him and make him go home.

And he mucks it, God love him! Showing me Q♣ Q♠, he seems both proud of his laydown and irked at the gall of me, slick little East Coast book-learned weasel that I am, even if it's his goddamn book I've been learning from. It's impossible not to think of Jack Palance staring down Billy Crystal: "I crap bigger'n you. . . ." Amid the ensuing buzz, I overhear Andy Glazer speaking about "how spooky things are getting. A few minutes ago he was a writer trying to hang on, and suddenly he's messing with T.J. and Kathy?!" With T.J. perhaps. I certainly didn't think of myself as messing with Kathy. I read them both as messing with me, each time with less than a premium hand. All I did was refuse to lay down my strong hands just because they were who they were and I didn't have the absolute nuts. So even after I get pocket kings cracked by Appleman's K♣ 10♥ when the board makes him a straight, everything's still copacetic. A few hands later an unfortunate gentleman at another table gets busted in forty-sixth place and it's time to call it a morning. And this time I do wake up Jennifer.

Eight and a half hours later I have unwelcome company in the pool on the roof. The strong swimmer splashing away my tranquility is a big, dark-haired guy with a mustache. When he finally climbs the hell out, I recognize him as Umberto Brenes, a Costa Rican player I met, along with his younger brother, Alex, back on Monday. He'd shown me his World Series bracelet, for the 1993 seven-card stud event, and invited me down to his poker club in the Hotel Corobici in San Jose. I saw him at Ferguson's table last night, so I knew he was still in the running. It turns out we're both in our forties and have kids. I have four, Umberto has two; he has a World Series bracelet, I don't. But my $276,000 is good for third place, just behind Liebert's $283,500 and Englishman Barney Boatman's $282,000.

Downstairs we learn that Umberto, with $101,000, is at Table 48, the most hazardous of the five—plenty of chips to win if you catch cards and play well, but with Boatman and Liebert wielding big stacks, you risk being set all-in each time you enter a pot. Tom Jacobs's $229,000 makes him the bully of Table 47, which has four stacks under $39,000. Duke, Habib, and Mike Sexton are all at Table 54, the second most chip-laden group and perhaps the most talented. Duke and Habib are both hot, and Sexton is fresh off a victory at the European No-Limit Championship. In seat six of Table 55 sits its putative bully, yours truly. I've fantasized for decades about having a World Series stack big enough to make brutal sport of my opponents, but I have zero actual experience in the role. I spent the first two days gasping and thrashing to keep my nose above water, and it isn't so obvious how to skim along the top with the current.

Another problem is that my four most chip-laden opponents sit immediately to my left. Larry Beilfuss in seat seven, with $121,500, is a bespectacled, all-business guy around my age. Then comes Dae Kim in eight with $127,500, Meng La in nine with $197,000, and Anastassios Lazarou in one with $125,000. Since chips tend to flow clockwise around the table, I'm in lousy position to kick any serious butt. On my right, I have a curly-haired Parisian by the name of Angelo Besnainou, who has what sounds like Cuban salsa leaking from his earphones. He's about the sunniest person I've met in Las Vegas so far. Even sunnier is the fact that he has only $64,000, which I plan to relieve him of stat.

At Level 11 the antes alone are $1,000 (five times the buy-in for my home game) with blinds of $2,000 and $4,000. My stacks now consist of sixteen blue-and-white dimes, twenty-four orange five-thousands, and fourteen hot-pink ten-thousands. We've been told to keep our pinks at the fore so that opponents can gauge whom they do or do not want to tangle with.

As expected, the first player eliminated, over at Table 62, is Eric Schulz, who started with a single $500 chip. An old poker adage says that all you need to win is a chip and a chair, but starting from so far behind at a table with Mel Judah, T.J. Cloutier, and Jesus Ferguson, that's what it remained for Mr. Schulz—an old adage. Yet that yellow-and-black chip of his just earned him $15,000, the same prize the next eight eliminatees will receive. Meanwhile, at our table, Appleman has just raised all-in. Angelo folds, and I'm not playing trooper with Broderick Crawford. After mucking, I have to brush away what looks like cocaine or powdered rock salt from the baize between my stack and Angelo's. Beilfuss calls Appleman, but Kim, La, and Lazarou all fold. (Was someone snorting lines or noshing saltines here last night?) Pair of fives for Appleman, A♦ 9♠ for Beilfuss. The flop comes A♥ A♠ 5♥, ruining Beilfuss's day while doubling Appleman through to $180,000. It seems like he was down to felt only a few minutes ago.

The white mess turns out to be sugar, and the culprit turns out to be Angelo. I discover this by watching him sprinkle out more of it. I stare at him, shaking my head. "For sweet life," he tells me. "You know?" He goes on to explain that Tunisian Jews, of which he is one, have a tradition of adding sweetness to life by sprinkling sugar on portentous objects: a new house, a tractor, a child . . . I have to admit it's a wonderful concept, but as its substance combines with the moisture on our fingers we're sugarcoating the cards as we play them. Isn't it bad enough that I've got either the suddenly ill-tempered Beilfuss or the ever-inscrutable Kim snapping me off with reraises each time I try stealing blinds? Have they no damn respect for the Bully? A few hands later Meng La comes over the top of me, all-in, this after I've made the heaviest wager of my life by raising his big blind eight pink—eight pink $10,000 chips. I'm forced to lay down the same red jacks that came to my rescue on Monday.

After licking my fingers and wounds for a round, I'm only too happy to call, with K♣ K♦, the last $28,000 of Ron Stanley, the player in seat 2. Stanley turns over K♥ 10♠. Oh yeah, I gloat, mentally pumping my fist. Time to get back in the lead! But the Q♥ 9♦ 3♦ flop gives Stanley a belly straight draw, and when, sure enough, the beardless jack of clubs arrives on the turn, my stack and my confidence plunge to $97,000, a piddling sum at this stage. Just in time, too, for Level 12, when the blinds jump to three and six grand. Worst of all, I get high-carded to a table with Habib, Sexton, Jeff Shulman (the chip leader, with almost $500,000), Jacobs, and Cloutier. In my humble opinion, it's over. Not that I've given up, but I have to be realistic before I get blinded to death. My only chance is to wait, not too long, for a monster to materialize between my knuckles, hope I get called by a worse hand and don't get sucked out on, and so double through. And then I have to do it again. And then I have to do it again. At least we have a ravishing dealer named Red, presumably because of her fox-colored shoulder-length locks, to go with wide hazel eyes and a sly grin.

T.J.'s $400,000 threatens to make him Boss Hoss, a role he was surely born to play. And with Shulman's vast stacks on my right, I'm developing a severe case of big-stack envy. A half hour later we lose Kathy Liebert. She entered a big pot with queens but lost to K♥ 10♦, then got bounced five hands later when someone called her K♦ 10♣ raise with a pair of queens, and that time the queens did hold up. Very brutal. But now I can barely keep from whooping when, sitting in the small blind, I find K♠ K♦. Even better is that Annie Duke, who's playing without shoes or socks, has already raised it four pink. I reraise eight more and flash her what I hope is a friendly but confident smile. Her response is to say, "I'm all-in." Terrified of aces, I call, timidly flipping my kings as Duke snaps down . . . Q♣ Q♥. This is good. What's bad is that our table has suddenly become the matrix of Annie Duke fandom, all of them training a miasma of estrogen on to my innocent cowboys, willing them to be bushwhacked by ladies. Bob Thompson's reminder that Annie's the last woman left only whips them up further. *Annieee! . . . You go, girl! . . . C'mon, queeeen!* Yet in spite of all this, my brag book decrees that the cowboys stand up.

We come back from dinner to antes of $2,000, blinds of $5,000 and $10,000, with the final fourteen reconfigured as such:

Table 1
1. MARK ROSE, $223,000
2. ANNIE DUKE, $130,000
3. HASAN HABIB, $330,000
4. CHRIS FERGUSON, $305,000
5. JIM MCMANUS, $450,000
6. STEVE KAUFMAN, $400,000
7. T. J. CLOUTIER, $540,000

Table 2
1. MICKEY APPLEMAN, $540,000
2. ROMAN ABINSAY, $330,000
3. ANGELO BESNAINOU, $70,000
4. TOM FRANKLIN, $450,000
5. JEFF SHULMAN, $440,000
6. ANASTASSIOS LAZAROU, $105,000
7. MIKE SEXTON, $385,000

What a player Appleman must be, having started the day with $6,000! I'm glad that he's not at my table as, once again, we play hand for hand, aiming to get down to six. Between shuffles I get up and watch Angelo get bounced when his A♣ 6♠ goes down to Shulman's A♦ 10♣.

I remind myself how much seven-handed action changes the value of pocket cards. Trouble hands like K♠ Q♦ or small pairs become cautiously playable, even from an early position. It's crucial that I not only adjust but account for the fact that my opponents will, too. The amazing thing to me is how calm I now feel, as though vying for the lead late on Day 3 of the Big One is all in a night's work. I can't see the stacks on the other table, but I figure I'm in fourth, third, or second, and I understand that I can win.

I watch as Chris Ferguson makes what has become our standard preflop raise, $60,000, and with J♥ J♠ I am happy to call, especially since I've read Chris's raise as positional. Kaufman and T.J. and Rose and then Annie all fold, but Hasan, in the big blind, calls too. This triggers the blend of "oh, shit" and "oh, well" that's been percolating down through my brain each time I play a big pot. I've risked only sixty so far, but we're likely to take it much higher. When the flop comes A♦ Q♦ 2♣, it's more like "oh, shit" and "oh, shit." The fecal sensation becomes more pronounced as Chris moves both hands behind his stacks, clasps them together with pale, bony fingers, and pushes them slowly toward the pot, making sure not to topple any of his precious pink towers. I ask him to count it. "Two-fifty," he says, without counting. I believe him, and the dealer confirms it. Do I call an all-in bet with two overcards already on board? I don't think so. At the same time, I don't want no Fred Astaire wanna-be shoving me off my two jacks. T.J. and Annie and Slim all have their share of the photographers' attention, but Jesus of late has become the new darling. Both the still guys and film people regularly zoom in on his badass Black Stallion hat with silver buckles adorning the brim, his wraparound shades whose convexity must make for some swank photographic effects—Fred Astaire meets Richard Petty, along with the Youngbloods hair and beard, the bona fide

Jesusesque features. I'm sure they're all pulling for him to win the whole thing, as opposed to some puffily unphotogenic dad-type like me. But darn it all, I'm bad as well! Haven't they noticed my space-age titanium shades, or the stain on my top right incisor from smoking Cambodian opium? And what about the four-color tatts of Sade and Genet on my scrotum? . . . I flip my jacks into the muck. Too many overcards, plus no read whatever on Chris.

But I only have to wait three more hands till I get my first chance at redemption, looking down to find what certainly looks like Big Slick. I peer in again to make sure. Yessiree, it's A♦ K♣. Swallowing as discreetly as possible, I wait my turn before pushing ten orange toward the unraised pot. The instant that Steve Kaufman mucks, T.J. shoves forward a tall stack of pink, snarling, "Raise." He may not have actually snarled, but that's how it registers in my soul. And whatever the participle or verb, it's another $100,000 to me.

In the final chapter of *Super/System*, Brunson claims that A-K are his favorite pocket cards because you win more with them when you make a hand and lose less when you don't; whereas A-Q, just one pip below it, is a hand he famously refuses to play under any circumstance. T.J.'s book stresses that you have to win both with and against A-K. "It's the biggest decision-hand in a tournament." He considers it so decisive that in four of his twelve practice hands, the reader is given A-K. And be still my computerized, book-learnin' heart and suck in my un-Christlike cheeks, but I just have a feeling that T.J. is making a play. And I want him to go on making it. Yet with four hundred large in the pot, what the hay is a feeling? The short answer runs something as follows: T.J. writes that when he gets raised holding A-K, his response depends on who made the raise. I've studied the passage so obsessively, I believe I can quote it verbatim. "There are times when I will just flat call the raise. There are times when I will try to win the money right then by reraising. And there are times when I will simply throw the hand away. It all depends on what I know about my opponent." Not to get overly granular here, but I think T.J. thinks he can push me around, so I feel I should give him a call. Playing against him these last two nights has made it clear he's a guy on whom nothing is lost—just his chips in this case, if I'm right. If I'm wrong, I'll be out of the tournament.

"Call."

The flop of my life comes a baby rainbow: 2♣ 5♥ 4♦. I still have boss overcards, plus a nice belly draw to a wheel; but I also have nada. Same draw for T.J., I'm guessing, since I've put him on a medium ace. He's not the kind of guy to reraise with A-3—unless he has Kryptonite testes or assumes he can bluff me with garbage, both of which are probably operative. I recall that in Practice Hand 4, the flop comes three babies. If Player A bets, T.J. quizzes the reader, what do you do? "You throw your hand away. Why? Because you have nothing. In no-limit hold'em, you never chase"—about the dozenth time he's restated the never-chase maxim. Assuming he knows that I know this, I chase. The instant I tap the felt checking, T.J. mutters, "Two hunnerd thousand" and his entire stack of pink chips disappears into his hand, to be deftly redeposited between him and the pot in four stacks of five. His fingers don't seem to be trembling.

"Call," I croak finally, making a virtue of necessity by trying to sound like I've lured poor T.J. into my trap, an impression I hope isn't risibly belied as my vibrating digits fumble to count twenty pink. I can't bear even to glance in T.J.'s direction, so I cannot say how he reacts to the turn card, the seven of diamonds, which as far as I'm concerned changes exactly nothing. I check.

"I'm all-in," T.J. says. No surprise here, since he's been trying to buy the pot all along. A third enormous bet doesn't scare me any less, or any more, than the first two did. Except now he has put me all-in.

"I call."

Thompson notes for the gallery that T.J. has me covered by a hundred thousand or so. What he doesn't say is that if his fellow Texan has even a pair of deuces, I'm finished. T.J. turns over an ace and a nine, muttering something I can't quite make out because of the buzz off the rail. When I turn over macho Big Slick, there are oohs, aahs, applause, and T.J. appears mildly shocked. Amid the gathering uproar, Thompson announces our hands. A trey will give us both wheels, a nine and I'm kevorked. Anything else, the pot's mine. My sense, as the dealer's right fist thumps the table, is that T.J. is going to catch. . . .

"Jack of clubs on the river," drawls Thompson. "Jim McManus wins eight hundred and sixty-six thousand and becomes the new chip leader." Benny Behnen and Amarillo Slim have been standing behind the table for the last several hands, and Benny now drawls, "Jesus Chrahst!"

"Ah'd bet on that boy," Slim drawls back. "He's got the heart of a cliff divah."

"T.J. taught me everything I know about this game," I announce. "Read his book and you'll see." If I had my copy on me, I would brandish it aloft for the cameras. T.J. stubs out a Salem, not pleased. "It didn't teach you that, boy," he growls, with what I hear as a trace of contempt. Now, the last man on earth I would taunt is T.J. Cloutier. I also remember how showing my queen to Kathy Liebert didn't seem to assuage her. Not that it's my job to assuage either one of them . . .

This former cliff diver, though, is gonna sit good and tight with his chip lead. After thirteen hours at the table and staring down T. J.'s three barrels, he's got cobwebby spermatozoa floating through his vitreous humor. So he's not even tempted to play a 3♦ 8♥, J♥ 5♣, or even A♥ 7♥. No, sir. He also decides not to raise but to limp. And Duke, one off the button, cooperates beautifully, raising to $60,000. Hasan and Chris fold. Hasan stands up, yawning and stretching, to watch. And then I'm yawning, too, just as I happen to start moving $150,000 toward the pot; judging by the size of Duke's stack, it's enough to have set her all-in. The next thing I know, both Kaufman and the dealer are citing me for a string raise, claiming I went back into my stack for more chips without saying, "Raise." I realize they're right and apologize. The dealer determines that the amount in my hand as it started forward was $60,000, which happens to be the minimum allowable raise of Annie's original bet. And boy, she's not happy. My raise doesn't set her all-in, but since she only has $140,000 left, she's been priced in. She turns to her entourage. "This is the worst thing that's ever happened to me in a tournament!" she shrieks—and *shrieks*, I'm afraid, is the word. "Let me call that myself," she chides Kaufman, and for a moment I'm cheering her on, till she adds, "I would've been glad to let him go to his stack for more!" She runs a hand up through brown bangs, jangling her wrist load of beads, braided leather, plastic bangles. That she would have been "glad" to let me put her all-in suggests she has a premium hand, and that she was so overwrought when she said it makes it impossible to believe she was acting. I have to put her on something better than a lousy pair of jacks, do I not? But so why, after my raise was scaled down to sixty, didn't she simply reraise me?

The flop comes A♣ Q♣ 8♣, about as bad it can be for my jacks, so I check to the shrieker. "All-in," she says, sliding her stacks in. She has a live human being inside her—her third—but that's not the reason I fold. No way can I call even a hundred grand more, though the pot odds declare that I should. Not with them overcards squatting pregnantly on the baize. It isn't the toughest laydown I've made, but it still smarts to have to muck johnnies again. This is, after all, two-card chicken we're playing, and things can change fast on fourth street and fifth street . . .

"I changed my mind," Duke announces, then graciously shows me an ace before mucking. "That's the best thing that ever happened to me in a tournament." Big applause from the rail. *Hang in there, Annie! . . . Chicks ruuule!* Yet who can I blame but myself and Steve Kaufman? If I'd been competent to set her all-in before the flop, when all she probably had was a medium ace, she almost certainly would have folded; but for only $60,000, she was still sufficiently tied to the hand to make a crying call correct. Then she caught that huge piece of the flop. So my little snafu while trying to put her all-in cost me $120,000 and handed Jeff Shulman the lead. If I'd simply said, "Raise," I'd be sitting on over a million.

To stem this new ebb tide, I resolve to enter no pots for the next fourteen hands unless I find aces or kings. I watch two rounds go by without a flop, a single raise being enough to capture the blinds. Meanwhile, at the other table, Sexton and Lazarou get bounced on consecutive hands.

Level 15 brings with it $3,000 antes and $15,000 and $30,000 blinds, but my chips are still copious enough to let me relax, await monsters.

Anyone in his right mind would follow this plan, yet when I find A♣ 9♦, I flash back to what Annie just did to me and call Chris's raise to $60,000. Hasan calls as well. When the flop comes A-Q-5 rainbow, Chris says, "All-in."

"Jim has about $700,000 in chips," declares Thompson, "Chris and Hasan, oh, I'd say about half that."

If I call and lose I'm out of the tournament; if I win I'll not only guarantee playing tomorrow but I'll have a huge lead in the sprint for the $1.5 million. Yet every last piece of advice I've received says no way do you call in these situations unless holding the absolute nuts. I do have top pair, but I lose to any kicker above nine. I wish I had some kind of read on this Jesus character. He's certainly capable of bluffing, but he's also extracted quite a few fishes and loaves from his butt in the last twenty minutes. My mouth for some reason says, "Call," and Chris turns over . . . A♥ 9♠. I pause long enough to give him decent psychological scourging before I let him off the hook and show mine. Shaking our heads as the crowd goes bananas, we triple-check the board for a flush draw; finding none, we both burst out laughing. His slender blond wife stands behind him, wrist to her forehead, recounting the split on her cell phone. In the meantime, on the very next hand, Annie goes all-in again, only to have Chris call and show pocket aces. Revealing the fateful A♠ 9♣, Annie never catches up, so she's out. As she slowly gets up, Thompson announces that Annie's tenth-place finish is the highest by a woman since Barbara Enright came in fifth in 1995, and the $52,160 makes Annie the leading female money-winner in World Series history. After watching her play for a week, I doubt this will cheer her up much. She's a cowgirl.

Down to nine men, we are ranged around one table: Ferguson in seat one with $800,000, then Habib with $400,000, me with $950,000, Cloutier with $550,000, Abinsay with $420,000, Appleman with $240,000, Jeff Shulman with $1,000,000, Captain Tom Franklin with $600,000, and Steve Kaufman with $220,000. Sitting just to my left, T.J.'s in perfect position to hammer his student, like he's been trying to do for two days. Plus he now has revenge as a motive.

For the next hour or so, the standard preflop raise is ninety or a hundred thousand, usually enough to take down the blinds. From time to time one of us reraises all-in, but in each case the original raiser gives the reraiser credit by folding. Then, in very short order, this happens: Abinsay, from under the gun, brings it in for $60,000, and Appleman calls with his last $58,000. With the J♠ 10♠, I'm tempted to make it a three-way, but I follow the no-chasing dictum. Thank God and Cloutier too, because none of my straight or flush cards appear on the board as Roman's A♠ K♠ easily holds up over Mickey's A♦ 10♣. Two hands later Captain Tom wagers his last $118,000 before the flop, and Ferguson calls him with tens. When the Captain shows fours and the board gives no help, we are seven.

One more unfortunate bet and it's bedtime, but nobody wants to finish in seventh. As in every WSOP event, the last nine players receive commemorative final-table jackets; there's also a hefty difference in prize money ($146,700 for seventh versus $195,600 for sixth); but the main reason for our lull in aggression is that tomorrow's final table will seat only six, owing to the Discovery Channel's need for compressed action in their documentary. Since we all want to be in the movie, not one all-in bet gets a call for the next forty minutes. The guy forcing most of the action is Jeff, and he steadily builds up his stack. I'd love to know whether he's doing it with legitimate hands, but I'm not catching cards to find out with. One mistake against Jeff and you're gone, whereas he can guess wrong and still play.

Finally, finally, one off the button, I find aces, the first time I've seen them all day. But my ecstasy ratchets down notch by notch as Kaufman, then Chris, then Hasan, muck their hands. At this point I'm tempted to limp, though I know it would be read as a trap. The $66,000 in antes and blinds I'll win by raising is hardly chump change, but when you find pocket rockets you want to eviscerate people. Masking my chagrin, I make the minimum raise to $60,000, hoping someone will come blasting back over the top of my show of timidity. Not this time. T.J. even shoots me a rare little smile as he folds, and Roman and Jeff are also untempted to call.

Three hands later, Jeff raises $200,000 from the button. Kaufman ponders defending his $15,000 small blind for a moment, then passes, leaving Chris, in the big blind, to reflect on his options for another thirty seconds. "What would Jesus do?" a shrill railbird wonders aloud, getting laughs. The answer is: move all seven of His tidy stacks toward the pot, reraising $650,000. Hasan and the rest of us scram. Jeff stares at Jesus for maybe ten seconds, then shrugs almost meekly and calls. When he turns over 7♥ 7♣—not really much of a hand to be calling a big stack all-in with—there are whispers and cries of astonishment. Then Chris shows us . . . 6♣ 6♠! In absolute crunch time, the twenty-three-year-old Shulman has somehow made a veteran read of his opponent, leaving Chris with two outs. As auto-advance cameras fire away and the railbirds go silent, the flop comes 10♥ 3♥ . . . 6♥! Having flopped a miraculous set, Jesus vaults from his chair. And yet Jeff, for all his hellacious bad luck, has a flush draw—nine outs right there, to go with the two other sevens. Jesus's lean, foxy wife, Cathy Burns, has her palms on her ears, a Munch screamer, as voices call out for sixes or sevens or hearts. When 5♣ hits on the turn, Jeff has a straight draw as well, though Chris is still the 2 to 1 favorite. The dealer turns fifth street: a ten. No heart flush, no seven. As Jeff slumps back in his chair, Chris dances out of his, the sooner to be locked in a tango embrace from Ms. Burns. No celebratory peck for these two, but a lingering soul smooch while they twirl one another around.

"Jesus Makes 6-6-6," I proclaim. "Takes Over Chip Lead, Molests Wife in Public."

"Molests Girlfriend in Public," a railbird amends me.

"Even better," I say. But the truth is, I'm dying inside. Not only is Jennifer not here to cheer me but it's starting to sink in that to win this damn thing I'll not only have to catch a few monsters; I'll need to catch them when someone else holds one a single pip lower. I'll have to play well for four days just to be in a position to get lucky when the big money goes in the pot. If only, if only, I snivel. If only I'd caught aces on this hand . . . till it dawns on me that if I had, I would've lost every one of my chips. But of one thing I'm certain: Smooching Jesus is due for an epic correction. Having bounced Duke with aces and Franklin with tens, he now spikes a two-outer and doubles through Jeff to the lead. What he needs is a quick crucifixion, if only to give his strawberry-blond Mary Magdalene something to hug him about. Everyone at the table would love to just nail him right now, yet we're terrified of taking him on. Not only does he have the big stack but he's got my old horseshoe lodged miles and miles up his ass.

T.J., of course, isn't terrified. He'd seen hundreds of rushes like this before Chris was even born. I fold Raquel Welch (3-8) in a hurry. "Raise," T.J. mutters as soon as the action gets to him, pushing in $290,000. Abinsay folds, but Shulman reraises all-in. Then Jesus not only calls Jeff and T.J.; he, too, reraises all-in! The big guy can't seem to believe what has happened, but he manfully lays down his hand, claiming it was jacks. We believe him. What are jacks, after all, once Jesus H. Christ gets involved? Turns out to be a pretty shrewd laydown when Jeff shows two kings, and Chris has . . . the aces again! Get the fuck outta here! The board renders no poetic justice either, because this time the best hand holds up. Just like that, Jeff is out. A couple of minutes ago he was running the table. He congratulates Chris and the rest of us, and then, with his dad's arm around him, walks away like a man with a future.

Ten hours later, the Horseshoe's vast tournament room has been converted to an intimate poker studio, if there is such a thing. In place of last night's four tables there are twenty rows of seats facing a thirteen-foot monitor. Bleachers were erected along one side of the final table, flanked by more rows of seats at both ends. The table is lit with four banks of lights, surrounded by cameras and monitors. Everyone else wants to interview the finalists, but the Discovery director has first dibs because of the shoot. One of his tech guys wires me for sound, winding the line up through the fly of my pants and clipping the mike to my collar.

Back behind the bleachers, I peruse the new sheet with Hasan. Chris is in seat one with $2.853 million, Hasan is in two with $464,000, I'm in three with $554,000, T.J.'s in four with $216,000, Roman's in five with $521,000, Kaufman is in six with $511,000. Between us we have $5.19 million in chips, with which we'll be vying for $3.74 million in prize money. The other $1.38 million has already been awarded to places forty-five through seven.

"Good luck to you, buddy," says Hasan in his buttery lilt.

"And good luck to you." We embrace. I'm startled to realize that I meant what I said. For eight days now, we've been throwing haymakers at each other over critical pots, but that makes me love him a little. Plus we'll both need some luck from now on.

Finally, a little after noon, Thompson introduces us one by one. Chris, at thirty-seven, has already won the $2,500 seven-card-stud event, to go with the 1999 Best All-Around Player at the California State Poker Championship and his new Ph.D., but lists his occupation as "student." I hear Andy note that his nickname stems not from delusions of grandeur but from his hair and the kindness of his features. I also hear that Hasan used to own a video store but has now, at thirty-eight, been a pro for four years; just last month, at the World Poker Open, he finished second in the $1,000 no-limit event.

Now me. On their live Internet broadcast, Glazer and Phil Hellmuth, the 1989 champion, are calling me the "family man's family man," mainly because of my brag book and frequent calls home. Thompson says I'm playing in my first poker tournament and that most of my no-limit strategy comes from T.J.'s book. Down I sit. T.J. needs no introduction but gets a rather lengthy one anyway, followed by a standing ovation. This is his fourth final-table appearance at the Big One; he's won four other WSOP titles, fifty-one major championships altogether. At sixty, he's the sixth-leading money winner in series history, but by placing first or second today, he'd move past Johnny Chan into first. Abinsay, a fifty-two-year-old Filipino now living in Stockton, California, has already placed second in the $2,000 limit hold'em event, so he's hot. Kaufman, fifty-four, is a rabbi as well as a professor of languages (Hebrew, Aramaic, and other Semitic languages) at Hebrew Union College in Cincinnati, sufficiently high-powered as a scholar to be a consultant on the Dead Sea Scrolls. After playing big tournaments since 1997, he made the final table at Tunica. He's also a bit of a noodge.

I may have the second most chips, but we're all basically tied for second behind Ferguson. And with a stack less than half the size of mine, T.J. is at least twice as dangerous. He sits bolt upright and smokes, his gray Binion's polo shirt tucked into beltless beige slacks. I let him know one more time how terrific his book is, but he doesn't want to hear about it. He seems to think it's some kind of gamesmanship, and maybe he's right. Yet it's obvious to him and everyone else who the novice is here, the book-learned tournament virgin. No question, these five other guys see my $554,000 as the most plunderable stack.

The blinds are still $15,000 and $30,000, with $3,000 antes, and will be for the next eighty-one minutes. T.J. can't wait long to make a move, but it's Hasan who puts in the first raise, to $70,000. I'm tempted to call with 2♦ 2♥ but come to my senses—duh!—in time to pass. When T.J. and Roman pass, too, it looks like Hasan may have executed the last day's first steal. But then here comes Professor Kaufman blasting over the top of him in a language we all understand: twenty pink. Once Jesus folds, Hasan has the day's first gulp-worthy decision. After gazing at Kaufman for maybe ten seconds, he lays down his hand with a sigh.

Hand 2: From the button, Roman makes it $100,000 to go, a likely positional raise. Chris says, politely but firmly, "All-in." Roman calls, pushing his entire half million, then turns over A♣ Q♣. Chris shows 8♦ 8♥. I want to observe Roman's face, but T.J. is blocking him out as Thompson narrates the 7♥ 2♦ 7♣ flop, followed by a jack and a trey. Roman stands up from the table to abundant applause. His ouster has just guaranteed me fifth-place money, though it's the last thing I care about now. What I want is to cast Jesus and the rest of these money-changers from the temple and rake in the serious shekels. What I don't want is to glance at a monitor and be forced to wonder who's the little homunculus hunched in the seat next to T.J.—this as, on Hand 4, T.J. is moving all-in. No one calls him, certainly not the homunculus with his measly J♦ 5♣. T.J. shows us A♠ 10♠. And now, on Hand 5, here comes Hasan moving in. I can't call with 7♠ 6♥, and neither can anyone else. Am I playing too passively? I've already bled away 10 percent of my stack while the others are letting it rip.

On my next hand Chris raises $50,000, Hasan folds, and with 8♣ 6♣ so do I; so do T.J. and Roman and Steve. We've thus let Chris extend his lead by $63,000. His chips are arranged in two massive triangles, one on top of the other: ten pink twenty-chip columns in a 1-2-3-4 configuration, topped by six of less-regular color scheme arranged 1-2-3. Very scary.

My next few hands are unplayable, but on Hand 9 I find A♣ Q♣. Hasan, in the small blind, has raised it all-in once again. Suited A-Q is a better hand to raise than to call with, but still. Five-handed, it can fairly be called, pace Brunson, a monster. Granted that Roman's A♣ Q♠ just got him beheaded, but my read of Hasan is that he's caught up in a spasm of all-in steal-raises. In the end I am happy to call him. Pushing my seven stacks forward, I believe that this puts me all-in. Hasan shows A♥ 4♥. I was right. When I flip up my A♣ Q♣, everyone sees why I'm thrilled. What a call!

But now comes the flop of Hasan's and my life: 9♠ 6♠ K♠. So far, so fantastic. Dead to the three remaining fours, Hasan groans, shakes his head. The other forty-two cards in the deck give me a $900,000 pot and a real shot at taking down Chris. The crowd's yelling hundreds of things, but all I can hear is the Habib Society pleading for fours. "Ha-san Ha-beeeeeeeb!" someone croons. They outnumber my own fans, such as they are, plus they have a specific card to pray for, but I've come to understand that I'm gonna win not just this hand but the tournament. One and a half million dollars. The heavyweight championship of poker. My faith is confirmed when fourth street arrives as the sacred, the numinous, the preternaturally chic five o'diamonds. Close to a four, I gloat to myself, but no sucking-out-on-me cigar. Hasan has stood up, getting ready to shake hands. My heart pounds spasmodically, but I'm still feeling thoroughly confident. So that when the fifth street card—what?—is—what!—4♥, I "reel," according to Glazer's column that night, "in stunned silence," even though a chorus of f-words and blasphemies and fours is howling like a squadron of Pakistani banshees on tilt through my skull. Glazer will also write that "Jim hadn't suffered too many indignities at the hands of fate in the last couple of days. Most of his leading hands had held up. But now, at the worst possible moment, he'd taken a punishing blow." Punished and reeling, then, away from the table, I have to be told by Hasan that I had him covered. "You'rrre still in therrre, buddy. I'm sorrrry. Keep playing. I'm sorrrry..." Although it feels like I died, I have life, if only $105,000 worth. Hasan and I are still clasping hands, shaking our heads in amazement. We realize that this is what happens in poker sometimes, that it could have just as—more— easily gone the other way, the towers of pink and orange chips being raked a foot to the left instead of a foot to the right.

A round or so later I find A♠ 2♠. I have barely enough chips for the blinds, so I probably won't see another ace, let alone a big pair. I move in. Kaufman—who else?—not only calls but moves in himself, trying to knock me out on the cheap while making sure it stays heads-up between us. Once Chris and Hasan muck their hands, Kaufman turns over... A♦ Q♠. It's perfect. That I'm now in the same spot Hasan was just in somehow inspires an ever-more bottomless gloom. Yeah, sure, when Dante was spiraling down into the frozen bowels of Hell he may have also been ascending, without realizing it, toward Paradise, but here in Las Vegas, another frigid desert peopled by faithless demons, three- outers don't spike twice in a row. Forget about the long odds against it—I know it's not going to happen. And indeed the nine-six-king flop gives me neither a straight draw nor a flush draw, let alone a sweet deuce. In the end, with an ace on the turn, a ten on the river, it's not even close. I am out.

Now that the Satanic Prince of Noodges has forked me down into the pitch, there's applause. Many zooms. Many clicks. I shake Kaufman's hand, then Hasan's, then T.J.'s. "You played well," T.J. says. And that's something. And now here is Jesus coming around for a hug. "You played great!" he says, bonily squeezing me. Walking away from the table, how- ever, it dawns on me how alive I felt while playing four days in the Big One, and now I feel dead. I mean dead. As Thompson and Glazer and Hellmuth and all the other commentators are making clear to the as- sembled and far-flung poker universe, I've won $247,760 by finishing fifth out of 512. What it feels like is fifth out of six.

Up on the podium, Becky Behnen shakes my hand, pets my arm. "You were wonderful, Jim. And last night! Congratulations!" Shaking my hand in his turn, her son Benny snaps me back to reality. "That four was brutal, man. Brutal. You were playing so awesome last night!" Yeah, last night . . . Tom Elias ushers me a few steps to the left, where the pay-out booth stands. From his unbashful spiel, I gather that "big winners" have to tip the dealers "between 2 and 8 percent." I have to decide that right now? "We have to take care of our people, Jim. So, I mean, yeah, you do." I decide to tip $7,800, 3.3 percent of my profit and vastly more money than I'd ever played poker for, or made in one week doing any-thing. After thanking me, Tom details a Horseshoe security guard to escort me downstairs to the cage. Passing a monitor, I see that Hasan has just been bounced, and I desperately want to keep playing! But I know it's all over when the technician starts removing the sound pack. "If you'd just undo your belt . . ."

At the cashier downstairs, I play hurry up and wait with bucket-toting slot players, then start signing form after form. I slide the tax forms, the tip receipt, and a trayful of five-thousand-dollar brown chips into my lockbox, keeping one of them back to rub against the coins in my pocket.

By the time I get back upstairs, it's down to T.J. and Chris. T.J. has one and a half million, and Chris has about four. It's hard to get close to the action because of all the film and press people. Then I see what the commotion's about: a phalanx of Horseshoe security has just deliv-ered the traditional cardboard box to the table. Benny's pulling out wads of cash and handing them to his mother, who stacks them at T.J.'s end of the baize. Each wad she takes from her son consists of five hun-dred Ben Franklins subdivided by five yellow and white paper bands marked "$10,000," these in turn held together with rubber bands dou-bled near the ends of the bills. When Becky has finished there are thirty such five-inch-thick wads stacked in a ramshackle cube three wads high, five across. She lays the gold championship bracelet across the second gray tier, facing T.J., and T.J. can't help staring back. It's the thing he wants most in the world.

I finally find Hasan and ask him what happened. "I had king-queen," he purrs wistfully, shrugging. "Chris had ace-king." Enough said. As we edge two steps closer, Chris makes it $175,000 to go from the button. T.J. calls. When the flop comes K♦ K♣ 6♥, T.J. checks. (In heads-up action, the player on the button bets first before the flop, second on subsequent rounds.) After thinking for over a minute, Chris bets $200,000. When T. J. says, "Call," there is eight hundred grand in the pot. Fourth street arrives a red trey. Check, check. Street five: J♦. No straight draw, no flush draw, but do either of them have a king? T.J. at least represents having one by betting $600,000. Chris takes a while to decide, then calls and turns over a jack and a six, only to watch T.J. turn over K♥ 10♥. His check on the turn, letting Chris catch his jack for "free," earned him an extra six large and put himself into the lead, with 2.6 million to Chris's 2.5.

"Only in no-limit," says Andy.

A couple hands later, Chris raises $175,000, prompting T.J. to come over the top for another half million. Chris shows how frightened he is by responding, "All-in." Without a blip of reluctance, T.J. calls. Whoever takes this pot wins the championship.

At Thompson's official request, they show us and the cameras their hole cards: A♥ 7♥ for T.J., A♠ 2♠ for Chris. An uproar, then relative silence. From six feet away in his booth, I hear the Discovery director whisper, "Camera Two, give me Jesus." Because Jesus is dead to a deuce or a flurry of spades and we all want to see his reaction. From my vantage point he looks nervous, unhappy, and pale. The flop comes 3♠ 10♠ Q♥. Although still a 3 to 2 underdog, Chris's four-flush gives him nine extra outs to go with the two other deuces. Both guys have proven they have solid brass balls, but right now all four must feel clammy. When the turn comes K♥, T.J. picks up his own flush draw. But when 10♦ shows up on fifth street, yielding ten-ten-ace-queen-king for another chopped pot, the vibe suggests that maybe they'll play on forever. Chris looks tapped out. How many deaths and resurrections can the Son of Man suffer per hour? Even the Texas centurion pretends to wipe sweat from his brow.

The next two small pots go to T.J. when Chris is unable to call even modest $100,000 raises, but on the following hand Chris wins $400,000 with a raise on the turn. The hand after that brings no pre-flop raises, and when the flop comes K♥ 3♥ 8♣, Chris checks again. T.J. bets a mere hundred grand, Chris calls, and we all sense a trap being set. The question is, who's trapping whom? Because when 7♠ hits on the turn, this time it's Chris betting a puny $150,000 and T.J. who's warily calling. Four of clubs on the river, and both of them check. While they stare at each other, Chris flashes what must be a king. T.J. mucks. They've been at it now for four and a half hours—a long time with this much at stake and dozens of lenses and mikes jabbing into your poker space.

Ten minutes later, on Hand 93, T.J. raises to $175,000. When Chris reraises six hundred thou, T.J. moves in like a shot. The pulse in his cheek makes me think that he feels like he's finally got Chris where he wants him. Certainly, if Chris manages to call him, this will be it— unless we get another chopped pot. Chris scratches his beard, shakes his head, exhales. Two minutes pass. I can't speak for T.J., but no one else seems to begrudge all the time he is taking. "Call him, Jesus!" shouts a rowdy fan twenty rows back. T.J.'s eyes narrow as he drags on his umpteenth Salem. He puts his left fist to his mouth, clears his throat. Won't anyone give him a lozenge?

"T.J. likes his hand," Andy whispers to me, "and I think Chris has ace-nine." I remember the matching A-9's Chris and I turned out to be holding last night, how the untranquil mood had been scalpeled by laughter. I watch now as Chris takes off his hat, then his sunglasses— whoa—in an instant defanging his aura. The thinning hair above his temples accentuated by the length of the strands, brown eyes a tad bloodshot and sunken, he also looks much more like Jesus.

He calls. As the low-decibel buzz from the previous five or six minutes rises to a crescendo, he turns over A♠ 9♣. T.J. immediately shows him A♦ and . . . Q♣. The crowd gasps and whistles.

"Pretty astonishing call," I tell Andy.

"Chris's?"

"No, yours."

He nods modestly, as though he hasn't been making reads like this the whole tournament, then elbows my arm. "Ace-queen look familiar?"

"Oh, boy . . ."

The flop—4♥ 2♥ K♣—keeps T.J. in the lead. When K♥ falls on the turn, Andy groans, "Not again!" Because now any deuce, four, king, or ace will give us another chopped pot. Exuberant Ferguson boosters entreat the poker deities for a nine. Cloutier fans are more numerous, but it isn't clear what they should beg for. Hollering "Let's go, T.J.!" is pretty much all they can do.

Jesus leaps from his seat with his fists in the air and T.J. thrusts his big paw across the table before I see the last card. What else could it be but "A nine!" Bob Thompson ejaculates. No one, especially Bob, seems able to believe it. Chris reaches across the table and clasps T.J.'s hand. "You outplayed me," he says. T.J. shakes his head, disagreeing. That he just got harpooned through the ventricles doesn't register on his vast, craggy features. He's smiling!

Cathy Burns and the Fergusons are all over Chris now. Hugs, kisses, pogo hops, shimmying. Chris still makes his way around the table to where T.J. is standing with his wife, Joy, inside a crush of reporters. While Chris is almost as tall, when the two men embrace their difference in mass is straight out of vaudeville: the burly tight end hugs the sinewy swing dancer, steel-wool ringlets meshing with yard-long chestnut locks. "Are we still friends?" Chris asks.

"Of course. Don't feel bad. You played great." But once they let go of each other, T.J. asks, "You didn't think it would be that tough to beat me, did you?"

"Yes, I did."

I congratulate Chris, then try to tell T.J. how brilliantly he played. "There's a lotta luck in poker," he rumbles, "and if you're gonna play this game you better get used to that."

Needing oxygen and sunlight, I go for a walk down on Fremont, then head south along First Street. Strip joints and flophouses, pawnshops and T-shirt emporia, a few dozen down-market tourists. In Las Vegas, Fifth Street is Las Vegas Boulevard South, which also is known as the Strip. Family Vegas. We are far, far away from that world. Already the scorching southwest wind has driven some grit through my lips and made my pale forehead feel crisp. I think of my children, my wife. By this time tomorrow, I'll see them.

At the far eastern tip of the Pacific time zone, Las Vegas sunsets come early. Even at five-thirty or so on a May afternoon, even through polarized lenses, there are horizontal shafts making you squint and ricocheting dazzlements that make you shade your eyes, and then there are glares that make you duck. And then there are thermal traps where it must reach 130 degrees. And when these are interrupted by gelid blasts from gaping casino doorways, it's a little like wandering along the perimeter of the eighth and ninth circles of Hell—all of this, mind you, while heading a block north toward Paradise.

But the thing is, I maybe could've won the damn thing.

RANKING OF POKER HANDS

STRAIGHT FLUSH: five consecutive cards of the same suit, such as 8♥ 9♥ 10♥ J♥ Q♥. The highest possible hand is an ace-high straight flush, called a royal flush.

FOUR OF A KIND: four cards of the same rank, such as 10♣ 10♦ 10♠ 10♥.

FULL HOUSE: three cards of one rank and two of another, such as three fives and two queens.

FLUSH: five cards of the same suit, such as 2♦ 5♦ 7♦ J♦ A♦.

STRAIGHT: five consecutive cards of mixed suits, such as 5♣ 6♦ 7♠ 8♥ 9♠. (In a straight, an ace can be used as either a high or a low card.)

THREE OF A KIND: three cards of the same rank, such as 6♦ 6♣ 6♥.

TWO PAIRS: two cards of the same rank and two other cards of another rank, such as Q♦ Q♣ and 9♦ 9♥.

PAIR: two cards of the same rank, such as 4♦ 4♣.

GLOSSARY OF POKER TERMS

ALL-IN: having all of one's chips in the pot

BELLY DRAW: a straight that lacks an inside card

BIG SLICK: ace-king

BOSS TRIPS: the highest possible three of a kind

BUTTON: disc that rotates clockwise around the table to indicate which player is the last to bet

CRYING CALL: a call with a hand you think has a small chance of winning

FLOP: the first three exposed community cards, dealt simultaneously

FREEROLL: to compete with other people's money

JOHNNIES: jacks

KICKER: a side card accompanying a higher card or cards

MUCK: to discard or fold

RAINBOW: a flop of three different suits

SEMI-BLUFF: to bet with a hand you don't think is the best hand but which has a reasonable chance of improving to the best hand

SLOW-PLAY: to check or call an opponent's bet with a big hand in order to win more money in later betting rounds

SMOOTH CALL: a call when a raise is expected

STEAL: a bet big enough to cause your opponents to fold, especially when your own hand is weak

SUCK OUT: to make a lucky draw on fifth street, especially with a hand you should have folded earlier

WHEEL: a five-high straight, such as A-2-3-4-5.